Active Duty

Letters to Home from Iraq

**The Longest 18 Months in the Life
of a National Guard Soldier**

9-24-05

SSG Jason Adams

Learnovation Press

Active Duty: Letters to Home from Iraq—The Longest 18 Months in the Life of a National Guard Soldier / Jason A. Adams

Hardback—   ISBN 0-9705790-5-5 EAN Barcode 978-0-9705790-5-8
Paperback— ISBN 0-9705790-6-3 EAN Barcode 978-0-9705790-6-5

Library of Congress Control Number: 2005923680

Editor in Chief: Anna Graf Williams
Production and Development Editor: Karen J. Hall
Manufacturing and Production Manager: David Morrow
Copy Editor: Cheryl Pontius

10 9 8 7 6 5 4 3 2 1

Published by Learnovation, LLC® 10831 Thistle Ridge, Fishers, IN 46038.
1-888-577-1190   http://learnovation.com

This book is dedicated to
Howard Adams and Paul Schauble

The first is my Dad, the second, my friend — together, they are
the two greatest people that I have ever had the honor of knowing.

This book is also dedicated to the men of Foxtrot Battery, 202nd Air
Defense Artillery. I will always be proud of what we accomplished.

Note

The views presented in this book are those of the author
and do not necessarily reflect the views of the
U.S. Department of Defense and its components,
including but not limited to the U.S. Army or the
Illinois Army National Guard.

Contents

Cast of Characters

SSG Jon Arneson – AKA "Bomb Magnet." Has three Purple Hearts– his first Purple Heart was one of the first my unit handed out, his third Purple Heart was one of the last that we handed out,. A great NCO, but very unlucky.

Bernadette – My sister.

1LT Tracy Doubler – Platoon leader of Second Platoon.

PFC Richard Douglas – AKA "Monkey." Part of my team for most of the deployment. A great guy and computer specialist– he helped many guys keep their laptops up and running so we could email home. Was promoted to Specialist-E4 during deployment.

Duke – Iraqi interpreter working for the U.S. military with my battery.

GQ – Iraqi interpreter working for U.S. military with my battery; 25 years old, married, his wife is pregnant with their first child, mechanical engineer, nicknamed GQ because he is well dressed, speaks impeccable English.

SGT Bruce Hartman – Ben's roommate. His life ambition is getting more horsepower out of Chevy V-8s.

Jaguar (Jag) – Iraqi interpreter working for the U.S. military with my battery. He is a tailor, is married, and has one son Evan. His father was arrested by Americans for threatening to kill him, yet he continued to work as an interpreter for us and live on the base. He exemplifies everything that America is fighting for– he is a good, honest man who believes in a free Iraq.

SSG James McGovern – An excellent NCO who hails from Michigan, ya-hey!

SGT Carlos Antonio Ortiz (Ortiz) – AKA "The Brown Kid." My roommate and driver. He is "Oscar Madison" to my "Felix," in that we are polar opposites when it comes to cleanliness. He is 23, single, and works at the Wal-Mart distribution center in Central Illinois.

1SGT Paul Peterson – Battery First Sergeant. AKA "Top." The senior non-commissioned officer at battery level who oversees troops and takes care of the "beans and bullets." He is married, has two children, and works as diesel mechanic for a farm implement dealer. He is the best 1SGT that I have ever worked for.

CPT Gregory Reinhardt – Unit XO (Executive Officer), second in command of the battery. He handles logistics as far as movement here and movement home. He served in Kuwait and Saudi Arabia in Desert Storm, and is also a stock broker and history teacher.

SFC Greg Remick – Platoon Sergeant for First Platoon.

SGT Ben Sleaford – AKA "Buford" (as in Buford T. Justice, Jackie Gleason's famous character in the *Smokey and the Bandit* movies.) My best friend in Iraq. We know each other from home and people think we look alike. He is a firefighter and county sheriff's deputy. He is an intelligent, loyal, and dedicated soldier.

Snake – Iraqi interpreter working for U.S. military with my battery.

Steph (Stephanie) – My wife. We married on 9-11-93, and we have two children– Teryl and Joanna.

SPC Eric Werkheiser – Fellow soldier and friend. AKA "Tonto," as he is part American Indian. He hails from Galva, Illinois. Eric is the clown of the battery. He is 22 or so, enjoys playing guitar, and is planning on attending Western Illinois University.

Military Rank Abbreviations

COL – Colonel	1SGT – First Sergeant
LT – Lieutenant	SGT – Sergeant
1LT – First Lieutenant	SSG – Staff Sergeant
LTC – Lieutenant Colonel	SPC – Specialist
MAJ – Major	WO – Warrant Officer

Introduction

The Stark County News first hit Main Street in Toulon, Illinois in 1856. "*The News*," as it has always been known, represented the archetypal small town weekly until the 1980s, when it succumbed to the discount stores and malls in nearby metropolitan areas, which had emptied the stores along Toulon's main street of their customers. Three years ago, I brought *The News* back to life out of a conviction that no self-respecting county, no matter only 6,000 residents, should be without its own newspaper, as was the case.

Our 2,000 subscribers relish the warp and woof of Stark County—the milestones, nuptials, heartbreaks (as recorded in the courthouse news), school and sports, and local government controversies. *The News* has a lively editorial page, where I opine rather tartly from time to time, as do guest columnists and letter writers. Jason's "*Letters from Camp Blackjack*" and other settings in Iraq fit neatly into that tradition. And our readers are much the richer, humbler and better informed because of Jason's direct observations and perspectives from the "frontline," which was everywhere around him and his unit. People have been struck by Jason's pointed, unvarnished, politically-incorrect, and heartfelt observations about his buddies from the unit, and those from Iraq with whom he has worked.

For readers of *The News* throughout the past year, Jason pulled the drapes back and guided us into an exotic world far away, where truth and fact are precious, often illusory, currencies of world affairs. Jason helped us sort out truth and fact as best he could, and provided a perspective that few Americans have been able to include in the mosaic that we call Operation Iraqi Freedom.

Five hundred of our subscribers are expatriates, you might say. These Stark County born-and-reared folks have moved away to seek their fortunes across the country and around the world, like Jason Adams' sister Bernadette, a television producer and a stand-up comic in an improv troupe in Boston. More than several of our expats have sent Jason's letters to their own newspapers. These fans have note to their editors, just as sharply as Jason might, that his is the news they want more of: the day-by-day rhythms, boredom, pulse-pounding action—and of the positive gains made among a people oppressed and brutalized for so long that hope, faith and charity have been squeezed out of them.

Jason earned a commendation for valor while in Iraq. But Jason is not the type to boast. It's just part of his job as a "citizen soldier," he would say, and then let it drop. Jason Adams represents the best of what we in America want to be. Thanks for inviting us to share your personal experiences, Jason. You have proved you are a fine soldier. We always knew you were a good man.

Jim Nowlan
Editor and Publisher
The Stark County News, Toulon, Illinois

Notice 10/12/03   Training   Deployment 3/1/04   Home leave 9/26-10/14/04   Back Home 3/19/05

Prologue

I had tried to get in the army when I was 17. At that age, parental consent is required to join. The recruiter came up to talk to my mom and dad and painted this magnificent mental collage of army life. He spoke of travel, great pay, great benefits, and the like. Young, and for the most part stupid, I took it all in and practically handed my dad the pen for him to sign the consent form. When my dad spoke, his words stabbed me like a knife, but in hindsight would prove almost sage-like. He said, "Let's let the boy think about it." Let down that he lost the "sale," the recruiter slithered back home empty-handed. Dad turned to me and said, "I know I have been out of the army for a number of years, but that guy was full of shit." Thanks dad, yet again you protected me, and I didn't even realize it.

Fast forward to 1991. I was sitting in my apartment up in Sterling, Illinois, watching TV, contemplating how I was to survive after being laid off from my job as a fencing installer. I had only been out of high school for a few months, and there I was– broke, with no job and the bills just kept on coming in. I was going to college at the time– a junior college just outside of town called Sauk Valley Community College– and majoring in criminal justice. I remember thinking to myself, "So this is what dad always felt like when a strike would break out at the factory." It was no fun at all.

As I sat there pondering my next move, the old "Be all you can be" commercial came on and interrupted my soaps. I thought to myself, "What the hell!" My phone hadn't been shut off yet, so I thought I should put it to good use. How could I have known I would be making what was to become the single most influential phone call of my life.

I picked up the phone book and looked up the number of the armory in Rock Falls. The line was busy, so I just dialed the number to the armory in the next closest town– Dixon, Illinois. I took my oath of enlistment on December 19th,

1991, and became a member of Charlie Battery of the First Battalion, 202nd Air Defense Artillery.

Skip ahead to March 2003. It is about six o'clock at night and I am at work, welding on a coal truck bulkhead. The side door to the factory opens and there stands my wife. My wife doesn't just pop in on me at work for any reason, so immediately I worried. She said my unit had called and said we were on alert. This means we have to drag every sock and handkerchief we were ever issued into the armory to be inventoried. We have to go through a comprehensive medical screening and a detailed records review as well. All of this has a sin- gular purpose– getting us ready to be deployed. I spent four days on active duty going through all this, and believe me, it was a pain in the neck.

For the next few weeks, my family held its collective breath, waiting for the phone to ring. The war in Iraq was in full swing, and it was looking like more troops would be sent over soon. It was in these few weeks I started to see the inner strength my wife has, for she retained her composure through it all. Finally, after what seemed like ages, my unit was taken off alert. We were able to exhale– for the time being anyway.

Later on in that same year, September I think it was, we were again placed on alert. Same story— inventories and medical screenings. Four more days of fun and excitement. We waited with crossed fingers, hoping and praying the inevitable would pass us by. Steph and I spent the next few days wondering if we could dodge the bullet twice. It was not to be. Thirty-five men from what was now Echo Battery, First of the 202nd ADA, were to be attached to our sis- ter unit down in Galva, Illinois. It is bad enough having to be deployed, let alone with a unit one is unfamiliar with. Needless to say, we were all on edge. The men from Dixon wondered the same thing as the guys from Galva were wondering; how would we all get along?

I entered active duty on October 12th, 2003, as a soldier assigned to Second Platoon of Foxtrot Battery of the First Battalion, 202nd Air Defense Artillery. Most of my buddies from Dixon were in Third Platoon. I felt alone, but the guys from Galva proved to be the consummate professionals, and quickly I was assimilated into the platoon. Early on, we had to list our civilian skills on a roster that was passed around. It was discovered I knew a little bit about emergency medicine, so I was tasked with developing classes for presentation in our train-up period.

I spent my time at the armory by day, packing and loading and teaching. By night, I sat at my little computer in the basement of my house, pouring over such books as Mosby's *Medical Encyclopedia* and Brady's *Emergency Care* and simultaneously writing classes on such topics as burn management, penetrating trauma, hypovolemic shock, and heat injuries– to name a few. Steph was getting steamed I wasn't spending time with the family, but I think she understood that where we were headed, the information I was trying to give to the guys might, someday soon, save a life– maybe even mine.

We left home and headed for Fort Hood, Texas, on November 1st. Fort Hood was to be our home for the next few months while we went through a more focused trainup. The time spent at Hood was characterized by classes, field training, packing, equipment issue, and of course, the last beers we would be drinking for quite a while. We left Fort Hood around the end of January or early February and headed by bus to Fort Polk, Louisiana, where JRTC awaited.

JRTC stands for Joint Readiness Training Center. I had been through JRTC once prior with the guys from my old unit in Dixon, but this trip would be different. This time, we focused on clearing buildings, interacting with "Iraqis" (local civilians hired to dress funny and pretend not to speak English), finding IEDs, reacting to ambushes, and other "army stuff." Personally, and I know many of the guys share this same thought, the time spent at Fort Polk training wise was a joke. Only about 1/64th of the information we were given at Fort Polk was true upon our arrival in country.

We left JRTC and said goodbye to our home soil at the end of February 2004. Some of us came to Kuwait early on a giant air force transport plane. Some people complain about flying coach on a trans-Atlantic flight. Let me tell you, riding the same trip in an air force cargo plane that can also haul tanks is not exactly comfy. I couldn't feel me bum, and we hadn't even made it to New England for our first fuel stop. There are also no flight attendants on these puppies. The flight was horrid and lasted for about 15 hours. We stopped in Germany, I think, for a bit and got to stretch our legs. When the plane landed again, we were in the desert.

When we got off the plane in Kuwait, we had to hand in one empty M16 magazine per man. After we went through our first "in country" briefing, we filed out of the circus-like tent, and two soldiers handed us our magazines back. Only now they were filled with bullets. When we took the fully loaded magazines in our hands and looked down at the green tipped bullets, any illusions any of us might have had about what lay in store for us were shattered. This is the real thing.

I remember lying in my cot one night trying to sleep and thinking: What would the days ahead hold for me? How would I react when that first bullet whizzed by me? Would I ever see Toulon and my home again? We all felt it. Anyone who suggests anything to the contrary is a liar. We started to really bond as a unit in Kuwait. The nightly "Cigar Pit" tradition was born in the sands of northern Kuwait. We put off the worries of what lay ahead and busied ourselves with the tasks at hand and with the camaraderie that only soldiers in war can ever really know.

Contact with home was sporadic at best in Kuwait. There was only one phone tent there and the line was always long and, of course, we had no Internet there. Soon, our days of preparation came full circle and we loaded up into our trucks, beginning the three-day trip north. As we prepared to leave, we went through sand tables of the route north. Every person knew the timeline, the route, what to do if we were attacked, and how to call for the medivac choppers. My good buddy Ben Sleaford and I went to church one last time. The chaplain, a Catholic priest, led the service. I took communion one last time and at the end of the service, the priest gave us all blanket absolution. I felt better knowing if I should get my arse blown off, at least I did so with a clean soul. This was it, and there was no turning back. Those many months of packing and preparing for every possible contingency was about to be put to the test. Word spread quickly that the convoy that had left the day prior had been hit already. None of us liked the sound of that, but we put our fear in our pockets and drove north.

Our hodgepodge of vehicles lumbered northward, with each of us, in our own way, praying for a safe trip. I was driving the truck in which 1SGT "Top" Peterson was riding. It was just me and Top. I felt good knowing he was riding shotgun– having a battle buddy close by gives you a sense of security, especially if happens to be Top. As we drove into the center of Baghdad and, as the traffic started to thicken, I noticed Top skinning his Beretta and holding it in his hand as we navigated the midday traffic clogging the streets of this ancient city. People were walking among our convoy, and the sight of these foreign people so close to me and my truck did not set me at ease. For the last few miles through the city, I drove with my M16 lying across my lap. We didn't have any doors on our truck at that time, and the thought of someone walking up and plugging me in the side of my head didn't make me feel all too good. We made it to the airport with no problems and started to get settled in.

Once settled into our trailers and running missions, we started to find ways to occupy our time. The PX at that time was nothing more than a tent with a few shelves stocked with the bare essentials– shoelaces, soap, toothpaste, and the like. No DVDs, no PS2 games…heck, they didn't sell much of anything. They had a bigger PX a few miles away, but we couldn't always get there. All I had to keep my mind occupied were the books I had packed and my laptop. Playing cards became a nightly affair, but I had no such appetites for that kind of thing. Soon, we decided to inquire into the possibility of acquiring an Internet system. Money was collected, satellites, cable and server computers were purchased and, in no time, we were up and surfing the web.

From the start, communication with home was paramount in my mind. I needed to talk to my friends and family as much as possible to help me deal with being so far from all I had known thus far. The highlight of my days was an email from home. Soon, I was in almost daily contact with my wife, my two little girls, and my buddies from school. Every night, I would sit and pour out my thoughts and my worries to anyone who would listen. My three closest friends from school became my rock. To them went all of my fears and my hopes. I would not have made it through this with my sanity if it had not been for them.

Although very expensive at first, having the Internet was fast proving to be one of the best purchases I have ever made. People back home would ask me constantly about what I was seeing, what we were doing, how the people of Iraq were reacting to our presence– it seemed even though in this information age, as it is called, people had no idea of what it was like over here! So, what started out as my attempt to enlighten my buddies back home, soon turned into an almost therapeutic nightly ritual for me; chronicling what would become the most intense and educational experience of my life.

As time passed and by reading what the media outlets were reporting, I found myself growing increasingly incensed at the bias and almost myopic manner in which the news from over here was being fed to the American public. I remember thinking, "What about all of the good we are doing over here?" "This trash the media is spewing is nothing more than a body count!" What about the schools we are building? What about the fact these folks don't have to live in fear of Saddam Hussein anymore? Why doesn't the news stations show footage of happy children rather than the latest car bombing? The negativity that is ever present in this world is not going to go away if people keep adding to it. The media has the privilege and the responsibility of letting the world know what is happening. They are charged with the unending task of letting the people know what is going on! But, I have come to believe such news should be presented in a truthful and unbiased manner. Responsible journalism to me is honesty and integrity, coupled with impartiality in the stories covered. This, in my mind, was not being done. So, with time on my hands and among men and women doing great things, I decided to tell our story.

At first, I just wrote to people on my email "friends list." I would write about our day's missions, within the parameters of security concerns, of course. I told the stories the newspapers did not. I told people about the good things our unit was getting done. Water purification sets, playground equipment for schools, medical assistance for the locals who would otherwise go untreated, delivering clean water to entire villages, obtaining wheelchairs for kids who otherwise had to be carried to and fro– these are the stories that needed to be told. This is what the men from Foxtrot Battery were doing, all while fighting with the insurgents. We are just a bunch of farmers, truck drivers, stockbrokers, factory workers, and students thrown together– taken from our civilian lives in America, ripped out of our comfort zone and thrown into a place thousands of miles from home, handed a rifle, and told to help a people we had never seen. We have done so with unwavering determination and compassion. Our side of this story had to be told!

And so I wrote. Every time I had a minute, I fired up my trusty laptop and poured out my heart. After a few of my letters made a tour of cyberspace, my dad, unbeknown to me, sent a copy of a letter to the local paper. The editor was kind enough to print it in its entirety, and soon people wanted to hear more. Dad told me one day what he was up to, and I was taken aback at first. I couldn't understand what the big deal was with my writing. Then it hit me: This is what the average American citizen really wants to know about. It isn't the carnage here, it isn't the flag-draped coffins coming home; it is the justification of those flag-draped coffins people want to know about. It is like seeing a return on an investment. You put money in for so long, and soon you'd like to see a return. Here, the money is the soldiers and sailors of our nation. Our youth, our pride, our sons and daughters are the investment. What we are doing for the people of Iraq is the return. We must, in our minds, be able to justify the loss. We must validate the loss of life, as well as the time spent away from home! In writing of our accomplishments, I was doing just that, and people wanted more. It was my belief if people could see what I saw, then maybe this war wouldn't be so unpopular.

America has always been the great beacon of hope. We have always tried to help others. The recent tsunamis in Indonesia are the prime example. In 2001, we were dealt a great blow at the hands of terrorists from fanatical Muslim sects and yet, rather than stereotype all Muslims as terrorists, we send a carrier group over to help a predominantly Muslim corner of the world. We are doing the same thing here in Iraq. We are helping those who were powerless to help themselves. America and Iraq alike will benefit from our efforts, and I tell you; our soldiers and sailors have not died in vain.

What follows is a compilation of letters that tells our side of this war: The good times, the hard times, hardships endured and hardships overcome, humorous times and reflections on how this war has impacted my life and how I view the world in which I find myself. But, it is also the story of a small number of people from Central Illinois. The men of Foxtrot Battery have a story to be told.

The stories that follow are written from a firsthand point of view. I have tried to paint a picture with words of what we see here. I have tried to remain pragmatic, but I freely admit, at times, I digress. I would be remiss if I did not forewarn you, the reader. I must admit, as well, I am pretty proud of my fellow soldiers here. So, forgive me if I seem a little biased.

At some points in the text, the dates may get a little cloudy. Sometimes, during this deployment, if it hadn't been for my watch, I would not have known what week it was, let alone the day. Any misquotes, inaccuracies insofar as dates, times or places; any errors of any kind are mine and mine alone. As you read, please do keep these things in mind.

SSG Jason A. Adams
Camp Cooke, Iraq
February 2005

Training
for War

Notice   Training   Deployment   Home leave   Back Home
10/12/03   3/1/04   9/26-10/14/04   3/19/05

Half Time in Texas

Today is November 28ᵗʰ

Hey everyone!

Hope all of you had a great Thanksgiving! We all had a great time at the Dallas/Miami game. More on that in a bit. We left Fort Hood at 0700 hours on Wednesday. It was a three-hour drive to Dallas. I managed to get a nap on the bus, and so it didn't seem like a three-hour ride. However, my butt was hurting pretty bad after three hours, so I am really glad I went ahead and bought the plane ticket home for Christmas! It is a 17-hour ride home by bus, and I don't think even I can sleep that long.

We went directly to the stadium once in Dallas and started practicing for the half-time show. The first couple hours we were in civilian clothes, but they wanted to do a complete dress rehearsal, which was recorded live on TV. They told us to go and get changed into our BDUs. We figured we would have to change on the bus, which would suck, but they sent us into this tunnel and told us to use the locker room. Yeah, that's right, we changed our clothes in the Dallas Cowboys' locker room!!! I have a picture of me standing right by Quincy Carter's locker! I told my buddies this was one place we would never be again!

We went through a few more practice runs, and then we got the chance to mingle with the Cowgirls! I have some pictures of them, too. We also got to meet Jerry Jones, who owns the Cowboys. He was very nice and told us when we get back from Iraq, we and our families can attend a game for free. We learned later he is a very big supporter of the military and frequently hands out free passes to soldiers. It is nice to know people like that still care about us.

At about 1800 hours, we boarded the buses for the hotel. I envisioned staying at the local Motel 6, but what a shock it was when the bus pulled up in front of the Dallas Marriott! Marble walls, people holding doors for us, valet parking, all the bells and whistles!! Our room was very nice. Yes, there was a mint on my pillow, too! We were on pass until 0100 hours.

We went down to the lounge to have a beer, and I asked the waitress if they had a piano there at the hotel. She said "yes," and pointed me in the right direction. I hadn't played a real piano since I left and was starting to have withdrawals. The piano was in a cubbyhole adjacent to the bar so I tried to play quietly so as to not disturb the other guys. I failed in my attempt, and soon had several guys standing around me. I felt like Liberace, minus the candles. By then, I was starting to get bloated from starvation, and all I wanted was food. We asked the doorman for a good restaurant. He recommended Duke's Roadhouse, so I reached for my cell phone to call a cab, and he said the hotel shuttle would take us!

Duke's was great. I had the best chicken sandwich ever (plus, the beer was cheap). Then we went to a place called Big Doug's Sports Bar where I spent most of the time playing air hockey with my roommate (I schooled his butt six out of seven times, by the way). I was back at the hotel by 2330 hours, polished my boots, and watched the History Channel — I am such a loser!

Game day started at 0800 for us. I came down from my room and was looking for some coffee, and wouldn't you know it, but there is a Starbucks right in the hotel! I have a weakness for their White Chocolate Mocha, and I spent five bucks on a cup of joe, but it was worth it. I figured those two days would never happen again, so I was gonna live it up.

We then went to the stadium and got our seats. We sat behind the end zone in the 17th row. Great seats, especially for free! We practiced for the half-time show a few more times and had a hot dog and nachos for our Thanksgiving Day meal. We took a lot of pictures on the field. I have a bunch with me on the 50-yard line and some with the cheerleaders. The game started, and Dallas was getting their butts kicked from the start.

We went down to the tunnel in the stadium to get ready for the half-time show and out walks Toby Keith! I didn't get his autograph, but I got to shake his hand and got a pretty good picture of him, too. The half-time show was great. It was very exciting to be taking part in the second biggest game of the year! It was also an honor to be representing my unit and my country. I talked to my dad after it was all over, and he said during the show the cameras didn't show anything past the 40-yard line. I was standing on the 20-yard line. Oh well, it is probably for the best anyway. I look pretty darn hot in my uniform, and if 50 million Americans would have seen me, I would be getting all that fan mail and reporters shoving cameras in my face every time I was out in public. That stuff just isn't my style.

After the game, one of the security guards hooked us up big time and told us the players exit the stadium at Gate Nine. Some of us went over there and got autographs and pictures of some of the players. I got autographs from three guys I didn't know. I don't get into pro sports too much, but the funny thing is while I was standing there, this lady started talking to me about the army. She said her son played for the Cowboys and I thought, "Whatever lady, dream on," then she asked me if I wanted to meet "her little Joe." I said "Sure... sounds great." This huge guy comes out and she yells, "Hey, Joey!" He walked over and hugged her, and she introduced us. This guy was No. 77 or 88, not sure, but he looked like Shaq, only three feet wider. He was really nice; I got his picture with his mom and me. He thanked me for serving my country.

Oh, I forgot, the Salvation Army uses the Thanksgiving Day game to kick off their Bucket Campaign for the holiday season. We went up to the food vendors' area to get some chow,

For every pushup we did, they put money in the kettles. I don't know how many I did, but people just started putting money in left and right.

and these people were ringing their bells and everybody just walked by. It pissed me off. So a group of about 10 soldiers and I asked if we could help them. They gave us bells, and we started barking like carni-rats! Then we got the wild idea to start betting people money for pushups. For every pushup we did, they put money in the kettles. I don't know how many I did, but the folks with the buckets were very happy. People just started putting money in left and right.

The bell ringers said they had never seen such a sight as army guys doing pushups to help them. It made me feel good to help them. I can't stand the thought of a little kid not having enough to eat or a warm coat, especially at Christmas. I think of all of us soldiers who will be away from our families, but at least we had good food to eat and a warm bed. I am so thankful for what I have.

After the game, we got back on the buses and drove back here. I slept most of the way, but my butt still hurt when I got back! We pulled into Fort Hood about 2330 hours, and went straight to bed. Today we have off. I am just hanging out and doing laundry. Sounds like fun doesn't it? Anywho, that's about all the typing my hands can take for one day. I hope you all write me soon. I can't wait for Christmas.

Later, Jason
Fort Hood, Texas

Notice
10/12/03

Training

Deployment
3/1/04

Home leave
9/26-10/14/04

Back Home
3/19/05

Getting Ready

Today is December 3rd

Hey all,

Started my Combat Lifesavers class today, I expected it to be nothing more than a good review for me, but I about died from sheer boredom. However, I realize that to 90 percent of the people in the room, it is all new and confusing stuff. The instructors are all in the medical field on the civilian side so they have a vast amount of hands-on experience with which to teach. We went over various types of injuries such as heat casualties, cold weather injuries, bleeding and shock, head and neck trauma, and some other stuff.

Luckily, our classroom just happens to be located right smack across from the A&W Root Beer shop! Which is proving to be quite a morale boost for me personally, as I am becoming addicted to their chili cheese fries. The irony of that is the fact I am fully aware of the health hazards associated with a diet of such items, yet, I find myself craving them regardless. I am a moron!

Anywho, class got out around 1630 hours, and we came back to the barracks and had mail call. My wife sent me a care package with about 10 lbs. of beef jerky in it. I love a woman that will buy her man beef jerky! What a gal! She also sent me an assortment of coffee creamer and sugar cubes. I am so stocked on coffee and condiments I could open my own Starbucks right out of my barracks room. I might have to check into that, you know, as a second income while I am here.

They sent us to get our Hepatitis B shots tonight, but I got out of it because I already have mine from working with the Stark County Ambulance. Speaking of that, today in class, we learned how to make a C-collar out of a SAM splint. What a joke! I was dumbfounded when I saw what they were doing. I thought to myself, "Why not just use a wet paper bag and some duck tape?" I guess it is better than nothing, but I am gonna try to scam a few C-collars while I am home on Christmas leave.

That's about it for tonight; I miss you all, and am counting the days till I come home. Keep me in your prayers, as you all are in mine.

Later, Jason
Fort Hood, Texas

Notice 10/12/03 | Training | Deployment 3/1/04 | Home leave 9/26-10/14/04 | Back Home 3/19/05

In the Field

Today is December 13th
  Good morning!

Another day down, and seven to go till I come home for Christmas! Just a quick note to tell you all I am doing fine, and that we came in from the field for a day to get warm and to clean up. I can assure you all of us take for granted the luxury of a hot shower and a real "flush type" toilet. The field set-up we have is not bad. There are field showers and port-a-potties, plus these big tents with heaters in them and plastic tiled floors. It is not as bad as I expected, but it still sucks.

It rained all day yesterday, and we were all soaked to the bone. It is a miracle we all don't have pneumonia. We have to ride around in the back of a Humvee with no roof or doors. It is very windy and cold. But the good thing is at least we don't have to walk. My point is this: Things can always be worse, and we need to be thankful for what we have, rather than lament that which we do not have.

I am not sure what is on tap for today, but I stuck my head out our door a little bit ago and it is cold and windy. So whatever fun we get to experience today, it should be cold. Rumor is we are coming in from the field for good on the 17th rather than the 19th. This would be good, because we need some time to clean up and get ready to come home. There is a lot of work involved with coming in from the field! Everything is dirty and must be cleaned, we have to pack our bags, and we need to rest up. This cannot be done in one day, so I hope the rumor is in fact true.

That is about all the time I have for writing today. We have formation in 45 minutes and I am sitting here in my skivvies. Steph tells me Angela Davis sent a Christmas card to our house. That is so cool! I hope all of you are doing great, and I will see you in a week!

Later, Jason
Fort Hood, Texas

Notice
10/12/03   Training   Deployment
3/1/04   Home leave
9/26–10/14/04   Back Home
3/19/05

Return to Fort Hood

Today is January 3rd

Hey all,

Just a quick note to let you all know I made it back to Fort Hood safe and sound. My travel experience was eventful to say the least! My flight was supposed to leave Peoria this morning at 0853 hours, but because of the fog it did not take off until almost noon. We sat on the runway for at least an hour. So, we obviously missed our connecting flight in Chicago. We managed to get a later flight at 1400 hours, but that meant we had to pretty much rush to our next gate. We finally left O'Hare en route to Austin around 1430 hours and landed in Austin around 1700 hours.

As if that wasn't bad, the stinking airline lost my bag due to all the shifting of flights. It is not just any bag either, it has my digital camera and all my medical software in it, plus all my music CDs. The airline said when it comes in, they will get it to me here on post. I think the screw up had to be in Chicago, as that was my only flight change. Anywho, I am not happy about it! The funny thing is our time at home flew by, and now that I am here, it does not feel like we ever left. But, the longer we stay at home, the harder it is to come back.

I am glad I was able to see most of you while I was home. I am also humbled by the fact a lot of you took time out of your schedules to see me. I hope all of you had a great Christmas. I know I did! I look forward to your emails, but be advised the military server I use has outlawed the forwarding of mail out of our accounts. These emails that want you to "forward this to at least 10 people or your toilet won't flush, and you will get herpes" can no longer be forwarded. I still like to read them, but I cannot send them on, just so you know. That is all for tonight, I have to get to bed as I am tired.

See you all later, Jason
Fort Hood, Texas

Notice   Training   Deployment   Home leave   Back Home
10/12/03   3/1/04   9/26-10/14/04   3/19/05

Training Days

Today is January 8ᵗʰ

Hey everybody!

Just a few lines regarding our last training block. We just got into the barracks today, but we are going back out tonight and won't be back until the 13th. The training is pretty good, and for the most part I am having fun. We are still going to rifle ranges and firing our weapons, but we are doing it differently than I am used to. For example, yesterday, we were riding around in the back of a Humvee shooting at pop-up targets. We are supposed to be refitted with different weapons also. They told us we are getting 10 shotguns and 9 sniper rifles, plus 40 more 9mm pistols. I hope to get my hands on at least a 9mm to carry along with my other weapon.

We are going to be getting our desert uniforms soon and are preparing to send a lot of extra stuff home to Galva, Illinois. This is good because we would have a ton of junk to haul around with us. I hate having to keep track of all that junk! The less stuff I have to sign for, the happier I am. When we get back from the field, we should be in the barracks for about 10 days. This is a good thing, as we will need a day off by then.

Not much time to write now; I will try to write more when we get back.

See you all later, Jason

Fort Hood, Texas

Packing for Battle

Today is January 17ᵗʰ

Hey everyone!

Just wanted to take a minute to tell you all I am sorry for not having written much lately, but we have been working until midnight all week, and getting up early, too. I haven't had a whole lot of time to do anything let alone sit down and type!

Today, like this whole week, was crazy! We had to get all the trucks ready to go overseas. If any of you have ever done that task, you will know how much it flat out sucks. Everything has to be banded down; all the places that metal touches metal have to be isolated with cardboard. All the trucks have to have EXACTLY three-forths tank of fuel or they have to be drained and/or driven until the gas gauge reads three-forths. I don't really understand the logic behind that idea, but there is a lot that goes on here that does not make much sense. We loaded our individual equipment boxes today, also. Boy, that was sure fun carrying a 200-pound crate down three flights of stairs! On the other hand, at least we were going down the stairs instead of up.

Tonight, we are supposed to have the night off, but we can't have formation until the idiots from first platoon figure out how to work the banding machine and finish their trucks. I shouldn't talk bad about my fellow soldiers, but watching them use the bander is like watching a drunken baboon trying to get a square peg into a round hole. Rumor is we are getting tomorrow off, but I also heard we just don't have first formation until noon. We all could use a night off to blow off some steam and a chance to get some good sleep. It will be a long time before we get to do it again.

Well, change No.14,235! I was supposed to carry an M16 into Iraq, but I was told today I would now carry an M249 (SAW). Normally, this would make me mad, but under the circumstances I am warming up to the idea. The SAW is like an M16 that is belt fed. It will lay down some serious lead. The only drawback that stands out to me is how carrying this weapon will hinder my additional duties as medic. The SAW, while a great weapon, is rather cumbersome.

The armorer here at my building refit all our SAWs with a scope, flashlight with the I/R filter on it so I can use it while wearing NVGs (night vision goggles), plus they put on a new sling that allows me to carry the weapon in the "ready" position.

I should probably go and try to get to chow before final formation, but I am too lazy and tired to walk the 2 1/2 blocks to the chow hall. Having been working so late into the night the last few days, we haven't been to the chow hall at all. I have been living off pizza and pop-tarts. If I don't get scurvy or some other nutritional-related disease it will be amazing. I have also been drinking a ton of coffee lately. That is not good either, but it sure helps offset the effects of sleep deprivation. The bad thing is I had to pack up my coffee pot today, so I will probably start having caffeine withdrawals pretty soon.

I hope you all are doing great, and I will try to write more later.

See you all later,
Jason
Fort Hood, Texas

Firing Range

Today is January 19th

Hey everyone!

Well, today was not what a normal person would describe as fun. We went to the M249 range today, and it was the most unorganized, screwed-up mess I have ever seen. The people running it were late, it was freezing out, and to top it all off, we didn't get to finish firing. The range did not open up until noon, and we had been there since 0830 hours! The ammo situation was all messed up and we wound up leaving in disgust. We pretty much could have sat in our rooms all day asleep and accomplished more things than we did at the range. The only good thing to come from all this mess is the fact that we learned how to use the M145 optical scope for the M249. This scope is awesome! It is a scope, range finder and point sight all rolled into one unit. It also has a backlight for use at night.

I still can't get my DVD player to work, and I can't send it in to get fixed either. If I were to send it in, I don't know where I will be when it is sent back to me. As if that were not bad enough, there is no heat in my side of the building. Our room is not too bad, but it is chilly. We opened the bathroom doors that connect our rooms and turned the ceiling fan on reverse to draw heat from the other room. I lit our two candles to try to add some heat, but my efforts are proving to be in vain.

We don't have formation until 0800 hours in the morning, so at least I can sleep in an hour. That is about it for tonight, see you all later!

Jason
Fort Hood, Texas

Notice | Training | Deployment | Home leave | Back Home
10/12/03 | | 3/1/04 | 9/26-10/14/04 | 3/19/05

Cell Phone

Today is January 27ᵗʰ

Hey everybody,

Well, I called today to cancel my Internet, and they said I could just do it on Friday. This is good, as I am not looking forward to turning it off. Having Internet capabilities has proven to be such a good thing as far as communications go. We were given last night and all of today off which was good because we have not had a full day off for about 24 days. Most of the guys went out to the bars for the night, but I did not. I decided rather to go out with all of the "under 21 crowd."

We had a great dinner at Red Lobster, and then we went to a pool hall right outside the east gate of Fort Hood. We just spent a couple hours listening to music and shooting pool. It was quite fun, and we needed the time to unwind. I can't really understand the need to go out and get totally drunk and then spend the next day recovering.

I woke up at 0900 hours this morning and went to the PX to turn in my cell phone. The lady said I could take it to Fort Polk and then just inactivate my account while I am in Iraq. Then when I get back, I can just call them and they will reactivate it no matter where I am. That is good because we will probably not come back to Fort Hood to demobilize. But in any event, I will just keep it with me and start it back up once we get back in the states so I can keep in touch. I figure we will spend a month at a de-mobilization site. Plus, we will probably have to work in Galva, Illinois, for a week or two unloading all our junk, too. So just because I come back to the good 'ol U.S. doesn't mean I will go straight home.

I had lunch at Popeye's Chicken today. It was good, and I was getting sick of pizza and Chinese food. I am not sure what is on the schedule for the next few days here. I imagine my leaders will find some fun and challenging detail for us. Man, I love the army! (sarcasm) Anyway, we will have to find a little time to pack all our junk and clean the barracks.

I had to laugh the other day when we came in from the machine gun range and they told us to clean our weapons. I asked for cleaning supplies such as oil and rags plus, I am out of bore patches. The dude in the arms room said they did not have any supplies because they packed them all away for the boat ride to Kuwait. I thought to myself, what a bunch of morons! How can you tell me to clean my weapon without cleaning supplies? I asked the guy if he had any toilet paper to use instead. I don't think he liked it too much, but who cares.

I heard a rumor the First CAV Division had a big parade today because they are getting ready to leave too. I also heard the only people that went from my unit were my commander, first sergeant and a guidon bearer. I would have liked to have known about it earlier as I think it would have been cool to see.

Well, that is probably enough for tonight, I have to rummage up something to eat. Maybe I will snoop around the dumpster out back and see what I can find. Just kidding, I am not THAT sick of pizza yet! Hope all is well with all of you.

Talk to you all later, Jason
Fort Hood, Texas

Notice 10/12/03 · Training · Deployment 3/1/04 · Home leave 9/26–10/14/04 · Back Home 3/19/05

Preparing to Leave Fort Polk

Today is February 29th

Hey everyone!

It has been awhile since I have been able to sit down and write all of you. We have been very busy with all that "army stuff," you know how it goes! So much has happened since we have been here at Fort Polk that it would take several pages and a couple hours for me to type it all. We made it through the JRTC portion of our time here. It went well, not exactly what I was expecting, but we made it nonetheless.

JRTC was designed to get different branches of the services used to working together; such as the air force and the army does in any war or deployment. So much of what we do is organic only to our respective branch that the right hand literally does not know what the left hand is doing. This training is supposed to be more stressful than real combat so it is actually a relief just to leave here. One good thing did come out of this time here – I got to have lunch with the president.

George W. Bush made a stop here last week, and a bunch of us got picked to have lunch with him. Only about 150-200 people got to go out of about 5,000, so I was pretty surprised I got to attend. I didn't get a picture with him as we were not allowed to take our cameras, but when he came in the tent we were in he passed right by me, and I could have grabbed his butt had I wanted to. Of course, I would have been tackled by all the secret service folks that were hovering around like vultures waiting for a wounded rabbit to die.

This post is pretty dead these last couple of days, not many people are here. Most of the guys are with their families that came down to see them one last time. I am on the advance party that will be departing before all the rest, so I am not able to leave the area. Plus, I don't want to have to say goodbye again. I would rather go and get this thing done and over with.

Some of the other guys and myself went to Wal-Mart today to get some last minute things to take with us. Then we decided that we should at least have one last good meal before we leave, so we decided on a Chinese buffet. This area is weird in that from the outside, most of these homes and buildings look rather dilapidated and ramshackle. Once you go in it is another story. The Chinese place we went to looked like all the other buildings but inside was very nice. The food was very good as well.

One thing I have noticed with the cuisine down here is that when the menu states an entree is "Hot and Spicy," rest assured they mean it. Case in point: In Kewanee, at the New China Buffet out by Wal-Mart, the General Tso's Chicken is labeled hot and spicy...not even close to hot. Down here, the General Tso's Chicken will burn through the top of the table if left unattended. This restaurant also served crayfish. Plus, every food joint serves hot wings.

I am ready to get the heck out of here honestly. I hate Louisiana! I mean the people are good people in general, but this whole place is a swamp! It has rained most of the days we have been here, and the soil here is mostly sand so it gets everywhere. I had to clean sand out of my gas mask which is sealed in its own carrying bag! Explain that one!

The last few days we have been preoccupied with packing up all we own. We have been putting everything on these huge air force pallets that will be loaded onto the plane. The only trouble was they are so big 20 men couldn't lift one, so we have to use a Skytrak forklift. The guy that was doing it for our unit was gone one day, and we couldn't move any pallets unless we had the lift. So I walked up to it and looked in the cab and said, "I can drive this thing." This dude asked me if I had a license and I told him "No." He asked if I was sure I knew what I was doing and I said, "Yep." He let me get in it and I just spent a few seconds playing around with the hydraulic levers to see which one did what and then off I went. In the army, it only matters that you have a license for something if you get into an accident. So I spent the majority of the day driving that monstrosity around. I had a good time, and by the end of the day, I found I was getting quite accustomed to the manner in which it worked.

The last couple of days have been spent sitting on our butts waiting for the air force to show up and take us overseas. They won't tell us when the plane is coming in or even what type of aircraft it will be. I guess they like to play their little cloak and dagger stuff whenever they can. My gut tells me we are not flying commercial, but rather will spend the better part of a day crammed into a C-5 or maybe worse a C-17. I have a master plan, however. I bought a bottle of Tylenol PM! I am not scared to exceed the maximum dosage either! I will go to sleep here, and wake up there! No problems! No, really though I won't abuse the stuff but, I have found in the past on long bus trips it makes them easier to bear. I bought a couple magazines to read also. I bought the latest copy of *Scientific American* and the latest copy of *Discovery*. Most of the guys bought "other" kinds of reading material (hint, hint) but that stuff isn't for me. If I am gonna read something, I might as well learn a thing or two in the process, don't you all agree?

I had better get going, I want to get some sleep before we leave. It is going to be a long trip, and I won't get a chance to catch my breath once we hit the ground either. Once there, we go to work unloading all our junk immediately. Anyway, I miss you all and am thinking of the day when I come home. Keep me in your prayers, and I will talk to you all later as soon as I get some Internet service over there.

Sincerely,
Jason A. Adams
Fort Polk, Louisiana

Settling In

First Impressions

Today is April 19th

Hey everyone,

I received notification just the other day that my Internet would be turned on soon. I had to update my virus protection and do some other stuff to my laptop (basically, I gave it a stiff laxative), and now I can email back and forth with you all.

For those of you whom I have not spoken to in awhile, I am now in Iraq and serving with the First Cavalry Division. We have been here for about a month now and are settled rather nicely in our little trailers. The rooms here are nice, and much more than I had expected. Our rooms are roughly 12 x 14 ft. and paneled. We have A/C and power outlets too.

I learned a hard lesson in universal power applications the first couple days here though. Seems as though the power here is 220 V rather than the 110 V that we are used to in the States. This presents certain logistical problems, as all the items I had requiring electrical power, I brought with me from the States. I had a universal power strip and a 150 W power converter, so I figured I was good to go for some old school joe the first morning here. I got up, plugged in my coffee pot, and went to shower. I came back and I had about 6 ounces of coffee. As it turns out, my coffee pot draws 1,000 W of power and I only had a 150 W converter. Do the math, and you can see the problem.

My alarm clock was a different story. I looked at the bottom of the clock and I could have sworn it was good for 220 V. Was I wrong or what! I plugged it in and it worked fine for about 30 seconds. Then it started smoking and the reading lamp on it got really bright and blew out.

So now I had no coffee, no alarm clock, and no converter. I blew a fuse in the converter, and you can't find them on post. So I got out another power strip and thought I would just plug it in the wall with my outlet adapter. My computer runs on either power supply, so I figured I would just run the power to my laptop through the power strip and that way I would have more outlets to plug stuff into. The power strip is one I bought at Fort Hood.

When I plugged it in, blue flames shot out of the power strip and the lights in the room went out. Scared me half to death! I had to go outside and reset the breaker, not to mention change underwear. So I had rendered all my electrical stuff useless, save for my computer, in two days. All is good now, I bought a 220 V coffee pot and my alarm clock is a windup.

The facilities here are adequate to say the least. The only problem is we have to walk quite far just to get to the phones and to chow. The phones are about 15 minutes away and you only get 10 minutes to use them. Chow is great, but again, long walk to get there. The PX is kinda dumpy for now. They are building a new one here but it is not open yet. So the only one we have is in an old tent. They don't sell much, but then again, we don't need much. I can't figure out their marketing strategies, however. They sell peanut butter and jelly, but no bread. They sell all kinds of makeup, but 90 percent of the people here are guys. (I hope they are not implying anything by that.) They don't sell any classical music at all! Can you believe that? What a bunch of heathen, podunk hillbillies! Luckily, I have almost 24 hours of music already loaded into my laptop. Now that I have Internet, I can listen to Internet radio anytime I want to. I like this station out of London. They play nothing but the classics with no stupid commercials.

Our days here are anything but normal. Our work schedule rotates; sometimes we work night shifts, and other days we start at 0400 and go all day. We don't get a lot of time to ourselves, but I think that helps make the time go faster. I have found the longer we sit idle, the more time seems to drag.

I am realizing several things as I am here though. We don't have enough equipment. Our trucks are armored, but not all of them. So, we have to share trucks. I

We only have four armored Humvees in our unit. The other trucks have what we call "Menard's Armor." That is, plywood and more plywood along with some sandbags.

am told the Clinton administration in its divine foresight saw fit to cut the budget, and the armored Humvees (M1114) got caught in the fire. We only have four in our unit. The others have what we call "Menard's Armor." That is, plywood and more plywood along with some sandbags. It works, but it really weighs the truck down and acceleration and maneuverability take a big hit.

I am also realizing that all the training in the world doesn't prepare you for this. We spent five months getting ready for this, and we would have been just as good coming straight here. The cultural awareness classes we went through at Fort Hood were worthless. I don't know what culture they were teaching us about, but it is not this one. The battle drills we learned are useless, and we don't even use them.

The area we are staying in is very pretty. It is part of Saddam's palace compound. There are several palaces here and many lakes. I am taking pictures as much as I can. There are many bridges here as well that look like something you would see in 18th-century France or Germany. The big PX over on the south side of the base camp is in a palace. There is a huge crystal chandelier that hangs right over the Pringles and beef jerky. The floors are marble and the doors are giant, hand-carved wood.

I see all this lavish, almost gaudy luxury, and yet a couple miles outside the gate people are starving. I can't get over the poverty here. Some of the guys are not upset over it. It really bothers me to see other human beings suffer. I don't care what race, religion, political alignment, or creed they are. They are still human beings, and I have not lost sight of this fact. When we go out, I take candy with me to give to the kids. They are the real losers in all of this. They have no choice in their situation. Yet they are all happy.

Many of them do not get the necessary medical care they need. I see a lot of physical handicaps and maladies I feel could be taken care of if adequate medical care was available. I can only do so much with my skills and the equipment I carry. I have treated a few of them as best I can, and I feel good as a result. I feel like I am really doing something for these people.

I hope when these kids get older, and they form their opinions about America that they remember us soldiers trying to help them. I hope they remember that many of us will never see home again because we fought for them. We fought for their freedom. I hope they realize this and don't forget it. Then we will have not fought in vain. These kids of today will lead this country tomorrow.

Well, I need to get off my soapbox and put my laundry away. Plus, I have to get ready for tomorrow's mission. I hope all of you can write to me when you get a chance. Soldiers can never get too much mail, you know. Just know I am well and doing fine over here. I miss all of you. Especially, I miss school. I never thought those words would come out of my mouth, but it is true. I miss school.

Gotta run, talk to you all later.

Sincerely, Jason

P.S.: My address here is:
Jason Adams
1 CAV 4-5 ADA
ATTN: F-202 ADA
2nd Platoon
APO AE 09379

Notice | Training | Deployment | Home leave | Back Home
10/12/03 | | 3/1/04 | 9/26-10/14/04 | 3/19/05

New Schedule

Today is April 23rd

Hey all,

Just a quick note to let you all know I am still doing fine. I have the next two days off. That is good, because I am tired. Our new schedule is two 13-hour shifts and then an eight-hour shift. The third day, we get 24 hours off. The only problem is the fact we still have to prep for our missions and recover from them, which takes a few hours too. So our average day on two of the three is about 16 hours.

What sucks is for the last three days they have been revamping the transformers here, and we have been without power during the day while the workers do their stuff. At night, they turn the power grid on, but we sleep during the day and we don't have A/C. It is almost too hot to sleep. I just pound some Nyquil and pop some Tylenol PM. I'm kidding, of course, but I have thought about it.

Anyway, all is well here, and I am thinking of you all. I hear the weather is turning rather nice back there, but you need rain. It rained pretty good here last night, hard to believe for the middle of a desert. It was lightning pretty good, too. That really looks neat through night vision goggles. Well, it is midnight, and I am beat. That's all for now. I will write more later.

Sincerely, Jason

Camp Black Jack, Iraq

Notice   Training   Deployment   Home leave   Back Home
10/12/03   3/1/04   9/26-10/14/04   3/19/05

Decent People

Today is April 24th

I know it is sometimes awhile between my letters, and I apologize for that. As you can probably surmise, the rest of us, as well as myself, are never short on things to do. Things have calmed down a bit here and that relieves us all. Oh sure, there is an occasional mortar round that comes in at night, but they never do any real damage. We are all fortunate the people we are fighting with really aren't all that intelligent.

We are still trying to get our Internet situation straightened out, but like anything it takes time. The guys that are working on it are members of my unit and have other things to do as well. But, our leadership realizes the importance of keeping in touch with our families, so they make provisions for the guys who are trying to get all this Internet set up. They have worked for the last three days just getting our laptops up to speed and putting in firewalls for virus protection. I told them all my laptop needed was a good stiff laxative; they just kinda stared at me. I guess medical lingo and computer lingo don't intermix.

Hopefully, we will be back online for good by tomorrow night. The trouble with the whole thing is the fact we are using satellite Internet. My understanding is like this: Our satellite here talks to a satellite in orbit, and that one talks to a receiver in Europe. Then it goes back to another satellite in orbit and then to a server in the United States. Even though radio waves travel very fast, that is still a lot of bouncing around.

There is an Internet café here, but it has been my experience with it that I would be able to communicate faster with smoke signals. I don't know why, but their computers run slower than a squirrel with no legs. Plus, there are only 12 terminals and the line is always long. I am so sick of waiting in line!!! Wait in line for chow, wait in line for mail, wait in line for gas! The only thing we do that doesn't require standing in line is the prostate exam. Just kidding, but it sure seems like that sometimes. That part of the military is eternal.

We have been actively patrolling our sectors for about a month now. Most of the people we meet are decent people. But, I have studied too many books about war to not realize the ones who wave at us as we pass could be the same ones that shoot mortars at us at night. I can't help being friendly to them though. I am still human.

We met a man and his family the other day while we were guarding a weed cutting detail. His name was Hebaz (pronounced Heh-baaz) and he spoke some English. Between him and his three brothers, they could form a sentence in English. That was helpful because between the four of us on my team, we can form a sentence in Arabic. Surprisingly enough, we talked for about a half hour. One thing I have noticed about these people here is their patience. We Americans tend to get frustrated rather quickly when we cannot convey to others what we are trying to say. These people just keep trying.

One thing I have noticed about these people here is their patience. We Americans tend to get frustrated... these people just keep trying.

While we were talking, we had our little Arabic to English books out and we figured out real quick they are worthless. I am sure the locals get quite a kick out of listening to us try to babble our way through "Hello" or "Good Morning." My driver, SGT Ortiz, was with us that day, and they thought he was Arabic. They must have thought he was an interpreter or something because they kept pointing at him and muttering to each other. We finally got it through to them that he is of Mexican origin, not Arabic.

We asked them if they wanted anything to drink and they nodded, so we gave them some water or *mai* as it is called here. We asked them if they wanted some MREs and they said, "No." I guess they don't like them either. They did ask us for some MRE coffee, which we gladly gave them. Personally, I think that stuff if nothing more than dehydrated vomit with caffeine added to it. But, they seem to love it. We started saving all we can, and the next time we see them we will give it to them.

Sincerely, Jason
Camp Black Jack, Iraq

Notice   Training   Deployment   Home leave   Back Home
10/12/03   3/1/04   9/26-10/14/04   3/19/05

Tootsie Pops and Beechies

Today is April 26ᵗʰ

Well, we made it back safe and sound for another day. Today we patrolled our zone again and it was quiet; more on that in a bit. Yesterday, Sunday, I got up and decided since I didn't have anything to do I would go to church. The Catholic chaplain here is really cool, though very hard to understand. His sermons are reminiscent of Father John's. That is, he talks at length about something, but I just can't figure out what it is.

Anyway, as I was walking back to my trailer, contemplating how to spend the rest of my day off, my gunner came running up and said we had just gotten a mission. I thought, "yee haw," there goes my day off. Then I found out we had to chauffeur the commander into a sector of Baghdad we had never been to. We didn't have any problems, and I must say I hadn't seen very much of the downtown yet and it was rather cool to see it up close.

It is not unlike any other city, except for all the open air vegetable stands. That and the makeshift gas stations. Surprisingly enough, there are very few gas stations here. I can count on one hand the number we passed in the 300-mile journey from Kuwait to Baghdad. The locals will fill up any kind of jug, pitcher or tub they can find with petrol and sit along the road and sell it. I understand what they are doing; I just do not understand where they get the gas.

No convenience marts here, kids! No crappy pizza, no hot dogs, no beer and smokes, nothing. Just gas. The other shops are the same way. They are all specialty shops. Sam Walton has not staked a claim here yet. That's right, no Wally World, Target, K-Mart or Sam's Club. I don't know how these people survive! After we got done with our VIP escort, we came back and relaxed.

Today, we had a long day (13-hour mission) and we are tired. But, I like the people and I love the kids. They are little swindlers though! When we give them candy, they pretend like we didn't give them any and try to get more. I can't help but laugh at their efforts! I remember when I was a kid and we would go to Kroger. They always had free samples of something, and I thought I was so sneaky by getting a snack, going over in the next aisle, taking off my glasses and hat, and going back again. I thought, "heh-heh-heh, they don't know it's me again. I get a kick out of them and I figure I will give them seconds if they want it.

Today, I handed out a full bag of Tootsie Pops, and some Beechies gum. I was having a good time with the gum. Mike Bigger sent me a whole box of Beechies, a State Farm hat (a really nice one,) and a U.S. road atlas. Don't really understand the road atlas part, but a nice gesture nonetheless. Anyway, as I handed out the gum, I told each kid, "Compliments of your local State Farm agent." Of course, none of them had a clue about what I was saying, but it was fun!

As I handed out the gum, I told each kid, "Compliments of your local State Farm agent."

We happened to go by our friend Hebaz's house again, and one of his brothers flagged us down. He said, *"Hawaan,"* and pointed to the north. *Hawaan* means mortar, so we asked *"Ayna?"* which means where. We followed him for about 50 meters and sure enough, a mortar shell was lying in the dirt, intact. It looked really old, but hell, if you shot me out of a tube and I went flying through the air, thinking the whole time that when I hit the ground, I will explode, and survive all that; then I guess I would look really old, too.

Anyway, we found three more in the area. We called the bomb squad, and marked the area with tape. By this time, Hebaz came walking up with a herd of sheep. His other brothers were not far behind. They kissed SGT Ortiz again, heh-heh-heh, then to my utter shock one of the dudes kissed me.

If I can change only one person's view of the USA, or make only one person's life better while I am here, then my time will be well spent.

Everybody thought that was the funniest thing they had ever seen. But, in this culture, it is a sign of friendship, and I am glad they consider us their friends. Today, two of their kids were with them. Ahmed and Omar are their names and they are cute as buttons. We gave them candy and some Matchbox cars we bought, and they thought that was the greatest thing ever. I took some pictures of them; they were amazed at my digital Kodak. I guess they aren't used to seeing the picture right after I took it. We talked to all of them for awhile, and then we left. They sell instant coffee in the PX, like they put in the MREs that Hebaz and his brothers like so much. I think I might pick some up to take to them. Like I said before, if I can change only one person's view of the USA or make only one person's life better while I am here, then my time will be well spent.

Please don't send anymore stuff. I am running out of room to put it all! I have enough Q-tips to last the whole time I am here, plus I have enough baby wipes to open my own nursery. If you want to send beef jerky, well, then I might be able to find a little room in one of my drawers. Speaking of drawers, today we got buzzed by an AH-64 Apache. We were sitting on an overpass on the interstate outside Baghdad. Given our constant proximity to the airport, there are always aircraft near us. Today was no exception, so I was glad I had brought along my camera.

I noticed an Apache flying our way, so I reached into my truck and grabbed my Kodak to catch it on film. As I stepped from behind the truck, I could hear my gunner yelling Holy $#@*!. I looked to my left and coming straight at us was a second Apache I did not even know was there. The pilot was flying so close to the ground that, because we were on the overpass, he was actually below us! He did not pull up on the bird until he was only about 100 feet from slamming into us. He shot upward and cleared my Humvee by little more than 15 feet. I swear I could see him laughing at us. I tried to take a picture, but that is difficult to do when you are ducking for cover at the same time. Let's just say it is a good thing I carry a roll of toilet paper in my medical kit!

Got a letter from Roselyn Ham today, along with a box full of food from Dad and Steph. For the love of God, please don't send anymore food. I have very little room in my trailer, and I don't need it. The chow hall here is more than adequate. I am trying to lose weight, not gain. I did like the cookies, though. I also got a kick out of the pictures from Christmas. The look on Grandma's face holding that giant underwear is priceless.

Well, I have to write some more letters, so I will close here. We have to go out on another mission in a little bit, so I have to get ready. I guess we are raiding some poor bastard's house tonight. Sucks to be him. But, in a sick twisted way, I sorta like it. The more assholes we arrest, the less there are to cause us trouble.

Thanks for everything. I love you guys.

Sincerely, SSG Jason Adams
(Check out the rank before my name, I got promoted too!)
Camp Black Jack, Iraq

Notice   Training   Deployment   Home leave   Back Home
10/12/03   3/1/04   9/26–10/14/04   3/19/05

Helping, Not Hunting

Today is April 28ᵗʰ

Hey everyone!

Just sitting here enjoying the beautiful heat of Iraq, and thought I would write you all a letter. We are on standby right at the moment, so we have some time to relax. We don't have to go anywhere or do anything unless we are needed. At 2100 hours, though, we have a mission that will last until 0500 hours tomorrow. The power has been sporadic for the last couple of days, for reasons unknown to me. It has been off three times today alone. While it is on, I figured I had better write. We still don't have Internet in our rooms. All the network is in place, but for some reason, it isn't working. Last night, we caught some action, but nothing serious.

We also went into a market square to take pictures of the owners of all the shops. Most of the owners were compliant, yet I caught a hint of hatred in their eyes. Not all of them, just a few. One guy didn't want his picture taken, so trying to be nice, I asked again. He muttered something in Arabic and turned away. Now that I was pissed off, I said, "Hey jackass, I have a machine gun and you don't, turn around!" He didn't have a clue as to what I just said, but he heard me talking to him and turned around. I already had my camera at my cheek, and as soon as he turned, I got his picture. That pissed him off, but hey, it isn't the first time I have made someone mad, won't be the last.

As we were coming back from the market, we saw a bunch of people crowding around a semi-truck that had broken down on the interstate. We thought they were beating the driver, but as it turns out, the driver was nowhere to be found and they were just looting the truck. We pulled up and told them to get lost, and many of them did, but some of the people were pretty brazen and stayed around. Most of them were kids.

It was hot out, and one of the kids, a teenager I am guessing, spoke pretty good English. He asked me why I wore so many clothes as it was very hot. I told him I was wearing a bulletproof vest and my equipment. He didn't know what a bulletproof vest was, so I decided to have some fun. I turned to my buddy, SPC Eric Werkheiser of Galva, Illinois, and said, "Punch me." He hit me in the sternum, but I didn't feel a thing. All the kids' eyes got really big and some of them were muttering to each other. Then, I punched him and got the same response from the kids. Then I pulled out my bayonet, showed the kids what it was, and stabbed myself in the chest plate. One of the kids let out a scream, and I am not sure, but I think another started to pray. I started laughing, and so did Eric. The kids were amazed and laughed too, once they realized I wasn't trying to perform some kind of ill-aimed *seppuku* ritual.

Problem with the truck was we couldn't figure out who owned it. It wasn't military or government contractor, so we said goodbye and "have at 'er." We weren't half a mile down the road and they were all over the truck like ants. These people here are so poor, they will cannibalize anything. Watching them makes me remember stories I have read about America in the depression years. How nobody threw anything away, indeed, the rural parts of this country is like looking at America not too long ago. Many of the homes don't have power; none have indoor plumbing, one car per family, and maybe a tractor. Ninety percent of them are farmers, and illiteracy is at least 40 percent.

I met a guy yesterday who used to be an officer in the Iraqi army for 11 years. Today, he drives a taxi. We were able to talk for a bit, and I found no animosity toward me or any other member of my unit who was in the area.

...had we met a little over a year ago, we would have been trying to kill each other.

I found it ironic to say that had we met a little over a year ago, we would have been trying to kill each other. Yesterday, we met on different terms.

We are not enemies anymore, rather, the members of my unit and I are more like protectors. He lives in our area of influence, and our job is to help keep the countryside safe for the people who live there. I feel so bad for these people sometimes, I wish these assholes would stop shooting at us and allow us to assume more of a humanitarian mission. The ones who shoot at us are not from this area. I can't go into details, but trust me, they are not. The ones who live here are trying to simply live through it.

Well, that is about all the time I have for tonight. I hope this letter finds all of you safe and happy. Don't worry about me. We are all doing fine, hot, but fine. Many of you have asked my wife, my parents, or myself what to send to me. Please, I beg of you, no more food. I am thankful for all of it, make no mistake.

This morning, I opened a package full of candy and cookies. What are you people trying to do to me? Do you know how hard it is for a fat kid who is on a diet to give away food? I did it, but it was hard. Anyway, all kidding aside, I am in your debt for all you have done, but please, no more food.
If you wish to send anything, I could use some classical music. Chopin or anything baroque will do nicely. Other than that, I do not need anything. Of course, a letter would be nice, but I understand you all have lives, too, and are busy. Just keep me in your thoughts and that will suffice. I will write as time permits, right now though, I have to go and bring peace and democracy to the Middle East!

Sincerely, Jason
Camp Black Jack, Iraq

War Is Eternal

Today is May 6th

Hey everybody,

Just sitting here enjoying my day off. Not too much went on today for me, but the billowing towers of smoke that have become such a common sight did not cease (there is a battalion of self-propelled artillery stationed not too far away). I guess somebody's day wasn't going too well. Now that we have Internet, I can read U.S. newspapers. One thing that strikes me as odd is the fact they are reporting "Fierce fighting in Baghdad and Fallujah." Sorry to disappoint, but I am right in the middle of that area, and I am just not seeing it. Perhaps, those reporting the news are directionally challenged and do not realize where they are at. I don't know, but I would not term the fighting as "fierce." We still have mortars shot at us quite often, but not to let us down, they are still not accurate. We would be in a world of hurts if the morons shooting at us ever figure out how to aim them.

Also, I see the scumbags that are whining about this war are still spewing venom. I love how they tell everyone we don't need to be here. Are they learning impaired? Did they eat a bowl full of stupid for breakfast? We are doing so much good here. As I wrote to my cousin earlier tonight, ask the little kid that gets to eat a decent dinner tonight only because of the food I gave him today; ask him if we need to be here! Ask the person whom I rendered medical aid to because she was bleeding; ask her if we need to be here! Ask them! Every time one of these folks looks out their window, they can see an American Humvee rolling past, with a sole purpose of keeping them safe. Ask them! These people are learning what it is like to not live in fear.

Yes, as a matter of fact, I am on a soapbox, deal with it.

We have no idea of what it is like to live like this. I had no idea until I got here. Now, my eyes are open and I see what needs to be done. It is being done, but just like Rome, a new Iraq will not be built in a day. Think of the things we Americans have. I am not talking about MTV, Martha Stewart, or "Survivor." I am talking about our freedoms, our way of life. Think about it being gone. Scary, isn't it? These folks don't even know what it feels like to live free. Some of the older ones might, but there are many who don't. Soon, if all the world will be patient (either be patient and shut up, or pitch in and help), this will all work out. Things are slowly starting to get done.

Today, we saw a bunch of workers picking up litter along the interstate. There were also several bulldozers and maintainers out reworking the shoulders of the interstate. In a couple of weeks, we are going to start working on a new school for the kids. The one they go to now has dirt floors and no windows. We are going to build it from scratch. I am so happy to be helping these folks. My vocabulary does not possess words to describe to you what it feels like for me to be able to do so much good. It is almost overwhelming.

Okay, I am done. It just makes me mad, no, livid is a more accurate term, to see and hear people yelling about things they do not understand.

Our interpreter, code-named Jaguar, had a son the other day. The army, being the compassionate organization it is, gave him the day off. We took up a collection for him and also bought some baby toys for the little guy. Not much of a selection of

Our interpreters put themselves as well as their families in great peril by helping us. We trust them so much.

baby stuff at the PX, but we did our best. Our interpreter is one hell of a guy. We could not do our jobs without the staff of interpreters we have.

Another interpreter we work with, code-named "Snake," has been shot twice by snipers. The people we are fighting against don't like to see Iraqis helping us, and it is not too hard to pick out the interpreter in a crowd full of Americans. Luckily, Snake has a bulletproof vest, and aside from some bruised ribs, he walked away unscathed. Both of these men, and the rest of them as well, have my eternal respect. They are putting both themselves as well as their families in great peril by helping us. We trust them so much, and because they are such an integral part of our team, they carry a weapon with us when we patrol. If we lose our interpreter, we will be up that well known tributary, without a means of propulsion.

My sister, Bernadette, sent me some new CDs to listen to the other day, and let's just say she has been bumped up on my Christmas list, big time! Vladimir Ashkenazy playing Chopin and Yo-Yo Ma playing Bach. What a caring, kind, saint-like person she is. She also sent me some food, but I gave it to my roommate who has this tapeworm problem. Just joking, but the only other guy I have ever seen put away so much food and not gain a pound is Rob Whittaker. People like that make me sick. I see a billboard for Taco Bell, and I gain weight. It is not fair.

I have received several cards and emails in the last week, and I thank you all from the bottom of my heart for thinking of me. Steph is sending me a printer for my laptop so if my Internet goes down again, then at least I can still write letters home. I feel guilty about my being less than punctual in my return correspondence. But, I must beg your forgiveness as I don't type that fast, and time is not an asset I possess.

As I am sitting here rambling on, the helicopters keep flying overhead. Sometimes they fly so low I can actually hear the rotors cutting the air. The UH-60 Blackhawks, when directly overhead, make a very distinct sound. It is like a high-pitched "wheek-wheek-wheek" sound and is only heard when they fly low and fast. I see the Medivac helos come in sometimes, and they always fly right overhead my trailer. It is rather sobering when they come in 100 feet off the deck cruising about 150 kts. It is sobering because I know why they are flying way.

The air force hospital is not too far away, and it is where they take the wounded. There is no mistaking the Medivac helo, especially because of the big red cross on the belly of the aircraft. Those pilots are fearless and are masters at their trade. They save so many lives with their daring rescues. Easter Sunday, we got into an ambush that rivals those seen in the movies. I can't go into details, but it was bad. When my platoon got through the first ambush and arrived at the people we were sent to rescue, they had already had two men hit. I helped treat them, and the medivac helo came out of nowhere and landed right in the middle of the interstate we were on. As I, and three others loaded the wounded onto the bird, we could here bullets whizzing by us, but the chopper pilots just waited for us to get the wounded onto their helicopter. I am sure they were about as nervous as a prostitute in church, but they waited. Then they took off, and went out the same way they came in, hard and fast.

The whole engagement was almost surreal, but I remember thinking what would have happened if they hadn't come when they did. Those guys knew the area was hot, I mean hell, an AH-64 was blown out of the sky in the same place not too long after that, but they did their jobs and helped those that were hurt. I will always remember that.

Speaking of wounded soldiers, we went to a battalion awards ceremony today. Since my battalion, 4-5 ADA, has been in country, we have taken seven casualties. Four of them are from my unit. Three of them were back on duty in a couple of days, and the fourth is fine, but will need some further care. Anyway, the brigade sergeant major got up and gave an impromptu speech I wish everyone in America could hear. Had William Jennings Bryan or Teddy Roosevelt heard the same speech, they would have said, "Damn, that guy is good."

He put into words what all of us are feeling about being here. He quoted Benjamin Franklin and Samuel Johnson. He said, "The full measure of a man can be judged by what that man is willing to give up for someone who is of no use to him." Not to be misconstrued, but I think what he meant was we are bleeding, fighting and dying for a people to whom we owe nothing. His speech was reminiscent of one that would be expected from GEN George S. Patton in that it was very passionate, powerful, and full of colorful language.

Anyway, I was very moved by what he had to say. In today's society it is considered wrong to be less than politically correct. The sergeant major laid it on the line and didn't care if you liked it or not. That is one of the reasons I love the military; sugarcoating what you say is not a major concern.

The weather here is starting to change. Last night we had a pretty good thunderstorm complete with hail. That's right, I said hail. I never thought it would hail in the desert. I was walking out of the shower trailer and I got pelted pretty good. I ran into my buddies' room and waited out the worst of the hail. Some of it was as big as golf balls! I knew the storm was coming, as they broadcast stuff like that over the radio. I was sitting on my porch watching the storm come in. It reminded me of home in that you could smell the rain and hear the thunder get closer.

I started to wonder about some things, really deep stuff, that I think some people never think about. Not that I am some budding protégé of some philosopher or anything. I just kept thinking that until the world ends, nature is eternal and so is war. I also was thinking about that no matter what is going on down here, on earth, the cycle of life continues. The seasons change, the skies open up with rain, the leaves fall. In winter, the earth sleeps and in spring, she wakes up again to give us such beauty. No matter what we humans are doing, nature doesn't seem to be concerned with it. It has been this way forever. But, there is a correlation between nature and warfare.

How many times have the forces of nature been decisive, if only by chance, in the defeat or victory of an army? Napoleon's Grand Army was decimated because of a harsh winter, for which he was ill prepared. Hitler lost Russia, in part because of a bad winter. Kublai Khan lost Japan because of a "divine wind" or *Kamikaze* that sank many of his ships, and left him unable to attack. Even here, a sandstorm will screw some things up rather efficiently. It is funny how nature and warfare seem to sometimes work together. I realize I probably should seek therapy, but it is hard to find a good headshrinker around here, one who speaks English anyway.

Tomorrow, my buddy and I are going to go to the post office again. It is funny that going to the post office back home never seemed like a big deal. To be quite honest, sometimes it felt more like a burden as it was just one more thing I had to do. But here, it is different because it simply gets us out for a bit. We get to go and just saunter down to the post office and not have to think about missions, ambushes, or anything we don't want to think about. It is my time, and no one else's. We went there tonight but they were closed for the day already. It was only 1600 hours and they were closed! My buddy was so mad he couldn't even cuss right. He was just chattering like a squirrel on a bad meth trip. It didn't help matters that I was sitting there laughing like a maniac.

I asked him why he was so mad and he said, "We work 24/7, why don't they?" He makes a valid point, the post office is in fact run by the army. Anyway, we plan on trying to get there in the morning to see if he can mail his letters. It is a hassle though, I mean they search every package, and I mean every package! I sent a couple CDs to one of my best friends from school. They searched the little box I had like I was trying to fit an Uzi in it. I guess it is their job, but talk about overzealous!

Other than that, nothing is new here, same old stuff. Oh, I forgot to tell you about my chow hall experience tonight. After the little post office drama, Ben and I decided to grab some chow. As we walked into the chow hall, we saw a big stainless steel kettle that was full of ice. It had a sign on it that read "Cold Beer." I thought to myself, "No way!" Ben and I looked at each other and made a dash for the pot. When we got there, it was full of beer all right, near beer, you know, nonalcoholic beer. What a sick, twisted, and cruel thing to do to us soldiers. I mean, what is the point in drinking fake beer?

Anyway, after that little letdown we ate, came back to our trailers, and just decided to relax. Everybody is doing fine here and we are all happy. I hope when you all read this email you are happy, too. I hope to hear from you soon. Until then though, just keep me in your thoughts and prayers. Pray, too, this war will end. Not for my sake, but for the sake of all the Iraqi people who have no choice but to try to live through it.

Sincerely, Jason
Camp Black Jack, Iraq

Caring for Locals

Today is May 9th

Hey everybody,

Just got back from a rather eventful day. Our mission ran today from morning till night; 12 hours in the sun. Things are starting to heat up over here. I would say that in the sun, the temp had to be at least 115 degrees. Not too long into our shift, my truck had a flat tire. It was kind of funny how it happened. We spend a lot of time driving up and down these canals and aqueducts that are laced like a wicker basket all over the countryside. Some of the roads are nothing more than donkey trails.

We were just getting ready to cross the most miserable excuse for a bridge I have ever seen, when we heard a high-pitched whistle and the sound of rushing air. My gunner, Ben, and I both started yelling at the same time. It sounded just like an RPG coming at you! So here are two grown men yelling at each other, "What the hell was that?" while my driver was yelling, "Who's shooting at us?" and trying to drive at the same time. We must have looked like the Three Stooges at a stag party.

We could now hear the familiar "whump, whump, whump" sound a flat tire makes, and we all felt kind of silly once we realized it was only a flat. So now we were stuck with a problem. That was the fact we were some distance from our base, and we don't carry spares. Humvees are designed to be able to run on a flat tire, but only if you have to. At this point, I figured we had to, because I didn't feel comfortable out in the middle of nowhere with a broken truck.

We started driving into base and got 9/10ths of the way there and had to pull over because the tire was catching on fire from the friction. So I, being a fireman and all, decided this was my big moment to save the day. I jumped out, drew my knife, thrust it into the burning tire, and cut a hole. Then, disregarding my own safety, I proceeded to douse the tire with water. Yep, I saved the day. Okay, it wasn't that dramatic, but we did pour water on it. We made it into our base and got it fixed and headed back out to patrol.

Later on in the day, we got a call from some Bradley Fighting Vehicles that were stationed down by a bridge. They called us because they needed an interpreter, and we happened to have Jaguar with us. We drove down to where they were and got out of our trucks. An old man was standing by the Bradley trying to talk to the crew, but all efforts were proving to be in vain. Jaguar talked to the man and said that his wife was sick. My platoon sergeant yelled at me to grab my bag and move out. Jaguar said she had heart problems; I informed my platoon sergeant I didn't carry much for that, but he said to do what I could.

As soon as I walked into the house, all the women seemed to get very nervous. I then realized I still had a hold of my assault rifle. I handed it off to my buddy and began to talk through Jaguar to the husband of the sick woman about her problem. Jaguar told him I was doctor or something to that effect, and the man shook my hand. He then produced a stack of papers from a hospital regarding his wife. I saw ECG strips, a CT scan, prescriptions, and a diagnosis. I was astounded to find the report was written in English!

Her ECGs were a mess, the QRS complex was screwed up, and her P wave wasn't right either. It looked like she was in V-Fib when the scans were done. The CT scan was focused on her brain and brain stem. The prescriptions were for Valium, aspirin, and something else I wasn't familiar with. I gave her a look and found an 84-year-old woman with a 90-year-old body who was scared out of her mind of me and from hearing the Bradleys roll past her house. I figure the Valium was to calm her down, and the aspirin was to keep her blood thinned out a little. We tried to explain to her we were not here to hurt her. We told her the reason she hears the tanks outside is because they are protecting her as well. The women here are very timid.

I spent quite awhile talking to Jaguar today. Before the war, he was a tailor in Baghdad. In this country, a tailor specializes in one thing. If you make suits, then that is all you make. If you make ties, then that is all you make. He told me that in the Muslim religion, the two most important professions are writing and making clothes. He also said he could make us all suits. He said it takes 10 days to make one, and he would do it for $150. I was amazed he could make me a tailored suit of my choosing for 150 bucks. You can't touch a decent suit at J C Penney for that! He also said he and his family had made 138 suits for the unit that was here before us. I asked how he learned to sew, and he said his family were all tailors before the war.

Before he started making suits though, he only was paid $6 a week. Now, he is paid $600 a month to be our interpreter. He said he has never

Jaguar is paid $600 a month to be our interpreter. He said he has never lived so good.

lived so good. I told him if he were in America he could make as much money as he wanted. He is bilingual and is a professional tailor. He could make a killing. He said he wants to bring his family to America but cannot afford to. I wish I could figure out a way to help him. He has done so much for us already. We could not do our jobs without him.

He also said he was upset because his father and him have an ongoing argument over his new baby. (I mentioned he recently had his first baby not too long ago.) He and his wife decided to name him Evan (pronounced Ee-Vahn). Jaguar's father wants the child to have an Arabic name. His father will not negotiate this at all. In fact, he told Jaguar if he did not name him with an Arabic name, then he (Jaguar) would not be part of the family anymore. Jaguar said, "If I name him "Fahed" like my father wants, then everyone who is not Arabic will think that he is a terrorist, and he will not be able to find work or go to a good school." I can't imagine having to contemplate such a thing! My heart goes out to him, and I hope he can find a solution to his problem. But here, family ties are very strong, and more important than most anything else.

As we were coming in from our patrol we found out the hard way one of our trucks' gas gauges doesn't work very well. It ran out of gas about a mile from our base. We had some extra gas cans with us, so we filled them up so they could get back to base. We were a little late coming in as a result, but we all made it back safe for another day, and that is the main thing. I will end here, I still have to take a bath and get some sleep. Tomorrow is another day, with another mission. I hope all of you are happy and well. I am doing fine, don't worry about me.

Sincerely, Jason
Camp Black Jack, Iraq

Notice 10/12/03   Training   Deployment 3/1/04   Home leave 9/26–10/14/04   Back Home 3/19/05

We Are Not Barbarians

Today is May 25th

Just sitting here listening to some music. I just finished watching *U-571* on my newly repaired DVD player. My laptop DVD has been broken since Valentine's Day. You might ask yourselves why I had not fixed it since then. Simple question, simple answer. I had the two computer gurus from our unit look at it, and they both were in agreement that I need to send my whole computer into the factory for repair. I don't know much about computers so I figured they were correct in their diagnosis. However, I had a sneaking suspicion my problem was not hardware in nature but rather software. My CD player still worked the entire time. Both DVDs and CDs play out of the same drive right? Why then would it not play movies but it would play any CD I put into the drive? CDs, CDRs, CDRWs would all play, just not DVDs. I went online and talked to a COMPAC rep in a chat room and his suggestions I had already tried. I decided to try to find a DVD program online. The other night, I was messing around and downloaded Realplayer 2.5. I figured I would try it, why not? I put in a DVD and it worked! I was so happy!

The enemy here is proving to be most obdurate. The problem with warfare such as this is not that we are outgunned, outwitted, or ill-equipped. The problem is we don't know who the enemy is. We had to go to a mandatory lecture yesterday on the laws of war and rules of engagement. What a crock! I am divided in this respect. Half of me says, "Our enemy disregards laws and rules, so why do I need to adhere to them." That is the angry side of me speaking. The other half, the side of reason and logic, is saying, "Because you are an American soldier who is held to the higher standard. Who kills only when he has to. We are not barbarians. Regardless of the negative publicity we are getting, as individuals we are expected to do the right thing." As good as it would feel to just nuke this whole place and be done with it, we cannot. Sometimes I feel like the only allies I have are the guys standing next to me, my buddies, my fellow F Battery troops.

Every time I fire up the old computer and look at the news, I see the media is focusing once again on negative things rather than the positive. Don't they get it? Are they so obtuse they do not realize the enemy reads our papers too? Do they not understand that Al-Queda fighters watch CNN and the BBC? Every report they broadcast that paints what we are doing in a negative light, every time they broadcast public opinion polls that show public support dwindling, every time they show a picture of flag-draped coffins, these things give the enemy hope. History has situated what hope can do to an army or a people in general. By their reports, the media is costing more soldiers' lives. Do they not see this? Or, perhaps they do not care. After all, people love others' dirty laundry and whoever has the most of it gets the most ratings, which equates to the most money. So it all boils down to greed.

Reporting the news is a responsibility and a privilege. But, it should be done unbiased, honest, and without personal agendas. I do not believe this is the case. Because of this, people like me and my buddies are dying as a result, because the enemy still has hope. Even *The Stars and Stripes* newspaper is swinging to the left side! We get *The Stars and Stripes* free at the chow hall, but most of us have stopped reading it. Ernie Pyle would puke if he could see what they are putting in it. Articles full of conjecture and sensationalized stories that only tell half the story. News stories taken from second-and third-hand sources. It makes me sick. I am not a journalist, so it may be the case that writing a bunch of junk is easier than actually investigating a story before reporting on it. I don't know the answer to that question. But, many of us here find ourselves wondering whose side the media is on.

Most of us take this in stride. We are a strong bunch of guys. We can handle hardships and letdowns. Yes, of course we complain, that is human nature, but we can also deal with it. Sometimes, things suck so bad over here that it is almost fun. We joke about it. I think that is because we all suffer together.

> **Sometimes, things suck so bad over here that it is almost fun. We joke about it. I think that is because we all suffer together.**

The other day, we got one of our trucks stuck while trying to cross a canal. I mean stuck good! We had to dig out around the back end so we could even get a tow bar hooked up to the towing pintle! It was mid-afternoon, the temp was well over 100 degrees, and we were out there swinging picks, shovels, and axes for almost an hour. We had all our equipment on, and it was miserable. Just to give you an idea, my body armor with my ammo, grenades, and other junk weighs almost 70 pounds. We were all dripping with sweat by the time we got the truck out of the canal. We were so hot that I was concerned with heat injuries. It sucked so bad, it was fun. So, what did we do? After we were done digging, we started flinging water at each other. Yep, a good old-fashioned water fight. We laugh at our misery. We can deal with it. What we can't deal with though is people talking trash about us, when they are not really educated about what they speak.

Some of the men here are starting to take their leave. Unfortunately, there is not enough time to get every man home to the States. So to be fair, our first sergeant held a lottery to figure out who would go home and who would not. The names of all the men in the battery were placed in a hat. Top held the hat up high, and one of the men from the unit drew out names. The names drawn were written down, and that was the order in which the men would go home on leave. As for me, well, I was lucky. My number was 42, which means I hope to be home in the latter part of the summer or perhaps early fall.

Those that were not drawn still get leave, only not at home. They can either go to the Green Zone here in Baghdad or they can go to the island of Qatar for a few days. I have read a little about both places, and the facilities at each spot are very nice. Gyms, TV, sports, swimming, good food, and time to relax. Qatar has a beach and lounges; the Green Zone does not; but either place is not here and that is what matters.

Other than that, things here are progressing very well. It looks like the new school is a go, and we have installed another water purification unit. I even saw crews picking up litter along the interstate the other day. There is a mosque that must have been damaged in the first part of the war not too far away. We are rebuilding that structure as well. Well, I must go for now. My buddy and I are going to the PX to snoop around a bit. It is our day off and we are bored. I hope all of you are safe and well. I miss you, but don't worry about me.

Sincerely,
SSG Jason Adams
Camp Black Jack, Iraq

Memories to Come

Today is May 28th

This past week has proven most uneventful. We continue to patrol our sectors day and night. I am curious to know how many miles will be on our trucks when this deployment is over. We drive constantly, stopping only a few minutes at a time to stretch our legs. There are several little shops along the interstate that sell pop and goodies. Sometimes we stop at one of them and get a cold Pepsi.

I know you must be envisioning an interstate like I-80 back home. This is not the case here, I assure you. Yes, it is a six-lane highway. Yes, it resembles what one would consider an interstate. But, this one has unlimited access from the sides. Not like in Illinois where you have to go and find an on ramp. Also, there are little stores that dot the sides of the road. These are not like "Quickie Marts" or Casey's; these are little huts made out of mud or reeds. The shop owners are the only employees; there is no power, no fresh baked doughnuts or pizza either. They mostly sell soda and cigarettes.

It is not uncommon to see a farmer driving his tractor down the interstate either. Many of the shepherds run their flocks of sheep and goats right along the shoulder of the road as well. Motorists really aren't all that concerned with what side of the road they drive on either. It is a common sight to see a truck going southbound in the northbound lane. Why, you might ask?. Well, we are still trying to come up with an answer for that one. We have stopped several motorists who were drunk beyond belief as well. I didn't think Muslims drank but all evidence is to the contrary. The median is littered with many beer cans.

It is harvest time here, and the countryside is dotted with golden fields of wheat. It is actually a very serene sight to see. Perhaps this can be attributed to memories of home. Only here the farmers don't have much in the way of farm implements. Most of the labor is done by hand. I have seen a few combines, mostly Massey Ferguson's and some German machines. They do not have wagons here, and the grain is dumped into the backs of pickup trucks.

One other thing I have noticed is the fact they have no haybalers. They just pile the wheat straw in piles and come by later and pick it up. Women do most of the fieldwork. Every day we see women in the hayfields with hand scythes cutting grass for the cattle. They load what they cut into these huge bags that look like giant garbage bags, load them onto their backs, and carry them back to their homes. Arduous physical labor is commonplace here for the women. They do not drive either. I have only seen one woman driving a car since I have been here. The men drive and usually the women sit in the back seat.

Massey Ferguson must have done great business here because most of the tractors are Masseys. I see some New Hollands, and Fiats, but mostly Massey Ferguson's. I would bet one or two have a Martin Implement sticker somewhere on them. I will have to check that one out a little more and get back to you all. There is an implement "dealer" not too far from us out on the interstate. I guess that to call it an implement dealer is really giving it too much credit, but that is the best way I can describe it.

It is a ramshackle structure with a thatched roof and mud walls that refurbishes plows, dirt blades, and trenchers. I don't know what the locals call a "trencher," that is just what I call them. It looks like two plowshares welded together at the front that forms a "V." They are used to dig the irrigation trenches in the fields. Pretty crude farming practices over here. The locals do not rotate crops; use any kind of fertilizer, pesticide, herbicide or anything else. They just sow the seed and hope for the best.

The military here is starting to prepare to turn the airport back over to the Iraqis. I am glad to see this, as it is another positive and obviously necessary step toward rebuilding. We are hearing rumors that a local entrepreneur is trying to make this area into a resort area. It would sure be nice to see!. Many of us have talked about making this area into a resort. It would not take a whole lot to do either. The lakes and buildings are already here. All you would need is some tennis courts and an 18-hole golf course and you would be in business. This place used to be part of Saddam's game refuge so it is very nice. There are three huge palaces within three miles of here as well. One of them needs a little fixing up, if you know what I mean. (Those pesky darn cruise missiles you know.) This particular palace sits in the middle of a big lake and the bridge that goes to it is blown to bits.

Speaking of bridges, the new one the engineers are building is progressing nicely. They are doing it the same way they do back home. They are building a substitute passage to facilitate motorists while they work on the main span. It is pretty neat to see them work. It is also nice to see Caterpillar and John Deere machines out working in the dirt, as it reminds us of home. The machines they are using, albeit camouflaged, are the same type we see around home. A couple of the bulldozers (Cat D9s) are totally armored, which is certainly unique to the army. I hope the locals can at least appreciate what we are trying to do for them.

Our zone has recently been enlarged to cover more area. On our first patrol into the new sector, we were out on the interstate and we went under an overpass. Off to our right we observed a large fenced-in sprawling complex with razor wire, block walls, and guard towers. It only took us a second to realize we were looking at the Abu Ghraib prison compound. I had no idea it was just a stone's throw from our old patrol zone. Because of the overpass, we could never see it prior to that day.

Seeing that prison which is in the global spotlight right now, helped to put into perspective the magnitude of our jobs here. All eyes are upon us.

It looks just like any other state pen at home, except of course for all the Humvees parked around it. It is hard for me to understand sometimes that what we are doing here is being watched by the entire world. Seeing that prison which is in the global spotlight right now, helped to put into perspective the magnitude of our jobs here. All eyes are upon us. It makes us proud I think, and yet, at the same time we are in awe to think we are taking part in such a monumental task. Many of us have never been outside the U.S. Now, here we are thousands of miles from home doing jobs that will have a profound impact upon the future of a nation. Not too many people can make that claim, and for that we are proud.

All of us wish we were home, but that goes without saying. But, years from now when all of us are old, and the days we are living now are but a distant memory brought up over coffee, we will still be proud of what we have done. We are soldiers, we are Americans, we are but a small part of a long lineage of men and women who have put on this uniform and done what others are unwilling to do. To quote George Orwell, "People sleep peaceably in their beds at night only because rough men stand ready to do violence on their behalf."

SSG Adams
Camp Black Jack, Iraq

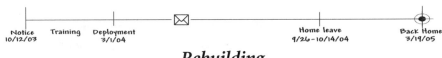

Rebuilding

Today is June 7

Yesterday, the 6th of June marks the 60th anniversary of D-day. Sixty years ago, my grandpa was fighting so I can live free. I have never met him, as my freedom was purchased, in part, with his life. Many other people can say the same thing as well. We all can think of someone who took part on that day. We owe them so much. All across America during the past few days, services were held to commemorate Memorial Day and the anniversary of D-day. All of those things can never repay those men and women who bought our freedom with their blood. It seems weird that we are still fighting. True, it is a different war, but in the end, are not all wars really the same? We just fight them different ways and in different places. War is still war; today we just kill with much more efficiency. World War I was called "The war to end all wars." We still don't get it do we?

This past week has seen some significant things happen over here. A new person has been selected to lead the interim government, one that (from what I hear) makes everyone happy. That is the nature of the game over here, the ability to compromise. I can't understand the divisions between the Sunni Muslims and the Shiites. It seems to me they are both Muslim, but they can't seem to get along. I have talked about this to our interpreter "Snake" at great lengths. I told him that in America, we have divisions in Christianity, yet we get along. Why does it not work here? He said it is about power, not religion.

Snake is an interesting guy. He had to move onto base with us because of death threats and attempts on his life. So now he lives right by us. We gave him his own room, and he has just become one of the guys. The other night, he came to my room and asked if I could fix a burn on his shoulder. He said the bulletproof vest rubs on it, and it is hurting pretty bad. I looked at the burn and decided it looked like a cigarette burn. This is odd because Snake doesn't smoke. I asked him about it, and he said his girlfriend had done it. I said, "Why would your girlfriend do that?" His reply was, "I did something really stupid, I had it coming anyway." I said, "Yeah buddy, men are stupid, shallow creatures aren't we?" Anyway, I patched him up and he went back over to another guy's room to play video games. I think he is becoming addicted to PlayStation©.

We have been going around to all the schools in our zone this past week and obtaining demographic information such as number of students, number of teachers, age groups of students, number of classes, etc. We also have been assessing the conditions of the schools, the quality of materials, the quality of water at the school, and other things along those lines. The purpose is to establish need. Some of the schools are in better shape than the others and need only minor things. Others need complete overhauls.

One school in particular needs nothing more than a playground for the kids. There is ample land right across a canal, but the kids cannot get to it because they cannot cross the canal. We are going to see if we can coordinate with the Civil Affairs Detachment and get some equipment out there to build a bridge and put in some playground equipment for them.

We not only have to help rebuild this area, but in many ways, we also have to gain the locals' trust.

The man in charge of the school was elated. We told him we couldn't promise anything, but we would sure try. He said, "That is more than the last group of soldiers did."

This statement aroused my curiosity and others there as well. We asked him to explain, and he said that in the months since Saddam's fall, we were the first soldiers to even so much as stop by the school and introduce ourselves. This made most of us mad and led me to believe what I had already suspected. The unit that controlled this area prior to our arrival did not do a whole lot of things. I think they just sat here and waited out their time before returning home. This inadvertently and instantaneously made our jobs harder upon our arrival. We not only have to help rebuild this area, but in many ways, we also have to gain the locals' trust. We had hoped some of that legwork would have been done for us upon our arrival, but no such luck.

It seems as though the use of car bombs is picking up around here. We have had several in the last week. All of them that have been placed in our sector have been discovered prior to their detonation. We remain ever vigilant, and the reward for this is lives saved. Read the papers and you will see how devastating these mobile bombs can be. Some of our fellow soldiers up north were not so lucky the other day. Most of us see things getting a little worse here prior to, and following the June 30th handover of power. We don't know if our role here will change or what. We are supposed to start working with the ICDC soon. The ICDC stands for Iraqi Civil Defense Corps; it is akin to the National Guard back home. Only here, it is not exactly the same. The men of the ICDC, for the most part, don't speak English, and quite frankly, I don't trust them. Perhaps this will change with time, but we have to be cautious.

We have been restructuring our platoon as of late, and the teams have been shuffled around a bit. I am now head of third section of second platoon. My gunner, SGT Ben Sleaford of Geneseo, who was recently promoted, now is in control of his own team. I am glad for him. He is one of the best soldiers I know. The funny thing is people are always mistaking us for one another. From a distance we look identical. So identical in fact, when we were having our pass and review ceremony in Galva, Illinois, prior to our deployment, one of my friends thought that he was I. They were waving and yelling until we got closer, and they realized it was Ben and not I. What a riot! Ben is in my section now and should perform admirably as a team chief. I am sorry to lose him off my team, but it would be very selfish of me to keep him as my gunner and not let him move up the career ladder.

I know I have mentioned the new PX several times in my letters, but it is such a big part of our existence here that I am compelled to mention it yet again. The other day, Ben and I were over there snooping around for "bargains" when to our utter amazement we saw these big chest type freezers. I thought, "Who in their right mind would buy one of those gargantuan things?" Not too mention, where would they put it? Then we saw the sign that said "Omaha Steak Company." The look of realization that flashed across my face was blatantly obvious! Sure enough, T-bones! Huge, delicious American USDA choice steak! They are rather expensive at $14.95 a pop, but who cares! It just so happens they sell little Weber grills and charcoal too. People went nuts! It looked like J. K. Rowling at a Harry Potter book signing. We are going to get some today and have a cookout. We might even choke down some fake beer too! A little piece of home is such a welcome thing here. It really makes us realize how much we take for granted back home. Plus, it is a good way for our teams to get together outside of work and just sit around and shoot the bull. We don't do that much. Most of the time our efforts are all geared toward our missions. Strong teams make for a strong unit, which is very important.

We have all been getting loads of packages from home, so many in fact, that our bathroom has become somewhat of a little PX in itself. This is where we take all the stuff that we don't want. At first, it was just extra pens and bars of soap. I went in there the other day and found a whole box of junk food! You know people are getting spoiled when they are giving away Oreo Double Stuffed cookies!

The support we soldiers have received from all of you at home is almost overwhelming. We all know what we are doing is not the most popular thing in the world right now. I speak for all here when I say, "Thank You."

I received a package last night from my old boss at Kress Corp. in Brimfield. Inside were no less than 10 CDs full of classical music! I was ecstatic to say the least! Everything from Beethoven to Wagner to Strauss and many others as well. The support we soldiers have received from all of you at home is almost overwhelming. We can never repay you for your kindness. We all know what we are doing is not the most popular thing in the world right now, but your support is unwavering, and we are eternally in your debt. I speak for all here when I say, "Thank You."

Still though, there are constant reminders of why we are here. We are here to help the people of this poor country. The other day while on patrol, we were taking a break under some palm trees to try to cool off. It was dreadfully hot out, which seems to be the norm here these days. A man approached our trucks from the rear and just stood silently about 30 meters away. I was suspicious at first. I mean most of the people come up to us and talk. He wasn't armed and appeared rather disheveled in appearance, which is not the norm for the men here. His hair was unkempt, his beard was ragged, and he was dirty. All of these things led me to believe he must be homeless or at least on the verge of being that way. Finally, he crept forward and bent over and picked up an old MRE carton and looked inside. Then it struck me he was hungry. He was just looking for food and meant us no harm.

Ben was the first of us to call to him, and as he came over I could sense also that perhaps he was simple-minded. He started to talk to us, and of course, I could not understand a word of it. I called for our interpreter Snake to come and talk to him. Snake said, "I have no idea what he is saying, he is just babbling." My suspicions proved to be correct. I felt such pity for him. It was so sad to see a person have to beg to survive. We gave him two MREs out of our own supply and some water. He seemed very happy and just kept chattering at us. He left us after awhile and walked away, I don't know where he went but I am glad he came to us and that we were able to help him. As I watched him walk away, I said a prayer for him. It would be hard enough, even in our society, to walk through life like that, let alone trying to do it in a society like this. But, that is the reality we are seeing here. I don't think it bothers all of us the same, but that night while I tried to sleep, I couldn't get his face out of my head. I said another prayer for him, and I hoped I might see him again so we can help him some more.

Other than what I have already written, not too much has been happening here. All of us are doing fine. We still miss home but, that along with the heat, are the two main constants here. The mercury is starting to creep higher as we move into summer. Yesterday, I sat on my "porch" in my shorts and tank top and was fried like a bucket of KFC in a matter of minutes. The sun feels good on my skin until I start moving, and then I instantly start to sweat like a prostitute in the front row of Sunday service. Many of us have started to compute when our leave time will come, and I feel sorry for the guys who go home in the winter because they will absolutely freeze in Illinois! When I came home for Christmas from Fort Hood, Texas, I told Steph to make sure and bring my heaviest coat from home. I was so acclimated to Texas weather that I couldn't get warm for a couple days upon returning home. Oh well, we would rather choose being cold and home over being hot and here!

SSG Adams
Camp Black Jack, Iraq

Notice 10/12/03 | Training | Deployment 3/1/04 | Home leave 9/26-10/14/04 | Back Home 3/19/05

Violence Is Easier than Peace

Today is June 17th

Hey all,

Many things have happened since I wrote last. More time has passed us by, more miles of patrols have been logged, and we have moved steadily closer to the hand over of power at the end of this month. I sometimes sit and think about what a daunting task it must be to get everything ready for this to happen. Somewhere here in Baghdad, someone is working longer hours than I, to make this transition happen. I think, too, that people's anxiety levels are starting to inch ever higher as well. How can they not?

Nobody knows what is going to happen July 1st. Maybe nothing, maybe civil war, perhaps things will remain the same as they are now. I hope peace finally sweeps through this land. These folks have seen and lived through enough. But, sometimes I think peace is harder than war. Peace means putting down your weapons and living together. Peace renders your differences irrelevant. This means also sometimes you must swallow your pride, let the wheels of justice take care of civil matters, and so forth. Now, if someone wrongs you, you can just shoot them, and there is no state agency that is going to do anything about it. Violence is easier than peace.

Last week started out just like any other week since we arrived here. We received the updated wanted list and were told to be on the lookout for several specific automobiles. The trouble is this: There are four major types of cars here. Volkswagen Passats, Kia Bestas, Mazdas, and orange and white taxis. Oh yes, there are more than that, but these represent 50 percent of the cars we see on a daily basis. Our report said we should be on the lookout for a white Mazda. It was suspected of being used as a suicide car bomb. "Oh sure, which one?" was our reply. So we stopped every white Mazda we saw and found nothing.

We got to go into the chow hall for lunch that day and were sitting at the tables eating and watching CNN. The talking head that happened to be anchor that day was blabbing about a car bomb that had just blown up in downtown Baghdad. Any guesses as to what kind of car it was? Yep, a white Mazda! Our platoon sergeant said, "Well, scratch that one off of the list!" One would think sooner or later these morons would run out of explosives! They must have a pretty good stockpile and have it very well hidden.

I get a kick out of some of our pep talks we get from some of the staff flunkies here. They tell us about how much stuff we are finding and how we are doing such a good job. That may be, and I believe that it is, but we can't stop them all. I remember reading about the underground in France during World War II. They were doing the same thing the enemy here is. Many of them had some rather intricate hiding spots and elaborate methods of screwing up things for the Nazis. This was all done right under the Germans' noses, too. Bottom line is simply the fact we cannot catch everyone.

One of the simple pleasures we indulge ourselves in periodically is sitting under a beautiful group of palm trees along the interstate. Our patrol route is 28 miles round trip. After several trips we get pretty antsy, and we can't feel our fannies anymore because the seats in our trucks are not what one would describe as "comfy." The palms are situated approximately 100 meters off the road, so we can still maintain our line of sight with the interstate. There is a roadside stand nearby that sells pop, candy, and cigarettes as well. Right in front of the trees is a soccer field, well, not like you would envision a soccer field. It is just a large area of dirt without rocks or grass that has a makeshift goal at each end. Many times there are people out playing soccer when we sit there, and we like to watch the kids play.

One day last week, we were sitting there trying to get out of the relentless sun, and this little boy came walking up and pointed at the soda stand and said, "Pepsi." At first we thought he wanted us to give him a Pepsi. As it turns out, he was taking our "orders." He works at the soda stand and thought he could turn a buck off us soldiers. So we got out our wallets and gave him some money, and he ran off at a dead sprint to his store. A few minutes later he came back at a dead sprint with a little bag full of Pepsi. We wound up sharing with him, and we all enjoyed some soda together. Then he noticed a soccer ball we had in the back of one of our trucks and pointed and said, *Tow-bow*, which means, "ball."

My driver, SGT Ortiz got the ball and started to kick it back and forth with the little boy. Then several other boys showed up, and SGT Ortiz had a little game of soccer with them. It was really a good time. It is amazing how two people who do not speak the same language can still interact and have fun. We got a kick out of the little boy that sold us the Pepsi! He was trying to play soccer and hold onto his soda at the same time. By the time the can was empty, more of it had gone down the front of his shirt than had gone in his mouth. What a riot it was to hear all the little kids laughing and giggling.

Prior to our deployment, I had been a welder at Kress Corporation in Brimfield. We had been working on some 10,000-pound forklifts we were converting for military use. In order for a forklift of that size to be airlifted, it is essential for the cab to be removed. But, it is also essential there be the necessary system onboard the forklift to do so. Kress designed such a system, made the forklift carriage, relocated the trailer hitch, and repainted the whole unit. I was fortunate to have been able to work on the prototype.

Before I left, we had made many of these forklifts, and several of them had been painted Desert Tan. I had worked on the vast majority of them in some way. Mostly, I was the one who installed the trailer hitch or welded some of the other substructures. I was sure I would see one over here at some point. The other day as we were driving up and down the interstate, we happened to be up by Abu Ghraib prison, and out in front of the prison was one of these forklifts. I fumbled for my camera and took a hasty picture. I had hoped it would still be

We work in zones here, and we are very protective of our zone. The trouble is that so many units are operating around here, that every once in awhile we catch somebody in our zone and we have to chase them out.

there on our return trip so I could get some pictures of myself with this machine. No such luck, by the time we made it back up there, the forklift wasn't anywhere to be found. It still made me proud to see something I had helped to build. Now that I know these machines are here, I will be on the lookout for more of them so I can get a better picture of one and send it back to Kress Corporation.

One of the less than proud moments of last week occurred out on the interstate and involved a bunch of military police. We work in zones here. This is akin to a sales rep for a company back home. They have zones in which they work and are not to work outside of said zone. It is the same way here, and we are very protective of our zone. The trouble is that so many units are operating around here that every once in awhile, we catch somebody in our zone and we have to chase them out.

There is a certain unit of military police here that are more like cowboys than soldiers. A few weeks ago, we caught a bunch of them out in our sector, and when inquired as to what they were doing, got a rather snotty reply. It has been my experience military police tend to be rather ostentatious sometimes, for reasons unbeknownst to myself. The guy I happened to be talking with that day was trying to be pushy with me and acting as though because they were army cops, they could go anywhere, do anything, and did not have to answer to anyone. We got all their information and pushed it up through our chain of command.

The other day, the same company was changing a tire out on the interstate. My team was way up north by the prison patrolling. We got a call on the radio that some MPs had a car stopped at gunpoint, and they had fired at the car. My team was asked to find out what they were up to. I told my driver it was high time to find out just how fast our truck would roll. According to my GPS system, the answer was 72.9 mph. Not too bad for a diesel truck that weighs almost 8,000 pounds, and is about as aerodynamic as a Sherman tank!

Anyway, we got down to where the MPs were and found them with their guns stuck in all directions like an attack was imminent. In front of their vehicles, we could see a civilian car pulled over with an obvious flat tire. Luckily, our executive officer, CPT Greg Reinhardt, was with me that day. We approached them and inquired if they had fired a round. The lieutenant in charge said, "Yes." Apparently what had happened was as they were stopped changing their tire, a car had gotten too close to them, and they felt threatened. So she had ordered a warning shot. A warning shot, to me, is one fired in the air to get one's attention, not a round through a car's tire.

So here we had a bunch of morons in our zone shooting at passing cars! We are on very good terms with the locals in our sectors, and we are up and down this stretch of interstate 24/7. I said, "Ma'am, we have been out here everyday for three months now and have never felt the need to shoot at a car!" Luckily, CPT Reinhardt was there because I was ready to go ballistic on this lieutenant, which would have been inappropriate considering the fact she outranks me. CPT Reinhardt was rather incensed as well, but retained his composure through it all, which I found rather impressive.

The worst part about it all is the fact they never even talked to the poor guy they shot at to see if he was okay. They just went about their business as if nothing was wrong! I asked the lieutenant who had fired the shot, name, rank, unit, brigade, etc., all of the normal stuff, and we went back to our trucks and called it up to our headquarters.

She knew what she had done was wrong. I am glad she was scared. I just hope the people in our sector can differentiate our guys from those morons. We have worked too hard to build good relationships with these people and then have jerks like this roll through and ruin those relationships on account of a bad judgment call from an officer who does not have positive control over her people.

One of the more exciting moments of our week came two nights ago when we were ordered to execute a cordon and search on the house of a suspected set of brothers that were engaged in anti-coalition activities. We went out to their house in the middle of the night and drove right up into their driveway. They were all asleep out in their front yard upon our arrival. There were only two men there but about 10 females (women and children). The trouble is most of the people out in the country do not have any identification. These guys did, but it wasn't theirs. The pictures looked nothing like them, yet they swore up and down that it was them!

I, along with others from my platoon, searched the house while the interpreter and our platoon sergeant talked to the two men. We didn't find anything of significance in the house, save for a small sword that bore a faint resemblance to a Roman short sword, the likes of which were used by the gladiators! We searched this house and the one directly adjacent to it and, again, found nothing of any significance, except for a really angry goat, but that is another story. It was decided we would take the two men in for questioning based on the fact they had false identification. We told the men of our intentions and immediately they began to protest.

My platoon sergeant is a no-nonsense type of guy and he (through our interpreter) told the men plainly, "This can be easy or it can be not so easy, choice is up to you." My buddy SGT Ben Sleaford, is a Henry County Sheriff's Deputy at home, and he was just about drooling over the thought of getting to handcuff the guys. I gave him my set of

My buddy, SGT Ben Sleaford, is a Henry County Sheriff's Deputy at home, and he was just about drooling over the thought of getting to handcuff the guys.

handcuffs, and he looked like a crazed pit bull just waiting for his master's command to attack. It was pretty fun to watch! The men decided that, to quote *Star Trek*, "Resistance is futile," and consented to being handcuffed. Ben got to do the cuffing, and we had the interpreter explain to the women, who had begun to freak out, that they were just being taken in for some questions, and if everything worked out, would be back home in a couple of hours.

We asked the women to get the men some shoes and a couple coats to wear, as it was rather chilly out that night. Coats and shoes were produced, and we put the men into our trucks and left. I was guarding one of the men, and I put a coat over his shoulders and put his shoes on him. We stopped a mile or so down the road, and I got out two field dressings to use as makeshift blindfolds so they could not see our base or the route into it. The guys were obviously very nervous, and rightly so. I mean there they were asleep in their front yards with their families and we show up, toss the house, throw handcuffs on them, and yank them off into the night. I took out the field dressings and showed the man I was guarding what I intended to do with it. I put the blindfold on him and patted his back reassuringly and told him not to be afraid, and we would not hurt him. I just kept talking to him in a reassuring tone and patted his back again to keep him calm. We dropped the men off and went back on patrol.

The next morning, we had a formation and our commander commended my platoon on how well we had done. He said the men we took in were released back to their homes and before they had left they thanked him for treating them so well. These men actually thanked us for arresting them nicely! They had been through a traumatic experience and found it noteworthy to commend us on how well they

We could have just kicked in their door and smacked them around a little, but we can do our jobs effectively and still retain some shred of humanity in it all.

were treated. I took a special amount of pride in that. We could have just kicked in their door and smacked them around a little, but as I have said before, we can do our jobs effectively and still retain some shred of humanity in it all. That is what we try to do. Besides, if I whup your butt and drag you away from your house in the middle of the night, would you be apt to tell me anything? I don't think I would either.

Well, this is pretty much how our week had gone. The electricity is playing games again. It was off for 24 hours two days ago; it came back on for six hours, and then went off for another three. It has stayed on for about 18 hours now so it should probably go off here shortly again. I don't understand what the deal is with it. It is a serious blow to morale to get off a 12-hour patrol, wanting only a shower, and to sleep in a cool room and find the power is out. No showers, no water to shave, no air conditioning, nothing.

I don't know who the genius is who designed the power grid here, but they really need to find work in a different field. I am thinking maybe fast-food? Obviously, the "Get-Your-Degree-At-Home School of Electrical Engineering" isn't paying off for them. What did they think was going to happen when it starts hitting 120-plus degrees outside? Did they really expect people not to use their air conditioners? These blackouts are like what California experienced a few years back, so I can definitely sympathize with them! It really doesn't bother me too much. I just grab a book, my CD player, and a Pepsi and sit in the shade and read until the "gods of all things electrical" decide to bestow power upon us once again.

Our forefathers who fought on our behalf never had life as good as we have it here, so I can't complain too much. Matter of fact, we shouldn't complain at all. We should be thankful for what we have, and most of us are, but we still grumble occasionally. Sometimes I find myself wondering if certain people aren't happier if they have something to complain about.

Other than what I have already written about, not too much is new. There are some incidents I would like to write about, but it will have to wait a few weeks. I keep a little notebook with me and write down things I want to write about so I do not forget. Many things that happen here I can't talk about right now. But just know all of us are doing well here. We are all healthy, and for the most part, happy. I am coming to realize one of the ways in which we soldiers deal with all of this is by bonding with one another. I have never experienced such a thing before, and did not understand it until I was here. Friendships forged in war tend to last forever. I can attest to the fact I am serving alongside some of the finest people Central Illinois has to offer. I am very proud to be able to count myself among them.

Sincerely, Jason Adams
Camp Black Jack, Iraq

A Change in Power

Notice 10/12/03 — Training — Deployment 3/1/04 — ✉ — Home leave 9/26-10/14/04 — Back Home 3/19/05

Our Little Town

Today is July 1st

Not too much has been happening here lately. The big news is of course the hand over of power to the Iraqi people two days early. We went out on another patrol yesterday, and to be real honest, I can't see any change in the people's attitudes. Everything seems to be the same. In some ways that is good, and in others it is not so good. I read in the paper yesterday the U.S. is planning on handing Saddam Hussein back over to the Iraqi government next week. I am not so sure is a smart move. But, I don't get to make decisions like that. This country is so different than ours that it is hard for me to guess how the people here will react to Saddam being turned over to them. Many of them will probably be out in the streets shooting their guns in celebration. That is a new one on me, I assure you. I have never seen so many people shoot into the air every time something big happens. Do they not realize that when bullets go up, they have to come down? I wonder how many people get hurt from falling bullets here in any given year.

Last week started out like any week, except our patrol schedule changed again in preparation for the hand over of power. We used to run six teams on patrol at any given time. Due to increased security considerations, we increased the number from six to seven. What that means is we keep three teams on the interstate and four teams in the country. It also means we don't get as many days off anymore. No, we are not too thrilled about that part, but we are adapting to it out of necessity rather than choice.

One day last week, we were patrolling up on the North Loop (as it has come to be known), and one of our trucks was involved in a car accident. The problem with patrolling in designated zones is the boundaries are not always consistent with the roads we patrol, namely, the North Loop. When the boundaries were laid out, nobody thought to make sure there was an adequate turnaround point for our trucks. Many times, where we have to turn around is nothing more than a portion of mangled guardrail a tank had smashed down for us. This presents a special problem because other motorists are not planning on anyone turning around there.

We were turning around in one of these spots the other day, and an oncoming car was traveling entirely too fast and did not see us turning. I find it hard to believe you cannot see a big green truck with machine guns sticking in all directions, but evidently, that was the case here. The truck in front of mine had made the turn and was accelerating when it was struck from behind. The motorist had been traveling around 70 mph or higher and did not change lanes as we turned. When our guys made their turn, this particular car was at least 150 meters back. He did not lock up his brakes until he was only about 30 feet from the back bumper of our truck. He slammed into the back of the truck in front of mine at about 50 mph.

Our truck's seating arrangement is laid out so there are two men in the front and one in the back. The person in the back usually rides standing up so they can man the machine gun. There was only one man in the car that hit my buddies' truck so instantly there were four possibly injured people. We jumped out of our truck, I grabbed my medical kit, and told the others to block traffic. I ran past the civilian and noticed he had not had his seatbelt on. The two men in the front of the Humvee were out of their truck by now walking around cussing. The person in the back who had been manning the gun was just sitting there holding his chest. With help from some other guys, we got Pat out of the back of the truck and took him to the shoulder of the road. The man who had hit them was also out of his car by now and was covered in blood. It was his lucky day because even though he had not been wearing a seatbelt, his airbag had deployed which kept him inside the car at least. I told the man to come and sit by Pat so I could look at them both.

Pat was banged up pretty good but not hurt too bad. I put on a C-collar and packaged him the best I could, given the materials I had. I cleaned up the Iraqi man and decided his injuries needed more care than I could render. I told him we would get him an ambulance and he said, "*La, shukran*" which means "no thank you." Most of these people cannot afford doctors or hospitals. I bandaged him up the best way I could, and he just got in the front seat with the tow truck driver that had shown up to get his car, and they drove off.

We wound up towing the damaged Humvee back to base because it would not go into gear so we could drive it. By this time, another medic had shown up and helped me work on Pat. We got him onto a stretcher and started to head back to base. It was a long drive anyway, and when you are only doing 30 mph, it seems even longer. We made it to the med station and Pat was examined. As it turns out, he had only a minor shoulder separation and some bumps and bruises. He is very lucky.

We raided another house this week and just like the last one, we came away empty-handed. The problem here is that informants are paid by the army for information about arms caches, anti-coalition activities, and wanted persons. Personally, I think people give us names of others in hopes we will find something and then pay them. The only exciting thing that came out of this particular house was the fact my buddy and I were almost lunch for some really angry dogs. There are dogs running loose everywhere over here, and most of them run in packs. In the Islamic culture, dogs are considered unclean and none of the people here pet them. They keep them around for guard dogs but they don't pet them, bathe them, or take care of them in any other way. I am sure you can imagine how nasty most of the dogs look!

This particular house was home to about six dogs. My buddy and I were out walking the perimeter of the house when these dogs came out of thin air and were on us in a flash. I raised my rifle and was just about to start shooting when they stopped and just sat there barking. PFC Hipkins picked up a dirt clod and threw it at them, and they retreated a few feet and just kept barking. Everywhere we walked, the dogs followed. It is very hard to search for weapons of mass destruction when you have Cujo and his buddies following you.

Everywhere we walked, the dogs followed. It is very hard to search for weapons of mass destruction when you have Cujo and his buddies following you.

A few days ago while out driving around we were sent on several wild goose chases or "snipe hunts" as we have come to call them. Without giving away too much top-secret stuff, we have a camera that can see for miles, and sometimes they will see a person or vehicle doing something fishy, and they will send us to go and check it out. The problem is they don't give us very good descriptions to go off of. They will say, "Look for a white pickup." Do you have any idea of how many white Toyota pickups there are here? That is like saying, "Be on the lookout for a dark-skinned man that speaks Arabic!" We spent two hours chasing down that mysterious white pickup the other day and found nothing.

Yesterday, we were told to be on the lookout for a blue Kia Besta. Here again, there are so many on the road it is impossible to stop them all. It gets very frustrating to say the least. Vague intelligence is almost as bad as no intelligence. I have to laugh sometimes at how inept we must look to the locals. They see us flying down a dirt road after some poor farmer trying to get some straw to his cattle, stop him, search the entire truck from top to bottom, only to send him on his way upon finding nothing. We must look like buffoons, but one of these days our efforts will pay off.

The problems with the power grid continue to plague us this week as well. It seems the fuses in the transformers cannot hold up to the heat, and it is causing the fuses to blow out. We set up some camo net over the transformer to try to keep some of the sunlight off it. KBR, which is the major contractor here, brought in generator sets that are the size of a semitrailer and set them right by each transformer to act as a backup power supply. I don't think they have them up and running because just yesterday the power went out for an hour or so.

I used to wonder when I was little how people ever lived without electricity, TVs, indoor plumbing, and stuff like that. I couldn't imagine living like that. I can still remember my mom telling stories about living on the farm in Duncan, Illinois. She would tell about going outside in the middle of December to use the bathroom. I can remember my Grandpa showing me how to splice rope together and telling me stories about farming with horses. So much has changed for us in America. But here, people live like this even today. Many don't have power, and fewer yet have TVs.

One thing I am realizing is the fact that without all these conveniences, people are still happy here. The families I have met are, for the most part, content. I believe part of this is due to the fact they do not know any different. But by watching these people in their daily lives, and the fact that many days we also go without simple things such as power and running water, I am learning you can still be happy. You don't need all these luxuries to survive. I have noticed also these families around here, as poor as they are, are still happy. The only reason for this I can come up with is because they are all together. Divorce is very uncommon here. Families stay together. I think we Americans can learn a lesson from these people in that respect. We get too tied up in life's little stuff and forget what is really important.

The army is really starting to improve our quality of life here. The camp where I am is organized into "pads." There are many pads, and each pad is comprised of many more trailers. Each pad is getting a gym, phone center, and Internet café. Some of my buddies have started working out every morning at 0500 hours. I hate getting up that early, but it feels good to be getting in shape. Some of the weight equipment we are using has really made the global circuit! There are stickers on one of the machines from the United States, the Balkans, and now Iraq. I guess they send this stuff wherever the troops are. I am glad the army realizes the need to keep the men occupied. Boredom can give way to some bad things. Over at the bazaar by the PX, there is a man that sells all kinds of sporting goods. Everything from basketballs to punching bags to golf clubs are available, and the prices are really reasonable. I don't think I will find any golf courses here, but the equipment must be selling or he would not have them in stock.

Harvest time is approaching here, and the open-air markets are teeming with produce of all kinds. Every morning we see many pickups laden with tomatoes, cucumbers, melons, onions, and any other kind of vegetable you would want all headed into Baghdad for the day. This place isn't like back home where you just go to Eagles or Wally World for all your groceries. Here, you shop at the market and make many stops before you get all you need. I think the people like it, too. They will stop and talk to each of the stand owners for a while prior to going on to the next shop and repeating the process.

It reminds me of when I was a kid, and I would go uptown with my mom to Rashid's grocery store. Mom would stand and talk to Mr. and Mrs. Rashid and my sister, Bernadette, and I would have to wait while mom chatted. In hindsight, it was fun. Ted Rashid was quite a salesman, and mom usually walked out with enough beef to feed the crew of an aircraft carrier. Many of the men here have taken to purchasing watermelons and musk melons on our way in from patrolling. They put them on ice and after the sun goes down, they stand around and eat them. I don't like watermelon, otherwise I'd be right there with them. It is good they do this as it builds unit cohesion and it helps the locals earn a living. We usually pay the American price for something when we buy it just to help them out.

Well, the power just went out again, so perhaps I will continue this letter at a later time.

The power came back on just now so I will continue this letter. The other day, I had almost as much written and the power went out. Unfortunately, I was typing online and when the power went out, I lost everything I had typed! I was not too happy about it, but I know now to type in a word processing program and then save it. I can then copy and paste onto my email later. In the past few days, my mail volume has almost doubled. It seems my letters are making quite an impression back home!

I have gotten mail and emails from all over the country telling me how much people like what I write. Letters from people I have never met or letters from a friend of a friend are coming in, and all of them share the same theme. They all say, "We support you." I find strength and comfort in letters such as these, because I can't judge public opinion based solely on newspaper reports and media surveys.

I had worried the military was becoming forgotten. I was feeling the only time the military is important was when it was needed. I am realizing this is not the case. Many people, while not particularly supportive of the war, still support the men and women fighting it, and I suppose that is the main thing. A soldier that does not have the support of the nation they serve, really has nothing.

Many people, while not particularly supportive of the war, still support the men and women fighting it. A soldier that does not have the support of the nation they serve, really has nothing.

One lady wrote me recently saying her life was really going terribly. Single mom, two kids, no car; all of what she wrote made me sad for her. Then she said that even though she had so many problems, none of them compared to what we soldiers face on a daily basis. God bless that woman! I wrote back to her hoping to ease her suffering, but I realize my words can do little to ease the problems she faces. What really struck me is the fact she took the time to write me. Things like this really mean something to me, and I will not forget the love all of you at home have, and continue to show toward your soldiers. Thank you.

Jason Adams
Camp Black Jack, Iraq

The Enemy's Trust

Today is July 3rd

As we came in from another long and hot patrol, all the men on my team, me included, were thinking about two days to ourselves. No patrols, no driving, no sweating for 12 hours straight. All that was on our minds was sitting in air conditioning, writing letters, watching movies, and anything else we wanted to do. Usually on our days off, we go to the PX and treat ourselves to Burger King and cruise through the bazaar to see what the locals are selling. There is one vendor there who sells real Cuban cigars, and every once in awhile, I like to indulge a little and just sit in the shade and read one of my books. These and other thoughts were running through my head as the MP at the gate checked my ID and waved us through. Upon reaching our trailer, LT Doubler, my platoon leader, came up and said he had some bad news for us. He said we had to go to the Green Zone in the morning to take Jaguar, our interpreter, to get a new ID card. I thought, "Oh great, there goes our day off." Crestfallen, we unloaded our truck and started to put our things away when SSG Troy Wolford came up and asked if I had heard the news. I said I had and he then said he also had to go on the same mission in the morning, on his day off as well.

The Green Zone is only a few minutes away and is situated in downtown Baghdad. It is comprised of many of Saddam's former governmental buildings and palaces. A sprawling compound covering more area than all of Toulon, it now houses the new Iraqi government and many other U.S.-controlled buildings. In one of these buildings, less than a week ago the Iraqi people gained their sovereignty once again.

We have gotten rather spoiled in many ways with our current patrol route. The interstate is much easier to patrol than congested streets. There is more room for maneuverability out in the country than there is in an inner city layout, especially given the fact it was during the day and the streets were clogged with pedestrians as well as vehicles. The problem with so many people is we have to be of the mindset that any one of them could be a potential threat to us. All this in mind, coupled with the fact we would be going into unfamiliar territory, I was a little apprehensive about the whole trip.

As we left the relative security of the airport and headed out into traffic, the truck I was in assumed the rear guard position and my driver stepped on the gas. At this point, I loaded my machine gun and put a magazine in my M16, which was slung across my back, right next to the rocket launcher. Today, unlike other days, I was the turret gunner. We swapped trucks for today's mission and traded our "Menard's armored" truck for an actual M1114 armored Humvee. The added protection set me at ease a bit, and for that I was glad. The short trip was uneventful, even at high speeds, and we arrived at the main gate in less than eight minutes.

The first sight I saw as we pulled into the area was a gargantuan entry monument that with its high walls and arched underpass bore a faint resemblance to the Arc de Triomphe in France. The inside of this structure was a visually stunning mosaic of tile and gold. Several enormous lamps lit the arch at night and, before the war, must have been an impressive site to behold. Today, the reminders of war were ever present as we could see shell holes in the uppermost parts of this structure. We parked our Humvees nearby, and Jaguar got out and started to act as an impromptu tour guide. There was a palace nearby that was shelled pretty good, and we

As we were walking, the smallest of the three boys took my hand in his and we just walked hand-in-hand back to my truck. No words were spoken between us as we walked, besides, I couldn't have talked if I had wanted to.

were told Saddam built it for his first wife. Jaguar left us and went to see about his ID card, saying he would return shortly. While we were waiting, I inquired if we were permitted to take pictures in this area. Permission was granted, and my Kodak came out. We took pictures of each other, the buildings, and some trees. I looked closer and discovered that in the middle of some palm trees were several pine trees! I could not believe my eyes! There, in the middle of a desert, were several white pines! As I looked at the trees, I found myself wondering how many other soldiers had made the same discovery as I. I wondered if their minds were flooded with memories of home as mine was as I examined a pine cone that had fallen to the ground. I just stood there for awhile thinking of home and it felt good to do so. Soon however, the moment's respite was shattered as a pair of Apache gunships flew overhead. I was right back in Baghdad again, but I was happier than I had been minutes before. I took more pictures and decided it was time for a Diet Coke break. As I was walking back to my truck to get a soda, three little kids were walking toward me on the sidewalk. They were just little guys, with the oldest one being maybe 10 years of age. I stopped and asked them, "*Kefa Haluka*" which means, "How are you," and luckily for me, they spoke some English. I knelt down and asked them their names and I told them mine. Then I asked them if they wanted a treat. Of course they said yes, and I reached into my pocket and pulled out some Slim Jims I had been munching on during our sightseeing tour. I opened them up for the kids and then they just stood there for a moment munching on them. The kids were so adorable I couldn't help staying there longer. Finally, I asked them if they wanted a soda. They all said yes, and I told them to follow me to my truck so I could get them one that was ice cold. What happened next will stay with me for a long time. As we were walking, the smallest of the three took my hand in his and we just walked hand-in-hand back to my truck. No words were spoken between us as we walked, besides, I couldn't have talked if I had wanted to.

I read once a soldier in war faces a cornucopia of emotions as they go about their trade. Hate, fear, anger, happiness, hope, and love are all present here in Iraq. It is hard for me to put into words what I felt walking with that little boy. Needless to say, I was deeply moved by his gesture. There I was with a rifle and grenades thrown about my body armor standing at least two feet taller than he. A soldier from a foreign land that had conquered his country. A man whom other little kids had run from in fear. But this little guy wasn't concerned with any of that. Perhaps he does that with all the soldiers he meets. Perhaps his gesture meant nothing to him. I don't know, but I believe that by his actions he showed trust and love. Such pure and honest sentiments in a country so full of unrest and struggle will certainly stay with me for a long time.

After about an hour, Jaguar returned and we decided to do a little more sightseeing. Jaguar, or "Jag" as we affectionately call him, suggested we might want to see the parade grounds. We climbed back into our trucks for the five-block trip to Saddam's former parade field. As we drove, in the distance I could see two giant swords crossed high in the air, each one brilliantly reflecting the midday sun and my mind hoped what I was seeing would be the parade field. As we neared the swords, I could see another set farther down the road as well, both of them just as majestic as the first set. As the trucks stopped, what lay before me was one of the most spectacular sights I have seen in many years. The swords each originate on both sides of the road thrusting skyward in mammoth hands made of beaten copper. The tips of the swords must have been at least 60 feet in the air! At the base of each sword was a net full of old battle helmets that were strewn about the base as if they had been in a bucket that had been kicked over. In the road directly under the swords were hundreds of old helmets set in concrete. To the left, farther down this stretch of road, I could see a large grandstand area with many rows of seats. The middle of the grandstand had a large outcrop that was covered with a large green roof. Jag told me this is where Saddam would stand and shoot his pistol in the air, as the army would pass by during parades. Farther yet, approximately a third of a mile down at the other end of the parade grounds was the other set of swords.

Off to our right was a rather odd looking building that was of unusual design. I asked Jag what it was, and he said it was the Tomb of the Unknown Soldiers. It seems this whole place was a monument to the Iran-Iraq war during the 1980s. The hundreds of helmets that littered both the roadway and the base of each sword were collected from the battlefield. I walked closer and saw many of the helmets had either bullet holes or shrapnel marks on them. It was then I realized these helmets had belonged to men who had died in battle. Most of them were probably on the heads of their owners when they fell.

As the other men from my unit ran here and there taking pictures, I started to feel awkward. I was standing on hallowed ground. I was standing amid a memorial dedicated to an army of men who had died for their country and their way of life. While I may not agree with many things Iraq has done over the years, I can still appreciate the sacrifice soldiers have made. This place I was standing is to the Iraqi people what the Mall in Washington, D.C., is to us. A place to remember. A place to pay respects. A place Iraqis of all faiths can come together and say, "This is our history."

I stood there talking with Jaguar, and it suddenly occurred to me Jag had been a soldier in the Iraqi army. I felt even more awkward at that point, no– sad would be the better term. I asked him if he had ever marched down this road under the swords. He said, "Many times." Sometimes I think about things entirely too much and this may have been one of those times. I began to think about what Jaguar must feel coming here. Two soldiers, each from different worlds, one the victor, the other the vanquished, standing next to each other talking amid a memorial dedicated to this man's brother in arms. I began to realize Jaguar probably knew some of the men who wore the helmets that were now part of this memorial. I noticed Jaguar wasn't saying much as we took it all in. His mind undoubtedly racing with memories from a different time. All I could say was, "These are different times, are they not?" I patted him on his shoulder and left him alone for a while. Jaguar is my buddy, but I still wonder what kind of emotions he wrestled with prior to taking the job as our interpreter. I trust him entirely, but he loves his country as much as I love mine, and I cannot imagine, nor do I ever want to imagine, myself in his shoes.

We spent about half an hour there, and as we drove past the guard shack to the parade field, we stopped again because the guard was selling pictures of Saddam from his days in power. All of us want some type of souvenir to take back with us, and a real picture of Saddam would be pretty cool. I asked the guard what all he was selling, and he said pictures and army items. I asked to see the other stuff, and he produced an old steel helmet. In my zeal for all things army, I never thought to ask where he got the helmet. I paid him what he asked and went to put it in my truck. As we left the area, I could see the guard walking back from the base of the swords, en route to his little guard shack with another couple helmets in his hands. Had we not been in a convoy

I would have turned the truck around and went back. This man was selling, piece by piece, a monument to soldiers who paid the ultimate price for their country! For a measly five bucks that guy sold part of his country's history. I understand times are hard for people here, but this man works for the Iraqi police, and they get a weekly paycheck! He is just turning an extra buck by selling something he is paid to guard and that he doesn't even own! This would be like me selling the little bronze plaques that have the names of soldiers on them that are all over military bases to commemorate soldiers who have served their country. Each one of those helmets represents a person who served, and their memory should not have a price tag affixed to it and sold to supplement some jerk's income.

As we drove back to Camp Black Jack, the anger I was feeling did not subside. Even now as I type, with Beethoven flowing in my ears, I am still upset at a man who would do such a thing. It is despicable to say the least. I told some of my buddies what had happened, and they agreed that it was wrong. But aside from the helmet incident, what started out to be just another day off gone bad, turned into a great morning of sightseeing and time spent with my buddy Jag.

Jason A Adams
Camp Black Jack, Iraq

Notice 10/12/03   Training   Deployment 3/1/04   Home leave 9/26-10/14/04   Back Home 3/19/05

Democracy: Rebuilding Iraq

Today is July 4th

Today, across America thousands of people will be gathering with family and friends, grilling hot dogs and eating countless pounds of homemade potato salad, fresh apple pies, and all the other foods that scream "America." The day will end with a trip to a fireworks show to commemorate our nation's independence from British rule.

In those first few years after the first Fourth of July celebration, I would imagine the people of the colonies really thought about what it meant to remember the significance of that day. Many of them lost loved ones in our fight for self-rule. It was the birth of a new nation, built on Christian beliefs, and the thought that all men are equal, free to pursue life, liberty and happiness. This "Grand Experiment" as it was called, meant no longer would some monarch across an ocean tell us what to do, tax us unfairly or impose their idea of government upon us. We were free! Free to do as we wish, within the limits of the law, of course, but free nonetheless.

Democracy, self-rule, the rule "of the people, by the people and for the people!" All these ideas embodied this fledgling nation. Many in the world thought it would never work. But, all evidence is to the contrary! It does work, and we have been the light of the world ever since! People continue to come to our land to find a better life for themselves and their children.

A few days ago, in a small room in downtown Baghdad, a new nation was born. The ceremony was simple, without political rhetoric, hoards of reporters or glamour and glitz. Gone is the tyrannical rule of a man, who for 30 years ruled not by the consent of those he governed, but by fear and persecution. Anyone who spoke out against this man disappeared, never to be heard from again. The country of Iraq is once again free. Their future is like a blank slate, a *tabula rasa* if you will. They govern themselves now, and it makes me happy to think they too can now experience the things that make our nation so great. Where they go from here is up to them.

Just like when the United States was born, there are those in this world who say this will never work. It may not, I mean, I can't predict the future! But, I hope it will. People say this is nothing more than a feather in our president's cap. They are saying this is just a ploy to get re-elected. Do you want me to tell the people I see daily that we really don't care about them and that we gave them freedom just so one man can keep his job? Are there people in America that are really that obtuse? We know what we have, and that it is the right way to live. Why then, should we keep this gift, and it is a gift, to ourselves? Why should we not bestow a little of what we have on others who do not?

The media likes to portray us as monsters. Although there are things people in this uniform have done that are less than keeping with the traditions and the standards of our armed forces, we are not monsters. Monsters behead people. Monsters cowardly set off car bombs in crowded neighborhoods in desperate hopes of killing one of us. Monsters fly airplanes into buildings and blow holes in the sides of our naval ships! Monsters act with wanton disregard for their own people and attack in the name of a God they don't really know that much about. No, we are not the monsters; we are the ones who are trying to show these people how to live as we do. We are not forcing it upon them, but rather guiding them. They are free to choose how they wish history to remember them. While I, along with everyone else here, miss that which I left, I for one am glad I am here. When I am old, I will look back upon this deployment and be proud to have done my part to give someone whom I have never met a piece of our way of life. I think I will never want to do it again, ever, but after we are home, I will be glad I was here.

This deployment has made me rethink some of what I thought I knew. I realized how much of my life I took for granted. I realize no matter how bad my life seems to be going, someone, somewhere, has things worse. I realize our liberties can be gone in a flash and that sometimes doing the right thing is not the easiest course of action, let alone the most popular. It is not my intention to sound as though I am on a soapbox. I just think people need to stop and think from time to time what life would be like if we did not have the liberties and freedoms that we do. I also would like people to remember that it is the

> **I realized how much of my life I took for granted. I realize no matter how bad my life seems to be going, someone, somewhere, has things worse.**

American soldier who bought and paid for these freedoms. I have been reading some online news services, and I would also like to remind some of those people that it is pretty easy to sit in the bleachers and yell at the quarterback! Get out of your comfy office, put on some boots, come over here, look at what I see, and then tell me I am the bad guy! Stand here and tell us what we are doing is wrong!

Okay, enough of that. Now on to the latest news from my neck of the woods. The past few weeks have seen some exciting things take place. Some things I have seen have made me sick and realize we still have a long road ahead of us here. Not just as it pertains to the army, but to the government of Iraq. Mostly though, as I look around me, I see progress.

We, along with Civil Affairs, have been running several medical missions out in our sector. Many of these people can't afford to see a doctor, let alone go to a hospital. Some of them don't have cars, and it is pretty hard to ride a donkey and a cart to downtown Baghdad just to get to the hospital. So, we have been taking a team of medical professionals out into the countryside to help heal some of the locals that are either sick or injured. Several people in our zone are confined to wheelchairs. Most I have seen are children. To speculate, I would say most of them are the result of birth defects or as a result of an untreated childhood illness.

The saddest thing I have seen to date was a boy dragging himself to the roadside in an effort to get some of the candy we pass out. You see, he had no wheelchair and was carried where he needed to go by family. Seeing that little boy crawling just to get a Jolly Rancher was almost too much for me to witness. We reported it, and we managed to get a brand new wheelchair for him. Now, at least he has some limited mobility and no longer has to crawl on the ground.

The saddest thing I have seen to date was a boy dragging himself to the roadside in an effort to get some of the candy we pass out.

Three days ago, while we were leaving post to go patrol, I saw a beatup Toyota pickup go by with a little boy in a wheelchair strapped in the bed of the truck. The little boy looked like he might have had muscular dystrophy or something like that, but it saddened me to think he must ride down the highway strapped in the back of a pickup like an animal going to market. My best friend is in a wheelchair, and I know the struggles he has gone through, so I can only imagine what it must be like to be in a wheelchair in a country such as this. I wish there was more I could do to help.

After receiving many packages from home filled with candy to pass out to the children here, I thought I had done pretty well with keeping up the demand here. Then, the other night when mail call time came, my platoon leader pulled his Humvee right up to the door of my trailer and said, "Adams, you got a box out here that weighs a ton, you can get it yourself!" Perplexed, I came out of my air-conditioned hovel and proceeded to try to lift the box out of the truck. The box weighed at least 40 pounds and, glancing at the postage, saw it had cost $46 just to send. I got it inside my trailer and looked at the return postage and saw my uncle and aunt from Roanoke, Illinois, had sent it to me. I remembered my mom had mentioned my Uncle Mike had secured "some" Tootsie Pops for me to distribute to the little kids that line the roads as we pass. I opened the box up and it was full of Tootsie Pops! Hundreds of them! I have been handing them out to anyone who wants one for the last few days, and I have barely made a dent in the box.

The last patrol before our day off, we found ourselves out on a dirt road, a million miles from nowhere, and I was busy throwing those Tootsie Pops when a man flagged us down. He spoke very good English, which I found surprising for a rural farmer. He told us his electricity had been off for some time and was wondering if we could get it fixed. The only reason he had power in the first place was because he lived under a set of high wires and must have spliced in somehow. We are not electricians, but we told him where to go for help, and that we would try to pull some strings on our end and see if we couldn't get something worked out for him.

We stood there talking for a few minutes and soon his kids came up with a little dog. I was surprised they had the dog, especially as a pet, because we were told the Muslims here consider dogs unclean and don't touch them. He was a cute little puppy, so I knelt down and petted it. I played with the little dog for a few minutes while LT Doubler talked with the civilian man. When I rose from playing with the dog, the man invited us into his home for food and tea. He said we must be hungry from working and he would be honored to have us as his guests. We politely declined, as we have a schedule to maintain and prepared to say our goodbyes. He just kept saying "Thank you, thank you, thank you," then he grabbed a hold of me and kissed me on the cheek. We all started laughing, and then he grabbed LT Doubler and planted a big man-kiss on him, too. All the other guys thought that was the funniest thing they had ever seen. We hurriedly said goodbye and jumped in our trucks before the crazed man-kisser could grab another one of us. I still cannot get used to this whole "kissing guys" thing, but it happens all the time, and I have said it before it is a symbol of friendship in this culture and I am glad these folks consider us their friends.

Earlier in my letter, I spoke of progress here, and I just wanted to mention some of the good things I have seen here over the past few days. At last count, I have seen four water treatment stations up and running. I don't know how many liters of water they are able to treat a day, but they are pretty good-sized structures so I am guessing a few hundred liters per day. Speaking of liters, the big gas station is open again. There are not many gas stations around here. Most travelers stop alongside the road and buy gas from people selling it out of old plastic jugs and worn-out "jerry cans." There is a large gas station out in our zone, but it has been closed since we arrived here in late March.

While patrolling the other day, we noticed a line of cars in front of it about 100 meters long. We stopped and asked how much a liter of gas is. Okay, I figured the stuff was dirt-cheap, but I had no idea of how dirt-cheap. Gas is 20 dinars a liter and diesel is 10 dinars a liter. You are **Another sign this country is heading in a positive direction is the fact the Iraqi police have started assisting us with the locals.**

probably wondering how much a dinar is, well when I checked last, a U.S. dollar equaled one 1,250 dinars (give or take). Do the math, and you will then know the meaning of dirt-cheap!

Another sign this country is heading in a positive direction is the fact the Iraqi police have started assisting us with the locals. The other day, while sitting under an overpass, we heard sirens approaching. I hadn't heard a siren since I was back home, so I wondered what was going on. Sure enough, here came three brand new Iraqi police vehicles with lights and sirens going. Jumping out of my truck, I grabbed my rifle because I figured something was up. The police went right past us just waving at us with all their might! A few minutes later, they came back by! They passed us a few times, and it began to dawn on me they were just having fun! They had brand new police cars, and they were just messing around with them. Boys will be boys, in any country!

We have a couple extra rooms in our pad of trailers that were unused for awhile. One, we made into a makeshift weight room, and the other is our day room. I am not sure, but I think the family support group back home got some money rounded up and now we have a large couch, chair, table, and a television! The best part is we have a satellite, too! I must confess I am a History Channel junkie! I sat in the day room the other night watching the History Channel until I was falling asleep! I had not seen that station since I was home at Christmas, which is far too long! The commercials are all in Arabic, which does not bother me too much. The main thing is it is one more piece of home that makes our lives here all the better. Like I said in a previous letter, the soldiers of yesteryear would cry if they could see how well we live here. Even when the power goes out, it is still better than living in a smelly old tent.

Jason A. Adams
Camp Black Jack, Iraq

Duke

Today is the 14th of July

Another week is gone and closer yet is our plane ride back across the ocean. In a few days, we pass the one-third point in our time in country. These next few months will prove to be very trying on the men. It is akin to the dog days of summer. The newness of being here is starting to wear off, we are very familiar with our zones, and most of us are focused on getting to go home for leave. Time seems to slow to a crawl. Our missions are the same thing day in and day out. We get up, go on patrol, and come back. The cycle of monotony is only broken up with a day off here and there. But for me, time is still going by rather fast. We get so busy and our days are all the same, it is hard sometimes to remember exactly what day it is. Luckily for me, being here is just that way. I mark days off on my calendar, and it seems like I don't just mark them off one at a time, rather I am finding I am marking them off in groups of three or four! That is a good thing, too!

Last week a funny thing happened to us while we were driving up and down the interstate. It was about midnight, and we already had four hours of patrolling under our belts. My truck was in the lead as we were going north up by Abu Ghraib, when one of the other guys called on the radio and said he had a little problem. He said he had lost a tire.

I thought he was referring to the spare tire that rides in a rack on the outside of the rear tailgate. To our surprise, he had been talking about the right rear tire on the truck! Not just the tire either! The entire wheel hub, bearings, seals, and axle shaft came out! I talked to the guys, who were luckily all okay, and they said they were just driving along, and they felt what they thought was a huge pothole. The next thing they knew, they saw a tire pass them! We found the tire off the road about 30 meters. We laughed about this unexpected Pepsi break as it soon turned into.

We called the wrecker to come give us a tow and decided we had better set up the reflective triangles to alert other motorists. It soon became apparent, however, Iraqi people do not understand what those things mean. We had to send a couple guys with chem lights down the road a bit to direct traffic into the other lanes. The wrecker showed up, and the truck was towed in for repairs without further problems. I talked to one of our mechanics soon after and he asked, "What in the heck are you people doing to these trucks?" He said in all the years he had been turning wrenches, he had only seen one other truck break like that. We drive the tar out of these trucks, averaging almost three hundred 300 miles on some days. Some of the driving is on the interstate, while other times find us on the bumpiest excuse for a road there is! Some of the roads here are nothing more than a set of tire tracks that may or may not lead anywhere. We spend a lot of time turning around on some patrols when we decide to go exploring.

One of the platoon sergeants here, SFC Greg Remick, is a carpenter on the civilian side and has been working on a large swing set for the kids at a local school. We managed to scam some 4x4's and some other wood and he has built it in his spare time. The kids are going to be so happy when they come off summer break and find this thing in their schoolyard. We had a hard time coming up with some of the bolts to build it. When you are bolting two 4x4s together, you need a long bolt, and our maintenance section did not have any that large. We spoke to one of the vendors at the bazaar, and he found them for us in Baghdad.

We have had a new interpreter working with us these past few weeks. Jaguar is still with us, but since we are so busy we needed another, so we were assigned "John Wayne." That is not his real name, obviously, it is his code name. We just call him "Duke" for short. Yes, it is kind of corny, but I think he likes it. Especially once we explained to him just who John Wayne was. He is only 19, but I have found him to be a very level-headed, straight talking, and honest young man. He is a college student and is studying music.

As a fellow lover of classical music, we hit it off right from the start. I asked him what instrument he was focusing on, and he said he played the lute. For those of you who may not know what a lute is, the best way to put it is that it is a string instrument that resembles a guitar. Once again, while talking to Duke, I have seen why our country is so longed for by those who aren't Americans. He had many questions about what it is like to live there. He asked what winter looked like and how cold it gets. He asked about what our cities are like. He asked about what we do for fun. Many questions came out of him as we talked, and he was captivated by our answers. He looked like a child being told a tall tale by his grandfather.

He asked me, "Do you think that I would like America?" I thought to myself, "I think America would like you," but I told him he would love it. I told him about how our system works. I explained the Constitution and Bill of Rights to him and he was amazed at them. Duke is not an isolated case here either. Many of the people I have talked to want to come to our land to find a better life, go to a better school or because they can live as they wish there.

One of his questions bothered me a bit. He asked, "Will people be afraid of me?" I didn't understand his meaning at first, but it became apparent he was referring to his ethnicity. What could I say to that? How do you explain something we feel when standing in an airport and a man of Middle Eastern descent gets on the plane? It is not right to stereotype, but we do it. I don't know what it feels like to be in his shoes in that respect. I hope I never do.

How does it feel to walk in a world that automatically labels you just because you are Arabic? It is a label that makes Hester Pryne's scarlet letter look rather infinitesimal, especially by today's standards. Duke is a good kid, and I am trying to do a little networking and find him a way to America. The army trusts him enough to let him carry a pistol, and he is proving to be a valuable asset to our team. I hope I am successful in my attempts to help him. I am constantly reminded about how much I take for granted to be able to live in America. Examples such as Duke, Snake, and Jaguar serve to reaffirm the fact we have it made. Some of us just don't realize it.

I did some digging last night, and I received replies to some emails regarding this subject. It seems the process to apply for a student visa originates at the U.S. embassy and is rather long and painful. Who would have imagined that? I think I have found a way for Duke to get his wish. The downside to this is just like everything else, it takes money. The average Joe in this country doesn't have money.

People like Duke, Jag, and Snake constantly put themselves and their families in jeopardy on our behalf. They volunteered to help us. Their skills in language are vital to our mission accomplishment, and quite frankly, we couldn't do what we do without them. Therefore, do we not owe them something for that? Yes, of course we pay them, but that is the norm when someone works for you. I hope to find a way to help them by the time we leave. What better gift could we give them as we leave than the gift of living in our country?

We have had several cookouts over the last few days. We cooked hot dogs on the Fourth of July. We had steak the other night, and last night I grilled out with some of the guys to celebrate my 31st birthday. I went to the PX, bought a giant T-bone, and we got some baked potatoes from the chow hall. It wasn't exactly Lone Star style, but it was a little bit of home I had been missing.

Some of the guys made shish kebobs the other night, too. They bought a T-bone and cut it into cubes. The fresh vegetables, well that was a different story. We can't get fresh produce on base. So, we did what all soldiers do at times, we improvised! We all have seen trucks laden with produce of all kinds heading toward Baghdad and its markets. As we patrolled, we kept our eyes peeled for trucks that were loaded with what we needed to make our meal.

When we saw a truck with tomatoes in it, we pulled it over. The driver thought we were going to search him, but we reached into the back, held up a tomato in one hand, and some money in the other. He took out a crate of tomatoes and held it out for us. We picked out six good ones and said *shukran*. The man wanted us to take the whole crate! I asked SSG Glisan, "How much cash did you give the dude?" He said he only gave him four bucks, but apparently that is what a whole crate goes for in town. The crate was twice the size of a milk crate too! We finally got it through to the guy we only wanted a few tomatoes and not the entire crate. He tried to give some of the money back, but we let him have it all.

I am rather certain it was the first time the driver had ever been pulled over in the middle of the night by a bunch of GIs with guns, just looking for some grub!

Needless to say, he drove off confused, yet happy. I am rather certain it was the first time he had ever been pulled over in the middle of the night by a bunch of GIs with guns, just looking for some grub! Later in our patrol, we had to get sweet corn. We saw a field of corn so we stopped, set up security, and went to talk to the landowner. After a few minutes, the guys came walking back with a baker's dozen of sweet corn and a huge watermelon! The farmers here are pretty nice to deal with, and the guy picked the sweet corn for us himself. It took us all night to get all the ingredients, but we were successful.

Two days ago, we had an awards ceremony to recognize the soldiers who were involved in the Battle of Holy Week. Several different engagements happened that week, and there were many awards handed out. We fought quite a bit with the enemy, had four men wounded, and while I have never heard an official body count, the enemy hasn't really messed with us since. The men who were hurt all got Purple Hearts, and three of them were back on duty in a day or two. One was sent home, but he is doing fine. Eight of us were awarded the Army Commendation Medal for valor. That is a pretty big deal!

I already had been awarded the ARCOM as it is known, but never for valor. It is the highest award many of us have ever gotten. It is a very good feeling to be recognized in front of your peers. The Brigade commander, COL Formica, pinned the medals on us and gave a short, yet impassioned speech. His words exemplified what we all already knew. He said he was eternally proud to serve alongside such great men and he is glad we realize the need to fight here and now, so our kids never have to watch another airplane crash into a building.

If my being here will ensure we never have to worry about another attack, then it is time well spent. We must finish what those morons on September 11th started.

While I try not to get caught up in loud, flag waving type speeches like that, sometimes it is hard. Especially when every single word that came out of his mouth was true and felt by every man and woman in attendance. We have a choice to make as a country. Do we realize what a stable democratic country in the Middle East will do to these terrorists? If my being here will ensure we never have to worry about another attack, then it is time well spent. So my kids can go to school and not have to worry about a bomb in the lunchroom's macaroni and cheese, I will stay. We must stay until the job is done! Regardless of what happens in November, we must finish what those morons on September 11th started.

Spain left us, big deal they weren't doing anything anyway. Now, I see some other country wants to pull out because one of theirs is being held hostage. This is a war, folks! People die in wars! Is their resolve that weak? I think it was Ben Franklin who said one time that the tree of liberty must be watered from time to time with the blood of patriots. The way I see things, we have to stay the course. We have to finish what we start or we will lose in the eyes of the world. Just like Vietnam or Somalia, if we pull out because it is not politically advantageous to stay, then we invariably lose.

The soldiers who have died, and the scars the living bear, both physically and emotionally have done nothing to help neither our country nor our cause. It just doesn't make sense to me. Then again, I am just a simple soldier who does what he is ordered to. I am not a person who is caught up in votes or electoral colleges. That is one of the beauties of being an American. The people have a voice, and we can make choices, too.

SSG Jason Adams
Baghdad, Iraq

Headphones, Dead Dogs, and Hand Grenades

July 24ᵗʰ, 2004

Where has this month gone to? The weeks have been a blur and the days have flown by at supersonic speed. Some of the guys have been home and are back already from leave. One thing they all said was the humidity of Central Illinois almost knocked them down. I have spent time in the desert before, but never this long. I would imagine it must be quite a shock to return to such humid weather. But, given the chance, I don't think any of us would turn it down. We could have our stuff packed in minutes!

My buddy Jaguar tells me July and August are the hottest months here, and I am glad to say that as July draws to a close we are all still hanging in there. One of my buddies has a little thermometer outside his trailer, and we keep track of the temperature to see how hot it gets. This morning, as I was helping him set up his new web cam, I checked the mercury and it said 118 degrees. Not too bad, but then again, it was only 1100 hours in the morning.

This past week again saw us working alongside the ING (Iraqi National Guard). We set up traffic checkpoints, went on patrols, and did some dismounted patrols as well. Although they are mostly inexperienced, what they lack in know-how, they make up for in motivation. The only problem we have is the language barrier. But, with the help of modern technology, we are learning to overcome that as well.

A few weeks ago, my platoon was issued what is called a "Phrase-O-Later." It is a small hand-held device that resembles a PDA only slightly bigger! What it does is nothing short of amazing! I speak into the microphone in English, and it spits out the exact phrase in Arabic!

A few weeks ago, my platoon was issued what is called a "Phrase-O-Later." I admit, not a good name for a product, but it is proving to be well worth the $6,000 that it cost. It is a small hand-held device that resembles a PDA, only slightly bigger. What it does is nothing short of amazing! I speak into the microphone in English, and it spits out the exact phrase in Arabic! Just like that! It also has a touch screen that lets you choose frequently used sentences such as "Where do you live?" or "Give us your wallet." Just kidding about the last one there, but you get my point.

Because we run patrols 24/7, it is not possible to have Jaguar or John Wayne with us all the time. Mostly at night, we do not even have an interpreter with us, unless we have a special mission to do such as raid a house. Thus, this "babble box" as I call it, has become priceless. The locals sure do get a kick out of our technology. The first time we used it at a traffic checkpoint, we had trouble getting it to work. So here are three guys, at 0200 hours in the morning with a carload of locals stopped trying to get this thing to tell them we must search their car. As we were all trying to get the thing to work, the locals were muttering to one another, and we were visibly frustrated. Finally, we got it to work, and I wasn't sure who was happier, us or them.

The best part about it is that it translates either way. If I speak English into it, it spits out Arabic. I then hold it up to the man I am talking to and he responds in Arabic, which it in turn spits out English for me. You can actually carry on a conversation with it! Plus, it can be programmed for many different languages. Needless to say, it is a welcome tool for the men of Foxtrot Battery.

I have always thought the indigenous people here were less susceptible to the weather than we are, given the fact they are the ones who live here and are undoubtedly used to it. The other day, I was proven wrong, and in a very scary way, I might add. We had just come back from the ING compound with a fresh batch of troops to help us run a traffic checkpoint. It was very hot out that day and we were all sweating profusely. We had just set up the TCP (Traffic Check Point) and the air force team that was with us had just sent up the UAV (unmanned aerial vehicle) to scan the countryside. We let the ING run the checkpoints themselves, and we just critique and act as mentors to them. So I was back at my truck with my team.

The call came across the radio to me saying an ING soldier was sick up ahead, and I was ordered to come forward and examine him. I told SGT Ortiz to hand me my medical kit and off I went. Upon arriving at the man who was sick, I saw him doubled over and vomiting. Of course he spoke no English, but luckily for me, one of his buddies spoke a little. I asked him what was wrong with his buddy and he said, "No problem, just bad stomach." I thought, "Okay, a little Pepto Bismol should do it." I opened my bag, got out some of the pills, and grabbed a bottle of water for him. When the dude stood up, I noticed he wasn't sweating at all. I took his pulse and noticed that, besides his elevated heart rate, his skin was hot and dry. I asked him how much water he had drank that day, and he said one bottle. He said he felt really tired and his stomach felt like a "fist," which I interpreted as muscular cramping. I hurriedly readied an IV set and proceeded to prep the infusion area.

At that point, he began to vomit violently and looked as though he would pass out. A couple of his buddies helped him and got his clothes loosened up while I got the IV going. I yelled at LT Doubler and told him we needed to get this guy to the hospital quickly. We loaded him into an M1114 truck (they have A/C) and got underway to the hospital. Unfortunately, we were pretty far out from anything remotely resembling civilization and the trip took about 20 minutes, even at full throttle. While en route, I started pouring water on him and put a couple field dressings soaked in cold water in his armpits in an attempt to cool him down. The hardest part of the whole trip wasn't trying to treat a patient in an already cramped area; it was trying to keep him awake.

We made it to the hospital, and they gave him two more bags of fluid and kept him for awhile to make sure he would be okay. I stayed with him and talked to him through an interpreter who happened to be stationed at the hospital. I admonished him pretty good about the need to drink water and staying hydrated. I couldn't believe he had only one bottle of water the whole day! It was 1600 hours when this all started! I told him bullets weren't the only thing that could kill him here and that he scared the heck out of me. I am just glad we were able to treat him and that he returned to duty the next morning.

Funny story about the interpreter in the hospital. As I was continuing to evaluate and treat the injured ING soldier, the interpreter approached to my rear and began to speak to the soldier. I didn't even look at the man speaking as I was more concerned about my patient. As I was attempting to spike another bag of IV fluids, I handed the empty bag over my shoulder to the interpreter and said, "Get rid of this." He took the empty bag, and I said,

"*Shukran.*" Then in plain English, the man says, "Dude, I'm from America!" I turned and looking at him, realized he was in fact an American. I felt like the village idiot and apologized as fast as I could. He just laughed and said it was no big deal. Sometimes I get so focused when dealing with sick people that Mr. T could walk by in a nightgown with a feather boa around his neck and I wouldn't notice it.

The other morning while patrolling, we came across a dead dog in the middle of the road. The enemy here likes to use dead animals as booby traps. They will get a dog or a sheep, kill it, and cram it full of mortar rounds or howitzer shells. Then they put it along the road, hide nearby, and wait for us to drive by. It didn't take us very long to figure out their tactics. We stopped prior to reaching the dog and dismounted. SPC Werkheiser and myself approached the carcass (cautiously, to say the least) and examined it. After deciding it was just a dead dog and not a bomb, we threw it off the road and into the ditch. LT Doubler called on the radio and said he could see what looked to him like a hand grenade alongside the road as well.

Sure enough, a few meters away from where the deceased pooch had been was an old pineapple grenade. We called our headquarters to get instructions on how to handle this. Usually, the bomb squad comes out and blows things like this up for us. That day, however, they must have been busy because our HQ told us to get a grid coordinate for it and place a sandbag on top of it. Somewhere in the back of my head was a little voice reminding me of how unstable old munitions can become, so I was a little nervous about the whole idea of disturbing it with a heavy sandbag. But, orders are orders.

We got a shovel, filled up a sandbag, and walked towards it. SPC Werkheiser and I were about to place the sandbag, and I noticed the fuse and pin were missing from the grenade. Werkheiser noticed, too, the composition B explosive that usually fills the grenade body was missing as well. That didn't make any sense, but we called it in anyway. HQ told us to just chuck the grenade body in a ditch and move on. By now several locals were standing around us, probably wondering what we were doing. The road that we happened to be on that day is well used by us, and the locals are all pretty cool. So the fact they were milling around us caused us no concern.

One of the guys followed LT Doubler, SPC Werkheiser, and me back up to the grenade. I bent over to make sure it was empty before I picked it up. I took out my flashlight and was trying to look inside it, when the civilian man started chuckling and waving his hands as if to say, "Don't worry, I got it." To my surprise, he bent over, picked up the grenade, and threw it in the ditch nearby. Then he looked at us, smiled, shook the dust from his hands as if to say, "That takes care of that," and said something I didn't understand. I was rather embarrassed a local did my work for me, but it was kind of funny to see. I just gave him a sheepish grin and walked back to my truck.

The school we are building for the kids is located along this stretch of road as well and is progressing nicely! The foundation is done, and they are starting to lay the brick for the walls. Obviously, wood is rather scarce over here so the majority of buildings are fashioned out of brick, stone or mud. I hope the workers can get the school done by the end of the summer so the kids can get to use it this year. We were originally supposed to build the school ourselves, but Civil Affairs managed to get some money and was able to hire a local contractor to do the work for us.

Either way, it is through our efforts this idea has reached fruition. It is just one more step of progress that is being made here. I am so proud to think all those little kids can at last have a new facility that will be more conducive to learning than the former structure ever was. If anything is going to turn this country into something great, it is education. A poorly educated, populous country makes for a poor nation as a whole. It is good we realize the need to guide those in power now, and we must also prepare the way for the leaders of tomorrow. The only way to do this is through adequate education.

If anything is going to turn this country into something great, it is education. A poorly educated, populous country makes for a poor nation as a whole.

Three days ago, while returning from another arduous day of patrolling, we decided to stop by the PX and get some Pepsi. My wife can attest to the fact I rarely come out of any store with only the item I went in for. Today was no different. While looking for bargains, I came across some headphones that were on sale. My roommate came up and noticed them as well. They looked pretty high tech, like some futuristic headgear one might see on *Star Trek*. They wear on the back of your head in the same area a baseball cap would. The earpieces are small and fit right into your ear canal. The weird thing about them is the headphones themselves run on a single AA battery. They are called Panasonic VBSS, which means Virtual Bass Sound System. I did need a new set, as my old ones were pretty beat up. So, I decided to buy myself a little birthday present and took them to the counter to check out. My roommate also decided he needed a set, and at $30 a pair, we figured "What a value!"

As I read the package on the way back to our trailer, it said they vibrate in rhythm with the music! The biggest problem I faced was what song to listen to first. I chose Tchaikovsky's magnificent 1812 Overture in E flat major. As the music played, I was amazed at the sound. Every crash of the cymbals resonated in my head and, as the canon fired, I could almost feel the concussion from the blast. What an experience!

It took me back to a few years ago in Toulon. July Fourth fireworks were rained out, and we decided to watch the Boston Pops special on TV instead. I remember they played the 1812 Overture and a U.S. army artillery company had their cannon on top of a hill near the amphitheater. The soldiers were attired in their dress uniforms with all their medals on their chests. All the men wore white gloves and all stood at attention by their guns, with firing cords in hand. As the music progressed, they loaded their cannon and fired shot after shot, all in time with the music. What a rush to hear!

While listening to that same music, I was right back there again. I closed my eyes and saw it all. As the shots of the guns filled my ears, goose bumps arose on my arms and I could feel my breathing pattern alter some. It was truly a remarkable and breathtaking experience all for the low, low price of $30. It is funny how a certain song can conjure up memories of days past. All it takes is the right song and some meditation and I am home again. What a wonderful thing to feel.

Many people have asked me how I deal with this deployment and I tell them all the same thing; I just get lost in my music. Some of us play cards, others watch movies, some read constantly, but for me, music and writing get me through. My computer on which I write these letters hears all my thoughts. It is like a

Music and writing are powerful vents for my fears, frustrations, and thoughts. Each of the guys here has to find what works for them.

really expensive diary. Some of what I write is only for me and no one else sees. Other times find me offering advice to my friends back home. Either way, music and writing are powerful vents for my fears, frustrations, and thoughts. Each of the guys here has to find what works for them. I am just thankful I already knew what to do.

Headphones, dead dogs and hand grenades aside, we are all doing just fine here. The care packages keep streaming in and so do letters. We can never repay all of you at home for your love and support you have shown us. I know I speak for every man in Foxtrot Battery when I again say, "Thank you." This deployment would be so much harder if we didn't know you were all behind us 110 percent.

SSG Jason A. Adams
Camp Black Jack, Iraq

Divine Intervention

Today is the 30th of July

This past week has seen many things. Some of them have made me laugh, and some of them have made me pray. Mostly though, things are going along really well.

One day last week, some members of Third Platoon came back from patrol with these rather large cylinder shaped objects with short, stubby fins on them. The objects were approximately 12 inches in length and 6 inches in diameter. Being the curious sort, I asked what they were. SSG Arneson explained they were the flares the artillery shoots to illuminate the night sky. I knew the artillery had such munitions; it is just I had never seen one.

He went on to explain they had to raid a house the night before and had coordinated with the artillery battery for some illumination flares so they could see the house and the surrounding area during the raid. These were parachute flares which have an actual parachute attached to them to slow their descent and allow the flare to produce more light for a longer period of time. When the flare burns out, the parachute burns up as well, and the metal case falls harmlessly to the ground… well, in theory anyway. Unfortunately for the guys of Third Platoon, the men figuring the coordinates for the guns are really good at it, and they dropped the flares right above them. Which in most cases is what you want, just not *that* close.

Apparently, as the guys were moving toward the house, the first volley of flares were burning out. Then suddenly a distinct "thud" sound was heard and then another. The empty canisters from the flares were falling right on top of the guys! One of them landed only a couple feet away from one of the guys! They all started running to the house to get under a roof. Nobody was hurt, and they all wound up laughing and joking about almost getting thumped in the head. They brought back a couple of the canisters as souvenirs and have them proudly displayed outside their trailers.

Another day last week found us out in the middle of nowhere, doing a house search for suspected weapons. The air force had their dogs out there, and while we were making jokes about Benji and Cujo, one of our trucks got stuck in a canal. It seems they had been trying to cross a culvert and part of the culvert collapsed rendering the truck mired and in a big way too, I might add. I was ordered to return to our base and escort the big eight-wheeled wrecker out to our position to pull out this truck of ours that was now halfway in a canal.

We returned a short while later with the wrecker and proceeded to get busy. The problem was that while no one could see it, the Humvee's frame was caught on the edge of the culvert. The wrecker is usually used to pull much larger equipment than a Humvee and using one to pull a Humvee out of a canal can be likened to using a sledgehammer to build a birdhouse. The driver of the wrecker lay on the gas and yanked the truck out of the canal with no problem, but it dragged the culvert out of the ground along with it. We all stared in disbelief as we looked at the mess in front of us.

The locals who had been observing the whole mess looked like they were in shock and started talking among themselves and pointing at the debacle we had created. What made matters worse was the fact the road on the other side of the culvert was a dead end and all the locals' cars were parked over there as well. Luckily, the wrecker has a knuckle crane on it and carries a ton of log chains, as well. LT Doubler told Duke to tell the locals not too worry, and that we would fix it.

So with the aid of the knuckle crane and some old-fashioned manual labor, we soon had the dirt dug out and the culvert reset. Then we started to backfill the culvert with loose dirt so they could again get their cars over it. The head of the family told us not to worry about that part saying, "That is what grand-children are for." We said our goodbyes and prepared to leave.

We decided we should check the truck's undercarriage for damage resulting from the culvert. We crawled underneath the truck with our flashlights and found everything to be in order. Man, those trucks can take a heck of a beating! Which is good, because that's what they usually get! On our way back to base, it occurred to me that is the second time we have had to pull that same truck out of a canal. I told SPC Bomleny he now is qualified for the coveted "Golden Dipstick" award for excellence in driving ability. I won't give the specifics as to his reply, but you can imagine what he said.

After all the jokes about putting his truck in a canal again, we realized it was getting close to chow time so we headed into the chow hall. While the men were in eating, I was guarding the trucks when a pair of marines came up and started asking all sorts of questions about my truck. I usually stay out and watch the trucks so I can read one of my books, and one of the guys just brings me a carryout plate of food.

The marines, one a private and the other a lance corporal, asked about all the armor on our truck. They were amazed at the bulletproof windows, the heavy doors, and the sandbag and plywood "Menard's Armor" on the back. They were also amazed at the weapons we had in the back and said, "Geez, you dudes don't mess around, do you?" I said, "Nope, we come ready for about anything." Then I wondered and asked, "How long have you been in Iraq?" The corporal looked at his watch and said, "About three hours." I just laughed and told them a little about how it goes here. They seemed sort of nervous but I told them they would be fine. It is funny, but I myself have only been here since March, and it feels weird to have newbies asking me for advice. We continued to talk for awhile and soon they left, but I hoped I had set them at ease a bit.

"How long have you been in Iraq?" The corporal looked at his watch and said "About three hours." It feels weird to have newbies asking me for advice.

Our interpreter, Jaguar, has set up a suit shop in one of the empty offices here on base. Before the war, Jag was a tailor and made custom suits. We talked to the commander to see if Jag could set up shop here and sell his wares. Permission was granted and Jag soon was taking orders. He explained to me that over here, unlike America, if you are a tailor, then that is all you do. It is sort of like the caste system one would find in India, yet not as confining.

To expound a little, if you make suits, that is it. You make nothing else: not shirts, not neckties, not sweaters. You just make suits. The same goes for the guys who make shirts. But, with that in mind, it is rather safe to say the products these people turn out are perfect. The perfection stems from the experience one can derive from performing the same tasks day in and day out. You would think performing such repetitive tasks everyday would soon become rather mundane, but Jag doesn't seem to mind. Folks over here don't have such an insatiable appetite for advancement and prestige like some in our country. I guess it all boils down to what you are used to, and since that is all you know, it must not be that big of a deal here.

The material selection he has is from all over the world; Italy, Germany, Britain and France, just to name a few. Plus, the dollar is so much stronger than the dinar that a three-piece, tailored suit costs around $150 to $200 (U.S.), and Jag is still making a good profit. I have seen the fruits of his labors, and I must say his work is most amazing. My roommate, SGT Ortiz, just got a new suit in time for his leave, and it is very sharp. He purchased a three-piece suit, plus a pair of awesome leather shoes for under $200. I plan on doing the same thing prior to my leave. I am glad Jag can make some extra money doing this, as his plans to bring his family to America after this is all over will undoubtedly cost a lot of money.

Most of us try to keep our birthdays as secret as possible around here. The reason for this is not that we are so vain as to not want people to realize we are a year older, but rather, we don't want practical jokes played on us. It is a defensive mechanism of sorts, you see. One of the platoon sergeants here, SFC Greg Remick, was not so fortunate the other night. It seems members of his platoon, et al., made the discovery his birthday was coming up and they all began to conspire as to what to do to help him "celebrate."

Soldiers historically possess two main qualities. One, they are resourceful and two, they are mischievous. These days, things are no different! Some of his guys went to the local marketplace and bought a live chicken. They took a box our water bottles come in and fashioned a makeshift cage. While SFC Remick was taking a shower, he made the mistake of leaving his trailer door unlocked. The men slipped into his room and put the chicken in the middle of the floor. Then they all went outside and pretended to be waiting to talk to him about platoon business.

SFC Remick did not notice most of them were holding cameras and walked past them into his room. As he opened the door, he saw the chicken and jumped a bit and then just stared in disbelief. I don't think he would have been more shocked if he had opened the door and found John Kerry standing there wearing something from Victoria's Secret! The whole time the chicken just sat there. SFC Remick turned around and yelled something I can't repeat, while all the men were laughing and making chicken noises.

If that in itself wasn't funny enough, he couldn't get the darn bird out of his room either. He finally grabbed a broom and tried to shoo it out the door. The chicken started clucking and flapping its wings, and SFC Remick jumped and screamed like a little girl who just saw a spider! SFC Remick is not a little guy either! Well, that caused the chicken to run under his bed, and SFC Remick couldn't get it to move. Finally, SSG McGovern regained his composure and walked in and reached under the bed and grabbed the thing and put it back in its cage. SFC Remick has a really good sense of humor and thought the whole thing was pretty funny, but I have a feeling he will not be denied his revenge if the opportunity presents itself.

On a more serious note, and all chicken jokes aside, some things that happen here still remind us we are in a war zone. When we all got pinned with our medals a couple weeks ago, many of us did not say anything to our families. We did so to protect them and not cause them anything else to worry about. It is then clearly obvious I wrestled with whether or not to include this next piece as part of this letter for quite some time. I do so now, not to scare anyone, or strike fear into the hearts of loved ones at home, rather, I do it to explain what I feel. Which is one of the main reasons I write these letters in the first place.

Two weeks ago, our patrol was out in our zone again, like always, driving around looking for the bad guys. My section of the patrol had to escort another vehicle back into the base. Our patrol split up, and the others continued on in sector, or so I thought. As we arrived at the perimeter of our compound, my section pulled over and waved the vehicle we were escorting into the gate. We were in a large parking lot with some concrete parking barriers in the middle of it. I happened to be standing up in the front seat of my truck, as I usually am, and I heard a low thud. I looked to the southwest and all of a sudden, I saw a geyser of smoke and rock hurtle skyward less than a football field away, followed by an earth-shattering explosion. I did not even have time to yell, "Incoming," when the voice came over the radio yelling for a medic.

I have dealt with some pretty hairy things as a medic here, but you never get used to hearing the call for a medic come over the radio. The minute you hear it, your pulse quickens, adrenaline starts to flow, and your mind goes into hyper drive. Millions of possible scenarios flood your thoughts as you try to get to the scene. It is your turn, *you* are center stage, and you either save life or you don't; it is as simple as that. Thus far, I am eternally proud of all the guys in our battery who carry the same bag of lifesaving items I do. We have treated many a wounded soldier and have managed to save them all. But, you never get used to it, and I think as weird as it may sound, it is good we don't get used to hearing it.

I also have come to believe in predestination. I feel each of us has a path to follow, and each of us has a time to leave this world, and as for the men of F Battery, that day was not it. As I answered the call on the radio, I realized it was one of my platoon making the call. While we had escorted the vehicle to the gate, LT Doubler had led the rest of the men to the other side of the parking lot to rendezvous with my section and resume patrolling. They were all standing outside their vehicles when the rocket came in. The 127mm rocket had impacted less than 20 yards from where they had parked. Not a single man had so much as a scratch on them. The blast knocked many of them to the ground, which is what prompted the call for a medic. We hurriedly made sure all were okay and then beat feet out of the area in case anymore came in.

Immediately, my thoughts turned from saving life to taking it. Rage filled my body, and the only thing I was concerned with was finding the person responsible for my friends' brush with the Reaper. As we left the area, we could see smoke not too far away, and since these rockets usually leave a scorch mark on the ground, we proceeded with haste. As we drove towards the smoke, reason began to overpower emotion, and I realized rockets of that size could not have been fired from such close proximity to where we had been. A long story made short, we didn't find those responsible for the rocket.

But, I am convinced I witnessed a miracle that day. I replayed the events in my mind over and over, we returned to the site of impact, and we could see the tire tracks from our

I am convinced I witnessed a miracle that day. It's as if God himself reached down with his hands and said, "Not today."

trucks and the crater from the blast. I can't explain how no one was killed, much less at least hurt. It is as if God himself reached down with his hands and said, "Not today." I am sure there are physics and science behind any explanation, but for me, it was nothing short of divine intervention. In a way, I am glad I was there to see it.

So you can see that even in war there is beauty to behold (in the case of the little boy holding my hand) and miracles do in fact take place. Sometimes, it is a matter of interpretation, and other times one just needs to open their eyes and look around.

I receive many letters and emails from all over the country. All of them share a common thing; we soldiers are prayed for constantly by hundreds, if not thousands of Americans. As you can see from the events of that day, your prayers are being heard. Keep 'em coming.

SSG Jason A. Adams
Camp Black Jack, Iraq

Salam Alakim

Today is August 10ᵗʰ

This past week continues to see much activity here and around the city. It seems our old buddy Moqtada al-Sadr, the head honcho of the bad guys here, is mad at us again. It seems he was behind much of the fighting that took place during Easter week. I am not really sure what it was that made him mad this time and frankly, I really don't care.

The funny thing about some of these folks over here is that whenever somebody yells "*Jihad*," they all come 'a running. It is like a college rugby player running into a frat house and screaming, "Free beer!" I know what they are thinking; they are figuring if they keep fighting us, then we will go home. Quite to the contrary! If they would stop fighting, then we would go home!

I know what the insurgents are thinking: they are figuring that if they keep fighting us, then we will go home. Quite the contrary! If they would stop fighting then we would go home!

One of the guys in my unit is a talented artist and has been drawing cartoons illustrating some of the events over here, and that last thought was recently the center of one such cartoon. I wish they would get the picture! This mess would be so easy to clean up if they would just put down their RPGs and machine guns. But, until they do, or we kill every last one of them, we aren't going anywhere. As I have said before, war is never the right answer; it's just that sometimes, it is the only thing left.

This cleric dude, Sadr, is quite the fanatic. My take on him is he is a little punk that wants to be in charge, but none of the elders think too much of him. Therefore, he figures if he can cause enough trouble, then the elders will have to at least recognize him. It is all too political for me. But this just goes to show politics and religion are like oil and water, they just don't mix, regardless of how much you stir them.

Most of the things I would love to write about, I can't. Not yet anyway. In time though, I hope to write more about the events that are shaping how things are going here. I keep a little notebook and when something happens, I make note of it and save it for future use. In time all of the stories will be told, but for now, security is still foremost in my mind. I hope all of you understand.

Last week, we again found ourselves out with the ING patrolling in our sectors. Around midday, with the temperature trying desperately to break all records, we decided to look for some shade. We had found a secluded group of palm trees alongside a field some time ago. We just couldn't find a road that would take us there. That day, we did some exploring and found that indeed, a road did lead to the trees, but it was very inhospitable to vehicles. We put our trucks into four-wheel low gear and made it to the trees.

We sat in the beautiful little grove of trees for quite some time just talking with the Iraqi soldiers. It was a very serene place, with the wind blowing in the palms, the birds chirping and, most importantly, shade from the sun. The trees were laden with dates almost ready to be picked and there were some beautiful flowers growing nearby.

As we sat in the shade of those palm trees, we could see a house not too far away. The Iraqi soldiers decided it looked "suspicious" and decided to search it. Personally, I think they were either bored out of their minds, or they simply wanted to look adept at their jobs. Either way, we get a kick out of their over-zealous attitudes. They came back a few minutes later with the owner of the house. The owner carried with him an antique Russian sub-machine gun. It was in mint shape without so much as a scratch on the finish. I have seen pictures of guns like this in my books at home, but only pictures. This was the real thing, and it was truly a remarkable firearm.

We spent a few minutes looking at it, and I think the farmer was rather surprised, not to mention proud, we had taken such an interest in something like that. He returned to his home, and not 10 minutes later, came back carrying a large tea service and a pitcher of iced water for us. He had his brother and two children with him as well. So, we had tea and talked with them for awhile.

His little boy, the youngest, was just plain adorable. Maybe five or six years old with a big cowlick in the front of his head. He didn't know what to think about all of us soldiers and wouldn't come near us. We gave them all a box of

MREs and some candy for the little boys. I have never had a taste for tea; I have always been a coffee sort of guy. Tea always seemed too weak for my taste. Not over here! The tea these folks brew makes Juan Valdez and his pet donkey look like amateurs. It is really good, but you had better use plenty of sugar!

The man and his family stayed until all the tea was gone and then left us. I am glad we get to interact with the locals. It sets me at ease to know most of them do not harbor

They are honest folks. If they say "salam alakim" to us, they mean it.

any animosity toward us. If they do, then it doesn't show on the surface. Plus, they are honest folks. If they say "salam alakim" to us, they mean it. That means "peace be upon you." I find it to be a most beautiful way in which to greet someone and I, too, mean it when I say it.

Some of the people who live in our section of mobile housing are former military folks, who now work for a civilian contractor. Most of them are former army, with one exception. A female that lives here used to be a colonel or something like that in the air force. I had to patch her up one day when she fell off her front steps and nearly snapped her ankle in two. She used to be part of some top-secret base out West. She wouldn't say which one, but I sensed some sort of "X-files" type stuff.

The problem with the civilian people is that if they get sick or injured bad enough, then they get sent back to the states and subsequently lose their jobs. Therefore, they are very apprehensive about seeking medical aid from their doctors. So, having found out I am sort of qualified in that area, they come to me for everything ranging from headaches to sinus infections to sprained ankles, and large festering cysts.

A couple of the guys have become my good friends, and we spend a lot of time together. One night, Dave came over and said he was getting a rash under his arm. I took a look and decided it looked like heat rash. I gave him some ointment and some powder and told him to keep it clean and as dry as possible. Not having mentioned it again, I thought it had cleared up. Quite to the contrary, one of the little pimples turned into a large cyst! The thing was huge and nasty. He wanted me to cut it out and manage the wound for him. I

said, "Hey dude, I don't feel comfortable going at your armpit with a scalpel."
Nothing in my medical books gave any instructions on how to deal with
something like this, so I convinced him to go to the doctor. I told him I could
manage him after the doc got done. So that is what I did.

Dave came by twice a day for two weeks, and I had to pack the cavity with
saline-soaked gauze. It was rather disgusting to look at, but it was cool to see
a wound in all stages of healing. He is better now, and the incision has only
minimal scarring, considering they never stitched it up. All of those guys are
between a rock and a hard place in some respects. If they get sick and have to
go to the doctor and wind up getting sent home, then they run the risk of losing a job with a six-figure income! I think I could live with a few maladies for
six figures!

This past week also saw another trip to the Green Zone and to the parade
field as well. Over the past month, what started as a bug bite on my left cheek
slowly turned into a rather odd-looking lump. I did some research on it and
decided it looked like Leishmaniasis, which is the dreaded disease caused by
the sand flies over here. Needless to say, I started to worry.

I went to the doc, and she said she would put me on antibiotics for 10 days.
That didn't set me at ease because I knew Keflex would not help Leishmaniasis. Like an idiot, I decided I would just cut the thing off my face. I grabbed
some stuff out of my kit and headed for the bathroom. En route, I was stopped
by one of my buddies and, of course, they inquired as to my intentions with all
the stuff I had in my hands. As I explained my idea to them, they just said
"Your nuts," and walked away. I should have listened to them. I cut it off all
right, but it bled for two hours! Then it grew back before I had finished my
medication.

I finished the Keflex with negative results. I made the mistake of telling the
doc I had cut it off once, and she told me I was a moron, too. The doc decided
to put me on Cipro floxacin, or something like that, for another 10 days. I
looked up that medicine in my pharmacology book and it told me it was used
to treat infections of the respiratory tract. I began to wonder what kind of a
voodoo doctor I had been seeing! It also said it was used to treat some types of
skin problems, so I thought, "Okay, we will see what happens." In the mean-

time, I did some more digging and decided since I didn't have any of the other signs or symptoms of Leishmaniasis, then that couldn't be what it was. Long story made short, it turned out to be a pyogenic granuloma, which is nothing more than a lump of overactive skin cells. In layman's terms, no big deal.

The doc was all ready to cut it off herself, but decided since it was on my face, she had better let the dermatologist do it so it would look nicer. I agreed with her, since I am still hoping to land that modeling career when I get back. We scheduled an appointment with the other doc and went down to the Green Zone again.

The dermatologist's office was really pretty nice considering it was situated right next to a building that had been blown back into the Stone Age. He is an army doctor, but he has a private practice out in Philadelphia, Pennsylvania. His office looked like any other doctor's office I had ever been in. It even had the same smell. As I lay on the little elevated table waiting for the anesthetic to set in, I asked him if he had a mirror. He asked what for, and I said I wanted to watch him operate. That one threw him for a loop! He didn't know what to say!

He turned to his assistant and instructed him to get a mirror. By the time the assistant got back, he was just about ready to start suturing. He said, "Oh, here is the mirror." The mirror was rather large and rectangular with the backside painted olive drab green. I said, "Is this from a Deuce and a half truck?" He said, "Yes, I believe so." I was dumbfounded and could do nothing but chuckle to myself. Here I sat, in a doctor's office with everything sterile and packed neatly. No hint of the military could be seen, save for the uniform I was in. All of his equipment was top-notch stuff, too. Then the guy hands me a mirror off an old army truck! That was too funny.

After the minor outpatient type surgery, the two lieutenants and the lieutenant colonel that took me to the doc decided they wanted to go and see the swords at the parade grounds. I really didn't want to go back to that place, but I was rather outgunned in the rank department, so about all I could say was, "That's a great idea, sir!"

The view that presented itself was just as stunning as the first time I had laid eyes upon it. The men peddling helmets were still there so I volunteered to stay with the vehicles as a guard. As the officers ran here and there taking pictures, they seemed almost giddy, which is not the norm for lieutenant colonels in my experience anyway. I sat under some trees nearby and once again, my mind was flooded with images of yesteryear.

Nearby, between the swords and the Tomb of the Unknowns were several rows of street lamps. At the foot of these lights was a large area of ratty looking grass. I thought it odd lights such as these would be in the middle of a grassy area. But, as I looked closer, I could see it had once been a parking lot. I started to notice the entire place looked rather overgrown, like an Old West ghost town. I felt lonely all of a sudden. The light poles were not used anymore and looked like silent sentinels guarding a sea of grass. But, I wonder what they had seen! How many parades and festivals had they been witness to? How many soldiers had passed by them: each one just like me and proud to serve their country, just like me. It made me rather sad to think their day is over. A place forgotten by time whose glory days are long gone. It seems like such a waste. All of it, not just the lights, but the swords too. Maybe I think too much, I do not know. We left not long after we arrived so I had little time to ponder such things, and soon we found ourselves zooming back toward our makeshift homes.

Not too much is new here. The helicopters continue to fly over our trailers on their way to land. They started landing about three football fields away from my trailer, and they came in really low ever since. Most of the men don't like the excessive amounts of noise when the birds land. They usually fly in tandem or in threes and they all land together so it gets pretty noisy, not to mention windy when they land. I don't mind it, though. Matter of fact, I sometimes stop whatever it is I happen to be doing and go outside just to watch them. It reminds me of when I was a little kid, and I would hear the fire whistle blow. I would run into the front yard in hopes the trucks would come by our house. It was so exciting to see those red trucks with their sirens wailing race by on their way to save the day. These helicopters give me the same rush of awe mixed with excitement. The aircraft come in constantly and yet, I never tire from seeing them.

I should have been a pilot. My test scores were high enough, and I had my chance, but I didn't want to go to that long of a school. In retrospect, someone should have slapped me silly for passing on such an opportunity.

Good food, good company, and really bad baked beans will certainly be remembered years from now.

We continue to have cookouts here. Tonight, SGT Sleaford and myself bought brats and hot links for my section, along with pop, chips, and, of course, baked beans. Well, they weren't really baked beans, they were little cans of nasty Beanie Weenies, but we just pretended they were homemade. We can't get the good stuff to really do any kind of cooking here. So, we improvised, but you know what? It is times like these we will remember. Most of my section was there, along with Snake and Jaguar, and we had a great time. Good food, good company, and really bad baked beans will certainly be remembered years from now. Needless to say, we are all still doing just fine over here. Aside from the fact we miss home, we are happy, too.

SSG Jason A. Adams
Camp Black Jack, Iraq

Locals

Today is August 14th

The month is half gone already. Time is moving faster everyday. The half-way point for our time in Iraq will pass at the end of this month and the rest of it is all downhill. When I look at my calendar, the end still seems to be far off. But I know in reality, it will get here just as fast as the halfway point has, perhaps even faster. The other good thing I think of as I look at my calendar is the fact that as August draws to a close, so does the hottest part of the year here. What a welcome thing!

I have heard Mother Nature has blessed you with a rather mild summer. I keep track of the daily temperature at the Peoria airport, and I have been surprised at the lack of high temps that are usually characteristic of August. Here too, it seems the days are not staying as hot as they were. A couple weeks ago, the temperature would peak between 1200 and 1700 hours. Now it seems the hottest part of the day is not as long. In addition, there is a new wind blowing through this area. Twice a year the wind has a major shift. There is an Arabic word for it, but that word eludes me at this time. At any rate, the wind signifies a change in the weather. In the spring, the wind came on the eve of the thunderstorms and hailstorms that hit us in April and May. That was the last time it has rained here as well.

Not too much has been happening around here that I can write about anyway. Instead, it has been asked of me if I would write some about the life of the locals here.

As I have said in letters before, the locals here are mostly farmers and shepherds. Most of them are poor and even more are not literate. Their homes are modest at best, sparsely furnished and without running water. The men are the head of the household, and the women take care of the kids, cook, clean, and help with the chores. It has been said this society places women at the same rank as the cattle, but from what I have seen that is not entirely accurate. You also must consider cultural relativity. True, women over here have not a shred of the freedoms women from other parts of the world have, but if the man is the head, then the woman is the neck. The neck can turn the head anyway it wants.

Most of the farmers' time is spent in the fields. Without the luxury of modern farm implements, it is obvious the fields here are small and do not produce the amount of crops the same area would in America. But they seem to get by okay. Most of the labor is done by hand, and the tractors they do have are only used for plowing and irrigation work. There are a few combines I have seen, but I think the owners of those machines do a lot of custom work for others. As I have said, there are no wagons here, and the grain that is harvested is dumped into the backs of pickups and hauled away. The straw from the oats is piled up and hauled away later. The cows are tied up in the cornfields to munch on whatever the combine might have missed. They do not dehorn the cattle here, so they just tie a rope around the horns of the cows and put a metal stake in the ground to tether the animal in place. There are no fences here like at home, and the animals have a person who stays with them all day to make sure they are all okay.

Unlike at home, the holy day for these folks is on Friday. There are mosques all over here and every Friday they are jammed with tractors and other vehicles. The Iman, or "pastor" of the mosques sings the call to prayer five times a day. It was weird at first to be sitting out in the night somewhere and hear the singing off in the distance. It was almost otherworldly and made many of us uncomfortable.

In the summer, people do not sleep inside their houses either. It is just too hot. It is nothing to be driving around out here and see a whole family asleep in the front yard of their homes.

The homes these folks live in are nothing like I have ever seen. They are mostly made of stone, brick, or mud and most do not have glass in the window holes. Just a metal framework that lets in light, air and, of course, flies. The flies and mosquitoes around the houses are not as bad as one would assume. The trick behind this is rather gross, but effective. The locals save the dung from the cows and make little bins with it. Then they just keep adding more dung on the inside, and this draws the bugs away from the houses. In the summer they do not sleep inside their houses either. It is just too hot. It is nothing to be driving around out here and see a whole family asleep in the front yard of their homes.

Cooking is done in antiquated ways as well. Rice and flour are stored in large bags that sit in the kitchen, and the only appliance most homes have is a large boiler-looking thing that cooks the grain. The fuel for these boilers comes from propane tanks like you see on the front of camping trailers or forklifts in factories. There is a man and his son, I presume, who ride around on a tractor and hayrack that delivers the propane tanks to all the houses. The boy rides on the rack and bangs on the propane tanks with another piece of metal to signal their approach. The locals take them the empty tanks and get a full one in return.

I have only seen two or three refrigerators in homes here as well. Ice is used a lot over here and can be purchased in large blocks. There are several road-side stands that sell only ice. A boy with a bucksaw will cut you a chunk to your liking and then you haggle for the price. We have stopped there some-times to get more ice for our coolers, and we don't haggle. We just give the kid a buck and the deal is over and done with. A dollar to us is nothing, but to that kid with the bucksaw, it is an entire day's wages. We usually don't have a problem getting ice!

Regardless of the standard of living over here, the people seem to be happy. I have thought about this, and I have come up with a theory regarding this. Their lives do not move as fast as ours. More time is spent with family and friends. No one is chasing a career or worrying about their 401(k). The folks over here are one with the soil. It is everything to them. Without the fields, they starve.

Most of these people are deeply religious as well. Most of the men here carry little prayer beads with them at all times. They resemble a rosary and like rosaries, they come in many different styles. I asked Hebaaz one day what they were and he explained it to me. They use them to keep track of their prayers and also for comfort. Hebaaz said he feels closer to God when he holds the beads. Although a different God, the notion of such a thing to me is beautiful.

One of the major things I have noticed here is the divorce rate. You can say all you want about public stoning, wife beating, and all of the other rumors one hears about third world countries, but the bottom line is these people once married, stay mar-

Even I have noticed my life isn't moving as fast as it did when I was at home. I think if our lives would slow down a bit, we would be happier as a result.

ried. I think this has a lot to do with their level of happiness as well. But, I think all of these things start with the fact that their lives do not move as fast and their lives revolve around their faith. Even I have noticed my life isn't moving as fast as it did when I was at home. School, work, and all the other things that demand my time take its toll. Somewhere in there, I have to be a dad and a husband, as well. I think if our lives would slow down a bit, we would be happier as a result.

The locals can move about freely as they choose. They do not seem to be concerned with the fighting that has gone on here. It is sad to think about but perhaps they are just used to it. To elaborate a little: One day we were stopped talking to a man about a rocket or something when we were ambushed. We all hit the deck and started shooting back. We could see the dudes shooting at us so we called up our grenade launcher to put the hurts to the idiots shooting at us. We routed the losers that ambushed us pretty quickly. When it was all over, we turned around to see where the man we had been talking to went. To our surprise, he had moved back down the other side of a canal not more than a few feet away and just stood patiently waiting for us to get done "playing." I couldn't believe it! Anybody from home would have been on their face praying for their lives. This guy just got out of our way, let us do what we do best, and waited to finish our conversation.

Unfortunately, this lack of fear sometimes leads to what the government likes to call "collateral damage." That is a fancy term for a civilian caught in the crossfire. But on the same token, the locals aren't stupid either. If they know the enemy is planning an ambush, they pack up and leave. At least that is what they did during Easter week. Now, the enemy doesn't tell the locals anything, because the locals will warn us. They just ambush us anyway, and pay no regard to the civilians. This to me shows that the enemy, who pretends to fight for the people, really doesn't care about them. Then again, we already knew that.

I have also observed qualities in these people that are not all that common in our country anymore. They help each other in a way I am not used to. We have come across people stranded on the interstate, and complete strangers will stop and try to help them. If they are unable to help them get their car started, they then offer them a ride to their destination. We have seen strangers stop and pick up injured people due to car wrecks and take them to the hospital (I assume). These people have opened their homes to me and my fellow soldiers on countless occasions. Perhaps this is due to their faith; perhaps they are just being neighborly. I do not know. But surely sentiments such as these make this a better place for the people here.

The children, however, are a different story. I love them to death, but they are not reared in the same way as our children. Many of them will come right out and ask me for my *sa'a*, or "watch." Other times, they will ask me for my flashlight or my glasses. I found myself taken aback the first few times they did this. I remember thinking about the kind of lecture behavior such as this would elicit from me, had my daughters acted in such a way. But, I have to remember this is not America. Anymore, if a kid asks me for my glasses or my handcuffs, I just tell them to go and fetch me a goat and the glasses are as good as theirs. You should see some of the responses I get! It is quite comical!

Many people have asked me what our camp is like. Camp Black Jack is located adjacent to the former Saddam International Airport. Now it is just known as Baghdad International Airport. The airport itself is not as large as I had envisioned, considering this city is home to some five million people. But, after thinking about it for a little bit, I realized most of the people here can't afford to see a doctor, let alone fly anywhere. Plus, under Saddam, most people could not leave the country. Jaguar is in his 30s and has never left a country that is roughly the same size as California. People just weren't allowed to leave here.

Our living area is a couple miles away from the runways so the jets really do not bother us too much. We are not staying on former airport property, but the area we call home was part of Saddam's private game preserve. There are many lavish buildings here along with many lakes and canals. The architecture here is rather impressive. One of these palaces sits on top of a man-made hill and can be seen from miles away. The palace itself is beautiful to look at, but on the inside, it is rather gaudy and puts forth an air of arrogance and way too much ego.

Our little corner of the world is pretty much made up of these trailers we stay in and some headquarters buildings, which are more permanent. The chow hall is about half to three quarters of a mile away and so is the PX. The Burger King is right by the PX and so is the bazaar. What does take up a lot of space here are all the vehicles and conex containers we brought all our things in. There are several motor pools here and each is filled with tanks, howitzers, Humvees, and larger trucks. I have never seen the army on this grand of a scale, and I must say it is rather impressive.

The chow here is still top-notch. The chow hall we go to has an ice cream bar now too! You can go and get a dish of chocolate, vanilla or strawberry and get lots of goodies to put on top as well. They make milkshakes, too, but the line is usually pretty long for those and considering how impatient I can be at times, I rarely get one. Yes, they still have the kettle full of fake beer at the door, too. I am rather certain it is the same stuff that has been there all along. Not too many people like it. First of all, the stuff is just plain nasty and second, what's the point of drinking beer with no alcohol in it? We aren't allowed to have real beer, or alcohol of any kind for that matter. At first, we all thought it was a stupid rule. But I am old enough now that I can understand the rationale behind rules such as these. That doesn't mean I necessarily agree with them, but I can understand them. Considering we all have live ammo, grenades, and anti-tank rockets at our disposal, perhaps it is a good idea to not let us drink. The repercussions from such a lapse in judgment could be severe. The last thing you want is a bunch of drunken soldiers with guns!

Life here is pretty good. We didn't have a very good idea of what our living conditions would be like prior to our arrival. True, we

Aside from this whole war thing, life is good.

had heard rumors and unofficial intelligence, but we still weren't sure. Once on the ground and sure these nice trailers were in fact our housing, we were very happy. Many of the men who came and went before us lived in tents the whole time they were here. Up in Afghanistan, I am told there are still soldiers living in bunkers. We could shoulder that burden if we were forced, but we would certainly not be as comfortable and spoiled as we are here. I was always raised to be thankful for whatever I had, and needless to say, I am very thankful we have the accommodations that we do. Aside from this whole war thing, life is good.

SSG Jason A. Adams
Camp Black Jack, Iraq

Notice Training Deployment   Home leave   Back Home
10/12/03   3/1/04   9/26-10/14/04   3/19/05

Medic...I'm Hit!

Today is August 21st

Well, we have reached another turning point in our duty here in this country. Our missions have shifted some, and along with that, it allows us a chance to catch our breath some. This past week we have pretty much had nothing to do. Not too many of us were complaining about it either. The lack of work was due to our leaders trying to figure out what to do with us. Gone are the days of endless patrolling out on the interstate! Now, our mission has shifted to other areas, and with it comes an entirely new set of challenges. Some of these challenges are nothing more than a battle with boredom.

My platoon has drawn a QRF duty, which stands for Quick Reaction Force. Basically, we sit around and wait for something to happen. Yes, we still have to make a sweep through a zone from time to time, but that is no big deal. This past week was spent grilling out, reading, playing video games, and sleeping in. We had a cookout one particular evening, and we

My platoon has drawn a QRF duty, which stands for Quick Reaction Force. Basically, we sit around and wait for something to happen.

invited Snake and Jaguar to come. Ben and I went to the PX and bought brats, hot links, cheesy brats and some chips and other stuff. We made sure to grab a pack of beef hot dogs for Snake and Jag, as they don't eat pork. We were able to scam some buns from the chow hall and some mustard as well. I made grilled hot dogs for Snake and Jag, and they went nuts! They absolutely loved them. Last week was also a time of reflection. Many events have shaped our memories here, and the week preceding our mini vacation was no exception.

We were all set to pull our 12-hour shift out on the interstate. It was a night patrol that meant we wouldn't be back until the next morning. We left the security of the walls and wire, going by way of the same route we have traveled a hundred times since we arrived here. Our platoon broke up into two groups as usual and proceeded to drive up and down the interstate looking for bad guys. My truck assumed the lead, and Ben and SFC Hess followed. We had been out about two or three hours. Honestly, I am not sure. The whole night was a blur. There is a patch of interstate that was blown up a few months ago and since has been patched with gravel. It is really bumpy, and we usually drive around it to the right or to the left. If you drive over the middle part of it, it will rattle the teeth right out of your head! On the first pass, we went right as we traversed the gravel. The second pass, we, for whatever reason, decided to go left. It is not a decision we usually dwell upon. Either right or left, doesn't matter.

As my vehicle cleared the patch and returned to the center lane, Ben's truck was crossing. At that instant, we heard an extremely loud explosion. We knew what it was instantly; it was an IED (improvised explosive device). I remember yelling, "Get the (bad word) out of here!" to my driver and then I asked my gunner if he was okay. He

I remember yelling, "Get the --- out of here!" to my driver, and then I asked my gunner if he was okay. He just calmly said, "Dude, I'm hit."

just calmly said, "Dude, I'm hit." I grabbed the radio to report to SFC Hess about our status. Then I heard Ben come across reporting his gunner was hit as well. We gunned our trucks and tried to squeeze every ounce of power out of the engines. The enemy likes to ambush you after they hit you with an IED, and we had no intention of giving them an opportunity to do any such thing. We drove out of the immediate kill zone and stopped to assess the wounded.

As we stopped, I grabbed a flashlight to assess my gunner, who was by now holding his right side and in obvious pain. I could see no blood on his uniform and upon a quick exam, I knew it wasn't serious. I could hear SFC Hess yelling for me to get my medical bag and come back to Ben's truck. As I left our vehicle, I didn't even look to see how damaged it was; I just sprinted back to Ben's gunner. I could see his truck was blown to hell, and the passenger side window was covered in shrapnel marks. SPC Nick Welgat of Kewanee is also an EMT and is Ben's driver. He had his bag out and was helping the gunner out of the truck. We got him laid out on the interstate and started to assess him. He had a big gash in his face and his right arm looked as if he had fallen off a motorcycle at 60 mph wearing nothing but a T-shirt. We are trained to expose injuries to get an idea of how bad they are and treat accordingly. Nick started to get an IV ready while I took care of the wounds. Nick and I work well together, and we each set about our tasks without getting in each other's way. I put a bandage on the facial wound and several places on the right arm. I had my trauma shears out, cutting away his uniform and I came to his hand. I was about to take his glove off when I could see the extent of his injuries. I decided to leave the glove on, what was left of it anyway. I splinted his entire right arm and applied another bandage. Nick couldn't find a vein to start an IV, so he decided to go "fishing" You can imagine what that term implies. No luck in the left arm, and you are not supposed to start an IV in an injured extremity. We decided to go for his feet. Nick was already getting another needle as I cut off a boot and removed his socks. We each tried to find a vein on his feet but none were to be found. You know, looking back, it is amazing we managed to put the doggone bandages on right let alone get an IV started. We each had just seen our lives flash before our eyes, plus it was dark and we were trying to work by flashlight. Not exactly what one would consider ideal conditions!

By this time there were two helicopters circling overhead, and they wanted a report on the injured to forward to the inbound Medivac. I ran over to a radio and gave the report while they looked at my gunner. My gunner was lucky and had only sustained three shrapnel wounds. Two were superficial and the third was rather deep, but not in a vital area. The concussion of the blast had knocked him against the ring of the turret pretty hard, and he was also complaining of his shoulder and right arm hurting. I carry a shoulder sling with me and applied that as the medivac helicopter landed. We loaded Ben's gunner onto a stretcher and told him to say "Hi" to Germany. He just smiled and said "Yeah, they have beer there, don't they?" When he said that, I knew he would be just fine. Ben and I, along with Nick, grabbed the stretcher and ran to the helicopter. As if my adrenaline wasn't already flowing good enough, running under a Black Hawk chopper just itching to take off, is a rush unto itself. The wind from the rotors feels like standing in a hurricane. You can feel the raw power the engines produce vibrating off your chest. What must it feel like to be in control of such a machine! We loaded the stretcher first, and then my gunner stepped into the bird. I glanced at the pilot, and he just gave me a casual wave as if to say "Later, dudes." The pilot pulled back on the stick and the chopper was gone in a flash.

Our jobs weren't done, by any means. We still had to get the damaged trucks back to base. We had to hook up a tow bar to Ben's truck, as it would no longer run. My truck had a blown-out tire and a broken drive shaft, which didn't decide to fall off until we reached base. It took us awhile, but we all made it back to base and changed my tire there. As we got into my truck to leave, it wouldn't go. Ben, SGT Hartman and I crawled underneath to look, and saw the drive shaft was messed up. We called the wrecker, and they just unhooked the drive shaft and we limped back to our trailers. What started out as just another patrol, ended up being one I will never forget. The irony of the whole night was we had been up and down that interstate a hundred times with no problem. That night was also our last patrol out there as well.

By the time we made it back to the trailers, it was almost 0700 hours. The attack occurred before midnight. My gunner was already back in his room with a really big bandage and a big bag of drugs. He said Ben's gunner was just fine and was going to be okay. He also told Nick and I to not feel bad about not getting an IV started. He said none of the flight medics on the bird could get one started either. Once again, we all came through.

Looking back at that night, I have come to think of many things regarding what happened. What would have happened if our truck would have gone to the right of that gravel? We would have driven right over the top of that IED. Why did they wait and blow the thing until our second pass? Why did they not blow it as my truck passed? Had they done so, I would not be sitting here typing this letter. What made Ben decide to leave his window up? Most of us run with them down. These questions are mine to ponder, and I think they will remain unanswered. We all came away from a potentially lethal situation with only two damaged trucks and two wounded. We can always get more trucks, but I am just glad those that were wounded made it through alive. In retrospect, the men of my platoon acted like a machine out there. Everybody pitched in and did a job that was just as important as anyone else's job. I don't know who called in the medivac. All I know is someone did. Nobody got tunnel vision and focused on the wounded. Whoever wasn't holding flashlights for Nick and I as we worked was out pulling security, just like they were trained. Nobody had to be told what to do, they just did it.

Two days after that, part of my platoon had to patrol part of another road, one that we were unfamiliar with. After the events that were still fresh in everyone's minds, we were, needless to say, more than a little apprehensive. But, we loaded up in our trucks, confident we could handle whatever the day would bring. It was the same deal as before. We drive up and down a stretch of road looking for bad guys. We had a couple of BFVs (Bradley Fighting Vehicles) with us that day for added security, which made me almost hope the enemy tried something stupid. I said, "Almost." Bradleys will bring down the finger of God, given the chance.

We had just made the turnaround point, and we could see a huge cloud of dust in front of us. I hadn't heard an explosion, so I wasn't sure what had happened. SFC Hess was driving and I was in the turret. I heard him yell, "Hang on," and he gunned the truck. When we got up to the now dissipating smoke cloud, we could see one of the Bradleys flipped over onto its side with fuel running out everywhere. I thought, "Oh, goodie, here we go again," as I yelled for the passenger of our truck to cover the gun while I grabbed my bag and went running. Ben and Nick got to the tank before SFC Hess and myself and were already helping people out. I could see a track was missing but, I had no idea what had happened! An RPG? A mine? Another IED? Bradleys don't just flip over! The driver was trapped in his compartment and could not get out. SFC Hess and I ran back to our truck to get an axe to bust open the hatch. Upon our return, Ben had already busted it open with a sledgehammer. To my amazement, no one was hurt. That is not the norm. I have heard stories about tanks going over and somebody usually dies. With everyone safely out of the Bradley, we were concerned about it catching on fire from the puddle of fuel we were standing in. It did not catch fire, but we got the heck out of there anyway. We had to stop traffic so the recovery track could come out and get the thing back to base. People were getting pretty mad about the traffic jam, but we could not help it.

The recovery track took an eternity to get there. Secondly, the men of the recovery crew reminded me of Beavus and Butthead of MTV fame. They didn't have a clue as to what they were doing. This whole time, remember we were in the city; the perfect place for an ambush. After about an hour of watching Larry and Moe try to get this mess cleaned up, I had had enough. Ben and I used to be part of recovery teams, and we could see exactly what needed to be done. I went up and asked the head of the recovery team if they needed help. He gave me an emphatic, "No." I had to state the obvious to him and said people would soon be shooting at us if we didn't get out of here pretty soon. He knew this and was visibly frustrated with the whole debacle in front of him. I know how mad I used to get when I would be working and somebody interjects their two cents. But, usually when that happens we were not worried about ambushes. Another two hours went by. By now, a car bomb had been found about two miles down the road, and four of our trucks had to go and close off the roads. So now we were down to my truck and the other Bradley for security. Visions of the movie *Black Hawk Down* flashed through my head, I could see that SFC Hess was thinking it, too, and so were the recovery guys. Finally, after four hours of trying to get this Bradley flipped back over, we were ready to move. The recovery team had to drag the tank back to base because it was missing a track. Our speed back to base was a blistering 10 mph. We got to see them blow up the car bomb, which was pretty neat, not to mention loud. We all made it back to base without any problems.

Another couple interesting days under our belts and all our arms and legs are still attached. A couple more have Purple Hearts, but they will fully recover shortly. I can think of a hundred scenarios with tanks flipping over and IEDs going off. None of them are pleasing. Considering the nature of the events I have recounted, what did happen are the best-case scenarios I can think of. We are so very fortunate. Thank you all for your prayers.

The guys here take all this in stride and are not demoralized by it. Spirits are still high. Our deployment is over halfway done! The rest is downhill. I should be home some time next month for my two-week leave. Life is good!

SSG Jason A. Adams
Camp Black Jack, Iraq

Thoughts of Home

Today is August 25th

Wow, it is 0900 hours in the morning, and the temperature is already 110 degrees. So much for an early fall. The sad part is that even though I am dressed in my boots and uniform, I am not sweating. The nice part of all this is the high for the day will hit around 1500 hours, but unlike weeks past, it doesn't stay that hot for long. I have been up since 0600 hours, which doesn't seem like any big deal, but I didn't get off my shift of work until 2200 hours last night. We didn't get back here until almost 2300 hours. Upon returning, we learned First Sergeant decided we needed to have an open ranks inspection bright and early. Rifle and barracks room had better be squared away when you have one of those formations, because First Sergeant is looking for some backside to chew, and you sure don't want it to be yours. I was up until almost 0300 hours getting ready. But, my stuff was all in line, and the backside chewing would be left for another day, at least mine anyway!

Our new missions are going pretty well. This QRF duty I have had is not too bad. Originally, we were skeptical of working with another unit, but so far, so good. Our day starts at 2200 hours at night and runs until 2200 hours the next night. We have to go over to the other side of the airport and sit at some of the former airport buildings. There is no power in some of these buildings; lucky for us they need power to run the radios, so our building has electricity.

It is a small stucco looking building, one story, with no indoor plumbing. The only lights in it are two large fluorescent lamps hung in strategic locations in the building to supply maximum amounts of light to all areas. There are a couple of rickety old tables, three folding chairs, and some cots. There are a few mattresses and a place to hang up our helmets and body armor. Since we are on shift for an entire day, we are allowed to crash out if we so choose. I must say the mattresses are the nastiest things I have ever seen. They look like they were dragged out of a liquor store dumpster somewhere in New York City. I asked Ben, who is a deputy with the Henry County police, if the mattresses in the drunk tank were better, and he looked down at the thing, wrinkled his nose, and said, "Definitely." But, when you are really tired…well, you know.

Most of our time is spent playing cards, reading, sleeping, and watching an occasional movie. My buddy has a portable DVD player and usually brings it with us. I have read several books since we took this mission a few days ago. Lucky for me, I brought a ton of books with me. Plus many people have sent me books from home. The PX here doesn't have much in the way of books that I like. Surprisingly, most of the ones they do sell are those cheesy romance novels. You know, the ones with the damsel in distress standing next to the dude that always looks like Fabio. Not exactly my cup of tea, besides, if I got caught reading one of those, serious questions regarding my sanity would surely arise, and rightly so.

Oh sure, we still have to make sweeps through our zones several times a day. But when and where is left up to us. We don't have to drive up and down that ridiculous interstate any more. Plus, we are basically on call for any con-

So we sit around and twiddle our thumbs. You know what? I kinda like it!

tingency that might arise at the airport. It is operating under civilian authority once again, and you never know what that could bring. The government of Iraq has its own airport police force now, but some things just need the army's level of, dare I say, "finesse"? So that is what we do; sit around and twiddle our thumbs. You know what? I kinda like it!

The other night, we had a little drama in our otherwise boring night. It seems some guy was driving along and rammed into a light pole. His car, a little Pontiac, flipped over, and he was trapped inside. We got the call to scramble and assist. We hurriedly drove to the grid coordinates we were given to render assistance. Upon our arrival, we found the civilian contracted security force was already on scene.

The car was on its driver's side and the driver was unconscious. Back home, if this scenario were to present itself, we would cut the top of the car off or cut out the windshield in order to gain access to the patient. Not these guys! About four of them pushed the car back upright, with the driver still in the car! I was flabbergasted! Anyone with any kind of accident response training will know actions such as those are on the first page of the "What *not* to do at an accident scene" textbook!

These men are employed by Global Security and are mostly British and Australian. The medic who happened to be working on the patient was an Aussie with a thick accent. "Bloody this, Bloody that" was all he kept saying. I had to fight back a chuckle as visions of Crocodile Dundee filled my head. He kept calling me "Mate" as well, but I couldn't help but like the guy from the get go.

As we pulled the injured man, still unconscious from the wreck, out of the car and put him on a backboard, the medics we had called said no ambulances were available for a civilian. We decided to load him in the back of the security force's pickup. As we loaded the stretcher and the medic jumped in, he thanked me for my help and off they went. As of yesterday afternoon, the guy's smashed-up car was still in the median. For all I know, the guy may have died from the wreck. From the looks of the car, he hit the light pole going pretty fast.

As you all know, the Olympics are currently going on. The Iraqi National Soccer team is competing for the gold as well. Soccer is to Iraq what baseball is to the U.S. and most of the kids here dream of being the next "great," just like every 10-year-old boy in America dreams of being the next Barry Bonds or Sammy Sosa. Unlike the U.S. however, over here when something big happens, people take to the streets and fire their guns in the air. It is nothing to see tracer bullets flying through the night sky every time there is a wedding or a birth.

The other night, Iraq won a big game at the Olympics, and the whole town went nuts. Ben and I sat on our front porch and watched with amazement as thousands of tracers went up in the air. They look like red glowing bottle rockets as they fly through the night sky. But, like they say, "What goes up, must come down." As we watched the tracer fire, we heard a loud smack against our day room

One night a rocket hit another of our trailers, bounced off a rafter, and landed outside. Luckily, the morons who shot the thing put the wrong fuse in it, which rendered it a dud.

trailer. We got up to investigate and walked into the day room. Inside, we found a bunch of guys playing cards with startled looks on their faces. One of the guys was holding a bullet. Apparently a stray round came through the ceiling, hit the floor, bounced up, and hit SFC Remick in the calf muscle. The bullet didn't hurt him, but had he been sitting a few inches to his left, well, this story might have a different ending. We aren't even safe from this nonsense in our trailers!

One night a rocket hit another of our trailers, bounced off a rafter, and landed outside. Luckily, the morons who shot the thing put the wrong fuse in it, which rendered it a dud. Several of us men were standing outside talking, not 20 feet away from where it hit. Thank God for stupid terrorists!

As the end of August approaches, so does my leave. These last few days, my thoughts are continually focusing on getting to go home. My leave is tentatively scheduled for the 21st of September through the 8th of October. Of course, this is the army we're talking about here, so that could change. Nevertheless, I am finding it hard to keep thoughts of home out of my mind. It is not clouding my mind enough to hinder my main focus, but when I get a minute to think, my thoughts always turn to Toulon, Illinois.

We were activated on October 12th, 2003. We spent a month of duty in Galva getting ready to go to Fort Hood. We left Galva around November 1st, I think. After a couple months at Fort Hood, we then came home for Christmas. I was lucky to spend 12 days at home before having to return to Fort Hood. Since then, I have not been home. According to my calendar, that equals eight months, give or take a few days.

Wow, eight months away! I have never been gone this long. It feels so good to think that in less than a month I can once again give Steph and my little girls a real hug, play with Buddy (my dog), sit on my patio, play my piano, along with all the other things I have been missing. I had gotten over being homesick many months ago, but those feelings of longing are starting to reappear as the days fall off the Rolodex. So much will have changed! I hear the Super 8 Motel in Galva is open. It was just a foundation when I left. My daughters and wife all celebrated birthdays during my absence. So much I have missed.

It is funny, but the saying "absence makes the heart grow fonder" is true. I miss Toulon! I miss the way Route 17 goes down into the Indian Creek valley just west of town. I miss the tree tunnels east of Elmira. I miss the smell of hay, or the smell of rain in the air. The sound of corn dryers whining in the distance on a cool fall evening! I miss the sound of nature's song I used to hear when I would go walking in the timber alone. To those of you sitting at home, surrounded by such things, it may seem like such trivial things. Imagine them being gone. How much would you miss them then? We take so much for granted, and when it is gone we want it back.

I think when I am home I will take time to savor the town I call home. If you happen to see me walking down the street with a dazed look on my face while I am home, fear not! I am not on drugs, and I have not lost my mind! I have to come back here for another few months before this is all over. I want enough mental photographs to last until my return is for good. It is these memories of home that reaffirm my need to be here. It is my job to keep America safe, as much as I hate to say it, our work is not done…yet.

If you happen to see me walking down the street with a dazed look on my face while I am home, fear not! I am not on drugs, and I have not lost my mind! I want enough mental photographs to last until my return is for good.

SSG Jason A. Adams
Camp Black Jack, Iraq

Tower Duty

Today is September 7th

Since I wrote last, several more days have fallen off the calendar and yet, my leave date still seems so far out of reach. That day is almost tangible. I can see it, I can almost feel it, yet I can't have it– not yet anyway. So that is my problem; anxiety! It can be likened to my world at 10 years of age. My sister and I would count down the days to Christmas, each new day dragging even slower than the previous. When Christmas morning finally got there, Bernadette and I would attack our presents like animals with such ferocity and quickness that any lion in the world would have stopped in its tracks and said, "Whoa, look at those two!"

With wrapping paper from the presents strewn throughout the house and mom and dad wondering why they went to all the trouble to wrap them, the rest of the family would show up, and the rest of the day we thought would never come was gone in a flash. So shall my leave be. I wait and wait, but the day eludes me. Then when I get home, my time will be like a bolt of lightning; gone in a flash.

One of the things that compound this frustration of waiting is this boring life my platoon has assumed these last few weeks. This latest duty we are doing is like a double-edged sword. On one hand, the work is like taking candy from a baby. It is very boring and mundane, yet it is relatively safe. On the other hand, I didn't come here to sit around. It doesn't feel right sitting on me bum while others are outside the wire. It is not right. There are enough troops here to run every Taliban-loving jerk out of this country.

Unfortunately, only a small percentage of the men here actually do anything. A great number of the troops here are what we call poogues. They get the same pay, the same combat patch, the same benefits, yet they don't get shot at…ever. Many of them are administration, postal, medical, finance, legal, or personnel soldiers. It is a thorn in all our sides, but who ever said life was in anyway fair? All of us knew we were joining a combat arms unit when we enlisted, so this is what we get, and boy, would we love to get our hands on our recruiter!

It is not my intention to negate the value of those of us in uniform that work in the post office or the public affairs division. All our jobs are like spokes in a wheel, you lose a couple and the whole wheel falls apart. But, we still feel a certain level of animosity toward those types of people. It is irrational to do so. We are a volunteer military, and we each got to choose the job we wished to perform. So in all honesty, it is my own darn fault I am not in an air-conditioned office getting coffee for some general.

Our new duties have been split again. We now rotate on and off the QRF duty. This is both good and bad, because sometimes you only get about eight hours to yourself between shifts, and that includes sleep. We have to man several towers on the wall, as well as provide troops for the QRF. The tower guard is terrible! Two guys stand in what is basically an oversized deer stand for 12 hours a day. The only time we get to come down is to use the porta-potty. Chow is brought out to us by the guys on QRF, and other than sporadic radio traffic, we are alone for the entire day.

At first, we would take books or game boys with us. One man would watch the perimeter while the other man took a break. That was until the sergeant major got wind of our little "at work time wasters." Now, we are not supposed to have books or anything in the towers with us. I have read 10 novels in the three weeks we have had these new duties.

Ben and I are usually stuck in a tower together, and we just write up our own work/rest cycle. One man watches the area outside the wall, and the other man takes a break. We have to wear all our gear in the tower, as well, which by the end of the day feels like it weighs 100 pounds. We keep a cooler in the tower so we can have cold water to drink and maybe a can of Pepsi once in awhile. The highlight of our day is the kids that come by the perimeter wall. They always want candy or a piece of our equipment. Some of them are little "wanna be" entrepreneurs and try to sell us whiskey or some other stuff. We play along with them, and I tell them to bring me a goat and we can talk business. That usually gets them to go away.

One of the other things we do for fun while "on the wall," as we call it, is baiting the dogs. There is a pack of wild dogs that roam the area we guard and usually come by once in awhile. We bait them in with MREs and then make bets on which one of them will be brave enough to come up to the wall and get the food. Yes, I know, pretty juvenile stuff, but hey, what else are we supposed to do?

The best part of pulling tower guard is the airplanes that come in. The towers are really close to the airport and the planes come in nonstop. The neatest planes to watch are the C-130s. These planes, although large, are surprisingly agile. They come in low, and I mean low, parallel with the runway, and then once they get to the end of the landing strip, they bank sharply in a 180-degree turn. Their wings straighten out about 30 feet above the runway, and then they touch down. When they take off, it is the same. They come screaming off the runway at full throttle, running only at treetop level. Once clear of the airport, the pilot yanks back on the ailerons, and the plane goes into an almost 45-degree angle and rockets skyward. It is so neat to see them fly like that! In flight, the aircraft looks so graceful. But, I have firsthand knowledge that the ride inside the plane is not what one would consider graceful! To the contrary, there is a reason they put barf bags in the seat cushions! The four engines on those planes produce so much horsepower that even on the ground in our towers, it still reverberates off our chests! I never tire of watching them.

Working so close to the airport, we get to see an abundance of aircraft from all over the world. Mi-7s, Mi-2s, Lynx's, Apaches, An-12s, you name it, we see it! Ben and I were discussing the other day how weird it felt to see the former Soviet Block aircraft fly over. As an air defense unit, we used to train on how to shoot aircraft such as these down. Back when I first enlisted, had we seen a Mi-7 fly over, we would have gone scrambling for our missiles! Likewise, at the chow hall, it is nothing to see the Estonian or the Polish army pull up in their BMPs. Not too many years ago, these vehicles were considered hostile. Today, they are our brothers in arms. It seems weird that time can change not only people, but nations as well. I hope the same holds true for Iraq.

It seems our beloved mass media is spouting off at the mouth regarding the fact that the 1,000th soldier has been killed in this war on terror. I would imagine the press releases for that little "milestone" have been written for weeks. Reporters drooling like starving dogs lying in wait to break the story. Yes, many soldiers have died in this war. I am afraid more shall follow before we are done. This number of dead is terrible, but as a history geek, I know that on many occasions more civilians than that were killed in a single air raid on London or Germany during World War II. As far as wars go, the casualties are really light. It is a sad day when we must resort to bombs to secure peace. As modern as our world is, we still act at times in medieval ways. We humans tend to focus on the negative side of things more often than not. Let me offer another view.

In wars of the past, territorial acquisition was usually the desired end result. Lands and peoples were conquered for king and country. Today is different. We did not muster our soldiers for new lands to populate. We did not cast off anchors for rumors of riches in faraway places! We didn't hoist up the colors to conquer and enslave a people! We took up arms as our fathers did to defend ourselves against a new type of enemy.

Victory in this war can be measured by what doesn't happen.

But, unlike wars past, victory is not as easy as who waves the white flag first. Victory is not a clear-cut case anymore; there will not be any armistice signed when this war is over. GENs MacArthur and Wainright will not be standing on the bow of the "*Mighty Mo*" waiting to accept Osama bin Laden's surrender. Victory in this war can be measured by what *doesn't* happen. Thus far, in our sector, attacks have almost come to a halt. America has not seen another major attack either. Therefore, we are being successful in our war on terror; we are doing our jobs. It is not pleasing to me that war must be our instrument to bring peace, but does the end not justify the means?

Over the past few months, I have been corresponding with a World War II marine vet in Florida. He and I first became acquainted through a project my sister is working on out East. She is working on the USS *Intrepid* Floating Museum project and has been doing so for many months. Her job is to put together the interactive movies that will be shown in the hangar deck of the World War II aircraft carrier.

Bernadette first came in contact with SGT Lesnett because he actually served onboard the ship during the Pacific campaigns. He has also been invited to speak at the grand opening of the museum in November. In their initial correspondence, Bernadette told SGT Lesnett she had a brother in Iraq who would love to hear from an actual World War II vet. SGT Lesnett has sent me many pictures of his days in uniform, including his commendation from G. E. Short, who commanded the *Intrepid* (CV-11) during 1945. SGT Lesnett was awarded two Purple Hearts, seven battle stars and was responsible for the destruction of many Japanese "Zekes" and "Betty" bombers. As an anti-aircraft gunner, he saw the action up close and personal! I feel like I really know him from his letters, and I can see him in my mind plain as day, standing at his Bofors 20mm cannon, with spent casings falling at his feet, cussing at the inbound enemy planes.

SGT Lesnett continually praises me for what I am doing. I do not feel worthy of his praise. Here is a man who fought in the greatest war our tiny little planet ever saw, stared death in the face countless times, managed to come out alive, and he is telling *me* how proud and thankful he is for what I am doing! I send him copies of these letters, and he reads them to his "Marine Lunch Bunch." Every week, he meets with former marines and reads my letters to them all. Then he writes to me telling me how proud he is of what I am doing! Compared to what men like him did, I am selling Girl Scout Cookies! I have been called a "hero" for what I am doing here. I am nothing of the sort! Men like SGT Lesnett are the real heroes. World War II vets are dying at a rate of almost 1,000 a day. They are a national treasure we will not have many more years. No, I am no hero. I spend my day sitting on a wall complaining because it's hot out.

SSG Jason Adams
Camp Black Jack, Iraq

Notice 10/12/03	Training	Deployment 3/1/04	Home leave 9/26–10/14/04	Back Home 3/19/05

Politics and War

Today is September 15th

Once again, this past week has found me stuck in my deer stand watching the grass grow. But, even though my duty would seem rather mundane, excitement never seems to elude me. I am still working the night shift in the towers, which runs from 0200 hours until 1400 hours. I have spent all this time with a soldier from Charlie Battery of the Fourth Battalion, Fifth Air Defense Regiment. The most interesting thing about him is he is from the island of Guam. I love talking to him about the places he has been. He has seen Korea,

> I felt like such a hick when I told him that aside from a border town in Mexico, this is my first trip outside the United States.

the Philippines, Japan, Australia, Indonesia, and many countless islands in the Pacific. I felt like such a hick when I told him that aside from a border town in Mexico, this is my first trip outside the United States. But, in trade, he has never seen some of the things I have seen either. He has never seen a cornfield frosted with snow or a deer and her fawn running through the timber, so it all averages out in the end.

Our tower is also occupied by "Alfred." Alfred is a rat and has become our most unwelcome guest these past few days. SPC Jasmin and I were sitting one night talking about Japan, and we heard something on the front deck of our tower. We could hear plastic crinkling, so I grabbed my flashlight. There on the front deck was this rat about a foot long from nose to tail trying to get a cookie out of its wrapper. The cookie was one of those Otis Spunkmeyer oatmeal raisin cookies, so it is rather large. This rat crawled inside the package, grabbed the cookie, and then backed up. The cookie slid off the edge of the deck and fell. Alfred wasn't about to let go and fell with it. We laughed for a bit over that and decided he would not be back because he must have fallen at least 15 feet to the ground. Later as we were sitting and talking, I felt something run across my legs. Sure enough, it was Alfred. I do not fancy the idea of rodents running across my lap in the dark, but there isn't a lot I am going to do about it. Plus, it gives us something to do in an otherwise boring shift. We have seen the little bugger several times over the last few days. We have christened him the "Tower 6 mascot."

We have had a lot of fun with animals since we have assumed the tower guard. One of the most interesting things we have seen is carnivorous wasps! I did not believe it the first time I saw it, but it is true. There are wasps here that love pork chops! One day SPC Jasmin and I were finishing lunch and there was a portion of a pork chop he hadn't eaten. There is always a mess of wasps flying around our towers, and we usually take turns swatting them with a fly swatter we brought to the tower. We decided to extend an olive branch to them and offer them some fine, quality army chow. We left the plate on the front deck of the tower, and sure enough, a wasp soon was hovering over it. The wasp landed on the pork chop and started to chew off a small piece. The wasp took a chunk off the pork chop about the size of a BB and flew away. Soon, it came back and tore off another chunk. We finally got tired of watching it, so we killed it with the fly swatter. I am not an expert on wasps, but I always thought they liked pollen from flowers and sweet things, not grilled pork chops!

I am told farmers are already picking corn in areas back home. There aren't exactly a ton of *Successful Farming* issues floating around here, so I have no idea of what the crop forecasts are this year. But I certainly hope the farmers have a good yield. The weather here is starting to change dramatically. A couple of weeks ago, the highs were still hitting in the triple digits, with the lows in the 90s or upper 80s. The last couple nights, the lows have gotten down into the 60s! Let me tell you, when you are used to 120° weather, 60° is downright cold. We have started to wear our field jacket liners at night. There is usually a nice breeze blowing from the north, and since our towers do not have windows, there is nothing to stop the cold air. It is refreshing to go through an entire day without sweating through my clothes.

Four days ago was September 11th. We were worried the morons we are fighting with might give us a little "party" in honor of our most infamous of

days. That day passed without incident, other than a call to my wife to wish
her a happy anniversary. Yes, our anniversary is 9/11. The only good thing
about that is I usually don't forget it anymore. It helps keep me out of the dog-
house! No, the morons waited until the 12th to remind us of why we are here.

SPC Jasmin and I have worked out a little
rest plan on our own in the towers. At night,
we take turns dozing off in order to get
enough sleep in an otherwise sleepless day. I
had only been asleep for a few minutes when
SPC Jasmin yelled, "Rockets!" The bad part
about being up in the tower is there is
nowhere to go during an attack. We certainly

**Sitting through
indirect fire is not fun.
There is nothing you
can do except pray the
rockets or mortars
either hit long or short,
left or right.**

can't leave our post, and even if we could, where would we go? There are no
bunkers nearby for us to run to for cover. Basically, we just hunker down and
hope for the best. We counted 12 impacts in the first salvo. Luckily, none of
them hit too close, but we could see them impact about 400 yards away. We
thought that was the end of it when we heard what sounded like a dump truck
at full throttle roar overhead. That is not a good thing, I assure you. We
ducked down, and we lost count of the explosions as the second salvo came
in. These hit closer and we could feel the blast wave from the explosions.

Sitting through indirect fire is not fun. There is nothing you can do except
pray the rockets or mortars either hit long or short, left or right. These rockets
are so big they are fired from several miles away. So the likelihood of finding
the jerks that shot them is slim and none. They are already in their trucks and
gone before the first one impacts. No one was hurt in the attack, and all the
rockets hit in a grassy area out by the airstrip. Nevertheless, neither one of us
were sleepy after that!

What these idiots don't realize is this: The airport is a source of revenue for
this new country, and if they continually try to blow it up, it will take longer
for it to get back on its feet, and therefore, take longer to get this country
going again. Like I have said a million times, these aren't the smartest people
in the world we are fighting against. Most of them are illiterate and the only
book they are allowed to have is the Koran, and even that is interpreted for
them by the Imam.

This war is so much unlike any other we have fought. Sure, we have fought guerilla wars in the past, but prior to Vietnam the United States allowed us to fight and win. It is different today. Today we again find ourselves in a guerilla war. Yes, we know the threat; we know the cities that give birth to insurgents and car bomb factories. We are allowed to defend ourselves, but basically prohibited from taking any real offense for fear of civilian casualties and religious backlash. This is what happens when politicians rather than soldiers run the war. Our hands are tied behind our backs, and then we are told to fight. To put it bluntly, bureaucracy sucks!

Unfortunately, the American soldier knows all too well about bureaucracy and how it works. That is the one thing that hasn't changed throughout the years. Who is to say the soldiers of yesteryear could perform to what society wants today? We soldiers of today wear many hats: Soldier, diplomat, liberator, protector, provider, police officer. All these jobs embody the U.S. soldier today. Our jobs are not limited to destroying the enemy by any means possible. Too many other things factor into our roles here. We cannot simply carpet bomb a city in order to root out a handful of bad guys. I am not suggesting carpet bombing should be among our tactics, but I am suggesting there comes a certain point where our leaders should get some backbone and decide this is enough.

We soldiers of today wear many hats: Soldier, diplomat, liberator, protector, provider, police officer.

We are like a bear being antagonized by a bee. The bee cannot destroy the bear, but it sure can make it mad! How many more rockets must fall upon us before we decide it is enough? At some point we must do what must be done to protect ourselves no matter what the political backlash. Let the politicians shed some blood, too.

One of my close buddies here recently left to go home on leave. Prior to his departure, we sat one day and talked about going home. He told me about an incident that happened to him in an airport when he was coming home from basic training. When a soldier travels under orders, they are usually required to travel in uniform. Coming home from basic is no different. My buddy was in the airport in his Class A uniform, when a man approached him, spit on him, and called him a baby killer. This appalling happening did not occur many years ago during the height of the Vietnam era, but rather, it happened less than 10 years ago.

This uniform I wear is not just a garment. A garment is something anyone can buy at Wally World. No, I have earned the right to wear it. There are millions of uniforms exactly like it, but mine is unique. It bears my family's name and is adorned with the rank and medals I have distinguished myself enough from my peers to be awarded. Nothing was given to me! I have earned it all! It is

> **This uniform I wear is unique. It bears my family's name and is adorned with the rank and medals I have been awarded. Nothing was given to me! I have earned it all!**

a reflection of me, and I consider it almost sacred. Its sharp creases and crisply starched collar command respect, the spit shine on my boots reflects the attention to detail that is one of the hallmarks of the army. I have had the honor of wearing it for almost 13 years, and even today as I put on the boots, the trousers, and the shirt, I am humbled. I am humbled to be able to serve all of you.

This uniform makes me a better person, a better husband, and a better father for I have a code by which I must live. It speaks loudly of who I am, what I believe, what I hold dear, and most importantly, what I am willing to do, or to give up in order for my kids to live as I have lived. But, not just *my* children! The countless millions of Americans whom I will never meet will also benefit from my service. To have someone disgrace it in such a way, to me equates to setting our flag on fire; it is disgusting, it is hateful, and it is almost unforgivable. The difference is this; our flag is an inanimate symbol of our country, whereas I am a living, breathing symbol of our country. A soldier's way of life is one of servitude.

We do not choose our missions; we serve all of you, even those of you who despise us for what we are. Perhaps, what is most despising to those types of people is the simple truth that in their hearts, they know fully well they could never fill our boots. It is their own cowardice and selfishness they find despicable, and it manifests itself in a hatred for those that *can* fill these boots. I can live with that.

Being spit on because of this uniform is not about the embarrassment of the act. Yes, it is embarrassing, but moreover, it hurts. It cuts like a knife straight to the bone, and the scars do not dissipate with time. We find ourselves asking, "Is this what I defend, is this the scum that my buddies died for?" These things are that which I fear; not bullets, rockets, or mortars. I volunteered to put myself in harm's way if need be. I did not volunteer to be defiled by some jerk so full of themselves they are unable to recognize what soldiers are all about. Thus far, I have heard only stories of warm welcomes, handshakes, and hugs from Americans back home. However, there is always some jerk just waiting for the opportunity to make a statement. Hopefully, my travel home will be looked back upon with happiness and thanks rather than sorrow and hatred.

At any rate, at last glance I had only 11 days left before that big airliner takes me back to the greatest place I know. It is good I am spending most of my time in a tower. I do not think I could concentrate enough to accomplish much else. See y'all in a couple weeks!

Jason A. Adams
Camp Black Jack, Iraq

Home Leave

The Trip Home

Today is September 28th

Here I sit, at Dallas/ Fort Worth International Airport. Thus far in my trip home, I have seen Kuwait, Ireland, Dallas, and I am heading for Chicago and then on to Peoria. It seems weird that to get home, I must fly over it twice. When we came through from Shannon, Ireland, we flew out over Greenland and then down across Canada. We flew over Central Illinois on our way to Dallas, and now I must fly back over Toulon to get to Chicago only to board another plane to take me to Peoria. It would be so much easier if the airlines would just issue me a parachute and kick me out over home. Life is not that simple.

Our trip started on the morning of the 26th in Baghdad at the Baghdad International Airport. We had to be at the Air Force Terminal at 0530 hours. That is rather early even by army standards. The bad part about it was we knew our flight would not leave until later in the day. Indeed, SGT Andersen and I wound up on chock No. 2, which didn't leave until 1630 hours. We sat in a semi air-conditioned tent for the better part of the day. What a waste of a day!

The flight to Kuwait was cramped and hot. The C-130 Hercules aircraft we flew on isn't exactly set up to accommodate passengers, so our trip was less than comfortable. But we didn't really care as long as the bird took us away from Iraq. Once in Kuwait, the silly games the army is famous for began. What could have been done in six hours, took all of 24. We had to go to ridiculous briefings aimed at making our leave as safe as possible. Next, we had to go through customs. Upon getting our initial leave brief back in Baghdad, we were told what we could take home and what we couldn't. We were brainwashed into thinking that any attempt to take contraband home would be thwarted, and we would be punished with the utmost severity. To the contrary!

When the air force security team went through our bags, I was astounded at the lack of thoroughness. I could have hidden 50 Cuban cigars plus the Cuban who made them in the bottom of my duffel bag and they wouldn't have been any the wiser. In hindsight, I am angry because I have some neat stuff I have collected that I wished to bring home. I could have sneaked it by with no problem, but I am glad I didn't try as my luck is not the best, and I would have looked like an idiot trying to explain why I had a bunch of illegal cigars in my bag.

We left Kuwait yesterday around 2350 hours and headed for Ireland. The flight was uneventful, and I spent most of it asleep. Once in Shannon, Ireland, we disembarked the aircraft and were allowed to venture into the terminal. Unfortunately, it was still dark when we arrived, and I was unable to see the surrounding area, which I am sure was a beautiful sight to behold. We stayed at the terminal for about an hour or so while the ground crews refueled and serviced the plane. The aircraft, a North American 737, took what seemed to be an eternity to refuel. The entire time, we weren't allowed out of the terminal because we had already been through customs in Kuwait.

By this time, I was ready to eat lead paint chips and ask for seconds. The only food available was sold out of a candy machine. I grabbed a pack of malted milk balls and a Fanta orange soda. My first experience with the euro was quite a shock. Granted, airports are airports no matter where you are and even the junk food is outrageously priced. Still, the grand total for a pack of Whoppers and a pop was almost four dollars. We reboarded the plane and were on our way. I hope on our return trip we can see Ireland in the daytime for I would really like to see some of the old castles that decorate the country-side.

Once back on the plane, I resurrected an old travel trick I had learned many years ago while traveling from Fort Chaffee, Arkansas, to Dixon by bus. It is a little something called Tylenol PM. I just take a couple of those and I am out cold for at least eight hours. When I woke up, the pilot was saying, "...and if you look out your window, you'll see Lake Michigan." I thought, "Great, not too far 'til Dallas!" The problem was the plane is operated by a civilian carrier, but is chartered by the army for soldiers going on leave. In other words, they get the most "bang for their buck" and the plane was packed. There were at least 200 troops on the plane and only four bathrooms. Do the math and you will see the problem. Everything worked out okay and we made it to Dallas around 1000 hours in the morning.

I wrote a couple weeks ago regarding my fears and apprehensions about returning from an unpopular war. When we landed at Dallas, what lay in front of me had me bursting with pride in a matter of seconds. There on the runway were two of those giant Osh Kosh airport fire trucks with their deck cannons raised up shooting water in giant arcs over our plane. Once inside the terminal, the welcome party came in droves to greet us. It was very special, and I was touched by their willingness to come all the way out to the airport just to greet a bunch of Joes they didn't know. Once again, I was humbled.

As I looked around at the men in the welcome party, I couldn't help but notice most of them were in their 50s and 60s. Many were wearing VFW and American Legion hats. I made the assumption many of them were Vietnam vets and, since many of their homecomings were less than happy, they were taking it upon themselves to see it didn't happen to us. Their actions upon our arrival home were heartfelt and sincere.

The USO had representatives waiting for us at the gate with free cell phones to use to call home. They also had free phone cards for us to use to let our families know we were back safe on American soil. The TSA employees bent over backward to make sure we got to our next gate, took care of any travel issues we might have had, and answered all our questions. The whole experience was great. I am not used to so many people catering to me. I thought to myself, "I could get used to this!" Unfortunately, this sudden and unexpected bliss was short-lived, as I still had to catch my next flight. My flight to Chicago left around 1400 hours and I had enough time to grab some mozzarella sticks from TGI Fridays and relax a little, and then I was off again.

Once in Chicago, I tried to grab an earlier flight to Peoria, but the only one was leaving as I was landing, so that was out of the question. The biggest pain in the neck I had was the fact the army provided me with a paper ticket rather than an e-ticket, which are so much easier. But hey, what is there to complain about when the ticket is free? I was concerned about the fact I flew to Chicago on United, but I flew with American Airlines to Peoria. I asked the lady at the ticket counter if they were going to lose my bag in the plane switch. She gave me the preprogrammed jingle about how, "We at American Airlines know how important your baggage is…blah, blah, blah." Needless to say, I wasn't convinced.

When I flew back to Fort Hood at Christmas, I didn't even switch airlines, and they lost my bag. I could only imagine where my duffel bag would end up by not only switching planes, but airlines, too. But I could only trust them as I already had a carryon and an army duffel bag doesn't exactly fit into the overhead compartment! The one thing the ticket lady did for me was ask if I had eaten. I said, "Well, if you count the mozzarella sticks I had in Dallas, then yes." She gave me a meal voucher worth twenty bucks that could be redeemed at any airport food vendor, including Wolfgang Pucks restaurant! Having never eaten at such a neat place as Wolfgang Pucks, I choose to get some buffalo wings at Chili's instead. What was I thinking? Nevertheless, free food is good food no matter what!

I roamed around O'Hare for awhile and looked through the shops and just enjoyed my freedom for a bit. It seemed so unreal; 96 hours before this I was riding in a tank in downtown Baghdad, having a hand grenade thrown at me! Now here I was loafing around O'Hare airport! As my flight time neared, I found myself unable to sit still. The batteries in my GameBoy were dead and I couldn't concentrate long enough to read, so I went to my gate. As if I wasn't anxious and jittery enough, I stopped at Starbucks for my favorite coffee, a white chocolate mocha; oh, and I bought some chocolate-covered espresso beans, too. So there I was, trying to be patient and wait for my plane while getting wired like an idiot on caffeine. Not the best idea in the world, I admit. I was so excited about getting home, like I was going to fall asleep anyway!

Anyone who has ever flown from the Windy City to Peoria knows it takes longer to say it than to do it. The flight was so short that the flight attendant was practically running up and down the aisle getting us a beverage before we had to land. I came through the gate and there stood Steph, the girls, Mom, and Dad. I was so happy. The girls are both about a foot taller and were bouncing up and down when they saw me. Mom and Dad had a look of utter relief on their faces and were overjoyed I had made it home safe. We said our hellos, and I decided to go to the baggage area to confirm what I feared. I walked downstairs and there all by itself was a green army duffel bag getting dizzy from going in circles on the carousel! I couldn't believe my bag made it!

The contents of the bag were very special and contained, among other things, my tailor-made suit that I will wear to my open house on Sunday and also a painting I had done of Mom and Dad for their anniversary. Plus, it had a ton of presents for the kids and my buddies that I could not replace over here. We left the airport as fast as we could and headed for Toulon. As soon as I got home, Steph and I headed for the patio for some time to chill out and talk. We spent a couple hours just sitting and listening to the fountain in our fishpond and watching the fire dance in our outdoor fireplace. After these many months away and the long trip home, I found that which I had been longing for; a return to normalcy.

But even though I am home, my buddies are still in harm's way. I worry about them, and I hope they remain safe in my absence. This time home will fly by at the speed of light, but that is okay. I have to go back to the armpit of the world, but when I do, it will be the last time I will have to say "goodbye." The next time I come home, it will be for good.

Jason Adams
Toulon, Illinois (for now)

Notice   Training   Deployment   Home leave   Back Home
10/12/03   3/1/04   9/26–10/14/04   3/19/05

Precious Time Home

Today is October 9th

Well, again here I sit out on my patio. It is so nice to be back into my old routine again. I have my favorite worn-out jeans and my camouflage John Deere cap on. My beat-up, rusty, eyesore of a truck is still running. Everything is just as I left it. Just like old times!

This past week has been exceedingly busy for both Steph and myself. We have been trying to get things done around the house, make time to visit with people, and in the middle of all of this, I am supposed to be on vacation. I am not really sure how one is supposed to feel on vacation. I have never taken this much time away from work before. It is just like I have heard though; you try to cram so much into so little time that you look forward to going back to work just so you can relax! The same is true with me!

Indeed, this past week has flown by, and I find myself more worn-out from being home than I was in Iraq. A lot of the time has found me engaging in activities I love. Tinkering in my garage, odd jobs around the house, playing my piano (I am very rusty at it though), running errands, and reading. But as I run to and fro, I have noticed I am either getting old or at least taking more time to enjoy the time that I have.

As I came back from the hardware store in Wyoming the other day, I got stuck behind a combine. In years past, I tried to get around the slow-moving behemoths as quickly as I could so as to not waste time. The other day, I just slowed down and followed it until it turned off by Dee Townsend's tavern. A smile crossed my lips as I realized what I was doing. It was so relaxing to take a minute and

In years past, I tried to get around the slow-moving behemoths as quickly as I could. Now I wasn't agitated in the least by its "blistering" 15 mph pace.

see the beautiful scenery that is everywhere in our small county. I wasn't agitated in the least by the "blistering"15 mph pace of the combine!

October 3rd was just like any other Sunday I have seen. Steph and I got up and went to church, I went out to the nursing home to visit with my buddies, and then I went home. That is just like old times. But later in the day, my parents and my wife had planned the best party I have ever had. They rented the News Room Bistro, decorated it, and sweet-talked Esther Macy into playing the grand piano for entertainment. I was very excited to hear she would be playing. I have played the piano since I was 10 or so, but my talent pales in comparison to hers.

My dad told me he was bringing some classical music to play on the stereo during Esther's breaks. I asked, "What kind of classical music?" He said, "Oh, you know the usual." That reply scared me since Dad and I do not share the same musical tastes. He likes the big band dance tunes of the early part of the 20th century. For me, unless the person who wrote it has been dead for at least 100 years, I don't usually like it. As we set up the candles, cake, and punch for the open house, I threw in one of Dad's CDs. As the music came over the speakers I said, "Hey Dad, since when is the theme to the *Godfather* considered classical music?" He just made a face at me and kept on with his duties with the coffee and punch. I told Steph I had better run home and grab some music before people started showing up.

One o'clock soon approached, and from that point on, I felt like a politician running for office! I did not have a chance to sit down for a second! The line of people coming through the door was endless. People I didn't even know came by just to tell me how much they liked my letters. One lady produced the notice for my party from the paper and asked if I would be kind enough to sign it! I must say was the first time anyone has asked me for my autograph! There must have been 300 people come into see me; many I hadn't seen in years.

As the afternoon wore down, the line of people slowed some, but not enough to let me visit much. I tried to apologize to folks as they left for not being able to spend much time with them, and I hope they all understand. I hope, too, they all know just what their presence meant to my family and me. I

Even today, over a week since my return, the posters in the windows of the stores on Main Street welcoming me home are still there.

am just a simple guy, and I cannot put into words how that day made me feel. It was almost too much. Even today, over a week since my return, the posters in the windows of the stores on Main Street welcoming me home are still there. The flags that line the road are still there as well.

Growing up in Toulon, I always swore I was going to leave and never come back. My sister, Bernadette, moved away for college and found her place out in Boston. She is happy there, and I, in turn, am happy for her. I, on the other hand, cannot imagine living anywhere but here. The love and support you all have shown for me is overwhelming and try as I may, I can't repay you for what you all have done. I guess I could babble about this all day, but I will just leave it at this: Thank you from the bottom of my heart. I will never forget the love you have shown me.

I had the honor of speaking at both grade schools since I have been home regarding my travels abroad. I spoke to most of the kids in Wyoming and again here in Toulon. My daughters thought having Dad come to school would be a big deal, so I went. I loved the opportunity to give the kids an idea of what the rest of the world was like. You just can't get the whole picture from a textbook. When I walked into the grade school in Wyoming, the first thing I saw was a big banner the kids had labored to make for me. The kids were really good, and I had a great time. The point I tried to drive home to them was simple; every morning you wake up in America, be thankful. The teachers were very receptive to my presentation and asked me to return to their classes when I am home for good. I look forward to doing just that!

My wife and I had an agreement regarding my return home. I promised I would not go out on any fire calls. Steph kept saying, "You are supposed to be on vacation!" She is right, but I

The bottom line is I need to help people, and I derive a great sense of satisfaction from doing so.

really do love being a firefighter. One of the first days back, the fire phone rang. I answered the phone and while I listened to see where the fire was, I was looking at Steph. I was begging her, and I felt like a little boy saying,

"Please honey, can I go play with my friends?" She just rolled her eyes and laughed saying, "You are so pathetic!" I ran out the door and made it to the fire station in record time. I grabbed my gear and jumped in the new tanker with Andy Colgan and Ryan Kelly. It felt so good to be back doing what I love! I felt like a kid in a candy store with a pocketful of money as we raced south of town to a combine fire. Again, a couple days later we had another call, this time to a rather bad car accident. The third call was a grass fire north of town. It feels so good to be able to still serve my community in any capacity I can; soldier, fireman or EMT. It doesn't matter which coat I put on, the bottom line is I need to help people, and I derive a great sense of satisfaction from doing so.

My wife and I, along with some friends, went away last weekend on a vacation of sorts. Well, we just went to Peoria for two days, but to me it was a vacation. We stayed in a really nice hotel, went hiking, ate at Jonah's Seafood Restaurant (our favorite), went shopping, and we even went for a spin on our roller blades! It was a good time. I had never been on roller blades before, so I didn't know what to expect, much less how to stop once rolling. Steph kept saying, "Shouldn't you practice some?" I replied, "Hey, if I fall and break my leg, I will get to stay home longer!" Unfortunately, I am more coordinated than I thought, and I didn't even so much as fall down, let alone break any bones. We went along the East Port Marina in East Peoria, and I didn't even fall in the river!

We went shopping at the Metro Center, and the new mall out on Route 150, Grand Prairie or something like that. We stopped at Sam's Club on our way back to East Peoria and while standing amid those aisles of plenty, it occurred to me how much I take for granted. I wondered what the average Iraqi would think if they could see what lay in front of me. What would they think? How would seeing so much make them feel? I have heard stories of immigrants coming to our shores for the first time and breaking into tears in the doorway of supermarkets. They have, in their country, never seen so much food.

As I sauntered through the aisles, I noticed employees offering free samples at every corner. People were running everywhere, talking on cell phones, some were tugging at their kids, and others were impulse buying, while some were just standing in the aisles talking to buddies. In the middle of all this I couldn't help but reflect upon what has been my reality for the last eight months; poverty, hunger, begging, people who do not know what it is like to stock up on groceries. I felt such sorrow in my heart because I knew that while I was standing there contemplating such things, there was a little kid somewhere in Iraq wondering whether or not he or she would eat dinner that day. Thankfully, most Americans never ponder such thoughts. But nevertheless, I have seen starving children, and I would rather bear witness to the horrors of war anyday than ever see a hungry kid again.

One of the things I have learned from this trip home is that time is a precious commodity. As most people go about their daily lives, I find myself wondering if we all value time the same. I would guess most take it for granted; I confess I used to. Both this deployment, and more importantly, this leave time have made me rethink some things. I have had to reevaluate my life and what I consider to be my priorities. I have missed a year of my kids' life! I have discovered my wife makes Bob Villa look like an amateur. (Steph and our friends, Carrie Taylor and Kurt Loncka, have redone our kitchen complete with new sink, countertop, floor, light fixtures, paint, and border! They also remodeled our bathroom and put in a new toilet! I knew they had been working on something, but the whole thing was a surprise to me!)

I now realize each moment we have with loved ones is precious. Every second I miss of my family and friends is one I will never get back. My leave is coming to a close and as I write this, the seconds tick away like a doomsday clock. I must soon start to think about going back to Iraq and back to the dangers my duty there entails. Even though I have tried to find some resemblance of normalcy with this leave, my thoughts are constantly on my buddies who are still there. I will soon be with them again, but I return with a positive attitude and a happy heart. I know what we are doing in Iraq is right.

I am glad our president had the foresight to undertake such a noble quest. It is a battle that must be fought not only for our sake, but also for the sake of the Iraqi people whom I have come to

Do not stop praying for my fellow soldiers and me. Your prayers keep us safe and give us strength.

respect, and in many cases, love. They are not all bad, regardless of what anyone here says. We have a duty to help them, and I am glad I can use the gifts I have been blessed with to make their lives better. By the time this letter is published, I will once again be patrolling in Baghdad. Do not stop praying for my fellow soldiers and me. Your prayers keep us safe and give us strength. With your support and God's protection, how can we fail?

SSG Jason Adams
Toulon, Illinois (for now)

Back to Iraq

Notice
10/12/03   Training   Deployment
                       3/1/04   Home leave   Back Home
                                                 9/26-10/14/04   3/19/05

Back to Iraq

Today is October 15th

Tonight, I find myself back in Kuwait after a long journey across three countries and an ocean. Even though we are all beat from the time change, the endless hours on the plane and the restless sleep that comes from trying to sleep sitting up, we are still not at the end of our trip. We still have to fly back to Baghdad tomorrow, and the sad thing is that as my travel buddy and I were discussing en route to here, "I would rather be back in Baghdad!" No joke! This place is no fun at all. We get prodded around like sheep going to the slaughter and we sleep in a giant warehouse on bunks that who knows how many other smelly grunts have slept on. Of course, the "disgustingly, nasty mattress thing" is not a new thing to us.

I left Toulon at 4 a.m. in the morning on the 14th. My flight left Peoria at 6 a.m. Mom, Dad, Steph, and the girls took me to the airport. Once in Chicago, I had an extra minute to grab a breakfast burrito at the Berghoff Café. It was extremely overpriced, but good nonetheless.

Our plane took off at 8 a.m. and we were in Dallas by a quarter after 10. The flight was uneventful, and I managed to sleep most of the way. The bad part about it was our flight out of Dallas did not leave until 8 p.m.! Talk about lay-overs! Let me just say there is not a whole lot to do at the airport in Dallas! Nevertheless, there were several things of note that took place while we were there, some good, some bad.

The USO people had a room set up so we could put our bags in and not have to carry them around with us. That was sure a nice thing for them to do for us. There was a cute little old lady working in the room, and she was trying to force feed us with Girl Scout Cookies. We declined her offer and headed for McDonald's. Many of the restaurants in the airport offer half-priced meals for men and women in uniform. McDonald's is not one of those restaurants. But, they did give us 10 percent off, and I won a small McFlurry treat from the Monopoly game they have, so it all averages out, I suppose.

Later on my buddy, Tyler, decided he needed to find the bathroom so I decided to go get a pop. While walking, a very smartly dressed middle-aged woman approached me and asked if I was coming home or going to Iraq. I answered I was indeed going rather than coming. Then, she just stood there for an uncomfortable length of time and stared at me. Then she said, "I am not a nut, but..." Okay folks, if a total stranger comes up to you and some of the first words out of their mouth are, "I am not a nut," you know you are in for a roller coaster of a conversation! She then proceeded to assail me with a barrage of conspiracy theories regarding the government and especially the military, which would have made Fox Mulder of the *X Files*, yell, "I don't believe you!" She was going on and on about the inoculations we get and how they are all poisonous, the supposed "$10 million life insurance policies" the government takes out on each soldier, the "fact" we are at war for money, and last but not least, my personal favorite, the "fact" the average Iraqi doesn't want us in their country. She asked me if I had seen *Fahrenheit 911*. Then she started bashing our president. I thought to myself, "Big mistake, lady!"

Being in uniform and standing in an airport, coupled with the fact this woman obviously needed some type of therapy, I had to choose my words carefully. Had I not been in uniform, I would have jumped on my soapbox, grabbed my megaphone, and let her have it good! Instead, I merely asked if she had ever been to Iraq and seen for herself what the average Iraqi wants. Of course she had never been there.

Question two: Do you really think the government is going to inject me with something potentially harmful and keep me from doing my job they have invested hundreds of thousands of dollars training me to do? No reply.

Question three: What kind of insurance company is going to insure me for $10 million when they know I am going to war?

Part two of question three: Given the fact we have lost over 1,000 soldiers in this war, if each one is insured for $10 million, what kind of insurer could handle that kind of payout? No reply. I also told her that in my opinion, had Michael Moore been born 100 years ago, he would have been shot for treason.

By this time, SGT Andersen was back from the bathroom and was listening in on our conversation. I was getting pretty steamed from listening to this woman's bantering. I maintained my composure and was polite throughout the exchange and finally she left. SGT Andersen asked, "What was up with that?" I answered I didn't know, but I wasn't about to let her win that little argument. In hindsight, I kind of feel bad for her, I mean, what must it be like to go through life that paranoid? I saw this same lady walk back by some time later, and I feared she would come and talk to us again, but she kept walking. I still felt sorry for her, even though she made me pretty mad. It was not my desire to get into a verbal altercation en route to Iraq, but some fights need to be fought.

Later on in our layover, we had a minute to grab some food so we went to Chili's Grill & Bar. As we finished ordering our meals, a man approached us and asked if we had paid yet. Keep in mind there were four of us there eating. We answered him and said, "No." He then told our waiter to make sure and bring our tab to his table. He stood and talked with us for some time. Most of what came out of our mouths were words of thanks. This man did not know us, nor did he owe us a dime, yet he took it upon himself to buy our meals. The total had to be at least $50, too! What a nice gesture! This is not a rare instance either. I have heard many stories of such instances from many of our guys who were coming back on the plane with me. It seems the folks back home still love their men and women in uniform.

I had worried prior to September 11th, our idea of patriotism had waned and was just a cozy thought brought up every July 4th. I remember thinking it had been so long since our liberties had been threatened that the military was just thought of as a tax dollar black hole. But like America on December 8th, 1941, America post-9/11 has burst forth like a phoenix from its ashes and is still shining forth with boundless patriotism. It is truly an awesome sight to behold. Patriotism is such a powerful thing! True, patriotism is just a word, but the ideology behind it is perfect and the power it wields is invincible. For as long as our spirit is not broken, we will not fail.

Patriotism, like democracy, must be cultivated and instilled in everyone's hearts and minds. Indeed, much like a garden, it must be tended to and cared for; an occasional weed must be uprooted as well. We must teach our children what that simple word entails. Our kids will take the reins of this country from us someday, and we must teach them what we all are feeling right now. That way this country of ours will forever remain like a lighthouse, a beacon of hope on the shore of the sea of oppression and injustice for the entire world to see!

As Tyler and I sat in Dallas we watched with amusement all the people coming and going. People frantically grabbing their baggage and heading to their cars, meeting loved ones, or business associates, but most importantly, going home. Here we sat going back to a place filled with uncertainty, danger, and loneliness. As I watched them, my heart was filled with happiness, serenity, and a dose of jealousy. I am happy to see all of them running here and there because in their doing so freely, it means I, as a soldier, am doing my job. We are keeping America safe, and that is the main thing to keep in mind.

Finally, around 8 p.m., we boarded our aircraft and left for Ireland. Once in the air, I popped some of my "sleepy time" candy and was out like a light. When we landed in Shannon, Ireland, it was daylight. What a sight! Even though we were confined to the airport, the surrounding countryside was easily visible from the terminal. The sky was full of low hanging gray clouds with an occasional patch of blue.

In the distance, I could see the ancient hills that are characteristic of Ireland. The whole place looked gloomy, but it was perfect and serene. It looked like a picture out of a storybook, and I was glad I was able to see it. Unfortunately, it took me awhile to wake up from the Tylenol PM that was cruising through me. I looked like a zombie for at least a half hour. SGT Andersen kept asking, "You gonna be all right there, buddy?" Then he and one of the guys who we were traveling with started making fun of me, asking, "Do you need a wheelchair?" You gotta love friends like that!

We met some soldiers that were en route to Iraq for the first time. They seemed pretty nervous, and rightly so. We tried to reassure them some and told them not to worry. Still, you couldn't pay me enough to be in their shoes! There isn't enough beer in all of Germany to get me drunk enough to come back here; voluntarily, that is.

We landed in Kuwait around 1900 hours local time and pretty much went to sleep. We got up the next day (the 16th) and went to the food court at the PX for breakfast. We found a doughnut shop there, and I had the best apple fritter I have ever had. Who would have thought an Islamic dude that hardly spoke any English would know more about apple fritters than Dunkin' Donuts! I am constantly amazed sometimes! After that, we got to our plane around 1600 hours. Once in flight, I started to feel rather weird, and my ears refused to "pop" from the altitude. Flying in a C-130 is rough. There are no windows to speak of and the seats are canvas webbing, and the flight to Baghdad usually takes well over an hour.

After only what seemed like an hour, I felt the landing gear go down. We landed, and when they dropped the ramp, I could see we were back in Kuwait. Apparently, something was wrong with the plane and the cabin wouldn't pressurize, which would explain the ear thing. We got off the plane, loaded back onto buses, and went back. A long story made short, we thought we would have to stay another night in Kuwait. But, around midnight, they found us a plane. When we got to the airport, we were in the plane and gone in a matter of minutes. Which begs the question: If they can get us on a plane and gone in 15 minutes, why did I stay there for darn near two days en route to home? I just can't win, no matter how hard I try!

We landed in Baghdad around 0200 hours and it was almost 0400 hours before I got back to my trailer. It was an arduous, miserable trip to and from home. But, in doing so, I was able to spend precious time with my family and friends. That time is priceless, and I would do it all over again for just one more day. It is in being without that we come to know the full value of what one more day is worth. Keep us all in your prayers, and we will all be home before the grass turns green in the spring.

It is in being without that we come to know the full value of what one more day is worth.

Jason Adams
Camp Black Jack, Iraq

A Soldier's Duty

Today is October 23rd

I have been back in Baghdad now for a few days, and already I do not know what day it is unless I look at my watch. While I was home, my old watch ceased to function due in part to too much time in the hot tub (I presume) and old age. It was a good old watch and had been with me since before I went on active duty. It had been through just as much as I have since the day I bought it. I am just glad I have managed to last longer than the watch!

When my watch broke, I was heading for the car to go to Wally World and get another one, but my wife reminded me I still had an old Timex in my desk I could still wear. So, I strapped the thing on my wrist and off I went. A couple days after doing so, I looked at the date and thought, "Darn, only three days until my leave is over." I commented to Steph about this and she said, "No, you have four days left." I looked at the calendar and wouldn't you know it but my wife was right again! Then I realized I had just gained 24 more hours! What a nice thing to realize! Most of the time here is not measured by what day it is, per se. Rather, it is measured by whether or not we have to go out on a mission. Our days off do not coincide with the weekends, at least not very often.

Luckily, since I left to go home and since coming back, our sector has been relatively quiet. Yes, there is an occasional RPG shot at us, but like I have said before, those who shoot at us are not very good with them. We still have small arms fire shot at us, but the armor on our trucks will stop most of it, so we don't worry too much about that. That is not to say I like it, but at least we don't have to worry about it like we have to worry about those doggone car bombs; those things freak all of us out.

The hardest part about all this is the fact that for the first few months we were here, we spent all our time patrolling a rural, agricultural area with an interstate running through it. It is analogous to Henry County up around Annawan or Mineral. An area sparsely populated and with minimal manmade structures is certainly different from the environment in which we now find ourselves. These two very different landscapes were broken up only by a stint sitting in a guard tower for a month and a half.

In essence, we were used to driving through the country, and then we got fat and lazy sitting in our towers with just the rodents to keep us company. Now we find ourselves patrolling the very road CNN declared, "The most dangerous road in the world." Pretty nice, don't you think? What does CNN know anyway? It doesn't bother us too much, we can adapt to just about anything. That is one of the prerequisites required to join the military, you know. Think about it: A year ago, I was sitting on my couch watching the History Channel, then I was crammed in a room with two other guys 10 years younger then I am for four months, then they sent us here, and through all of this we have retained our sanity.

Unfortunately, this patrol thing is really cutting into my chances to see the USO variety shows that come here to the airport. A few months ago Toby Keith and Ted Nugent were here. I was on patrol when they were giving a free concert. Some of the guys here got their guitars autographed by both artists. I didn't get so much as a crummy T-shirt!

Then, some of the NFL's cheerleaders or something like that came and had a dance review. Yep, we were working that night, too.

Today, Wayne Newton, Rob Schneider, Neil McCoy, and some comedian were here giving a free show at the PX. Any guesses where we were while this was taking place? Yep, you guessed it, working. Most of the people that get to go to those types of shows work in the post office, finance battalions, or some other administrative jobs here on post. I am not mad at those people for getting to go, a little jealous perhaps, but not mad. It all comes with the job. What does irritate us most is the fact the finance office is only open, well…you know, banker's hours. Plus, they are closed on Sunday. They have the life, let me tell you. Their jobs are so easy it makes Beetle Bailey look like Rambo.

Just like in the old zone, we drive constantly. After awhile we have to stop and stretch our legs. Plus, around 2000 hours or so, we start to get hungry. The other night, while out driving, we stopped by a sandwich shop to get some food. Some of my buddies found this place quite by accident. One night, they were patrolling and took a side street for whatever reason, and soon realized they were sort of lost. Not to worry though, we have good maps and GPS systems, and from any point in our zone we can see the "Space Needle" (this is a building that looks like the famed Space Needle out in Seattle), so we always have a point of reference to go by.

This particular sandwich stand serves up the best sandwiches in town, at least that is *our* opinion anyway. The sandwich is called a *shuwama*, (pronounced shoe-wamma) and is kind of like a submarine sandwich back home. The bread they use is the best I have ever had! Then they put on mayo, tomatoes, peppers, and fire-roasted beef. You can get a footlong sandwich and a Pepsi for a buck seventy-five. Not too bad of a price, even for somebody as cheap as I am. We aren't supposed to eat the locally made food over here, but we figure it can't be any worse for us than traditional army chow; you know, mystery meat, S.O.S., and my favorite, powdered eggs.

Unlike the old zone, we can't exactly just stop anywhere and eat. We have to wait until dark and then go and hide somewhere. If we sit out in the open, someone will shoot at us. So, we took our shuwamas and went to our "hideout." Snake was with us, and he and I talked quite a bit. He is sure a nice guy. We talked mostly about our roles in Iraq and Ramadan. I am constantly amazed at the similarities between Islam and Christianity. I won't get

Unlike the old zone, we can't exactly just stop anywhere and eat. If we sit out in the open someone will shoot at us.

into it here, perhaps in another letter one of these days I will talk about it more.

This month is Ramadan and is kinda like Lent back home. It is the Muslim holy month and is characterized by fasting and prayer. Snake can't eat or drink from sun up until six at night. While we were driving, he kept asking us, "Hey, what time is it?" We, being the ornery types we are, kept telling him different times. As soon as six p.m. hit, he was looking for a bottle of water and some chow!

Our break was cut short by a loud explosion, which was uncomfortably close to where we had been hiding. As soon as we heard it, SGT Sleaford and I looked at each other and said, "Well, break's over!" We jumped in our trucks and took off. As it turns out, some idiot shot an RPG at one of the Bradley's that was cruising the highway. We spent the next half hour driving through the alleys and side streets along the highway looking for the dude that shot it. Luckily, the RGP missed the Bradley and impacted on the opposite side of the road.

The TC (track commander) radioed and said it missed his track by at least five feet, so no big deal. Unfortunately, if you have ever actually looked for the proverbial needle in a haystack, you'll know trying to find the guy who shot the rocket was pretty much the same thing. Whoever did it was most likely in civilian clothes and just blended in with the other people on the street or was hiding somewhere. Either way, he didn't risk a second shot once our trucks rolled into the area.

Sometimes while driving, my mind wanders a bit. Tonight was no different. After the RPG thing, it was back to the merciless boredom that has become commonplace in my life for the last few months. As we drove, my mind drifted back home, as it always does. I was thinking about all the fun I had on leave, my family, and my friends in school. I think about them often and even though it makes me feel even more lonely and sad to do so, I can't stop. Sometimes, I think I enjoy solace in some freaky way.

It seems funny that even though the threat we face is indeed real, and the danger is always imminent, we can, even though only momentarily, forget about it. I am sure we all do it in some form or another. It is just one of the many ways we cope with the stress we all face. This stress manifests itself in different ways for different people, but we all feel it. For me though, I haven't had too hard a time dealing with it and for that I am glad. I have found that for me, music and writing helps tremendously. For one of my buddies though, it is art.

Dan Brokaw is quite the artist and is one of those guys who is always doodling. Since our deployment started, he has drawn many cartoons, some of which have been put into our monthly newsletters. His cartoon strip is titled "Outside the Wire," which is in reference to those of us who work outside the walls of our compound. His latest cartoon is pretty cool, if you ask me. It shows a caricature of Michael Moore, with a TV camera tossed at his feet, a microphone in one hand, and an RPG on his shoulder. The caption reads "Whoops." I cracked up the first time I saw it. For those of us in uniform over here fighting though, it is all too true. The media is proving to be our worst enemy. It seems they are more focused on making the military look bad, than they are in reporting about the insurgents who are killing both us as well as innocent civilians.

The latest hot topic for the news here is the story of those soldiers of the 343rd who refused to go on a mission. It is all over *The Stars and Stripes* newspaper and Yahoo news. It seems this unit in question is a transportation unit, and one of their jobs is to deliver supplies. They were ordered to take a load of stuff somewhere, and one platoon refused saying it was a suicide mission. They cited the lack of armor on their trucks as the main reason for this refusal.

While I don't know the whole story, the route they were supposed to go isn't unlike the interstate we patrolled for five months. Plus, according to the paper, it wasn't that long of a trip either. Most of the guys here are pretty surprised they refused. I, on the other hand, find myself to be rather incensed. We patrolled for the first three months here with little or no armor on our doors. Yeah, we had the "Menard's armor" on the back for the gunner and cargo, but the cab had regular windshields and the doors were made out of 1/8th inch mild steel which won't even stop a .22 long rifle bullet. Easter Sunday, the day of our worst gunfights, a couple of our trucks didn't even have doors!

A soldier's job is twofold. First, we are to obey orders. Second, we accomplish our mission. Period, end of story! One of my buddies thinks they should take those who refused, line them up against a wall, and shoot them for cowardice in the face of the enemy, an offense that, in the not too distant past, would most definitely have carried this punishment. Like I said, I don't know the whole story, but if those who refused are not punished, it will set a bad precedent for the rest of us here.

Sure, I don't want to patrol in Baghdad. I will admit it! It is dangerous, and it flat out sucks. But, when you are given an order, you follow it. Today's paper said the commander of that unit had already been relieved of her command. It would appear the heads are already starting to roll. It will be interesting to see where this story ends.

As for the rest of us, we are starting to see the light at the end of the tunnel. Only a few more months left and we will be coming home.

Jason Adams
Camp Black Jack, Iraq

The Tribal Dance

Today is October 28th

Well, we are all moved into our transitional billets as I type this. While home on leave, Bob Taylor pulled into my driveway with, of all things, the city squad car. Whether it be force of habit or an attempt at humor, I don't know, but I thrust my hands in the air and yelled, "I swear, it wasn't me!" He burst into laughter as he exited the car and just shook his head. The reason he had stopped was not to arrest me, but rather to let me know his son, John (a soldier in my unit) emailed him and said we were going to be moving. I thought this was weird as I had only been home a couple days, and there wasn't even so much as a rumor floating around about anything like that when I left to go home. Usually, we start hearing rumors and "I know for a fact," and such scuttlebutt weeks before any big bombshell (no pun intended) gets thrown in our lap.

Upon my return, I inquired as to the validity of said email, and it seems for once the rumors were correct. We are in fact moving. When we were activated, we were attached to the 39th SIB (E). (SIB stands for Separate Infantry Brigade and the E means enhanced.) We spent all our time at Fort Hood and Fort Polk with them. When we took the big plane ride across the water to Kuwait, we were still attached to them. Then something I still am not sure I understand happened: They went north to Camp Cooke, and we got sent south to Baghdad. I knew from the beginning we would have to link up with them at some point prior to returning home, but I wasn't sure where or when this would take place.

My best guess was we would link up with them in Kuwait on our way home. As it turns out, they really miss us and want us to be up North with them sooner than planned. When word of the move leaked out, you could hear groaning and complaining a mile away. Our guys have life pretty good here and to have to pack up all our belongings and clear post is no easy task. Much work goes into moving not only ourselves, but all our trucks and equipment.

Indeed, it takes many days of planning followed by a couple weeks of work to get everything ready.

Luckily, by the time I returned, some of it had already been done. The big kick in the pants came when I learned not only did we have to move, but we had to move *twice*! We had to move into transitional billets to make room for another unit that was moving into our trailers. So now, here I sit, in another trailer, a scant 400 meters from where I slept last night, with everything I own strewn about in various bags, waiting for the word to make the big move. We don't know when it will take place, but I, for one, am not unpacking any more stuff than I absolutely need to survive.

One of the problems with the army is there never seems to be enough room for all our junk. This is true for both individual items as well as larger unit items such as water cans or tents. We all fight the same monster when packing: We try to cram 50 cubic feet of junk into a bag made to hold 20 cubic feet. It is pretty funny watching some people try to pack!

The army duffel bag is a great piece of gear. In use for many years and unchanged in design, it is still the main way in which the individual soldier transports his gear. But, it has its limits. Some of the guys have

The army duffel bag is a great piece of gear.

to be reminded of this constant each time they pack. I get a kick out of watching them try to fill the thing up and then enlist the help of a buddy in trying to get it closed. It looks more like some tribal dance to ward off evil spirits than two guys trying to close a bag. They both grab it and lift it up as high as they can and then slam it down on the floor to settle the contents. The only thing missing is the witch doctor standing there chanting, "Oogah Chaka, oogah chaka!" They repeat the process until either one of two things happen. They are successful and the bag closes, or they work up a good sweat and decide the bag has too much junk in it. If the latter is the case, they take out a couple items and then repeat the tribal dance.

I learned long ago from my dad that organization is the key to space management. When I was a kid and we would go on vacation, Mom always let Dad do most of the packing. He was such a neat freak about it, but he could actually get 50 pounds of junk into a 20-pound bag. When I grew older and started to travel some, I remembered how Dad would pack and I, too, adopted the same habits. I roll all my socks the same size and then rubber band them together. I do the same with my T-shirts and underwear. In fact, I roll everything I can; ponchos, cold weather gear, uniforms, it doesn't matter! (My wife thinks this is a sign of some underlying obsessive/compulsive disorder.) Sure, it takes more time to pack up my things, but the payoff for my efforts is more stuff in less space and no tribal dance to get the bag closed.

The major downside of this move is the loss of my lifeline, my window into the world I left– the Internet. Obviously, since we moved, our Internet had to be shut off. Luckily, our leaders realize what a morale boost it is and have already made provisions to have it set up for us by the time we get to where we are going. The Internet has been like a cuddle blanket for us since we have been here.

True, we can send letters back and forth to home, but they take an eternity to go back and forth. Email, on the other hand, seems to lessen the distance we are apart from family and friends. It is worth every penny it costs to have. Initially, the cost was pretty steep, but with everybody pitching in and a lot of help from the family support group back home, we set up our network and were surfing the web in no time. SGT Taylor and a few other guys are techno whiz kids, and they built an entire network from scratch. They ran many feet of cable, hooked up server computers, and troubleshot the entire thing. I was, and am, pretty impressed with what they accomplished.

One of the things that makes the Army National Guard so strong is the fact that as soldiers we bring with us a vast civilian experience dossier full of skills from all walks of life; carpenter, welder, nurse, computer guru. All these skills combine to form a sort of "ability melting pot" that makes us a very self-sufficient and versatile fighting force.

Jason Adams
Camp Black Jack, Iraq

Twelve On – Twelve Off

Today is October 29ᵗʰ

The sky is overcast today for the first time in what seems like months. There is a hint of rain in the air; the sky looms dark with ominous clouds, but no sprinkles yet. As we loaded our trucks and prepared for another grueling 12 hours of doubt and apprehension peppered with moments of fear, Jaguar came over to my trailer and asked if I could look at his little boy. Jaguar said he was running a fever and was exceedingly irritable today. Given the age of little Evan, I asked if he was gnawing on his fingers, thinking this may be a simple case of him starting to teethe. Jaguar said he was teething, but this was different.

Upon further questioning, Jag said Evan had diarrhea as well. I took a look at the little guy and noticed the top of his head looked a little big. I hadn't seen Evan for awhile, but nonetheless, something was amiss. Unfortunately, I didn't have a lot of time to examine Evan because my first duty is to patrol. I am an EMT only second to the first. I told Jag to take Evan up to the TMC (Troop Medical Clinic) and see one of the docs up there.

While on patrol we see countless helicopters flying here and there. I never give a second thought as to who might be on them. I usually look up at the magnificent machines, consider where I am at the time, and then say under my breath, "I should have been a pilot." That day while out on patrol, none of us knew one of those choppers carried a precious cargo: My friend Jaguar and his son.

It seems Jaguar took Evan up to the docs at the TMC, and they didn't know what to make of it. One of them, a doctor on the civilian side, had the forethought to make a long-distance call back home to confer with one of his colleagues, a pediatrician, in Texas. He told the pediatrician the signs and symptoms, and the pediatrician knew exactly what had to be done. So they loaded Jag and Evan onto a Black Hawk right then and there and with haste, took them to the 31ˢᵗ CSH (Combat Surgical Hospital) in the Green Zone. Once there, a team of doctors gathered around Jag and his son.

It was confirmed by them Evan had an excess of CS fluid, and this was causing the fontanel or "soft spot" on the top of his head to bulge. This excess fluid raises intercranial pressure thus giving you one heck of a headache. The problem with the brain and spinal cord is they are in their own little world in the human body. This is kind of like a force field that only lets certain things across it. This helps keep the brain and spinal cord from getting diseases. Unfortunately, CS fluid cannot pass through this barrier and, because of this, excess fluid doesn't have too many places to go. They used a sterile needle and drained the fluid from the spinal cord. Although brutal to watch, spinal taps are performed regularly across the world everyday and the risk is less than it once was.

Luckily for Jaguar and, more importantly Evan, they were in the hands of some of the best doctors to be found anywhere, bar none. The procedure was successful, and we picked Jaguar and Evan up from the Green Zone around 2300 hours and took them home. Jaguar commented the next day how impressed and thankful he is for what the army did for him and his family. He stated he had never seen so many doctors in one place, and that had it not been for the army, Evan might have had to wait days for the treatment we got for him in the matter of time it took to get him on that chopper and to the Green Zone.

There was a time when our patrol shifts varied from seven to nine hours. I use the word *was* because that is not the case anymore. Back in the early months of our deployment, we patrolled twelve hours on and twenty-four hours off. It was a good arrangement and the guys had plenty of time to sleep and relax. Today finds us working twelve hours on, twelve hours off. With some men, depending on their place in the platoon, going five days without a day off, time seems to race forward at light speed, but it leaves one exhausted and not in the best frame of mind. This sadistic work schedule is not the status quo, but is something new in preparation for our elections back home and should be back to normal in another couple days.

The insurgents obviously feel an increase in attacks here could influence the elections back home. And for some people it may, but anyone with half a clue wouldn't let it change their minds one way or another. Nevertheless, we must remain vigilant here, and one way we do this is by stepping up our rigorous patrol schedule. There are those who would say 12 on and 12 off isn't that bad. Ha! I scoff at thee! That is 12 hours *in zone*, folks, not 12 hours total. There is a distinct difference, indeed.

Our day starts around 0800 hours, 0700 hours if we want breakfast. We have to load, fuel, and check the trucks

Murphy's Law is always in effect here in Iraq.

over, and then we have to load water, ice, and food. Then we have to be in the staging area at least one hour prior to SP (start point). Our mission runs from 1100 hours to 2300 hours, given nothing happens in our sector that would prevent us from coming in on time. And believe me, something usually happens. Murphy's Law is always in effect here in Iraq.

Once inside the wire, we have to unload, clean out, and park the trucks. Then we are on *our* time. We take showers and get ready for bed. After some sleep, we get up and repeat the process. So that is our day: Sleep, work, sleep work, etc. Once you get used to the routine, it is bearable, but not well liked. Hopefully, once the elections are over, things will be back to normal.

While out driving, I like to absorb the scenes of the city and contemplate what this cluster of buildings crammed with people must have looked like prior to the Gulf War. Some of the architecture here is just plain stunning. Beautiful buildings with marble and sandstone façades with tasteful hints of color here and there and driveways made of chipped marble which forms a mosaic of colors are not that uncommon in the more affluent sections of this city. The contrast of affluence and poverty in this place is most troubling for me. But I guess one can find instances of such in any society in the world. Every country has its "haves and have nots."

We noticed some interesting buildings off to our north today that are situated just a stone's throw away from the road that now constitutes our every waking hour. Needing a chance to stretch our legs and use the "facilities", we turned off the road and went in search of a road that would lead us to these structures. After a little bit of meandering through side streets and alleys, we found the road we were in search of. The grouping and differing architecture of these buildings set them apart from the surrounding area. My curiosity piqued, I asked Snake what they were. He said this was the embassy block. Snake said the buildings have been empty since just before the Gulf War.

The buildings stood silent, with no trace of human habitation to be found. The walls were overgrown with foliage, and most, if not all, of the windows are gone. The sight that lay in front of me looked rather forlorn and deserted. I could almost feel the loneliness emanating from the dark hollow shells of these once majestic structures. These ruins, set against the dark overcast sky, made the entire block look like a scene out of some post-apocalyptic movie set. These buildings, once the houses of representatives from foreign lands, now are home to pigeons and stray dogs. Nevertheless, we stretched our legs and then got back into our Hummers and headed back out to patrol.

There is a particular alley that sits adjacent to our patrol route, which to me looks like the perfect spot for an RPG attack. It offers good ingress and egress routes and is without streetlights. Every time we pass it, our gunner shines our three million candlepower spotlight down it to see if some jerk is harboring in there just waiting to take a poorly aimed potshot at us. A couple of days ago, one of our sister units here had an RPG fly out of that same alley. Luckily, the moron who shot it was, like the rest of his RPG-shooting buddies, a bad shot.

We thought it might be a good idea to patrol down the alleys and just see what is going on, search some cars, and talk to the locals. The alley in question was deserted upon our arrival and no sign of any insurgent activity could be found. A couple alleys away, we found quite a different sight, people standing everywhere and cars lining the streets.

It is reassuring to know all I have to do is yell, and a slew of 7.62mm jacketed bullets, like frenzied hornets, will come to my aid, should I need it.

We positioned a truck at both ends of the alley both for our protection and to stop any chucklehead that might try to run. The third truck we drove right into the center of the alley to provide over watch protection for our dismounted troops, and since I was one of them, I felt good knowing three M240b medium machine guns were watching my backside. It is reassuring to know all I have to do is yell, and a slew of 7.62mm jacketed bullets, like frenzied hornets, will come to my aid, should I need it.

After we positioned our security elements, we began the sometimes awkward task of searching cars. I have searched many automobiles since I have been here, but I still don't have a warm and fuzzy feeling about it. I think I would not like someone rummaging through my things, so it is then safe to assume these folks don't fancy the idea either. But that is why, as they say, I get paid the big bucks, so hesitantly I set about my task.

Much to my astonishment, the people in the alley came up and were very nice. They freely consented to our searches and even thanked us for helping keep their neighborhood safe. Their gratitude was genuine, I believe, and really makes our jobs easier. It is then safe to say I was not surprised when our searches produced negative results.

One of the people, a man of about 20 or so, invited us into his house for tea. We never seem to have time to sit down and drink tea with these folks. I feel like an ungrateful piece of garbage when I have to repeatedly decline these people's hospitality, but I have orders to follow and to have to explain to the colonel why I was sitting on my rear, laughing it up with the locals versus patrolling my sector is a place in which I do not fancy finding myself!

Nevertheless, we did stay there for a few minutes to chitchat with them. We bought some sodas from a little kid who was selling them out of a cooler and said our goodbyes. I felt good afterward about the whole encounter with those folks. There is a common misconception in America that the Iraqi people neither like us Westerners, nor do they desire us to be in their country. Most of this is due to biased media reports, reports that are, in many instances, the sole manner in which the average American educates themselves on current world events. I hope the stories I have recounted in these many letters will serve to lessen this train of thought and offer another perspective; one that is unbiased, candid, and from the heart.

Jason Adams
Camp Black Jack, Iraq

Notice
10/12/03

Training

Deployment
3/1/04

Home leave
9/26–10/14/04

Back Home
3/19/05

The Enemy Above

Today is October 30th

The other day while preparing for our first move en route to our next, and hopefully final, place of residence, I began the task of deciding what to take with me and what not to take. For many, this task is easy. But for a pack rat such as myself, this task is most daunting. I am not a sloppy pack rat, mind you. To the contrary, I am a very neat one, but nonetheless, I am a pack rat. I tend to accumulate items and then fry my brain trying to remember when, where, and most importantly, why I bought them. I fight an internal battle with myself trying to justify why I need to keep so much junk.

At home, I have a system of drawers and pegboard on my garage wall that is filled with odd screws, hinges, bolts, nails, and other oddities that I may or may not ever use. The logic behind my fixation with all things "pack-ratable" is simple: The minute you need it, you'll rue the day you threw it out. Having said this, it is easy to picture me standing amid all of my belongings trying to decide what to throw away.

Do I really need 3,000 baby wipes? I could start my own day-care center for crying out loud! In the garbage they go, save for a couple hundred, because you never know! Next come the Q-tips. True, they are handy to have around to clean all of the nooks and crannies on an M16, but four cartons? Bah! Away with you! And so it goes on like this for a couple hours. Extra shampoo, soap, assorted toiletries, boxes of envelopes that, thanks to email, I have never had to use; all of these things take up much needed space and, therefore, get pitched. At the end of the day, tired, dirty, and disgruntled for having had to waste so much stuff, I head for the shower.

In a rare case of absent-mindedness, I left my shampoo and body wash in the shower. I didn't even realize what I had done until the next morning when I got up to go shave and brush my teeth. Much to my chagrin, I walked over to the showers and, lo and behold, my shampoo and body wash were nowhere to be found. And so there I stood, in silent disbelief at the realization of, after breaking with tradition and throwing extra stuff away, fate reared up, and with a menacing smile and a big, steel-toed boot, kicked me square in the rear!

The inconvenience of having to use an old bar of Zest to wash my hair was short-lived. I was able to get to the PX later and bought some shampoo and body wash. They were out of regular body wash and the only kind they had was some fruity smelling, girly type Bath and Body Works stuff: Sweet Pea, I think the scent is. And so, like a new husband sent to the store to pick up feminine products for the first time, I tried to act nonchalant as I walked up to the counter.

It was pointless, I was in a crowded PX full of soldiers, other men trained to kill, in a combat zone, no less; and there I was with my Sweet Pea (shampoo). I felt like the essence of masculinity in a room full of bra burnin' lesbians. I quickly paid for my purchase and hastily exited the PX. As I crossed the parking lot, I stole a glance over my shoulder, certain I would see the masses coming at me with sticks and clubs, but no such mob appeared. I know they were looking at me funny though.

I was in a crowded PX, full of soldiers men trained to kill... in a combat zone... and there I was with my Sweet Pea shampoo.

The ironic part of this whole story is that later on in the night, when mail came, I had a package waiting for me. It was from the Wyoming American Legion Lady's auxiliary. Inside was... yep, you guessed it; shampoo and soap! There were many other items in the box, but when I saw the shampoo and soap I let loose with a string of obscenities peppered with slightly obnoxious guffaws. Needless to say, as I type this, the personal care items they sent me are nestled snuggly in my locker, where they will stay.

Later on during patrol, PFC Douglas was riding in the turret of one of the Humvees in our patrol. The turret is the most dangerous place to be in a Humvee. You are exposed to, and could be subjected to, any one of a multitude of things: IEDs, car bombs, small arms fire, RGP shrapnel, and nature. This last item is the focus of this story.

Nature is a broad term and can encompass many things. Rain, hail, snow, heat, birds; all these things can be encountered while in the turret. While riding along, it seems PFC Douglas and a pigeon looking for a bathroom crossed paths. The result of their chance meeting was, shall we say…. messy? PFC Douglas was our first casualty from flying poop. I heard it come across the radio from a guy who was laughing so hard he could hardly speak. The flying waste struck PFC Douglas, whom we affectionately refer to as "Dickdoug" (his name is Richard Douglas, hence the moniker Dickdoug) on his hand and given the fact he was in a truck moving about 30 mph, it splattered quite a bit. We laughed about this for awhile and some good-natured ribbing took place throughout the night's patrol.

As I chuckled to myself about his misfortune, I thought back to a family vacation my folks took my sister and I on when we were kids. Mom and Dad scrimped and saved for a whole year in order to take us to Disney World. The trip getting there is a story unto itself involving driving to the Greater Peoria Airport in December while riding in a 1970 International Scout, waiting on the runway for four hours while waiting for the fog to lift, and of course, let's not forget airline food from the mid-eighties.

Once in Florida, Mom and Dad were ready to hit the hotel and sleep, but Bernadette and I would have none of it. We were ready to go stir crazy just sitting in the hotel while Mom and Dad snoozed on the bed. The hotel Dad had chosen was…well, let's say…definitely *not* five star. It wasn't even one star and in hindsight, I am sure the proprietor would rent rooms by the hour if need be. The whole time Mom and Dad were enjoying their mid-morning siesta, my sister and I had nothing to do but watch the Cheese Channel or something along those lines on the little color TV that was so proudly advertised on the sign out front. This sign, a big neon eyesore also had the words "Air Conditioned" under the words "Color TV" and, it is no surprise then that the "Vacancy" word was also lit.

When it comes to power tools or any tool for that matter, my dad spares no expense. His workshop is adorned with many things that have Porter Cable or De Walt written on them. In contrast, regarding some things, he is flat out cheap, hotels being one of these things. The logic is that if you spend less on lodging, the more you have to spend on having fun; an apt method of thinking, I admit. In retrospect, it is no surprise that beside the bed they were lying on was a small box with a coin slot in it. At the time, I had no idea what it was for, but nevertheless I was curious and happened to have a quarter.

My sister and I stood next to the coin box with quarter in hand, giggling like two grade-school pranksters standing next to the locker room toilet with a cherry bomb and a book of matches. With Mom and Dad peacefully in slumber, I slipped the coin into the slot and immediately the bed began to vibrate. My sister and I jumped back and watched in horror at the mischief we had just committed. Mom was the first to wake and as she sat up, muttered a groggy, yet terse, "What the hell?" Dad was sitting up, too, and emphatically declared, "You ornery kids would drive Jesus himself crazy!" Needless to say, there was no sleep for them after that, and with some prodding from Bernadette and I, we were soon off enjoying Disney World.

Bernadette was in awe of the castle and just had to go and see it. So there we stood, like the quintessential tourists; Dad, with his shorts, black socks and tennis shoes, with his trusty Kodak 110 securely fastened to his belt; Mom with her purse that looked more like a five-gallon bucket than a purse; me with my mullet; and my little sister with childlike amazement in her eyes as we walked toward the castle. Halfway across the drawbridge, Bernie suddenly stopped, reached up, and felt the top of her head. Then came the screams as the realization of what had just transpired sunk in. She had fallen victim to the bane of Florida tourism, seagulls. With tears in her eyes and trembling in her voice she looked at Dad and said flatly, "I want a hat!"

It didn't help matters that by this time, I was doubled over with laughter, and I think even Mom was laughing under her breath. We left and went to one of the many vendors that dot the Magical Kingdom and Dad got Bernie a hat. To this day I remember it perfectly. A little pink and white, short-brimmed baseball cap, with a little pom-pom on top. I don't think Bernie took the hat off the rest of our time in Florida. I still bring that story up at Christmas time and other family get-togethers. Bern just rolls her eyes and says, "Let it go, man!" We never did get to see the castle.

There is a building not too far away from here we refer to as "the red sniper building." It is situated approximately 100 meters to the south of the road we patrol. It is a large building that looks rather out-of-place next to the surrounding buildings. The others are short one- or two-story structures but this one is seven stories high. We call it the sniper building because it is a landmark for us to maintain our bearings. That, and the fact that it looks like a building out of Stanley Kubrick's *Full Metal Jacket*.

It is empty these days, and judging by the looks of it, has been for many years. There are no windows, doors, plumbing, or electrical components to be found anywhere. Any that were there have long since been looted by scavengers. We were tasked with clearing the building, which is to say we charge in like SWAT teams with our guns at the ready. It is pretty neat to watch a trained group of guys execute a structure clearing operation. They move as one to the door, then with either a door ram or a good kick, the door flies open and the men rush in not knowing what danger lurks on the other side. The men move like machines as they cross the door threshold. Each man, judging by his position on the outside of the door, will go to a pre-positioned point inside the room. Each man has a section of the three-dimensional room that he is responsible for. When each man has ensured his sector is free of anything hostile, he will sound off with "Clear!" When all team members announce "Clear," the team leader will say "Room Clear," and they once again stack outside the next interior door and repeat the process until all rooms have been cleared. Then and only then, will they proceed to the next story, if one exists. It takes a lot of practice to be good at it, and since no two rooms are alike, improvisation plays a big part in the operation as well.

We enter the building from the basement, six of us in all, rifles pointed in all directions. We look like a desert camouflaged porcupine moving through the basement of what we hope is a deserted building. The difficult part of clearing the unknown is the unknown part. Are there men on the other side of this wall just waiting for me to come through so they can fill me full of bullets? Is there a grenade under this piece of wood I am about to move? What evil awaits me inside? Is there no one inside? Like a top-fuel drag car headed for the finish line, these thoughts race through my mind.

This time, however, those thoughts are mitigated by the fact that from the outside, the building looks to be uninhabited. Room by room, floor by floor we go about our dangerous work with skill and tenacity. My thumb never strays from the safety switch on my weapon, and my finger is but a split second away from discharging a stream of hot lead toward anyone I deem to be a threat. After the fifth floor we cannot go any higher. The south wall has been blown away by a bomb or something and the staircase is not traversable anymore. The building is in fact empty. We find no evidence of booby traps, enemy activity, or anything out of the ordinary. Except for the pigeons, we are the only ones there.

Next on our list of things to do is to clear the Russian embassy building. We climb back into our trucks and head off in the direction of the embassy block. It is but a short drive anywhere in our zone, and we are there in a few minutes. Our zone is very narrow, only a few blocks wide and about three miles long. Not much area, I concede. But, what our zone lacks in land area, it makes up for threefold in activity and attacks.

The road we are responsible for keeping free of insurgents, car bombs, IEDs, and RPGs is a major artery for the Coalition Forces. It is just as important as the sole interstate that leads into Iraq from Kuwait. The road we patrol links the airport and the Green Zone. Hundreds of convoys roll up and down it everyday and the job of keeping them safe falls to us.

It is funny when I think the responsibility for keeping this road open falls in the lap of a bunch of farm boys from Galva, Illinois. The First Cavalry Division surrounds us, which is arguably the premier armored division in the world. There are tons of special forces dudes here as well. We must be doing something right if all these people entrust this monumental task to a bunch of Army National Guardsmen from the Corn Belt. Either that, or we are the only ones dumb enough to do it.

We arrive at the embassy in less time than it took me to type the previous paragraph and jump out of our trucks. The Russian embassy is probably, in my opinion, the nicest of the embassy buildings. It is a square structure made of tan brick. The building is three stories high with a solarium-like structure on the roof. The corners of the building are higher than the middle of the walls by about four feet. The idea behind the construction gives the skyline of the building a concave appearance. This building is part of the ones we stopped by previously and is overgrown and deserted like the other buildings around it. But, through the dust and vines, one can easily see this building was once a beautiful sight to behold. There is an empty set of pools out back that once housed water fountains and fish. The steps leading up to where the front doors used to be at one time were marble. Today, only broken pieces lay strewn about these steps.

We stack outside the door in our room clearing formation and go in. Just like the sniper building, this one, too, is clear. This one, however, has more junk in it. The HVAC system or at least part of it is still somewhat intact. The power had long since been turned off, but light fixtures and wire still remained. Insulation and sheet metal along with bricks lay strewn throughout the hallways and make walking difficult, but we manage. After the job of securing this place is done, I have time to look at the building itself. I noticed at one time this place was very ornate. Evidence of intricate stonework and marble slabs is everywhere. The solarium I saw on the rooftop opens up into a hollow center that lets natural light in. There are the remnants of flower boxes around the center of the foyer. Even the bathrooms are marble!

There is not much time to marvel at this building as we have a tight schedule, especially since our commander was in tow that day. We got back into our trucks for the drive back to the airport. The day was uneventful, but I am glad I was able to take part in clearing buildings. One needs a change once in awhile from endless miles patrolling the highway. Even though the buildings were empty, the potential for catastrophe is always present. Any SWAT or SRT team member will tell you close quarters combat such as one would find in a building is no fun. But, over here, we are willing to assume risk in order to have a break in an otherwise monotonous day.

Jason Adams
Camp Black Jack, Iraq

Notice
10/12/03

Training

Deployment
3/1/04

Home leave
9/26-10/14/04

Back Home
3/19/05

Unhappy Halloween

Today is October 31st — Halloween

You just know if anything crazy were going to happen, it would be on this day. With this thought in my mind, we loaded up in our trucks and clamored out to the exit gate.

One of the guys in my unit is quite the budding comedian. In his repertoire of all things humorous, he has a clown wig, a Darth Vader mask and, my personal favorite, a George W. Bush mask. While out on patrol, he usually rides in the gun turret and so he is exposed for all to see from the chest up. It is nothing to see him go by with the clown wig sticking out under his Kevlar helmet. I wonder what the locals think. He also carries, in his bag of tricks, sparklers. I asked him once what he had the sparklers for. He laughed and said, "You know how the kids always swarm us when we stop, and then won't get out of the way when we have to leave?" I said, "Yeah….and?" He laughed even harder and pulled out a green apple from his backpack, stuck it in a sparkler, lit it, and as the sparks flew, proudly said, "*Koonbelah*", which in Arabic, means quite literally, "bomb."

The first of the day's events happened early on in our shift by one of the overpasses that cross our highway. The call came across the radio there had been an accident with no U.S. injured, but civilian casualties were present. We turned our patrol around to go and assist. Being an EMT, I started thinking about all the possible injuries I might find. I did a quick mental inventory of my medical bag and started to formulate a plan of attack.

Once on scene, we found the typical fender bender type wreck. The car in front hit the brakes, the car in back…well, didn't. Unfortunately, the autos in this case were a medium-sized truck and a small sedan. Suffice it to say in this country there are no enforced speed limits, and no one wears seatbelts. The occupants of the car, two of them, were banged up pretty good. No life threats, but one man was in obvious pain and holding his arm when we got there. My buddy, Nick, also an EMT applied a SAM splint, Coban wrap and an arm sling, but he was still in a lot of pain. His buddy, the driver, had a three-inch laceration on his forehead, so we put on a field dressing and had them both sit down.

The driver of the truck was chattering like a crazed beaver gnawing on an oak tree about the wreck. I had about enough of it, and someone told him to be silent, but their phraseology was not that polite. The problem is some people here think we are acting as traffic cops. They try to get us involved in their disputes and are baffled when we explain to them they have to call the real police to handle such matters as a car wreck. We are on scene to render medical aid and then get the road clear so traffic is not impeded.

The injured men said they had called their uncle to come and get them. The uncle, they told me, is a doctor. The man with the injured arm was really hurting, and I wanted to help alleviate his pain, but I don't carry anything like morphine with me. The most I could do for him was give him some Tylenol. I knew he would be at the hospital well before he would reap any benefit from the Tylenol, but it was the placebo effect coupled with the act of me trying to help that I was aiming to achieve. He gobbled the pills I offered and muttered *shukran, shukran* (thank you, thank you) in between gulps of water.

A few minutes had passed and the uncle showed up. He ran up to the injured men, kissed them and was obviously thankful they were not hurt worse than they were. Being an educated medical professional, his English was very good. I gave a report to him based on my initial assessment and focused physical exam, ran down the list of injuries, and helped him take his injured family members to his waiting car. He kept saying, "Thank you, thank you for helping." His final words to us as he got in behind the wheel were "God bless you all." It was in his departing words I found another chunk of what I have been searching for since my boots hit the sand those many months ago: acceptance.

Later on, while driving down around the Al-Sadr mosque, we had a call there had been a drive-by shooting. I was not present on scene but the gist of what transpired came to me via the radio microphone, which is never more than an arms reach away. It seems our other patrol happened to see a truck parked alongside the road and since one of our jobs is to keep the road open, they stopped to investigate.

The many bullet holes in the driver door and windshield of the truck were the first hint something was not the norm. The single occupant of the truck, a middle to late forties male, had been flat out gunned down. One of the members of the patrol that found him was a medic. Later on I asked him about the incident. He said the guy had a weak pulse upon his arrival, but he wasn't breathing and pretty cyanotic to boot.

One of the hard parts about our jobs as quasi-medical providers is when we encounter civilian injuries, we are supposed to let civilian ambulances and civilian hospitals handle the injured. Oh sure, we can provide treatment, but definitive care is not our responsibility. We cannot, nor would permission ever be granted, to tie up the medivac chopper with a civilian casualty. Whether this is right or wrong is debatable, but I understand the logic behind it.

When that chopper is en route to a scene, it is "in service." If, somewhere else the chopper is needed, whoever called it is second in line for a flight. In most cases it is a wounded U.S. or coalition soldier that was hurt in the line of duty. We can't ask, nor would I ask, a military chopper and a military trauma team to put precedence on a civilian over a wounded soldier.

The time it takes for a civilian ambulance to arrive on scene is many times very long. Of course, any firefighter or EMT will tell you the longest moments of your life are in waiting for advanced care to get there. The time it takes for the Lifeflight helicopter to make it from Peoria to Toulon is only about 15 minutes. But when an injured person is lying at your feet and you are the only one that is there to help them, those 15 minutes seem like an eternity. Many times, I have been at the scene of a car accident and have thought to myself, "Man, what is taking those guys so long?" when in reality, only five minutes have elapsed since the call went in for the chopper.

This particular night, the man was pretty much dead upon our arrival. He had multiple gunshot wounds to the torso and legs, and judging by the amount of blood in the cab of the truck, he had been there for a little while prior to the patrol finding him. In our medic bags, we carry a lot of things. Yeah, I have Asherman chest seals, Combi-tubes, J tubes, nasopharyngeal airways, a BVM and even some TraumaDex. TraumaDex is a powder that is applied right to the wound and is capable of stopping what is known as a "killer bleed" in a matter of seconds. I can manage a sucking chest wound, an occluded airway, and I can even breath for you, but, and the key word here is *but*, with serious trauma such as that associated with multiple gunshots, it is *time* that is usually the deciding factor between life and death. Early intervention, rapid transport, and advanced care are the things we try to provide, but the most important thing is getting to the patient quickly.

The Iraqi ambulance had been called, but they were told, "No hurry, patient deceased." My buddies got out one of the body bags we carry in our trucks and proceeded to put the recently departed man into the bag. The IP (Iraqi police) showed up and started to snoop around. As I listened intently to the situation unfolding, questions began popping into my head. First and foremost was Who killed him? and second was, of course: Why?

The most troubling scenario I could think of was he died at the hands of an American soldier. Convoys travel that road constantly, and it is not hard to envision a nervous, trigger-happy private in the turret of a gun truck letting loose a burst of machine gun fire because the driver of the truck got too close to the convoy in which he was traveling. Car bombs are our biggest threat here, and when you see a single man in a car trying to get up next to your truck, it makes the hairs on the back of your neck stand on end. I know. I have been there many times.

Car bombs are our biggest threat here, and when you see a single man in a car trying to get up next to your truck, it makes the hairs on the back of your neck stand on end. I know. I have been there many times.

That thought quickly exited my mind because had that been the case we would have heard about it on the radio before we ever found the truck. The next thought was evidence at the scene. Surely, there would be bullet casings lying about that would aid in determining who might have been responsible for the shooting. Indeed, there were. Our guys found a bunch of AK-47 casings lying in the road. There is no mistaking an M16 casing from an AK. The M16 fires a 5.56mm bullet and the AK-47, along with several other Russian rifles, fires a 7.62x39mm round. The guys gathered up the spent rounds as evidence, not so much for any forthcoming forensic investigation, but so there was no question that American soldiers were not responsible for this man's death.

There are more questions than answers regarding the events that occurred up to and right after this shooting. Why was this man killed? Was he an insurgent that was gunned down by a pro-American group of locals? Probably not. Most likely, it was the opposite. He was seen as a collaborator with the Americans and shot because of this. Perhaps, this was an internal family dispute that ended in bloodshed. This is not that uncommon over here. Was it a robbery gone bad? Who knows. What I do know is this– there is one less person in this world tonight who died needlessly at the hands of evil and hatred. When will it stop? When will peace finally spread its wings and blanket this country?

All over this city on walls and billboards I see messages that say "Islam is peace," "Islam is love." It may be the core teachings of these people's faith, but I saw no love out there on the highway tonight. When will the day come we *all* put down our weapons and our differences and embrace each other as brothers? When will the day come the color of our skin is of no more importance than the color of our eyes? When will the morning dawn that finds our religious differences of no more relevance than the type of car we drive? Oh, how I long for that day! When that day comes, in the words of the Garth Brooks song, "We shall be free."

Jason Adams
Camp Black Jack, Iraq

Notice
10/12/03   Training   Deployment
3/1/04   Home leave
9/26-10/14/04   Back Home
3/19/05

Out of the Frying Pan

Today is November 1st

Today started like any other day. Get up, prepare the trucks, go sit at the gate and wait for the start time of your mission, proceed to drive around and wait for something to happen. That is the norm. Everyday it is the same thing. For creatures of habit, this is not a bad setup. For me, it is agonizing. I like a little variety in my day. Back home I have heard stories of guys working at the Caterpillar plant who do the same task day in and day out for years. Arrgh! I would go nuts! Luckily, since we have assumed this new mission, everyday is different.

It used to be, in our old zone, nothing happened…ever. Okay, back up a minute, I shouldn't say ever; *almost* ever would be more apt. There was Easter week. I won't be forgetting that seven-day period anytime soon. And then there was our last night out there, the night we hit the IED and two of my buddies had to be airlifted to the hospital. Other than that, our five months there were pretty quiet. This new zone is a flurry of activity at all hours. Like the local Quickie Mart, our zone never shuts down. It used to be a question of *if* we get hit. Now, the more suitable phrase is *when* we get hit. Indeed, for the first few weeks that was the going rule. These past few weeks have seen attacks lighten up considerably. This is largely due to, and this is only my opinion, the fact we have gotten more aggressive and obstinate in our patrols. Don't give them an inch, they say. Truer words have never been spoken.

As we drove around the big loop that constitutes our patrol route, we noticed a car blocking traffic atop one of the overpasses that cross our route every so often. We exited the off ramp and drove to the front of the traffic jam to see what the deal was with this car. Two men were pushing the car, a newer Daewoo sedan, to the top of the overpass. Gravity being what it is, their progress was slow and tiring. We, being the good-hearted guys we are, decided to stop and render assistance. I was in the turret of the Humvee and told the men we would help them.

I yelled at two of the guys in my truck, SPC Mark Rathjen and SPC Justin Boelens, to go help push the car. They jumped out and went to the back of the car with the older of the two Iraqi men. The younger of the two was trying to steer the car from the driver's side window. I remember thinking to myself he had better open the door at some point so he could manipulate the vehicle controls as the vehicle rolled down the other side of the overpass, which was obviously what they were intending to do. Can anyone see where this story is going? As the car reached the apex of the overpass, the man steering the car reached an event horizon of sorts. He had a choice: Either act, or don't act. He chose the latter.

As Newton stated: An object in motion will stay in motion, unless acted upon by an outside force. The force in this case was a concrete Jersey barrier at the bottom of the overpass. As the car passed the top of the overpass, it started to roll freely. Rathjen, Boelens, and the older Iraqi man stopped pushing. The man steering was by this time at a comfortable jog beside his car.

Soon, this comfortable jog turned into an all-out sprint as the car continued to speed up. By this time, the man wasn't so much trying to steer the car, he was trying to stop it, but it was too late. Again, faced with the choice of acting or not acting, he chose to act. In a last ditch futile attempt to hold catastrophe at bay, he attempted to jump through the driver's window and position himself behind the wheel. His efforts were disastrous.

As he threw himself through the window, the steering wheel was forced to the right. The car jerked hard to the right, throwing him partially back through the window. By this time, the car was moving around 30 mph. with the man now half out of the window he had just jumped through, the car slammed into the Jersey barrier. The speed at which the car had been traveling forced the front end of the car up and over the concrete barrier. The crash knocked the man out of the car, and from my vantage point atop the overpass, it looked as though he had been run over in the process. We quickly ran down to see if he was hurt. He was, to my amazement, okay. He smacked his head pretty good, but I think he was more irked about smashing his car than anything else.

While I frequently castigate others for laughing at someone's misfortune, I couldn't help but envision Bob Saget on the set of *America's Funniest Home*

Videos saying, "And you thought your day was going bad…look at this next clip."

What we had there in front of us was a classic case of benevolence gone terribly wrong. We hooked up a tow strap to what was left of his car and pulled it off the Jersey barrier and towed it to the next side street. The front end was smashed up pretty good, and the right front wheel refused to turn, even though the car's transmission was in neutral. We tried to help the guys; we really did. It is really not our fault the guy steering didn't think about brakes, nor did he consider the effects of gravity. Out of the frying pan and into the fire……

As we crested another overpass, our commander came over the radio. "Destroyer 86, this is Archer 6, looks like we have another wreck down there on the right, better turn it around." We pulled a hasty U-turn and headed down the ramp to the road below. As we arrived, I could see a small station wagon that had obviously rolled a couple of times. There were 10 or so people mulling about and were centering their attention on two individuals.

Early on in my budding young career as an EMT, three letters were permanently tattooed in my brain: ABC. EMS uses many mnemonics to help people remember things. SAMPLE, DCAP-BTLS, APGAR, OPQRST are all aimed to help the EMT remember things to look for while assessing a patient. Sometimes, a call is routine. We have what we call "frequent flyers" in this business, and it refers to people that call the ambulance every time they have anything more than a hangnail.

Then there are other calls that try even the most seasoned of EMTs. Men and women who have years of service and hundreds of calls under their belts still freak out under the right circumstances. These are the veterans of the service who have been puked on, peed on, sucker punched by an old lady and pulled countless bleeding, deformed people out of what is left of their cars. Even they still get blind-sided by some calls. In come the mnemonics. They help us keep our wits about us while the rest of our body is panicking. Sometimes, it gets bad. There is a running joke about a rookie first responder arriving on the scene of a bad car wreck and yelling, "Ohmigod!" "Somebody call 911!" Then the seasoned veteran says, "Hey boy, we are 911!"

But all that aside, ABCs are easy to assess. The mnemonic stands for Airway, Breathing, and Circulation. Sometimes, this checklist can be done while walking up to the patient. If a guy is hurt and lying there screaming, you know you have (a) Airway and (B) Breathing. All you have to do now is make sure the reason he is screaming isn't because he is bleeding to death, thus the third part; Circulation. It is a snap. Where you go after the ABCs depends on a lot of things, but that is the start point.

Tonight, as I jump out of the truck and run to the scene with my M16 in one hand and my big bag of tricks in the other, I can see both of the injured men are walking around and talking to the other people present. I've got A and B, just waiting on C. One man from the group came up to me, pointed at the car and said, "No problem, mister." I thought, "Yeah, whatever buddy, from the looks of the car, they took a pretty good beating." I pointed at myself and said *"Ana tub-eeb,"* which means "I am doctor." I am not a doctor, but they don't know that, and I don't know the Arabic word for emergency medical technician.

I immediately thought of spinal injuries. Yeah, I carry C-collars with me, but I only have two. The two I have, I brought with me when we came to Iraq. I know how to make a makeshift C-collar out of a SAM splint, but I have to get the guys to hold still for a minute so I can rig one up. I approached the two injured men and began a hasty assessment.

Back home, I don't have to worry about getting shot while at an accident scene. Over here, it is not that way. There are many people here just waiting to end my life, and with that in mind, I set about my work. My problem is I care too much sometimes. In my quest to save the world, I have a tendency to jump out of the Humvee while it is still moving in order to get to my patient a split second sooner.

Right before my instructor taught me ABC, he taught me Scene Size Up. This means before you go into a house, step foot near an accident scene or even open up my bag, I check the area to make sure it is safe for me. My teacher said, "A dead EMT can't save anyone." Point well taken.

Scene Size Up is out the window here, because quite frankly, the scene is never safe. I have to rely on my buddies to provide security for me while I ply my trade. Tonight, the two guys are not hurt that bad. One guy had an abrasion on his head and was more mad than anything. The younger of the two had some cuts on his back that were bleeding so I taped on a couple 4x4s and a few Band-Aids. I looked in the car as I approached and noticed two things: (a) no spider web in the windshield, and (b) no head rest on the seats. A spider web is indicative of someone's head hitting the windshield. The lack of head-rests on the seats could lead to possible whiplash.

I gave them the best once over I could. I checked for bruising behind the ears, CS fluid in the ear canal, and I palpated their cervical spine for any obvious deformity. I grabbed my flashlight and checked their pupils, had them follow my finger up, down, right and left, had them squeeze my fingers simultaneously, checked some other stuff and decided they were indeed, lucky. All the while I was helping the two men, my commander was talking to the one guy who could speak English. I overheard part of the conversation.

He was asking, "So-ah, you like George Bush?" "What do you think of America?" I remember thinking to myself, "Gimme a break, sir!" This guy's friends just totaled their car, are lucky to be alive, and you are asking this guy if he likes the guy who is responsible for sending all us over here?" I held my tongue because; well… I might like to get promoted again. Besides, I still had two men who needed me. I remember the Iraqi man saying, "America good, Saddam bad, Bush bad." Then I felt a hand on my shoulder and I heard the man say, "This man good, he help us, he have mercy in his heart."

I remember the Iraqi man saying, "America good, Saddam bad, Bush bad." Then I felt a hand on my shoulder, and I heard the man say, "This man good, he help us, he have mercy in his heart."

Another chunk of that which I seek is added and it feels so right.

Balance. By some definitions it means, "equal." In a world full of war, hatred, violence, and uncertainty it is easy to fall victim to such emotions. Many of the soldiers here don't like (a) being here, and (b) the Iraqi people. They laugh at the poverty and make jokes about selling babies for food. They find the misfortune and terrible portion these people have been given by life, well, humorous. It sickens me to hear them talk. I retain my equanimity throughout their ranting, but it saddens me to hear such things.

Many of those who speak of such things are just chiming in with words that carry connotations they could not possibly comprehend. Many talk of "Cap-ping a raghead." They speak of them as if they were garbage, filth; people unworthy of our time, or our compassion. These thoughts are reminiscent of the racism that ran wild in our country not too many years ago. Yes, there is still racism in America today, but I believe the key to understanding is through education. I am not talking about classes designed specifically to quell racism, I am talking about higher learning in general. Acceptance and tolerance is born through knowledge.

Balance is the bridge between the thought of hate and the thought of love. I cannot single-handedly eradicate the hatred that brews here on either side of the walls of our compound. What I can do is work each day I live to help another person.

I derive an almost spiritual inner peace when I help someone, especially those who are in desperate need or find themselves in their darkest hour. Self-aggrandizement, boosting my ego, portraying myself as a saint: These are not my goals. My goal is to help offset the effects of hatred and to try to show these people that indeed, a brighter day looms ahead! There is hope! Don't lose heart! This is the message I have. I go about my day-to-day life helping one person at a time, but those I do meet go away knowing we are not all bad, that some of us do care, and they are not alone in their struggle.

I go about my day-to-day life helping one person at a time, but those I do meet go away knowing we are not all bad, that some of us do care, and they are not alone in their struggle.

There is a saying in the army that goes like this, "Lead by example, and your men will follow." It is simple, yet rather thought-provoking if one thinks about the implications of that simple group of words. For me it means this, if I act like a moron, how can I not expect the same behavior from the men under me? If I get drunk and then go on guard duty, how can I look my men in the eye and tell them it is wrong? If I mistreat a prisoner and laugh about it, then chastise my men for doing the same, am I not a hypocrite?

This method of behavior transcends military life and carries over into civilian life. I use the same method in raising my children. My kids see my actions and, hopefully, will emulate such beliefs, values, and norms when they are adults. It works. Where do you think I learned it? And so the cycle of mercy and compassion will perpetuate. Humans helping each other in their times of need, what could be more perfect? The hate that is ever present in this world is assuaged by love.

Jason Adams
Camp Black Jack, Iraq

Notice
10/12/03

Training

Deployment
3/1/04

Home leave
9/26-10/14/04

Back Home
3/19/05

The Clouds Cried

Today is November 2nd

The clouds that have hung over Baghdad today opened up with rain. It started before I woke and continued throughout the day. Roads that only days before had been dusty now turned to muck. Our trucks are a mess. As the alarm clock rang next to my head, I woke to the sound of raindrops pitter-pattering on the metal roof overhead. Such a peaceful sound. In my usual neat freakish ways, I dug out my wet weather gear, unrolled it from its rubber bands, and put it in the little backpack I carry with me on patrol.

Three weeks ago, the engineers here decided our compound needed more gravel. At first, many of the guys complained because walking in loose gravel can be likened to the old saying, "Two steps forward, one step back." Today, the reasoning behind the new gravel was completely obvious. No mud in and around our trailers. What marvelous forethought on the part of the army!

We once again set about the task of loading our trucks for another 12 hours of patrol. When everything was loaded, we headed for the gate. As we drove through Baghdad, the rain continued to fall. I found myself wondering aloud that this place had suddenly taken on a sight reminiscent of Fort Polk, Louisiana. Anyone who has ever been there knows what I am referring to.

On we drove, up and down the same three miles of road, looking for bad guys. About 1500 hours we decided to take a break and go hide for awhile. There is a place under one of the overpasses that is out of sight, out of the rain, and most importantly, relatively safe. The spot is about two football fields long by half a football field wide. Four lanes of highway shelter us from above; two-story houses protect us from the north, the on ramp for the interchange shields us from the south.

We don't even have to worry about RPGs coming at us because the on ramp has a 10-foot high chain link fence that lines the sides of it. RPGs usually are point detonating, and since the chain link fence is between any potential enemy and us, it offers protection. The chain link fence trick is nothing new. Tanks as far back as Vietnam used chain link fence to protect them from RPG attacks when stationary. The RPG-7, so I am told, is new enough that it has a built-in way around the chain link fence trick. It uses a shape charge, rather than the traditional high explosive material that is characteristic of the older variants. Lucky for us, we haven't seen too many RPG-7s over here.

We sat under the overpass for about 20 minutes and ate some MREs. There were some locals in lawn chairs sitting under the concrete as well, so we talked to them a little bit, too. We had some extra MREs, so we handed them out to the folks. We have been in this spot before, and the locals are all pretty cool. Once we had our lunch in our guts, we decided we had better get back to patrolling.

Once back up on the highway, the rain intensified. The trouble is even though I am inside the Humvee, the turret hatch is open for the gunner and rain has little in its way before it lands on me. It felt good to have the fresh rain upon my skin. Rain doesn't bother me. Life would cease without it. It is nature's way of breathing life back into the soil. It has been so long since any-one of us had seen it rain here, we weren't too upset by the showers. Soon however, the rain tapered off a bit and the sun shone through the clouds.

Off to the east, we could see a rainbow. Then the rain started again, but it was just a sprinkle. The sun was still shining and the rainbow turned into a double rainbow! It was magnificent to see! All the colors were there! I saw red, blue, yellow, and violet with such vivid intensity that had I been a poet, I might have broken out in verse at the sight. I can honestly say it was the most spectacular rainbow my eyes have ever seen.

For some reason, the sight of this, the most perfect of all natural phenom-ena, reminded me of scripture. "When I bring clouds over the earth, and the bow appears in the clouds, I will recall the covenant I have made between me and you and all living beings, so that the waters shall never again become a flood to destroy all mortal beings." (Gen. 9:14-15).

The rainbow is not just something that happens when light and water col-lide. Yes, it is a prism effect, but more importantly, what it creates is a reminder. It is a reminder of a promise that is as old as the story of Noah and his ark. It reminds me that no matter what carnage we humans create for our-selves, the big man upstairs is still at the wheel. He doesn't need a map; he knows where he is going. It reminds us we are not alone in this world. For me, it reminds me even though I am in a different world here and danger is ever present, there is hope. I sometimes wonder how many people in the history of the world have looked up at a rainbow and thought the same thing. The juxtaposition of a symbol of peace and tranquility among the RPGs and car bombs is truly one of life's little ironies.

Around 1700 hours we were coming out of the Green Zone headed west. We were going along an overpass when all of a sudden my peripheral vision saw a geyser of something rocket skyward. At the same time, I heard a loud boom. Next thing I know, we had a flat tire. I thought, "Damn, IED!" One of the guys in the back of the truck started yelling, "Floor it, c'mon get out of here!" I was already on the radio yelling for our patrol leader. Then SSG Glisan, who was riding in the truck behind me, called me and calmly said, "Hey dude, looks like you got a flat." I yelled back, "Naw dude, we been hit!"

I made sure no one was hurt as we sped away with our front right tire flopping in the breeze. SSG Glisan radioed back, "What are you talking about?" Then it struck me: I saw the plume of whatever it was on the *left* side, but it was our *right* tire that was flat. Something wasn't kosher. SPC Boelens, meanwhile, was wondering the same thing I was and said, "Maybe that car that just passed us hit a mud puddle at the same time that the tire blew." Then it all added up: a mud puddle, a car, and a blowout. Yep, that is what happened.

Then I wondered what had punctured the tire? Those tires are pretty tough and I, in 13 years in the army, have never had a blowout. Yeah, I have had slow leaks, but never a violent blowout such as the one that had just occurred. We limped along until we made it to a stretch of the median that was concrete and flat. We got out our jack, lug wrench, and jack handle. I loosened the lug nuts while PFC Hipkins worked the jack. I thought it odd that as the truck came up off the ground, the tire was tilting outward. I looked closer at the backside of the tire and then I saw it. The upper ball joint on the A-arm had separated, causing the tire to rub on the A-arm, which in turn, sliced through the sidewall, which in turn, made it go boom.

Now we had no choice; we had to call for the recovery team, which meant that we would be sitting awhile. I usually don't mind taking a break from the patrols, but sitting out in the open like that didn't exactly give me that warm and fuzzy feeling; too much exposure. The wrecker took about half an hour to get there, and surprisingly, they had us hooked up and ready to go in less than five minutes. The lead mechanic looked at me and said, "So where are you and your boys gonna ride?" I pointed at the truck that was now lifted to a nice 30-degree angle and said, "In there." He said, "Yer all nuts, but okay, let's get outa here!" I said, "We'll be fine as long as you go slow." He replied, "Screw that, it's dangerous out here!" Wow, say it ain't so!

So, with the big eight-wheeled wrecker and my truck securely in tow, we headed back to base. The driver was hauling about 40 mph and we just sat back and enjoyed the ride. I had never ridden in a car being towed like that. I am sure most people back home can say the same thing. Then again, this place is nothing like back home.

We made it back to the motor pool and the mechanics, obviously relieved to be back inside the wire, unhooked our truck. We offloaded all our gear, loaded up into another truck, and headed back for the gate. As we were leaving the mechanics, one of them said, "Hey y'all, be careful out there!" Duly noted.

We finished our patrol without incident and headed in around 2300 hours. One thing that was of interest to me while back outside the wire was a message that came across the battalion radio net. Our commander radioed all of us and said the battalion had just informed him IEDs were being found on all the major roads that convoys travel, except for the one we patrol. What does that tell you? The Army National Guard farm boys from Galva are doing just fine.

Outside of the army, we all live separate lives. We have different likes, dislikes, hobbies, and goals in life. But, when we put on the same uniform, we become one. We are indiscernible from our active army counterparts. Our affiliation with the Army National Guard is the nucleus that we form around. Everything else about us is, quite frankly, irrelevant.

Foxtrot Battery, 202nd Air Defense Artillery, from podunk Galva, Illinois, is causing many people to rethink any preconceived notions they had once regarding the abilities of the reserve components of our nation's armed forces.

I don't particularly care for certain men in this unit. I have my opinions regarding some members and they, likewise, have their opinions of me. The most important thing is this: We put our personal lives in the closet for the most part and do our job. I think, and I have heard this from more than one person that, Foxtrot Battery, 202nd Air Defense Artillery, from po-dunk Galva, Illinois, is causing many people to rethink any preconceived notions they once had regarding the abilities of the reserve components of our nation's armed forces.

Jason Adams
Camp Black Jack, Iraq

Four More Years

Today is November 3ʳᵈ

BUSH WON.

 And with that, you can be sure of a few things:

1. Four more years of freedom and democracy.

2. Osama bin Laden is still running for his life.

3. Saddam is as good as dead.

4. Fallujah is toast!

5. The army will get that pay raise it so desperately needs.

6. Watered-down socialism is held at bay for a few more years.

 Now, if I could just get home somehow, this would be a great day all around. Seriously though, I am glad "Dubbya" won. I think history has illustrated the importance of not changing presidencies during armed conflict. I am glad, unlike 2000, neither side contested the race. Childish actions like those displayed in the last election detract from the professional and serious idea behind the whole election process. Hanging "chads" as they were called is the bane of election workers everywhere. If you are too dimwitted to push the little pin all the way through the dang ballot card, well... I hate to tell ya, but your vote shouldn't count anyway.

 What I do hope to see is bipartisan cohesion. Yes, there will always be two sides to every coin, and politicians will always be debating about something, but let's not forget we are all in this thing together. As it says on the Great Seal of the United States: *E Pluribus Unum.*

Jason Adams
Camp Black Jack, Iraq

Notice | Training | Deployment | Home leave | Back Home
10/12/03 | | 3/1/04 | 9/26-10/14/04 | 3/19/05

A Rude Awakening

Today is November 5th

Yesterday morning, we were greeted with a most pleasant surprise. Our patrol shift was returning to normal hours. That means no more 12 hours of patrolling. Needless to say, Wahoo!!

Now instead of having to roll out to the staging area at 1000 hours, we do not have to be there until 1400 hours. What a good change of pace. We lounged about and drank coffee all morning, stood around and talked with the other members of this battery whom we usually don't get a chance to see. We just went about our day with no rush. It was kinda nice.

Once out on patrol though, it is the same thing. Drive in circles until something happens. Today, we had to wait a few hours for it, but it soon came. I am not sure what time it was, but I know it was after 1800 hours, because it was already dark. We were headed east toward the Green Zone, when we noticed the traffic starting to back up.

We, with our horn honking and headlights flashing, drove to the front of the fracas and found the Iraqi police blocking traffic. It appeared a civilian car was stuck in the median, and the police were on scene to assist the stranded motorist. Why they were blocking traffic remains a mystery, but nevertheless, traffic was tied up. With the memory of the last act of assistance still fresh in our minds, we cautiously approached to render assistance. I don't know how this particular car managed to go off the road. But, judging from the distance it had traveled through the median before becoming completely mired, it was going along at a pretty good clip when it hit the mud.

We got out our log chain and yanked the car out with little problem. SGT Ortiz had to get in the car and steer because the Iraqi driver didn't comprehend the whole concept of vehicle recovery; i.e., steering the car in the direction it is being pulled is really, really helpful.

So, my team is tied right now insofar as good deeds gone badly versus good deeds gone right. We managed to get the fellow's car out of the median without him having to drop some of his own money on a tow truck, and also without destroying personal property, killing little furry woodland creatures, or injuring anyone. I am feeling pretty good about myself right now.

Around 2200 hours, as we were coming off an overpass, a car was coming at us going the wrong way. I was in the turret again, so I hit the directionally challenged motorist with a beam of light from my trusty three-million candle-power spotlight. Having the power of the sun in your hand is truly an awesome feeling. Anyway, the guy hit his brakes and started acting goofy. He stopped, backed up, drove forward, then hit the gas, and pulled a U-turn in the middle of the road. Gravel rooster-tailed from under his tires as he sped away.

I thought that was pretty suspicious and, given the fact the type of car he was driving matched one we were supposed to be looking for, we decided to give chase. I yelled through the turret, "Hey Ben, this guy's running, get him!" I radioed the Bradley behind us and told them we were going after this guy. So, like Roscoe P. Coletrain, we were in "hot pursuit."

Having every reason to suspect this guy was up to no good, I fired a shot into the air to get him to stop. Yeah, that worked. By now he was pulling away from us and, in a last ditch attempt to stop him, I fired two shots at his tires. He still didn't stop. By this time, we were doing 65 mph or better, and this guy was still pulling away from us. All this time, we were all by ourselves on the highway. Otherwise, I would not have fired at his car. I certainly don't want an innocent bystander to be hurt as a result of a ricocheting round.

But now, we were approaching a curve in the road, and there was traffic around the curve. What impeded my acquisition of the target even more, other than simply trying to put an aimed shot into a tire from 50 yards and standing up in a truck doing almost 70, was the fact he had no taillights. He was far enough ahead of us by that time that he was out of the range of my spotlight, and I wasn't about to engage a target I can't see. That is just stupid. As much as I hate to admit it, the jerk got away. We lost him in the traffic as we rounded the curve.

What infuriates me the most is this: we were riding in an M1114, which costs almost $150 grand, and we were outrun by a scumbag in a rusty old Volkswagen that isn't worth three farts in a windstorm.

Still angry over losing the dude in the Volkswagen, our shift was finally over and we headed back to the gate, where a hot shower and my best friend, "Mr. Pillow," were waiting to greet me.

As I lie snuggled in my bed this morning, drooling on my pillow and with over two hours to go until my little travel alarm was set to go off, I was violently awakened by a loud "BOOM." Seconds passed, I wondered to myself, "Is that incoming?" "Boy, that sounded pretty close!" Then in my groggy stupor, I heard another thunderous explosion. This one, too, sounded just like the first. Then another,

We were riding in an M1114, which costs almost $150 grand, and we were outrun by a scumbag in a rusty old Volkswagen that isn't worth three farts in a windstorm.

and another…what the heck is going on, I wondered. Like an idiot, I walked to my front door and peered outside to see if there were people running about. Then and only then would I go to the bunkers. Otherwise, back to bed I go.

There were a few people standing outside looking north toward the chow hall. Then I heard another loud boom and saw a bright muzzle flash and then a large cloud of smoke. Then it dawned on me: the artillery was firing. I thought to myself, "Well, somebody's day is off to a rather explosive start!" The thought of insurgents screaming and running for cover as 155mm high explosive shells rained down upon them made me smile, and I laughed quietly to myself. I saw one of my buddies walk by and I told him, "At least those bastards know that Bush is still in office!" Another guy walked by and said, "That isn't a fire mission, the newbies are zeroing their guns. It came across the radio just a few minutes ago."

You have got to be kidding me. Of all the times of the day one can zero an artillery piece, for crying out loud, wait until mid-morning at least! You gotta love the army!

The artillery barrage lasted for about 10 minutes with about 20 rounds downrange, and then it stopped just as abruptly as it had started. By now I was wide awake, so I decided to go and get a shower and get dressed. No sense trying to go back to sleep now.

My neighbor has a refrigerator and I don't. We have worked out a rather one-sided agreement regarding that. He lets me keep pop in it, and I don't have to do anything in return. Not a bad deal. After my shower, I needed my morning Pepsi. I walked into his room, and he was watching *Fahrenheit 911*. I had not seen it yet, and to be real honest, it isn't actually on my list of things to do either. But, I stopped to see what the buzz was regarding this movie.

I know it caused quite a stir back home, and I think Michael (aka Bobby) Moore hoped it might influence the election. I am not sure how I came to refer to him as Bobby. I have used that name for him ever since that film came out. It just seems to fit. My buddy has the book titled, Michael Moore is a big fat stupid white man (or something along those lines). I've yet to read it, but he said that he really liked it. I know Mr. Moore thinks he is doing the right thing; that is his prerogative.

After a few minutes of the documentary, I left. My neighbor is in the next room watching it right now. Our walls in these trailers are paper thin, and I can hear every word. Please, somebody make the bad man go away! I think I will put on my headphones and listen to some music. Otherwise, a few more minutes of this and the men in the white coats are going to come and take me away.

Jason Adams
Camp Black Jack, Iraq

Notice
10/12/03

Training

Deployment
3/1/04

Home leave
9/26-10/14/04

Back Home
3/19/05

Change in Orders

Today is November 8th

Two days ago as we headed out for another patrol, we were sitting in the staging area waiting for our start time. We usually use this time to finalize radio checks, double check our equipment, and the commander has a little pow-wow to brief us on the preceding 24 hours activity. As we stood there, the commander's briefing just completed, we heard a loud explosion followed by a shock wave all of us could feel. Whatever it was, it was big, and it was close.

No sooner had the blast wave dissipated than the radios crackled to life. It seems the patrol we were all set to relieve had just fallen victim to another car bomb. MAJ Kessel yelled, "Let's move!" We hurriedly ran to our idling trucks and hastily drove out the gate. While en route, MAJ Kessel was giving orders via the radio regarding where he wanted our trucks to go. I was ordered to secure an overpass east of the attack in order to block traffic from getting out on the expressway and thus hindering medical aid to the wounded.

For the past couple months since we originally received the mission we currently run, the order from battalion was, let traffic pass, don't obstruct civilian movement with your patrols. That is, in my opinion, the most ludicrous order anyone could have given. We know we are vulnerable to these mobile bombs. We cannot differentiate a car bomb from any other car. There is no bright flashing neon sign that says "suicide bomber" on the

There is no bright flashing neon sign that says "suicide bomber" on the front of the car bombs. The only defense against these *kamikazes* is to not let *any* car come near us.

front of the car bombs. The only defense against these *kamikazes* is to not let *any* car come near us.

I don't understand the logic behind this order. I can honestly say, without hesitation, whenever a car comes near us, I cringe. The only person watching my back is my buddy. If I get my butt blown up, I am of no use to anyone. If there were another way to tell friend from foe, we would do it. But there is not. So where does that leave us? Between the proverbial rock and a hard place.

As we raced down the expressway, we drove past the scene of the attack. It is easy, even at high speeds, to see what had taken place. In the middle of the road was a Humvee with the doors blown off and chunks of what was left of the car bomb strewn about. Not too far away was another car, a taxi, that was blown to bits as well. We could see a body lying in the median. The driver of the car bomb was blown up beyond recognition and pieces of him were lying everywhere. The other body was of the man who had been driving the taxi. An innocent bystander killed simply because he was in the wrong place at the wrong time.

As we drove, I thought to myself, "Nice going, sir. How many more people must die as a result of your order? When will you get your head out of your butt and realize we can't let these cars get near us? How can you continuously tell the families of the deceased their loved one died bravely; that they died doing their duty? How can you say this? How can you sleep at night, knowing their death could have been prevented?" I have been to too many memorial ceremonies as a result of these car

I could feel the anger rising in my body. It is intense, it is uncontrollable, and in hindsight, I am scared by it. I am scared because for a second there, it felt good.

bombs. I have seen unit commanders reduced to tears as they spoke of the soldiers under them who fell victim to these suicide bombers. As these thoughts ran through my mind, I could feel the anger rising in my body. The same anger I felt that day the rocket almost killed half my platoon. It is intense, it is uncontrollable, and in hindsight, I am scared by it. I am scared because for a second there, it felt good.

It is hard to go out day after day and watch my buddies get maimed and die because of this war. When a country goes to war, casualties are expected, that is just part of the job. I am okay with that part. I know the risks associated with my chosen profession. I have not forgotten that when I joined the military, I did so as a volunteer. But, and I stress the word *but*, when casualties can be avoided, and the efforts to avoid them are not taken, I tend to get very angry.

Psychiatrists and therapists will tell you that to hold emotions bottled up is not healthy on one's psyche. We are told to let our emotions out, to not hold them in. But, tell that to a guy decked out with grenades, assault rifle, and anti-tank rockets who just saw some more of his buddies killed. In that moment of rage, everyone who is not a soldier is the enemy. Every civilian, every man, woman and child; every person of Middle Eastern descent is therefore, by proxy, my enemy.

Yes, it is not right to stereotype. I have written about this many times. As I sit here and type these words, I know to think any other way is wrong. But, in those seconds of blind rage, one is not thinking clearly. I can control my emotions. I still do not have any big issues in doing so. I know the difference between right and wrong under any circumstances, but I wonder how much longer my buddies can also make the distinction.

As I sat on that overpass blocking traffic, the radio came to life. It was my commander's voice saying from this point onward, no traffic is to pass our patrols. Thank God, wisdom has finally befallen our colonel.

Over the past few days, the new brigade that is to be our replacement has been showing up. The reason we had to move is so they could have room to stay. The motor pool that had for a couple weeks looked like a ghost town is once again a flurry of activity and vehicles. The only problem with their arrival is this, there are now 3,000 more people here.

The lines at the chow hall are now backed out into the parking lot. The lines at the PX are insane. They actually have quasi-traffic cops at the four-way intersections by the PX and chow hall with the sole purpose of directing traffic. We have taken to driving to a different chow hall a couple miles away just so we don't have to wait in line two hours for a plate of food. If we want to go to the PX, we drive five miles to the south fort and use the little PX there. Otherwise, half our day would be spent waiting in line.

One of the days last week, when the boys from Louisiana first started showing up, we were hit with some mortars. We were down by the motor pool for some reason when the shells came in. There were a bunch of the newbies down there as well. Perhaps we have been here too long, but mortars really don't bother us anymore. They only come in groups of two or three and are more of a nuisance than anything else. But, the Cajuns didn't realize this. The melee that ensued was, to us, quite comical.

The first shell hit about 200 yards away. The newbies hit the deck, started screaming, and a few of them jacked a clip into their M16s. We stood there laughing like residents of some loony bin and watched them as they went through their antics. None of the shells hit anywhere near us, as they usually do, and the whole thing was over just as fast as it had begun.

The newbies hit the deck, started screaming, and a few of them jacked a clip into their M16s. We stood there laughing like residents of some loony bin and watched them as they went through their antics.

Slowly, the new guys started getting up, clearing their rifles, and brushing each other off. I don't think the sight of us laughing helped matters too much, but the sight of them all freaking out was pretty funny. I think what makes it all the more comical is the fact that when we got here, we did the same thing.

Of course, with the addition of troops from Louisiana, you can imagine the jokes about moonshine stills in the backs of 5 ton trucks, the references to the movie *Deliverance*, and of course, the complaint cards in the suggestion box in the chow hall regarding the lack of crayfish and gumbo on the menu. Nonetheless, these guys are in for a year of fun and excitement just like what we have experienced. We are nearing the tail end of our deployment, and they are just starting. Midas does not possess enough gold for me to trade spots with them.

Jason Adams
Camp Black Jack, Iraq

Notice 10/12/03 — Training — Deployment 3/1/04 — Home leave 9/26-10/14/04 — Back Home 3/19/05

Taking Fire

Today is November 10th

Today is a special day. The cause for celebration is the fact that as I type this, our replacements are getting a guided tour of what is to become their home for the duration of their deployment. What this means to us is our days are numbered out there. Today, they are riding with us. Tomorrow, we are riding with them. After that, pending approval from the battalion commander, it is all theirs. They can have it.

The past couple months have seen us tackle the most dangerous mission that could have possibly been given to us. I can honestly say we tamed the beast. While Foxtrot Battery has been on patrol, in the last month and a half, there has not been one car bomb detonated in our sector. Oh sure, there are still car bombs in our sector, they just had two the other day. My point is this, while *we* are on patrol, there are no car bombs. Unfortunately, the RPG, IED, and small arms fire attacks are still there. Anymore, they really don't bother us. Yes, they are a nuisance, but that is about it.

I carry a little notebook with me at all times to write down thoughts, ideas, and observations while I am on patrol. This serves as a memory jogger when I finally get a minute to sit down and write. My notes are usually one or two words, rarely do they exceed three. I make a little tick mark and start the next note underneath. Sometimes, I write down specific occurrences such as "RPG" or "IED." Before the army decided to reduce Fallujah to a smoking crater, RPG attacks were down to a couple a week on average. Now, if I don't make a special note as to where the RPG attack occurred, I can't remember which one I am thinking of. There are that many! The last few nights have seen an increase in small arms attacks as well. (Small arms is a collective term that is to say… anything smaller than a 50-caliber machine gun). Small arms might be an AK-47, maybe it is an old Mauser bolt action or even a pistol, who knows. Last night alone, we were shot at on at least three different occasions with small arms and one RPG.

We kinda figured the attacks would increase since the army is removing Fallujah from the map right now. This increase comes as no shock to any of us. But, I think perhaps we have been here too long because last night we kept driving by the area where we had received fire in hopes they would shoot at us again. We looked more like the carnival game with the little ducks that go back and forth while you try to shoot them than an army patrol. That sounds pretty stupid to some folks, and that may indeed be the case, but anymore, destroying an entire city block seems like a pretty good idea.

As the night drew on, from my turret I could hear explosions all over the city. Some were very distant and sounded more like thunder than an explosion. Others were much closer to us, and in many cases, we could feel the shock wave from the blast. At one point, we rolled into the entrance to the Green Zone to use the porta-johns that are right inside the gate. Sometimes we go there to grab an MRE and chill out for a few minutes. It offers a little bit of safety and lets us shoot the bull a little before we have to head back out and patrol. While I sat enjoying my MRE, well, I shouldn't say enjoy, perhaps tolerate would be a better term, we suddenly heard several bursts of AK-47 fire.

The gate to the Green Zone is heavily guarded. There are many machine guns and even a couple M1 tanks that sit there. You would have to really want to meet Allah to try anything stupid there. But like I have said before, most of these guys we fight are a couple french fries short of a Happy Meal anyway. Plus, the guys who guard the gate are pretty green as far as combat is concerned. I mean, hey, it is not their fault! They spend their day guarding a gate and checking ID cards.

As the AK-47s fired, the men guarding the gate opened up with all their guns. What they were shooting at, I don't know. We were sitting a stone's throw away and I couldn't see where the fire was coming from. Of course, it is hard to see downrange when there are

This one sergeant yelled at me, "Don't go out there, man! There are people shooting at us!" Gee, ya think? I told him, "I got a Bradley and two gun trucks with me, we'll be fine, just don't shoot us!"

5,000 tracer rounds going the same way. We jumped in our trucks and fired them up and headed for the gate. Once at the gate, we told the gate guards to ceasefire. We told them we would go out and see what was going on. This one sergeant yelled at m, "Don't go out there, man! There are people shooting at us!" Gee, ya think? I yelled back, "No shit, Sherlock, why d'ya think we're goin' out?" I told him, "I got a Bradley and two gun trucks with me, we'll be fine, just don't shoot us!" I yelled back at the Bradley to start scanning with his thermal sights to see if there was anyone trying to hide.

We rolled out the gate, and just as I figured, whoever was shooting at us took off. It all happened quickly, and the whole thing was over in less than a couple minutes. Apparently what had happened was a couple cars pulled up to the first set of deceleration barriers, several guys got out and just started shooting toward the gate. By the time we got there, all we found were a bunch of shell casings. The enemy likes to use BMWs to get around in. There are a ton of BMWs in this country, and my Humvee has no chance of ever catching even a beatup 325i, let alone the bigger ones.

Looking back upon the actions of the gate guards, I have to laugh. They really freaked out. The funny thing is, I don't recall any rounds hitting any-where near us. But that didn't stop the gate guards from blowing off a couple thousand rounds anyway. We went back to the gate to report the area was clear of hostiles and to make sure everybody was okay. Regardless of how appropriate snide comments, insults and belittling might have been, we held our tongues. We have all been there at one point, and frankly, now wasn't the time. Less than five minutes earlier, we were being shot at. In essence: shoot first, make fun of panicking gate guards later.

At the beginning of the shift, I loaded up a fresh magazine with nothing but tracer rounds. The reason for this is twofold. One, it lets me see exactly where my bullets are hitting. Two, whoever I am shooting at knows I am shooting at them. This is most helpful in stopping traffic, especially at night.

Our method of stopping cars goes like this. First, I shine our big spotlight at them. If they don't stop, I put a warning shot in the air. If they still don't stop, I put a bullet through the radiator. Lastly, if they still don't stop, I have to assume malicious intent, and I shoot the driver. Simple as that. This whole process only takes a matter of seconds to do, and luckily most people get the hint I want them to stop when I hit them with the spotlight.

Some people, particularly the "tree hugger" type, might find this method too aggressive, bordering on just plain evil. But, I have to tell you, after you see your share of car bombs, knowing the car has to get up close to detonate, you'll think twice before letting any cars near you. It is pretty basic over here: my butt or theirs.

Back to the tracers. With my fresh clip of tracer ammo securely in my M16, we headed out to patrol. We made it down to our most southerly checkpoint and were preparing to turn. When we turn, we stop all traffic.

Our method of stopping cars goes like this. First, I shine our big spotlight at them. If they don't stop, I put a warning shot in the air. If they still don't stop, I put a bullet through the radiator. Lastly, if they still don't stop, I have to assume malicious intent, and I shoot the driver. Simple as that.

When we are stopped or slowed down, we are at our most vulnerable. Therefore, when we stop, so does everybody else. As I signaled to the oncoming motorists, I noticed one car on the inside lane wasn't heeding my commands. I shined the spotlight at him but still he kept on coming. I raised my rifle, switched the selector switch off safe, and pulled the trigger.

The loudest sound in the world is the sound of a firing pin striking a dud cartridge. I frantically worked the charging handle to shuck another round in the chamber, pulled the trigger, and once again heard the metallic tink as the firing pin fell on a dud. The car by this time was still coming at us and was less than 100 feet away. What made matters worse was the fact that historically suicide bombers are male, by themselves, and driving a junky car. This guy fit the profile to a tee.

Now I was starting to get really nervous. I didn't have time to load another magazine. That takes at least five seconds; five seconds which, at that time, I did not possess. I pulled the charging handle back one more time and pulled the trigger. The rifle let loose with a thunderous crack, and the guy hit the brakes and skidded to a stop less than 25 feet from the front of our truck. Had he been a bomber, he was close enough to at least maim us had he detonated himself. Luckily, rather than a suicide bomber, he turned out to be a very non-attentive driver. Had he not slammed on the brakes when he did, I wasn't even going to mess with shooting the radiator. I was planning on putting the next one through the windshield. As much as I would have hated to do it, there are four men in my truck who depend on me to keep them safe. I am not going to let them down.

That little escapade rendered me more than a little frazzled. I have not had a single misfire with my weapon the entire time I have been here. To have two in a row, at the moment you need the weapon to fire most, is a most frightening thing to have happen.

There are four men in my truck who depend on me to keep them safe. I am not going to let them down.

A couple hours later, we found ourselves driving past the Al Sadr mosque. I get nervous any time we drive past a mosque. Historically, we have not been able to fire on a place of worship. Unfortunately, the enemy knows this, and they hide weapons inside and use them as a fortress of sorts, because they know we are not allowed to fire at them.

Think of the media carnival that would create! I can see it now: CNN headlines showing American troops shooting up a mosque. That wouldn't be good for the public relations entourage! These days, our policy has changed. Rule of thumb around these parts is this, you take fire from *any* building, you shoot back, period.

As we passed the mosque, we heard shots ring out. I swung the turret of my Humvee around and pointed the 50-caliber machine gun in the direction of the reports. It was dark out, and although I couldn't see any muzzle flashes, I am pretty sure the shots came from the street that runs parallel to the main drag and not from the mosque. Regardless, the dudes hanging out around the mosque saw me charging the 50-cal, and they knew what was coming so they all scattered. I didn't shoot because I never had a target to shoot at. But, it would appear the word is out to the people. We will shoot up you and your mosque. It is no longer a safe house for the enemy.

On our next trip by the mosque, we took a serious amount of fire from the other side of the road. I mean serious. It sounded like 10 or maybe even 15 AK-47s just blasting away. There were tracers jumping across the road in front of, over the top of, and to the rear of us. I swung the 50-cal around and was just looking for a muzzle flash to shoot at. I couldn't see anything. The Bradley, with its thermal sights, couldn't see anyone either.

There is a wall that runs parallel to the road, and my best guess is the dudes were hiding behind the wall, sticking their guns over the top, and just firing wildly at us. They know we are better shots than they are, and they didn't feel like dying just yet. They were just hoping one or two of their bullets might hit one of us. Fortunately for us, no such luck. Our patrol went up the road, turned around, and came back by at a crawl in the hopes one of them would get stupid and expose himself for a better shot. When we went back by, nobody fired at us.

We have heard reports some of the people who shoot at us do so only because they get paid to do it. I think this may have been the case here. They will get paid because they, in fact, *did* shoot at us. I doubt the insurgents specify *how* one is to shoot at us!

If you think deeper about the events of the last paragraph, it serves to illustrate the desperation that haunts some of these people. Unemployment, coupled with the ensuing financial hardship, has led some people to risk death simply to provide for themselves, and perhaps, their family. What they don't realize is this, this pattern of behavior is self-defeating. The more they fight us, the longer it will take to get the unemployment rate down. Every IED and car bomb add hours and days to the time it will take to get this country back on its feet and stable. Why is it that I understand this and they don't? I am not the sharpest tack in the box, but this simple truth, to me, is unequivocally obvious.

Jason Adams
Camp Black Jack, Iraq

Fallen Soldier

Today is November 12th

As I type these words, I can say with all certainty I survived Irish. As I sit here typing in the relative safety of my cozy little trailer, I can say I am done with that patrol. It is over. I think when I get home, I will have Breedloves make me a T-shirt that has this written on it: I survived Irish. Problem is, the only people who will know what I am referring to will be those who have been here. Then, no explanation will be needed. To those of you who demand an explanation, there is none I can offer.

The process of integrating a new unit into taking over our mission happens in graduated stages. It is an intricate and neatly orchestrated chaotic event. Much planning and preparation must be executed prior to the first soldier stepping foot on the battlefield. Indeed, this project has been in the works for many weeks, and it was just three days ago we started what we call Right Seat Rides, or RSR for short.

Right seat rides is part of the integration process and is characterized by the leaders of the new unit riding along on our patrols, learning from the guys who are out there at the time. Platoon leaders, platoon sergeants, section sergeants, and such will go out with us on our daily patrols to learn the area, threat areas, and scheme of maneuver. We call it right seat rides because the new guys ride with us. After a couple days of this, we switch to Left Seat Rides, or LSR. This is the next step in the integration process where we ride with them. It is a productive and necessary process that, at times, is rather unique in that a private first class may find himself serving as a mentor to someone who seriously outranks him.

The simplest way to describe this transition would be like taking the roof of a building shingled with gray shingles and replacing them with red shingles a few at a time, until the whole roof is at last covered in red shingles. Tonight is the last night; tomorrow, the roof will be covered in red shingles. Tomorrow will find me packing yet again. This time, however, I will be done with the task in an hour or two. I never really unpacked from the last move.

The commander and some of the NCOs from the new unit were quite taken aback by some of our methods regarding our patrolling techniques. The commander's exact words were, "You guys are a bunch of cowboys who shoot too much." Last night, one of the NCOs who happened to be in my truck said pretty much the same thing. This unit that is replacing us has been guarding checkpoints and manning guard towers since they got here last March. They have no idea of what goes on outside the walls of our compound.

I told the NCO who was with me there is a method to our madness. I told him as politely as I could that even though he outranks me, in this particular situation, I am the teacher and he is the student. We act how we act out of necessity. Are we overly aggressive on our patrols? Perhaps. But, the reward for our aggressiveness is lives saved. I reminded this guy he has never been to a memorial service for a soldier from Foxtrot Battery. We must be doing something right.

I reminded this guy he has never been to a memorial service for a soldier from Foxtrot Battery. We must be doing something right.

As we drove, we found ourselves in the area where, only a couple nights back, we had taken large amounts of small arms fire. I told the gunner, "If you take fire from any building, fire at will. If you see an RPG shot at us, smoke the area that it came from." The NCO in the back seat said, "You can't do that!" I looked over my shoulder and said, "The hell I can't!"

What he didn't know is I, and all the men of my unit, have been given permission to shoot back with everything we have. Call it paranoid clairvoyance, but I think if the new unit, as a whole, has this timid attitude regarding their new mission, they are in for some hard days of patrolling. But, then again, we had to learn the hard way and so must they. I think what I was trying to pound into his brain began to sink in when he noticed the bullet holes in the hood of my truck and the shrapnel holes in the rear fenders and infrared panels on the trunk hatch. He asked what all that was from and I told him, "What d'ya think, sarge? This ain't no picnic out here!"

Toward the end of the night, we were headed west toward the airport when we happened upon a stranded group of men whose car had hydroplaned and went into the ditch. We stopped to make sure they were okay and call them a wrecker, if they so desired. They said they were all okay and they had already called a tow truck. Not wanting to sit in one place too long, we loaded back up in our trucks and headed out.

We had only driven a few hundred meters when, in my side mirror, I saw a blinding flash followed by a thunderous explosion. No sooner had I heard the explosion than my gunner yelled, "RPG!" and proceeded to empty his machine gun in the direction the RPG had come from. The Bradley behind me radioed and said an RPG had just struck their track and the track commander had been wounded. I radioed back to inquire as to the extent of both the damage to the track and the condition of the track commander or, TC for short. The TC came over the radio and told me he was okay, as was his track. Not wanting to give the jerks who shot at us a second opportunity to shoot us, I told my driver to get us out of the area and then we would stop and assess the situation.

We drove up to a set of concrete barriers that offer some protection and stopped. The TC had suffered some first-degree burns to his right forearm and two small lacerations to his hand. A lucky man, indeed. I put on a couple Band-Aids and jokingly told him to quit being a baby. As for the Bradley, the RPG had struck about 10 inches below the hatch where the TC had been sitting. The armor on those things is pretty thick, and the blast caused only superficial damage. Nevertheless, I, for one, breathed a sigh of relief. If the person who shot the RPG had chosen to shoot at my Humvee instead of the Bradley, the outcome would not have been so good. Once again, we were lucky.

Around 2200 hours, the patrol commander radioed and told me to take my patrol into the main gate and get fuel. I was glad to hear that as we had been driving for seven hours straight, and we were getting pretty low on fuel. I really had no idea how low because our fuel gauge is busted, and since my truck goes out everyday, the mechanics have never had a chance to fix it.

As we pulled into the main gate, with the fuel truck less than 100 meters away, my truck died. All efforts to restart it proved fruitless. So there I was, leading a patrol of one gun truck and two Bradleys and I was stuck in the middle of the main gate to Baghdad International Airport. I carry a five-gallon jerry can of diesel fuel in my trunk, so we put that in the tank and tried in vain to restart the engine. The problem with diesel engines is when you run the tank dry, restarting the motor is a pain in the neck. My gunner and I threw every trick we knew at it, but it still wouldn't start. We wound up pushing the six-ton piece of junk on through the checkpoint so we wouldn't be blocking traffic, and I called the wrecker. Luckily for us, the thing didn't run out of gas out in zone. If we stop out there, we are RPG bait.

Our battery first sergeant happened to hear me call for the wrecker and said he would come and get us. So, with our truck broken down and only an hour to go in our shift, First Sergeant towed us back to our trailers and said we didn't need to go back out. And so ended my time spent on Irish: A broken truck, a short patrol and....all of my fingers and toes securely attached. Not a bad deal.

This morning, the morning after my last patrol on Irish, our battalion had yet another memorial service for yet another fallen soldier. Another soldier, who had fallen victim to a suicide bomber.

The ceremony is simple. The whole battalion is present, as is the command staff and other VIPs. Even commanders from other units sometimes show up. The battalion is formed up in their respective companies with the First Sergeant up front. In front of the formation are several rows of chairs for the officers. In front of the chairs are the division flags.

I have always liked the flags. They are like snowflakes in that no two are alike. The flagstaffs are all the same; a wooden pole, varnished to a high luster and tipped with a silver arrowhead. Around the top of the flags are the battle streamers. These are ribbons that bear many names; names like St. Lo, Normandy, Iwo Jima, San Juan Hill, and Desert Storm. The names are battlefields where the battalion which bears the flag has fought. They stand as a constant reminder and a silent testimony to the struggles and trials the sons and daughters of our country have had to endure in the name of freedom. The streamers are like a time capsule. Some units have histories that go back to the Revolutionary War! Some flags have more streamers than others, but if you think about it, one is too many.

Seeing those streamers makes me proud. Proud because I know that forever more, I am a part of that history. Alternately though, I am saddened by them.

They remind me that too many times humanity has had to resort to the most ugly and ancient manner in which to settle disputes. We kill.

The American flag is all the way to the right of the flags, as is customary, but it is only uncased at the beginning of the ceremony. In front of these flags is the reason we are all standing here. We've all seen it in pictures and movies. The rifle stuck in the ground with the helmet on top and the dog tags hanging from the trigger guard. These items belonged to the dead soldier. It is in his honor and memory we now stand at attention and pay our last

Off in the distance stands the bugler. To the north of the bugler stands the firing detail with their M16s at their sides, ready to fire those familiar three volleys in honor of our fallen brother. It is, indeed, a somber time for us.

respects. To the left of the flags is the podium where the emcee and the guest speakers sit. In the background of all this, in a semicircle, stand the flags of all the individual companies. Off in the distance stands the bugler. To the north of the bugler stands the firing detail with their M16s at their sides, ready to fire those familiar three volleys in honor of our fallen brother. It is, indeed, a somber time for us.

The ceremony is simple and starts with the uncasing of the colors, followed by our national anthem. The chaplain then gives the benediction followed by scripture readings. After that, the battalion commander gives a few remarks, as does the company commander of the company from which the fallen soldier was a member. The speeches are usually short, and they try to encompass just what type of guy the soldier was. It is hard for me to bear witness to a captain breaking down in front of his guys over the loss of one of his troops. How must it feel to know you are the one who ordered this person into battle? What a heavy weight to carry with you the rest of your days!

Then comes the final roll call. The first sergeant of the unit from which the deceased soldier belonged comes to attention and yells out the name of two men in the formation. They both answer with, "Here, First Sergeant!" The third name is that of the fallen. It goes like this: "Private Doe?" Silence. "Private John Doe!" Silence. "Private John Allen Doe!" Silence. By the time his full name is recited, there is a lump in my throat. My feet hurt from standing at attention for so long but, I am reminded by the silence after the roll call there is a spirit among us that would love to be standing there too. The ceremony is concluded with a prayer, taps, and the rifle salute. After all this, the officers, one by one, approach the rifle, helmet, and dog tags, stop, snap to attention and render one last salute to their fallen comrade. It is not too often in the military when officers salute enlisted soldiers. The salute, though, is a symbol of respect. After the officers pay their final respects, they then execute a left face and exit to the side of the formation. When all the officers, guests, and VIPs have rendered their final respects, the rest of the soldiers are dismissed.

As I walked back to my trailer, I found myself contemplating many things. Why did this soldier die and not I? Why did a 20-year-old boy, with his entire life in front of him, have to be killed? To what end does this serve? Yes, he died bravely and without cowardice in the face of the enemy. This soldier shot the suicide bomber twice before he detonated the bomb. He did his job, but he still paid dearly. To me, this soldier, whom I never knew, is a hero.

Once back in my trailer, I did not stop thinking. I spent most of the morning listening to music and reflecting upon many things. Chief among these things was this: Did this young man have to die? I could not come up with any other answer than, no. Then, I thought about predestination. I trust God has a plan for all of us. It is not my place to question it. We all have a time to go, and we are powerless to alter this fact. There is an upside to this mornings events though. The whole battalion was able to get together and pray. The Bible tells us whenever two people come together in God's name, he will be in our midst. I am happy when I think about this because for many of us, memorial services such as these are the only time we get to see the chaplain. Most of us don't have time to go to church on a regular basis due to our erratic schedules.

Thinking about this, however, made me realize some things that up until now I had not thought about. Why is it our country seems to be, as of late, trying with all its might to push God to the back burner? Why does our society try with all its liberal might to remove God from all things? There are efforts to ban the pledge of allegiance because it has the word "God" in it. To pray in school is all but a crime! How is it a country that was founded with God foremost in its mind, can be reduced to what we have today? If I dye my hair orange, put a spike through my tongue, and use vulgar language it is because I am expressing myself. If I wear a T-shirt that has John 3:16 written on it, it is because I am trying to push religion off on others. Why is that?

As a whole, our society is in trouble. Our morals are in a downward spiral as of late. Abortion is not only legal, it, at times, seems encouraged. Gays wanting to marry, high divorce rates, murder, hate, and evil are everywhere. We need to be praying now more than ever, and yet, we don't. Why? It is as if we realize the manner in

Why is it we forget about God in our day-to-day lives, then when the day comes we face death or we find ourselves in great peril, we utter God's name?

which we live is wrong. So, rather than fess up and change our ways, we just tell ourselves we don't need God; that the whole Jesus thing is just plain passé. Out of sight, out of mind, right?

Tell me this: Why is it, we forget about God in our day-to-day lives, then when the day comes we face death or we find ourselves in great peril, we utter God's name? Why is that?

In comes the military. We pray before missions. We pray at memorial services. We still have prayer breakfasts. When we move into an area, one of the first buildings or tents to be erected is a chapel! We are one of the last arms of the government that hasn't eradicated God as if the simple thought of him were a disease. The military is one of the last bastions, outside a church, that embraces God. We fight for what is right. We fight for what is good. Our desired end result is always peace and freedom for those that are oppressed. Tell me, how is this different from what Jesus stood for? I am not making comparisons here, but, I find it odd our society tries to remove Christianity, not religion mind you, but Christianity from all facets of life and yet, the arm of the government whose sole purpose is to defend our liberties and way of life still embraces it?

Should the day come Christ is removed from the military, too, then that will be the day I no longer put on this uniform. But, I don't think that will be happening anytime soon. We deal with reality here. Our reality is a mortar shell could land in my lap at any second. We face our own mortality with every second that passes and with every breath we draw. We, therefore, turn to scripture for courage, for strength, for the promise that keeps us going into battle day after day, and for the knowledge that should we fall, as long as we have kept the faith, we will walk in darkness no more.

The young man whose memorial ended only hours ago died so you can live free. Scripture tells us the greatest love one can show is to die for our friends. Every man and woman who wear this uniform volunteered. When they raised up their right hand and took that oath, they, in essence, said, "I am willing to die, so others may live." How could anyone express more love?

Jason Adams
Camp Black Jack, Iraq

A New Home

Today is November 18th

The last few days have been a flurry of activity for both myself and the rest of the members of this unit. We moved up here on the 14th of November and immediately started the formidable task of unpacking and organizing all 200 tons of junk we have and, at the same time, started to prepare for our new mission.

Back at the airport, we shared a pad of trailers with a different unit and were crammed in pretty tight. Here, we have an entire pad all to ourselves. The extra space is nice. Heck, we even have our own mailroom now! Our trailers are closer together here, but the parking lot for our trucks is only a stone's throw away. Back at the airport, if I wanted to go see my buddy, Ben, I had to walk about 200 yards, down to the next pad. Here, I only have to walk about 100 feet. That may not seem like that big of a deal to most folks, but when Ben and I frequently meet for morning coffee, the less distance he or I must walk to get to the other's trailer means the less coffee we spill on ourselves.

Back to the move. It took only a fraction of the time to pack this time around. The secret is I never really unpacked. I hate living out of a duffel bag, but I hate packing and unpacking more. So, to lessen the task I loathe most, I chose to live as simple as possible. My next-door neighbors didn't follow suit. Even though we were only in our transitional barracks for a couple weeks, they had a fridge, TV, jumbo beanbag chair, and many other luxuries strewn throughout their room. Come moving day, they worked like woodpeckers on LSD in order to get all their junk packed. At first, I felt sorry for them, and I almost lent a hand. But, I was selfish. I was too busy enjoying watching them trying to fit a 30-inch TV and a dorm fridge in the back of their Humvee. Actually, they put that stuff on the five-ton truck, but nevertheless, they had trouble getting the hatch to close on the Humvee at any rate. Me, well…all I had were a few bags and my little bookshelf upon which my laptop sat. I loaded all that junk the night before, and in the morning I just casually sipped my morning Pepsi and watched with amusement while my neighbors tried to frantically pack. We waved goodbye to Camp Black Jack around 1300 hours.

As we pulled out the gate to leave, once again, I found myself reflecting back on many things. I was reflecting back on what had been my existence for the last eight months. What would this new place be like? Would it be safer? Would there be more fighting up there? Are the last few months of this deployment going to be worse than the first nine? And what of the people in our new zone, what will they be like? I know leaving Black Jack is a necessary step toward getting home, but I hate change.

What would this new place be like? Would it be safer? Would there be more fighting up there? Are the last few months of this deployment going to be worse than the first nine?

In my daily life back home, I tend to fight it sometimes. Whether that is good or bad is certainly open to debate, but here, I fight it even more. I was in my comfort zone at the airport. I knew how things went, where things were, and most importantly, the good areas and the bad areas. I could walk from my trailer to the PX and back with a sandbag over my head. That is how I like things, i.e.; simple. To pack up and move throws our lives into chaos for a few days, and I don't think any of us really fancy the idea of moving around a lot. But, such is the nature of the army. If I hated it that much, why am I still here?

The trip up here lasted only about half an hour. We looked like the Beverly Hillbillies heading for California, let me tell you! We had two five-ton trucks loaded to the gills with duffel bags, foot lockers, TVs, a couple of couches, and some homemade entertainment centers. Behind the gypsy wagons, our convoy stretched out for almost half a mile. One of the Humvees was pulling another Humvee with a tow bar. It isn't broken, but it doesn't have any armor on it and represents a safety issue if we were to have troops riding in it. So, we hitched it up and used it like a trailer to haul more junk. Backpacks and duffel bags were strapped in with the seat belts, and the back of the truck was piled up with coolers and odd boxes of junk. The only thing missing was the clown music blasting out of loudspeakers and a trail of confetti flowing behind our trucks.

We made it to Taji in record time with no problem. As our circus-like hodgepodge of trucks neared the main gate, I noticed some locals stopped along the road gawking at us. I have no idea what they were talking about, but I am rather certain it went something like: "Hey Omar, what is this, who are these people?" "I don't know, Achmed, but there goes the neighborhood!"

One consolation to the discomfort of having to move is our trailers are brand new. In fact, they are so new that when we walked into our rooms, we were surprised to find our furniture still in boxes! So, not only did we have to unpack and organize all our belongings, we also had to assemble the wall lockers and nightstands to put all of it in. So there I was, among the duffel bags and backpacks, trying to assemble a wall locker to put it all in. What a bum deal.

As I looked down upon the task ahead of me, I noticed on the outside of the box the three most hated words in the English language: *Some assembly required.* I couldn't help but chuckle and think to myself: All assembly would be more appropriate! Below that, it pictured a drawing of the two tools one needs to assemble this wall locker.

As I looked down upon the task ahead of me, I noticed on the outside of the box the three most hated words in the English language: *Some assembly required.*

The pictures seemed like they were placed conspicuously on the outside of the carton as if to say: Look how easy I am to put together! Ha! Yeah, right…all I need is a hammer and a screwdriver. And a drill, a pair of vise grips and some C-clamps, plus a third hand. A 12-pack of beer wouldn't hurt either.

As I opened the box full of pre-cut, pre-drilled pieces of particleboard, I saw the instruction leaflet glaring at me. Upon further inspection, I found three little boxes full of assorted screws, plastic doohickeys, and hinges. It is no exaggeration when I say there were about 10 or 12 different types of screws in one box. Why not make it easy and just use the same type of screws to put the whole thing together?

To make matters even worse, our unit was given two different types of wall lockers. It wouldn't have been so bad if the same manufacturer had made both types. But, different companies altogether made these and, wouldn't you know it, but the parts kits got mixed up somehow and I got stuck with the parts to a different locker. Talk about getting a round peg in a square hole! I would have been more successful trying to get a carburetor from an old Chevy to fit on a Mazda. So, now I faced a dilemma. I could either wait to try to get the right parts, or, I could try to get the right pieces of wall locker. I chose the latter.

Door to door I went, asking if anyone had any parts to an Olympic brand wall locker. It took me over three hours of begging, but I was successful in my quest. Around 1500 hours, I set about the task of assembling my wall locker. By 1900 hours, half crazy and ready to rip the spine out of the guy who designed the thing, I was done putting it together. The little nightstand was a cinch after putting the wall locker together. I didn't assemble the two chairs that came with the set. I have a nice office chair I found in a dumpster down by the airport a couple months after we got to Iraq.

I usually do not frequent trash dumpsters looking for stuff. I don't want anyone who reads this to get the wrong idea! This place is like a college dorm in that, when people leave here, they throw out everything. This chair was sitting on top of the dumpster and hadn't so much as a scratch on it, so I grabbed it. Besides, Ben has two chairs out in front of his trailer on his "patio." We sit out there a lot and get wired on Folgers. If I need another chair, he will let me borrow one of his.

After we spent a day and a half unpacking and assembling our furniture, the leadership of the battery had to start the Right Seat Rides process. This is just like what we did with the unit that took over for us when we left Baghdad. We went out on patrol with them, and they showed us how they do things, where the limits of our patrol route are, gave us an overview of what to expect out there and so on. The only disconcerting part for me was it only lasted all of 30 minutes. The unit we are replacing here only patrolled this area we are taking over, for two hours a day. Which meant the insurgents had 22 hours to plant IEDs, plan ambushes, and move freely about the battlefield. Not getting a warm and fuzzy feeling here, just so ya know.

Anyway, our new area is pretty small in dimensions. It is less than 10 miles long and only 1,000 meters wide. Basically, we drive up and down the same stretch of road for 12 hours, wait for some moron to shoot at us, shoot back, and keep driving. The only thing that is different from patrolling in Baghdad is this area is more rural in nature. The best way I can describe it is like this: If Baghdad were Chicago, we are just west of

Basically, we drive up and down the same stretch of road for 12 hours, wait for some moron to shoot at us, shoot back, and keep driving.

Elgin. What I don't like is the sides of the roads are pretty overgrown with vegetation. Which means anyone could crawl up to the road, plant a bomb, crawl away, and we wouldn't even know it. Well, that is until the darned thing blew up. We are working on that issue. Back on our old patrol route, we managed to get some maintainers and bulldozers and took care of that problem ourselves. Up here, we hope to do the same.

Sun Tzu once said you must know your enemy, but more importantly, you must know yourself. Yeah, we got that part down pretty good. He also said in order to be successful, you must make the enemy fight on your terms; you must shape the battle according to your abilities and needs. By reworking the roadsides, we are doing just that. Of course, Sun Tzu also said the best way to win a war is to never fire a shot. I guess nobody read that part.

As we came in from our down and dirty right seat ride, we passed an area that was covered, and I mean covered, with tanks, artillery, and assorted pieces of armor. The area is probably five football fields in size and straddles one of the roads that lead out to the gate we use. T-52s, T-62s, BMPs, self-propelled howitzers, large bore howitzers; you name it, it is there. It is all Soviet era stuff, which is no surprise. I was amazed at the sheer amount of war material!

Back at the airport there was an occasional anti-aircraft gun sitting here or there, but nothing like this. The entire first row, which stretched about 300 meters, was nothing but Russian tanks! As we passed the armor, I cursed myself for not bringing my camera, but I have a feeling it is not the last time I will be on that road.

As I marveled at the sight of so many machines of destruction, the thought occurred to me, where was all this during the war and how did it all end up here? Would the course of the war have been different had all this been factored into the equation? Once back in my trailer, I started surfing the web in order to find out as much as I could about the area where we now find ourselves.

Pay dirt! It seems this place was a major rebuilding and refitting yard for the armor corps of the Iraqi army. That would explain the tanks and such. This sprawling complex was also home to Saddam's long-range missile research facility. In addition, there are a runway for aircraft and two sets of train tracks that run in here to facilitate the movement of equipment. There are many bunkers that dot the landscape here. I can't help but wonder how many more are below ground. I wonder, too, how many exist we don't know about. It is really amazing to see the remnants of what was once one of the largest armies in the world. I've yet to have time to go exploring in the bone yard of tanks and whatnot.

One of my buddies has already been there. In front of his trailer is the nose cone of what was once a rather large rocket. He found it in a deserted building out by the airstrip. When he brought it back to the trailers, a bunch of us were standing around marveling at his treasure. The nose cone is about three feet high and about 16 inches in diameter at the base. On the inside are some electrical connectors and some information regarding where it was made. The words are written in French, hmm…interesting. Anyway, my buddy said there are tons of stuff sitting in this building, and while the chances of me getting to keep any of it for a souvenir are slim to none, some pictures might be in order.

As I said, this pad of trailers is rather new. So new in fact, they didn't even have time to spread gravel in among the trailers. The army was nice enough to dump a few truckloads of gravel out in the parking lot for us to spread ourselves. Two days ago, we spent most of the morning spreading gravel. Problem was we didn't have anything to carry the gravel from the parking lot to our trailers. Thank goodness for GI ingenuity!

Two days ago, we spent most of the morning spreading gravel. Thank goodness for GI ingenuity!

A couple guys took a stretcher off one of our trucks, put two Coleman coolers on it, loaded the coolers with gravel, and headed for their trailer. We did manage to scam a garden cart from somewhere. It is a dilapidated little thing, but it was certainly better than using a cooler and stretcher. We hauled load after load of gravel and built several walkways to our trailers. We just took turns; two guys would shovel gravel into the cart, one guy would push the cart to the trailers, dump it, and return for more. At the trailers, two more guys spread the gravel out in front of our steps. It took awhile to get it all done, but we did it. We were pretty tired and sore at the end of the day, but it was a task that had to be done.

While we were shoveling, we saw a guy drive by our pad in a little Bobcat. We thought about flagging him down, getting some cash together, and working out a little deal. But, by this time, we were almost done, so we let him go. But, seeing him on the Bobcat brought back memories of a particular summer camp at Camp Atterbury, Indiana, several years back.

This particular summer camp found three of us tasked with building the battery's fighting positions for our crew-served weapons. In other words, digging holes. Of course, traditionally, the army finds the worst, yet, cheapest tract of land upon which to build its camps. Camp Atterbury is no exception. There are about four inches of dirt on top of solid rock, so needless to say, digging is quite fun. Foxholes, traditionally, need to be armpit deep, so we had our picks and shovels out and set in for a long day of playing John Henry.

We had been digging one of three holes and were about a foot deep after about four hours of effort. We were taking turns with the pick and shovel. One guy would break up the earth with the pick; the other would shovel it out. The third guy would take a break and try to think of a better way to dig. On it went until we were all exhausted and it was well into the afternoon. First Sergeant told us to get as much done as we could, and that if we weren't done, not to worry. He said they would finish when the rest of the unit arrived there. Well, we were faced with an opportunity to get some serious butt kissing points: Imagine the unit showing up and the battery's defenses were already done! That would make us three dudes look like real studs. Unfortunately, the digging was going nowhere really fast, and with it, so were our hopes of getting those brownie points.

As the hopes of us looking like heroes were fading like the light from the setting sun, a glimmer of hope appeared on the horizon. It started off very faint, almost imperceptible, but soon the other guys heard it, too. A backhoe was coming down the road! Like manna from heaven, the backhoe lumbered toward us and we quickly formulated a plan. We figured it was range control coming out to do some earthwork on one of the ranges, but if we looked pathetic enough, we might be able to con the operator into digging our holes for us.

We got our canteens out, doused ourselves with water so as to look like we were sweating profusely, put on our best pitiful faces, and waited for the backhoe to get up to where we were digging. It turned out to be some master sergeant from Range Control, and as luck would have it, he stopped to see what we were up to. We told him we had been digging for hours and our commander was going to have our heads on a pole if he got there and the foxholes weren't dug. We told the master sergeant we would pay him if he would help us out. The guy thought for a minute, looked at the results of our digging efforts, and then said, "Where do you want your holes?"

If it weren't for my belief in proper military bearing, I probably would have kissed his combat boots. We pointed at three spots, and he set about making us look like studs. In the course of 30 minutes, he was able to dig more than we had dug all day. He was about three quarters of the way into the third hole when the backhoe ran out of gas. I thought, "Well, we are screwed, there is no way he is gonna finish now." But, being the consummate Good Samaritan that he was, he simply got on his little radio, had his buddy run out some gas, and finished digging. We thanked him and got out our wallets in order to compensate him for saving our butts. He chuckled and said, "Don't worry, guys. Just buy me a beer the next time you see me in the NCO club." I thought to myself, "A beer my foot! We will get you so drunk you won't remember where you parked your car!"

We said thank you again and the master sergeant left. Now, all we had to do is get rid of the backhoe marks on the sides of the foxholes and cover the tire tracks in the grass and we were home free. We finished with about an hour to spare. Our unit pulled in and Top was amazed we were done with the defenses. Accolades and praise flowed from both Top and the commander as they surveyed our work. We didn't tell them our little secret until a few days later.

One of the more obvious things I have noticed regarding our new base is the differing architecture. The area north of the airport that housed us for the first part of this deployment was beautiful. Buildings adorned with carvings, hand-carved doors and marble were commonplace. The reason behind this was the fact Saddam Hussein used them as a game refuge and a retreat of sorts for himself, as well as all his Baath party cronies. He lived in luxury while, just outside the 10-foot wall and guard towers that helped keep him in power, his people lived in squalor. While searching for a word to describe how this makes me feel, the word bastard comes to mind with ease.

Here at Camp Cooke, the buildings take on a more common look. They are built with necessity and cost in mind. Just by looking around me, it is easy to deduce these facilities were built for the military. But, unlike our military, the buildings do not all look alike and they are not dress right dressed like ours. Our military is unique in that if one were to sight down a row of barracks, they are all in perfect alignment. Trust me, this is fact. I have done it. The U.S. army goes to great lengths to make everything identical. Whether it be buildings, tanks, trucks, or even soldiers for that matter, attention to detail and uniformity is paramount in their minds. I love it!

Here, that is not the case. There doesn't seem to be any forethought on the part of the planners of this base. Buildings are thrown here and there in an unorganized manner. They are all of modest construction, without the decorations and bells and whistles their counterparts at the airport have. In essence, you are not going to find any gold-plated toilets here.

Jason Adams
Camp Cooke, Iraq

Notice 10/12/03   Training   Deployment 3/1/04   Home leave 9/26-10/14/04   Back Home 3/19/05

New Wheels

Today is November 20th

I cannot get over the fact it is only a few days until Thanksgiving. Just think, a year ago, I was sitting at Fort Hood thinking about coming home for Christmas. Now, here I am a year later, sitting in Iraq thinking about not coming home Christmas. How ironic! This will be the first time many of us have not been home for the holidays. But, with the passing of Christmas, we move even closer to our departure date, and that alone is cause for celebration.

We just came back from another mandatory suicide prevention briefing. I guess someone up in the head office thinks we are at greater risk of killing ourselves as the holidays approach. I kinda take a little bit of offense at the thought of the army resorting to blanket brainwashing for the troops. Besides, if I was going to off myself, I wouldn't wait until the last three months of this deployment to do it. But, I guess the need for such training exists, otherwise the army wouldn't waste the time or the money in doing so. Yes, people get depressed and, yes, they do sometimes take their own lives. Add to the fact all of us are armed and have access to ammunition, I guess the idea of suicide prevention isn't that ludicrous after all.

Two days ago, some of us had to go up to another base to pick up some more Humvees. I am not quite sure why, but my unit always seems to get the short end of the stick in regards to trucks. There are units here that are 100 percent outfitted with the M1114 trucks. Then there is Foxtrot Battery. For the first few months, we didn't even have armor on all our trucks. Yeah, we had plywood and sandbag boxes to protect the gunner, but that was it. Then, we were able to get some metal boxes built in the beds of our trucks and that offered a little more in the way of armament, but we were still behind the power curve compared to other units.

About three months ago, we started to get some M1025 series Humvees. They are not even close to M1114s, but they are definitely a step above what we had. But, the problem that plagued us was we didn't have enough to go around. Even here, we had to swap out trucks between teams so we could go on our missions.

When the 10th Mountain Division took over our old zone, they showed up for the Right Seat Rides driving M1114s. They were amazed at the "Menard's armor" we were driving. Many of them commented regarding the fact we must have been nuts to patrol with so little to protect us. What were we to do? You make do with what you are given. In all honesty, we never really thought that much about it.

Up here, we again were faced with a shortage of trucks. We found some extra M1025s at another base and decided to go up and get them. The reason the trucks were available is because the unit we were getting them from had just gotten some more M1114s. Yep, that's right, we get the hand-me-downs, the crap nobody else wants. The sad thing is we took the trucks eagerly and with many thanks.

The trip up to get the trucks lasted about 45 minutes. Top showed up in our parking lot on the morning we were to go in the Galloping Goose. That is the name of his five-ton. I wish all of you could meet 1SG Paul Peterson. I can say with no reservations he is the best battery-level 1SG I have ever had the honor of serving under. He is fair, he is open, he is honest; if he screws up, he is the first to admit it.

Easter Sunday, he led the assault on the houses the insurgents had been hiding in. He is of the mind no leader should ask their men to do anything they themselves would not do. He is the essence of leadership, the consummate professional. Every soldier, in their careers, comes across a few leaders they would follow anywhere. People like that are a rarity, trust me on that one.

1SG Peterson, or "Top" as we affectionately call him, is one of those people. Many of the guys in Foxtrot Battery feel the same way. The manner in which he earned our respect is simple. He loves the men of this unit, and in turn, he has our respect. It is pretty simple. Don't get me wrong, if I screw up bad enough, he would put his foot so far up my kiester it would give me a bad case of athlete's tonsils. But, if I do something really well, he would be the first guy to pat me on the back and tell me, "Good job." Years from now, when these days we are living are but memories of days past, 1SG Peterson will still be referred to as "Top." That kind of respect does not dissipate with the passage of time.

The so-called Galloping Goose is a five-ton truck we picked up at Fort Hood. It is a pretty good truck and is fitted with an armored box that fills the entire bed of the truck. It has a mount over the cab that will accommodate a 50-caliber machine gun, plus, the thing will get up and run about 70 mph. Not too shabby for a hand-me-down army truck. On the convoy up here, Top was in the lead driving the Goose. He told us he would plow the way for our Hum-vees, so we wouldn't have any trouble with the traffic. Usually, the upper leadership of a unit doesn't ride in the lead truck. That just isn't how Top does things.

We all jumped into the Goose and prepared for the trip up north. Of course, Top and the Goose were up front. The other two gun trucks fell in behind us. It was quite a sight to see us going down the road. Ten or so men in the bed of the truck with our weapons pointing every which way, Top in the cab with the air horn blaring, and SGT Sosa standing behind the machine gun. Needless to say, people got out of our way! We made it there around 1000 hours.

We drove to the motor pool where we were to get the new trucks and met with the supply sergeant. While Top took care of the paperwork, the rest of us checked over our new trucks. We kicked the tires, checked the oil, antifreeze, and brake fluid. We crawled over, under, and through the things to get an idea of their condition. While we were checking the trucks, we noticed a C-130 Hercules coming in for a landing. We didn't even realize we were right by an airstrip. Soon, we saw a C-17 Globemaster coming down for a landing as well. Man, the noise from that thing trying to slow down is deafening! We flew on one of those from Fort Polk to Kuwait, but from the inside the noise isn't that bad. Outside the plane, well, that is another story altogether.

As we were standing in the parking lot of the chow hall, we heard another jet taking off. The chow hall is several blocks from the airstrip, but the noise was still enough to make one's eardrums burst. I thought it was the Globemas-ter taking off, but to my surprise, two F-16s came screaming off the runway. I was amazed at the amount of noise they make! I had never seen fighter jets take off before and to see them like that was really something. It made the trip up there all the more worth my time.

We were doing our final checks on the new trucks when a soldier came up and asked where we were going. We told him we had come up from Camp Cooke to get some new trucks. He said, "Are those the trucks?" "Yes," we replied. Then he said, "Man, y'all are nuts, they don't even have bulletproof windshields! What are y'all gonna do if you get shot at on the way back?" "Duck," we said.

Jason Adams
Camp Cooke, Iraq

Notice | Training | Deployment | Home leave | Back Home
10/12/03 | | 3/1/04 | 9/26-10/14/04 | 3/19/05

The Nature of War

Today is November 21ˢᵗ

As we came in from another all night patrol, tired and hungry, we threw our equipment on our beds and went out to the parking lot to finish unloading our trucks. The morning's tranquility was shattered by a thunderous report, and then another and another. Oh great, I thought…mortars. But, as the explosions continued, it became clear to us they were all coming from the same area. Then it occurred to me it was artillery firing. The only problem with that is the fact the guns are only about 100 meters from my trailer.

Why does this keep happening to us? Back at the airport, we had some 155mm howitzers stationed close by. Here, we have the same thing. It is as if the person who decides where my unit is to live has some intense personal vendetta against us. I don't get it. I don't mind outgoing rounds. Matter of fact, I like them. Not because it is inflicting harm upon someone, but because of the awesome feeling I get from watching them fire. What I don't like is the ear-splitting explosions at two in the morning as I try to sleep.

It is really something to see an artillery battery open up with all of its guns! The smoke from the muzzles, the deafening concussion of sound as it hits my chest, the sight of the gun crews jamming round after round into the chambers, and pulling the lanyard is truly an awesome sight (insert Tim Allen grunt). It is as if some primal urge deep within my mind is suddenly satisfied.

As I watch the gun crews plying their deadly trade, I am taken back through time. I picture myself on top of Breed's Hill, watching the Revolutionary War. I can see myself at Verdun and Stalingrad. Waterloo, Normandy, and all of the great battles throughout modern history have used extensive amounts of artillery. The smell of the gunpowder mixed with the cool morning air is almost intoxicating.

Not long after some Chinese guy invented gunpowder, somebody said, "Hey, what if we made a really big gun that shoots a really big bullet?" Bingo, artillery is born. The artillery is one of the oldest branches of the army and even today is a very important part of any battle. The guns are bigger and surprisingly accurate. But, the concept of artillery today is the same as it was those many years ago: Destroy the enemy from a distance.

I know I have said many times war is a stupid manner in which to settle disputes. In fact, one of my favorite quotes is from Dr. Martin Luther King. Dr. King said, "War is a poor chisel to carve out tomorrows." That is 100 percent true. But in watching the artillery fire, I have to admit I love this stuff. Don't get me wrong; I hate the idea of fighting. What I mean is I love the tools of war, without the whole war part.

In watching the artillery fire, I have to admit I love this stuff. Don't get me wrong; I hate the idea of fighting. What I mean is I love the tools of war, without the whole war part.

Throughout history, men have been drawn to battle like sailors to the siren's song. What is it about war that is so alluring? Is it the smell of gunpowder? Perhaps, it is the bonds and camaraderie that is forged through the pains of combat. I know this bond. I have felt it. Powerful in nature, this bond is able to transcend time and space, lasting a lifetime in many cases. Is it because a man is tested in battle? Is it the question of what kind of men we are that draws us into combat? I am no philosopher, and I don't think there is an easy answer to these questions. There has to be something that draws us to this, the second oldest profession! It is possible it is just a simple testosterone thing, the likes of which we will never completely understand.

Last night while driving around, I found myself contemplating these thoughts. I looked up at the cloudless sky and was stunned at the intensity of the stars. Millions of them twinkled in the cold night air, and I found myself reflecting on the human race. I don't subscribe to the whole ET thing. I don't buy into the Roswell, New Mexico, conspiracy theories, but I can't help but wonder, if another species of beings were looking down at us, what would they be thinking? Would they be impressed with what they saw? Or, would they wrinkle their little green noses, come to the conclusion we are a bunch of morons, and move someplace else in the galaxy.

I find it more than a little ironic the same race of beings can give us people like Leonardo Da Vinci and, at the same time, Charlie Manson. It is funny the same mix of atoms, chromosomes, cells, and neurons can make up great figures like Ludwig Van Beethoven and, at the same time, genocidal maniacs like Adolph Hitler. We can fly to the moon, but we can't feed the hungry. We marvel at our own greatness! We can a take a person's heart out of their body, rebuild it and put it back in, and yet, we can't cure the common cold. We build airplanes that fly at mach 9.6, computers that make Tesla look like the village idiot, and yet we can't keep drugs out of the hands of our kids. We spend our days working to advance technology, then go home at the end of the day and sit in front of a TV and melt our brains watching shows like *"Who wants to marry a millionaire?"* The paradox is endless!

Sometimes, just sometimes, I think the only thing that separates us from the apes is the fact we eat with utensils.

Jason Adams
Camp Cooke, Iraq

Notice   Training   Deployment   Home leave   Back Home
10/12/03   3/1/04   9/26-10/14/04   3/19/05

Piecing Things Together

Today is November 23rd

Wow, only a couple days until Thanksgiving. Hard to believe a year ago I was sitting at Fort Hood getting ready to go and watch the Cowboys play. They lost that day…matter of fact they got spanked. The Dolphins pretty much walked all over them, with the final score something like 40 to 21. Another point worth making regarding this time of year is: one year ago is the first time I wrote one of these letters. I wrote a letter to my dad and some friends highlighting my trip to Dallas and unbeknown to me, dad sent it to the newspaper. They liked it and the rest is history. Try as I might, I just cannot get over the response to my brainless ranting. Letters and emails from all over the U.S. have been sent to me from people I have never met and all of them say the same thing, my writing is well received back home.

It is funny when I think about this response I have gotten. I have never considered myself to be a writer, and I have never had any appetites thereof. In all honesty, I never did that well in English back in school. Matter of fact, I did rather poorly. Don't get me wrong, I love to write and I love to read even more. It, at the time, just seemed I didn't like to read that which I wasn't interested in.

While home on leave, I ran into the husband of my high school English teacher. He told me how much he liked my letters. As we stood there chatting about an electrical problem I was having at home, one question was burning in my stomach like Tabasco, and I had to ask it, "What does your wife think about my sudden, hitherto unknown talent?" He stated flatly, "She can't believe that you're the one who is writing them." That made me feel good.

Yesterday, we pulled the day shift of patrols. Around lunchtime, as we stood by our trucks waiting for all our guys to come out from the chow hall, we heard a loud "whoosh" over our heads. Before any of us had time to react, we heard the rocket hit the building directly behind us. Luckily, it did not explode upon impact. Many of the rockets and mortars that land here are duds. Most likely as the result of age and improper use of fuses. I am not complaining.

The lone rocket was all that landed near us, but it was enough to freak out the driver of a bucket loader who had been waiting in the parking lot for his buddies to exit the chow hall. We all stood there like a bunch of idiots watching a monkey copulate with a football. We should have been looking for some cover. One should not stand idly by while rockets land nearby. But, it would

Around lunchtime, as we stood by our trucks waiting for all our guys to come out from the chow hall, we heard a loud "whoosh" over our heads. Before any of us had time to react, we heard the rocket hit the building directly behind us.

appear that we are not that smart. The driver of the bucket loader looked at us, looked at where the rocket had landed, then hastily put on his body armor and Kevlar. He then jumped in his earthmover, fired it up and expeditiously left the area. We got a pretty good laugh out of that, when in hindsight, we should have been a little more reactive to the incoming round. I guess we are just too used to it.

This morning, my driver and I took our truck down to the motor pool for some repairs. Since the truck is new to us, there are a few things that are not up to par and required a little more attention than I am able to provide with my modest tool kit. For starters, the headlight switch was all but useless. We had to finagle the switch for the last couple hours of our last patrol. Otherwise, the headlights would not stay on. The brake light switch would not engage unless you practically stood on the brake pedal. But, the worst part for us was the fact the fan motor for the heater only works on low and the duct work that carries the much wanted hot air from the squirrel cage to the heater vents was missing. In essence, since the blower motor is on the passenger side of the truck, I get all the heat and the other occupants of the truck get nothing.

Some time ago we received some infrared headlights to put on our trucks to use in conjunction with our night vision goggles. These are like driving with the regular headlights on, except no one can see them; unless of course you happen to be wearing night vision goggles. All they are is a fog lamp like you would buy at any auto parts store, except these have a dark red lens that only lets minimal light through. But, because night vision goggles amplify available light, they look like halogen spotlights when used with the goggles.

We haven't used night vision goggles, or NVGs for short, for quite some time. Back when we patrolled the old zone, we discovered driving down a major highway with our headlights off presents a rather flagrant disregard for safety. Not so much for us, per se, but certainly for the other motorists that happen to be on the road. The locals used to get quite a shock when we would pass them in the middle of the night in full blackout.

As I stated, we don't drive in blackout anymore. So, we really don't need infrared headlights on our trucks. But, what to do with all those lights? We can't just pitch them, so we are mounting them on our mirror posts to be used as "IED lights." We position them so they shine on the shoulders of the road to provide much needed illumination so should an IED be planted on the shoulder of the road, we will stand a better chance of spotting it before it goes off.

We are mounting lights on our mirror posts to be used as "IED lights." We position them so they shine on the shoulders of the road so we will stand a better chance of spotting an IED before it goes off.

The problem is all we have are the lights. There are no connecting wires to direct power from the electrical system of the truck to the lights. So, we have to improvise. Out in the bone yard, there are a ton of Iraqi tanks and whatnot. We took a little trip out there, and I was surprised to see several M113s. These are American-made tracked troop carriers. I had no idea the Iraqis used any of these! Most of them are pretty old, not to mention stripped to the bone. But, some of them have electrical harnesses in them. We should be able to use some of these to rig up some sort of wiring job that will enable us to use the lights.

While standing in the motor pool trying to decide how to rig up the lights, our thought process was interrupted by a ground-shaking blast. Another followed not long after. The walls of the shop in which we fix our trucks shook with each report and dust fell from the tin sheeting that constitutes the roofing. Five explosions in all were heard. After about the second one, I thought to myself, "Man, those are awful close." My buddy was up on top of one of the five tons to see where the shells were landing. He jumped down and said they were only 100 or so meters away. That is a little too close for comfort, and I started to think about finding something to crawl under when the radio crackled to life. They said the explosions we were hearing were not incoming rounds. They told us the EOD guys were disposing of some rockets that had come in a couple days ago. That was so nice of them to let someone know of their intentions! I mean, come on! What kind of morons detonates high explosive ordinance right by the motor pool and doesn't tell anyone?

After that little fiasco, we finished working on our truck. We didn't get the heater fixed, but we ordered the parts to fix it. I won't be holding my breath on that one, but one can always hope. I heard a rumor there is an area where they keep all the wrecked Humvees. It might be advantageous to seek out this area, as I am sure that between my buddies and my toolbox, we might be able to get all we need to fix my truck. It is not like I have never parted out a Humvee before!

A few years ago, back in Dixon, we had a truck we never used and it just sat untouched in a corner of our motor pool. If memory serves me correctly, that was the year the state of Illinois went broke. Parts to fix our other trucks were pretty scarce. Faced with the prospect of unusable trucks, we decided to part out the unused truck, use those parts to keep the rest of the trucks on the road, and just wait until the state got its finances in order so we could order the parts we needed. Yeah, it is a bad way to do business, but what were we to do? They don't exactly sell parts to Humvees at the local NAPA Auto Parts, plus, if they did, we would have had to pay for them out of our own pockets. By the time the state found some common ground and balanced the budget, the truck was sitting on jack stands with all the tires gone, no starter, no generator, no batteries, as well as various other parts that were missing. In the end, we managed to put the truck back in running shape, but it took some time to do.

After SPC Girkin and I got back from the motor pool, we stood in the parking lot of our trailer park and talked about the best way to rig up the lights. Without warning, we suddenly heard a long burst of machine gun fire that sounded like it came from not too far away. We could hear bullets ricocheting off trailers and concrete barriers on the other side of our trailers. I looked at

Kenny G (that is Girkin's nickname, his name is Ken Girkin, so we call him Kenny G) and said, "Wonder what that's all about." Later on that day, we found out what had happened. It seems one of the 50-caliber machine guns on an Avenger went haywire and started spraying bullets all over the place. The 50 on an Avenger is electric unlike the 50s we use which are mechanical. I heard a bunch of trucks were shot up in the melee the runaway gun had caused. No one was hurt in the accident, which is good because usually when someone gets shot by a 50, they lose whatever part of the body the bullet hit.

The new PX is supposed to open here on Thanksgiving. It is supposed to be the biggest PX in Iraq to date. I have seen the new building and yes, it is huge. Until the new one opens, however, the one we are using in the meantime is in an old Iraqi army warehouse. Don't get me wrong, it is still better than the PX we were going to when we first got in country. That was in a tent not much bigger than the trailers we live in. The only thing they sold was shaving cream, sun block and sunflower seeds. Once the big one opened up at the airport, their inventory and selection quadrupled. The same should apply here. Rumor is the new one here will be open 24 hours. That would be great since many of us work erratic schedules. Back at the airport, there was one PX that was open around the clock, but unfortunately for us, it was on the other side of the base.

Jason Adams
Camp Cooke, Iraq

Thanksgiving

Today is November 25th

Well, today is Thanksgiving. A day set aside by President Lincoln for all of us to count our blessings, be with family, and to reflect back upon the first Thanksgiving those many years ago as the Pilgrims celebrated their first harvest in the new land. So, here I am, sitting in a country, surrounded by people who are as different to me as the Native Americans were to the pilgrims. The pilgrims managed to make peace with some of the Native Americans. Sure, Manifest Destiny and greed soon brought about the slaughter of many Native Americans, but that is another story.

Today found me working yet again. We had to pull a 12 hour patrol, which meant we would miss the Thanksgiving meal. It isn't really that big of a deal to me, but for some, missing the turkey and trimmings is quite a big deal. Our commander made arrangements for us to rotate into the chow hall and get some holiday fare. The chow hall hours were adjusted so as to only serve two meals today, rather than the regular four. Breakfast was still served, but lunch was moved from 1100 hours - 1330 hours to 1400 hours - 1600 hours. Or so we thought.

We run our patrols in two teams. That way, we can cover more ground with less people. One of the side effects of this is we can rotate men in for chow without leaving our sector unmanned. The other group went in at 1400 hours and we were supposed to go in at 1500 hours. The empty parking lot should have been the first sign something was amiss as we rolled into the chow hall.

Now, keep in mind we had forgone breakfast and lunch so we would have more room in our bellies for all that wonderful, succulent bird; needless to say, we were ready to eat road kill and ask for more. Unfortunately, there was a mix-up in the scheduling and the chow hall closed at 1500 hours. So, we were late. Wow, you talk about a letdown! The folks that were running the chow hall felt bad for us as we lingered at the door like lost little puppies. They let us in so we could at least get a plate of food.

Since everyone and their mothers went to eat, it was no surprise they were out of turkey. We managed to get some canned ham and some macaroni and cheese. The folks serving the food were even dressed up in costumes! It was pretty weird, to say the least, to see a Filipino dude dressed up like a pilgrim. They must have trouble getting costumes over here because they were wearing tricorn hats rather than the traditional hats with the big buckle in the middle. They looked more like pirates than pilgrims. Yellow Beard was serving the ham, Captain Hook was manning the sandwich bar, and Black Beard was in charge of the desserts. I wonder how humiliating it must have been for those poor folks to have to dress for a holiday they don't even celebrate in their homelands. I thought it odd they had people dressed like pirates/pilgrims, but no one was dressed like Indians. If my memory of grade-school history lessons serves me correctly, there were Indians at the first Thanksgiving, but there were none in sight.

Because the chow hall was officially closed, we had to get our meals to go, rather than sit down and eat. We didn't complain since they didn't even have to let us in to begin with. As we wrapped our plates in aluminum foil and grabbed a can of pop, the pirates came up and wished us a happy Thanksgiving. I have really grown quite fond of the chow hall workers. Many of them are either Indian or Filipino and have not been home since this war started and yet, they are always happy and diligent while working. Some of them don't speak very much English, but "Sir" always follows what they do say. They work their tails off trying to give us good food and friendly service. I really admire them.

It was just so odd to see two Filipino guys standing there in full Indian dress, smoking Marlboros! I thought to myself, under different circumstances that would seem weird.

As we left the chow hall with our carryout plates, the mystery of the missing Indians was solved. Out behind the chow hall stood Squanto and Samoset taking a smoke break. I about dropped my plate due to my laughter. It was just so odd to see two Filipino guys standing there in full Indian dress, smoking Marlboros! I thought to myself, under different circumstances that would seem weird.

And so, to celebrate the start of the holiday season, we ate canned ham on the hood of our trucks out in the chow hall parking lot before going back out to patrol. But, you know what? I am still thankful. Regardless of the situation in which I find myself, I remain grateful for what I have, and I do not lament that which I do not. I am healthy. I am happy. I am employed and because of this, I can provide a nice life for my family. I am able to help people everyday. What more could I want? Too many times, people get all too caught up in things that do not matter. Little things, that are infinitesimal in the bigger picture, cause people sadness. Life is not meant to be spent unhappy. Sometimes we must pause, scrutinize our lives, and meditate upon those things that are really important. If we do this, life gets really simple. And it is this simplicity that can give way to unequalled happiness.

I was snooping on the Internet the other night and I came across one of the purported execution videos of a hostage here in Iraq. Words cannot describe what I witnessed. Naysayers might argue the video is a hoax. Yes, the thought did cross my mind. But, in this case, I don't think so.

The video shows three masked men standing behind a man on the floor, bound and gagged, also with a mask on. The man in the center is reading something in Arabic, which I cannot understand, but it seems to be a list of crimes this prisoner has committed along with the justification for his forthcoming death. The man on the floor is kneeling upon an American flag, which is spread out upon the floor as well. When the man is done reading the letter, the man on the left pulls out a knife, forces the kneeling man prostrate, and proceeds to saw off his head. I use the terminology saw, rather than decapitate. Decapitation conjures up thoughts of guillotines, pit and pendulums or perhaps an axe-wielding man. No, this is not that humane. It is brutal, it is heinous, and it is by far the most gruesome thing I have ever seen. As the executioner is sawing, all three of them are chanting, "Allah this, Allah that, yadda, yadda."

Thinking about this, I say this, every person in America should watch this film. If they choose not to watch it, they should be forced to see it. Why? Because it is the truth. It is reality. Nothing better illustrates what we are fighting here. Nothing better exemplifies all that most people would rather forget about. This video personifies the hatred and fanaticism that brews in the minds of some people in this world, and that hatred and fanaticism is made manifest in the killing of the innocent.

We live in a big comfort zone, folks. But the truth is this, we live in a world that is in chaos. True, our borders repel a lot of it, but the bottom line is this, there are people in this world who would like nothing more than to watch every last American man, woman, and child die. Whether one at a time or en masse, it really doesn't matter to them. They hate us for who we are, what we believe in, and the manner in which we speak to God. Go on and kid yourselves if you like, but they hate us because we aren't Muslim.

We live in a world that is in chaos. There are people in this world who would like nothing more than to watch every last American man, woman, and child die.

In all fairness, most of the people I have met over here are at least tolerant of us. In fact, many of them are pretty nice folks, if you take a minute to talk to them. They don't see us as a threat to their faith. In many cases, they see the Coalition Forces as liberators; because now, they can fully practice their faith; a faith which, up until recently, was suppressed by the ruling party. Problem is there are those in this world who don't see things quite like that. The people responsible for 9/11, the people responsible for the USS *Cole* bombing, the kidnappings of innocent civilians, and their subsequent beheadings as well as every other terrorist act worldwide: These people are our enemy!

Let us not forget the images of the planes striking the twin towers! Let us not forget the sight of that gaping hole in the side of one of our naval ships! I will not forget the images of that beheading as they held up the head of that man as if it were a battle trophy! Unless we are willing to hunt down every last terrorist on the planet and kill them like the animals they are, then this– this war on terrorism, as it is called, cannot be won. We cannot say to ourselves, "Oh well, we've done enough, we have had enough of this war bit. Let's bring our boys and girls home." Nice sentiment, but if we leave before we finish what we have started, then we have already lost. I believe in my heart this is a war America cannot afford to lose. The hardest part for me to swallow in all of this is my belief the American people do not perceive the threat of terrorism.

Complete and total annihilation of the threat should be our only acceptable end result. Anything less and it will only be a matter of time before that ugly beast rears its head and strikes again. We must realize life is not about company picnics and taking little Timmy to baseball practice. Yes, those things are important, but sometimes there are more important things to concern ourselves with. Protecting our nation and our way of life should be foremost in our minds. When the morning comes we find these things threatened, we must be willing to defend them in every way imaginable.

There is ample evidence in our society that proves there are many who do not realize the threat. Take our elections for example. Yes, John Kerry and George Bush ran against each other but, it was not just about the men running. It was a battle between those who do not perceive the threat of terrorism and those who do. Fortunately for all of us, those who see terrorism for what it is won.

I find myself missing my life back home with increasing intensity. I do not fancy the idea of being away from my family for so long. My wife tells me our youngest daughter, Joanna, is quite the budding basketball star. I wouldn't know. To be frank, I want to go home. But, I also wholeheartedly support this war on terrorism. I believe it is a fight that needs fighting. I believe we, as a country, cannot afford to lose. I believe our way of life, as we know it, hangs in the balance.

I want to go home. But, I also wholeheartedly support this war on terrorism. I believe it is a fight that needs fighting. I believe we, as a country, cannot afford to lose.

Therefore, I am here of my own free will. We must stay the course. We must finish what those cowards started. In the words of Winston Churchill, and I paraphrase: So you have enemies? Good! That means that, at some point in your life, you have stood up for something.

I believe I have made my point to the best of my ability. I am not an orator, nor do I consider myself an avid debater of political topics. My inadequate vocabulary and my unpretentious intellect have done the best they can to help illustrate just what kind of enemy we face. I can only close this letter with two quotes I feel best sum up my thoughts.

"The only thing necessary for evil to triumph, is for good men to do nothing." —Edmund Burke

"War is an ugly thing, but not the ugliest of things. The decayed and degraded state of mind that thinks nothing is worth fighting for is far worse." —John Stuart Mill

Jason Adams
Camp Cooke, Iraq

Moving North

Notice
10/12/03   Training   Deployment
3/1/04   Home leave
9/26–10/14/04   Back Home
3/19/05

The Police Station

Today is December 1ˢᵗ

Our missions have changed yet again. We no longer patrol the stretch of road that had been our home since we arrived here. We have moved farther north to a little town that sits on the banks of the Tigris River. Smaller than Baghdad by far, Al-Tarmiyah is reminiscent of many of the towns the soldiers of this unit hail from. It is roughly the same size as Galva, Illinois, in land area, but much larger in population.

Al-Tarmiyah is about an hour north of Baghdad, and by just driving its streets, one can see it is, indeed, a normal small town. The traffic is slower, more use is made of animals for transportation, and the streets are not as crowded as their Baghdad counterparts. In fact, many of the streets are dirt. Walking down Main Street, I get the feeling things move slower here. Nobody seems to be in a rush. It has a certain quaintness to it all. I guess, in some ways, it reminds me of home.

We have only been there for a few days, but I have to say I like it. I hope the insurgents stay away from us here. Not because I am scared of them, but because in their absence, we can focus on the humanitarian side of our jobs, rather than the bullets and carnage side. But, as we pull into yet another town, in another part of Iraq, doing the same thing, questions arise. How do we go about showing these folks we are here to help? How do we help without offending them? The Iraqi people are a proud people, and rightly so. How then, do we help without insulting them, causing them to perceive us as though we pity them and are there to offer a handout?

I am of the mind that to give a man a fish, you will feed him for the day. But, if I *teach* a man to fish, I have empowered him to feed himself for the rest of his life. I have spoken of this idea with all our interpreters and they agree. The key to

The key to really helping the people of Iraq lies not in giving them a handout and then leaving. The key lies in education.

really helping the people of Iraq lies not in giving them a handout and then leaving. The key lies in education. The problem here is that to do this, it will take time.

Sadly though, we live in a microwave society. We want things now. We Americans do not want to wait. How many times do we put in a movie and then get frustrated at the length of the opening credits? How often do we put something in the microwave and then stand in front of the thing and watch the timer, as if our presence will somehow make it go faster? Drive thru's, express lanes at the supermarket, faster downloads! We want things now! Unfortunately, for some things, we must be patient. For this country to recover from a singular thought process that lasted for more than 30 years is going to take time.

We first heard rumors of a change in missions before we left the airport. They were just rumors, so nobody gave them a second thought. When we got up here to Taji, the rumors increased in both frequency and in scope. Soon, it was fact. We were going up north. We were told we would be living in a police station and using it as a base of operations. This city, Al-Tarmiyah, has been called "East Fallujah" by some, which didn't set well with a lot of us.

We were issued maps soon after we learned of the new mission, and the first thing I noticed was the distance this town is from Taji. I really don't like the idea of being out in the middle of nowhere, by ourselves, but what are we going to do about it? Yep, that's right–nothing. Oh sure, we could embarrass our families, our country, and ourselves by refusing to go on this mission. We could cite poor armor, lack of equipment, even poor fuel, if we wanted to. It has worked for other units. But, we have too much self-respect to do anything as cowardly as that. All that does is give the tree huggin' anti-war protesters more to whine about. Quite frankly, I couldn't live with myself if did something like that.

Just like celebrities at the Oscars, the army, too, likes to make a grand entrance. It's the whole "shock and awe" thing. Moving up to Al-Tarmiyah was no different. As we waited at the west gate to Taji, with our trucks overflowing with ammo, food, water, rockets, and anything that we might need, four M-2 Bradley Fighting Vehicles pulled up. Ahh, it would appear our escort had arrived!

But wait, there's more, folks! Soon, our air recon assets were on station. Yes, we rolled out with nothing less than four tanks and two choppers! That was pretty awesome to see. Kinda made me feel pretty important at first. Then, the feeling of importance was overcome with the burning question of why we needed so much security. I started to wonder if we had brought enough ammo. Needless to say, I didn't have a warm and fuzzy feeling.

We made the trip up with no problems. As the column of trucks and tanks lumbered northward, the helicopters swooped here and there the entire way. Their air acrobatics

Like the waters of the Red Sea, the people and cars on the streets of Al-Tarmiyah parted as we approached.

could be likened to watching barn swallows dive for insects. I, for one, was impressed with their maneuvering. All the way north, people stopped and stared at us as we passed. Some were undoubtedly scared, others looked on unassumingly. I am sure some were wondering what we were up to. Like the waters of the Red Sea, the people and cars on the streets of Al-Tarmiyah parted as we approached. We drove to the middle of town, right in front of the police station. It was there we stopped and set up security.

The police station is set in the middle of town and is comprised of a two-story stone and brick building with a 10-foot wall surrounding it. In front of the station is a sliding gate, along with an outbuilding for gate guards, I assume. To the west is the parking garage for the police cars that were once there, but have long since disappeared. In their place are three old cars that are riddled with bullet holes. The windows and doors are all perforated with multiple holes and the interiors of the automobiles are stripped of any useful parts.

The building itself is pretty good sized. The Iraqi police occupy the first floor and we use the upper level and the roof. When we first got there, the place was a dump. Some other unit had been there before us and they left the place in disarray. The rooms upstairs were cluttered with garbage and the hallways hadn't been swept out in a long time. That kind of behavior by other units makes me angry. We are acting as ambassadors of America. The impression we make on these people is lasting, and I would like to think we care a little more about these folks than to trash their building, which, they are nice enough to let us use, and then pack up and leave. That is not professional at all.

The first thing we had to do is set up our defense. We placed our gun positions and improved the emplacements with sandbags and some plywood. While that was going on, other men unloaded the trucks and trailers and carried all our supplies to the second floor. We set up a supply room, a TOC or, Tactical Operations Center, designated sleeping areas, set up cots, set up the radios and did radio checks with the rest of our unit down in Taji, and started the formidable task of cleaning up.

It took us awhile, but we got the job done. The best part of the whole day was when we were pulling in the gate. As I was directing some of the trucks in, we all heard a loud explosion that was really close. I thought, "Oh goodie, there is the welcome committee!" But, it turned out to be an aerosol can that someone threw in the burn barrel out back, not a mortar. Since we have arrived, we have had not a single incident involving the enemy. Knock on wood.

The building, at one time, was pretty nice. A second-floor balcony that extends 30 feet off the main building covers the main entrance. There are remnants of flower boxes that line the sidewalk into the front doors. The double doors that make up the main entrance are large, wooden and decorated with carvings. The main floor is carpeted in a tight-weaved shag carpet emblazoned with the all too familiar Baath party symbol. The steps that lead to the second floor are tiled with marble chipped tiles, as is the balcony. The rooms are all painted and have ceiling fans and florescent lights. Some of the lights and fans work, some of them don't.

There are four bathrooms on the second floor alone, but none of them work. Our bathroom is an ammo crate with a toilet seat nailed to it that sits out back in a corner. Our living conditions are primitive, to say the least, but in a way, it is almost fun. Living like this puts into perspective how my grandpa lived in World War Two as he moved across France, en route to his untimely death. I feel close to the soldiers of yesteryear as I share in the inconveniences they had to contend with.

We make the best of things, as we always do. Last night, for example, found some of us huddled around a kerosene heater with our stocking hats on while one of the guys played the guitar. It was a good time. Most of the first couple days were spent setting up shop and cleaning. Of course we had to go patrol the city, but that is a given.

After the first few days, I had the opportunity to talk to some of the police officers that work in the station with us. They are a pretty neat bunch of men. They work for free.

Yes, I said free. You see, they, for some reason, haven't been paid in at least a month. We are working on that issue for them. The fact they show up and put their butts on the line for the people of their town, knowing fully they might get killed or not receive a paycheck, has

The fact the Iraqi police show up and put their butts on the line for the people of their town, knowing fully they might get killed or not receive a paycheck, has earned them my eternal respect.

earned them my eternal respect. They are committed to their town and the people of that town. That, in and of itself, speaks volumes as to their character. At one time, the police tell me, there were about 20 men on the force. Due to the lack of pay, today only about eight or 10 show up on a regular basis. They are underfunded, underequipped, and undertrained, but still they try as best as they can to do their jobs.

Their weapons are a sorry sight as well. Their arms room is modest to say the least, and its inventory is comprised of a few AK-47s; some of which do not work. Ben and I decided to help them out. Yesterday, we took up our cleaning kits and sat down and cleaned three rifles and seven magazines as well as the individual cartridges. The weapons were a mess, but we got them working. Tomorrow, we will work on a few more. Hopefully, we can get most of them working again. Some need parts, which my commander said he would try and get for them. I don't mind helping the men out. It helps them provide better protection for their town and it helps to build rapport with the policemen. Plus, it helps us pass the time.

Since we moved from the airport, I haven't seen Snake or Jaguar. They didn't come up north with us. I miss them, but we have been working with a new guy as of late. His codename is GQ- just like the magazine. I am not sure, but I think the reason he was dubbed "GQ" is because it is a reflection of how he presents himself. He is 25 years old and dresses to the hilt. He has a trendy black wool coat he wears everywhere, his hairstyle is reminiscent of Ashton Kutcher's, and he sports a pair of thick-rimmed black-framed glasses. Sometimes, he wears a stocking hat pulled low over his head like some rapper out of Compton, but not always.

His English is perfect and easily understandable. Plus, his personality is rather warm and outgoing. We have spent a lot of time talking as of late and the more I talk to him, the more I like him. He happens to be a very educated young man. He holds a degree in mechanical engineering with an expertise in heavy machinery. On a side note, his wife is also a mechanical engineer. Like Snake and Jaguar, he longs to live in America. We have tried to work those issues from our end and, unfortunately, we have met with little success. These guys put their lives on the line for us and we could not do our jobs without their skills in language. Do we not owe it to them to give them the chance at a better life? I think so. I just do not know anyone in the INS to get the ball rolling.

I am sure a company like Caterpillar would beg GQ to come and work for them, if not in engineering, then most certainly as an interpreter. We have talked of America and he has loved every bit I have told him. I warned him some facets of our society might shock him, such as gay people and pornography; not to mention bars and liquor stores. I told him about strip bars and I laughed as his eyes widened at my colorful description of what goes on in those places. He said, "Wow, that's awesome!" Now it was my eyes that widened! I said, "I thought that stuff was taboo over here." He replied, "What can I say, I am a bad Muslim!"

Last night, he took us across the street from the police station and bought some of us dinner. We insisted for him to let us pay, but he wouldn't hear of it. After a minute of resistance, we consented and he proceeded to buy four of us shish kebobs and *Tic'a*. The meal is served with lettuce, tomato, onions, seasoned with paprika, lemons and some type of pickled vegetable. What you do is this, you take the meat, which is lamb, put it on a piece of bread that looks like a tortilla, put on the lettuce, tomato, onion, pickled veggies and then squeeze some fresh lemon juice all over it. Then you roll it up and eat it like a burrito. I must admit, I really enjoyed it. The vendor that was selling it looked pretty nervous as the five of us walked up, but he seemed to mellow out when he realized he stood to make a few bucks off us.

Earlier that day while on a patrol, we stopped at three shops on the main drag and bought some kerosene heaters for our little clubhouse. Again, the people seemed nervous as we approached. Their behavior made me wonder how they were treated by the last group of soldiers that had been stationed at the police station. I hope through our efforts to help these folks, coupled with the interaction between us, we can overcome this apprehensiveness and get down to making these people's lives better. Nothing would leave me feeling more satisfied.

As we walked back over to the police station with our food, some of the policemen were standing in the entryway of the building. We asked them if they cared if we took pictures of the jail cells later on to send home. They said it would be no problem. After we ate, Ben and I took our cameras and headed downstairs. GQ did the talking for us, and the captain of the police got his keys and unlocked the cell door for us.

The cell is a room about 12 by 12 with a bathroom at one end that doesn't work. Needless to say, it is the nastiest jail cell I have ever seen. It makes the gulag look like Club Med. As we walked in, I was surprised to see a man sitting on the floor wrapped up in a blanket. I jumped back and said to Ben, "Dude, a prisoner!" Sure enough, some poor guy was in the lockup for some reason. He looked like he was about to freak out when he saw two U.S. soldiers walk in full battle dress.

He looked up at us as if to say, "Please, please....don't kill me!" So what did we do? Ben said, "How's it going, my man?" and then we pulled out our cameras and took his picture! What a riot. We asked the policemen why this man was incarcerated, and they said he had been caught fighting with another man. Not exactly a serial killer, but nonetheless, enough to land him in the slammer for a few days. I told Ben we could have been really ornery and knelt on either side of him and then yelled, "Boo!" That would have most likely sent the poor guy into cardiac arrest.

Tonight finds me sitting yet again in my chair typing out my thoughts and ideas. Every once in awhile, I stop typing and focus on the music that is playing. Tonight's fare is once again Beethoven. It is weird, but I can clear my mind of all things and just focus on music. I am not sure if others can do this; this isn't the type of thing that gets brought up over the chicken fried steak at the chow hall.

I consider myself lucky to possess an ability such as this. No thoughts, no pictures, nothing, just music. I can hear every note. I can feel every crescendo and decrescendo. I can focus on the violas but not the cellos. I can block out the strings altogether and listen to only the horns if I wish. I first realized I could do this while listening to Johann Pachelbell's Canon in D. I must have listened to that song 10 times in a row. Each time, I focused on a different melody or instrument. I was amazed at parts of the song I had never heard before. It is most relaxing and, at the same time, powerful.

Sometimes, it can be a most moving experience for me. There are times when listening that I shiver. Other times finds my hands moving to the flow of the music. If I want to, I can see an orchestra playing the music. I can smell the rosin on the bows and the paper upon which the music is printed. I can see the bows of the violins moving together in precise unison like the parts of a well-oiled machine. I can see the conductor waving his baton in the air as if he is swatting at imaginary bees.

Sometimes, being so lost in my music takes me to another place, away from here. Away from Iraq, away from the army, away from every other thing in this world. I am all by myself and I am surrounded by peace, perfection and unimaginable beauty. It is magnificent! When the song is over, my breathing returns to normal, the goose pimples go away, as do the shivers and I open my eyes. Back to reality, but what a trip! LSD and peyote can't hold a candle to Beethoven's Ninth! Not all songs will put me in this trace-like state, but the ones that do get played in my trailer quite often.

> **Sometimes being so lost in my music takes me to another place, away from here.**

Jason Adams
Camp Cooke, Iraq

Notice 10/12/03 — Training — Deployment 3/1/04 — Home leave 9/26–10/14/04 — Back Home 3/19/05

Life's Rages

Today is December 7th

Things here have been rather quiet for the last few days. Not that I am complaining, I assure you, I am not. But, the trouble is when things quiet down, it means two things. Soldiers get lazy, and the enemy could be regrouping.

Up where we are at now, things are going great. Well, as great as can be expected anyway! As many of you know, our shifts are 24-hours long. That means we are there, in that police station for an entire day. When the time comes for our relief to get there, we

When things quiet down, it means two things. Soldiers get lazy, and the enemy could be regrouping.

can't wait. For the last few days though, our escort has been exceedingly late. Today for example, they were three hours late relieving us.

The reason behind this tardiness is twofold. First, we are not allowed to move up this way without an armored escort; in other words, tanks. Second, the tankers and we are on completely different schedules. This makes coordinating escorts a royal pain in the neck. If we get to the gate and our escort is not there, we wait. Today, our replacements waited for two hours. Add that to almost an hour or so drive time and that makes our relief three hours late. When you are on duty for 24-hours, another three feels like an eternity.

The reason for this is pretty simple. We don't have a bathroom up there. Well, I take that back, we have an ammo crate out back that has a toilet seat nailed to it. But, the lavatory, as it is called, is rather drafty. That, and the fact that for the first couple days, all we had was MRE toilet paper. Trust me, Saran Wrap is more absorbent. Most guys just try to "hold it" as they say. This works for awhile, but willpower and control of voluntary muscles only goes so far, and sooner or later nature takes over.

I never thought I'd say it, but, happiness is a working toilet and a good, quality roll of Charmin.

Life here is getting better though. While shopping at the new PX today, we noticed the line for the Subway stand was pretty short. Since one of our little indulgences here is a break from army chow, we ran over to the stand and got in line. It felt like being back home for a brief moment as I gazed at all the sandwich possibilities. What kind of bread do I want? You mean I get a choice!? You serve Snapple here!? Yes! Yes! There is a God, and he is smiling down upon us today!

I ordered a footlong hot chicken sub on herbed wheat bread with marinara sauce, green peppers, tomatoes, cheese, pickles, and black pepper. For a drink, I had a pink lemonade Snapple. Man, it was good. As we sat at the picnic tables eating our lunch, it felt like we were back home, sitting at some outdoor café, eating our gourmet sandwiches with no other pressing issues to worry about. In short, we felt human again.

As we sat at the picnic tables eating our lunch from Subway, it felt like we were back home, sitting at some outdoor café, with no other pressing issues to worry about. In short, we felt human again.

After our brief break from reality, we headed for the PX to do a little shopping. We really didn't have anything in particular to buy, we just wanted to get away from the barracks and relax for awhile. While cruising the aisles, I remembered I needed a coffee cup. I went back to the coffee section, and to my dismay, I discovered they were sold out. Yeah, they have the traditional coffee mugs there like you would use at home, but I needed a travel mug that can go with me in my Humvee. I bought a very nice Eddie Bauer coffee mug a week or so ago, but that particular mug and I had a terribly short, yet violent relationship.

I confess, I have a temper. I mean, a bad temper. Most people who say they know me would argue this. That is because most people never see it. I am pretty good at keeping it in check and not letting it boil to the surface for all to see. But sometimes, I lose the battle against it, and I wig out. Most of the times it is over something really stupid. I admit it isn't pretty to see. My poor wife has seen this streak in me a few times. Usually I am out in the garage trying to fix something, and thankfully, I am by myself when I decide to act like a moron.

There I stood in my trailer with my brand new coffee mug. Guaranteed to keep coffee hot for two hours, it was well worth the 13 bucks it set me back.

As the Hazelnut Folgers brewed in my coffee maker, I figured I would put in the sugar and cream ahead of time. I took the mug out of the box and tried to take the lid off. No luck, it was stuck. It wasn't just stuck; it was if it had been glued in place.

I strained. I grunted. I tried to use my pliers. Nothing would get the lid off. By this time I was getting steamed. I was getting my butt kicked by a coffee cup! Not a proud moment for the human race, indeed. So there I was on the floor, with the coffee mug between my knees and my giant Channel Lock pliers in one hand and a hammer in the other, cursing like a sailor. Suddenly the door flew open to my trailer and in walked Ben. Ben looked at what I was doing, saw my face reddening with anger and the veins bulging out in my forehead and, like any good friend, immediately started laughing at me. I got up off the floor and headed for the door. Ben, sensing the possibility of great hilarity, was right behind me.

There is a row of cement barriers about eight-feet high that surround our trailers. They offer protection from shrapnel in the event of a mortar or rocket attack. That night, they offered a little more. They offered a way to smash that which had caused me this great anguish. Yes, I had decided my coffee cup was indeed possessed with a demon and must be destroyed. I strode up to within 15 feet of the barriers and, with a primordial scream, I threw the cup at the barrier.

It hit the side of the barrier with a crash, and plastic flew in all directions. The only part that survived my childish behavior was the stainless steel body of the mug. Ben was laughing so hard by this point he had to steady himself against a trailer to keep from falling down. In between his loud guffaws, he managed to blurt out, "What a loser!" and continued to laugh at my misfortune. Ben, being the consummate buddy that he is, decided to go tell everyone about my little breakdown. The next morning, as we readied the trucks for the trip up north, the entire platoon made an effort to ask me where my new coffee cup was…nothing like a bunch of your buddies pouring salt in your wounds.

So, as I left the PX coffee mug-less, I happened to pick up the latest copy of *The Stars and Stripes*. I usually skim over most of the articles in that daily rag, but today the headline caught my eyes immediately. Ben saw it, too, and our blood instantly began to boil. It seems the soldiers from the 343rd Quartermaster Company, the ones who refused to go on a mission, are getting a slap on the hand. I guess a little background information would be in order before I grab my megaphone, jump up on my worn-out soapbox, and begin my ranting.

The 343rd is a unit that transports, among other things, fuel and water. This particular mission they refused to go on would have taken them up the same stretch of road we patrolled for the first five months we were here. Eventually, their convoy would have taken them here, to Camp Cooke. The reasoning behind their refusal to follow orders stemmed from what the paper calls "…not all of the vehicles were armored, some vehicles were in poor condition and the route, known as Main Supply Route Tampa, was rife with ambushes, roadside bombs or both."

Give me a stinking break! First, let me say this: COWARDS!! Let me say it again: COWARDS!!!

The army operates off a little thing we like to call the Warrior Ethos. Now, Warrior Ethos is just a fancy term some staff officer came up with to give some general a warm, fuzzy feeling at night, but the gist of what that ethos states is this: Put the mission first. Pretty simple. What that means is, yeah, sometimes things don't go right. Sometimes, you are going off bad or incomplete intelligence. Sometimes, not all your equipment is up to snuff. But, you still do your job. You still go out and do your mission. Yeah, it sucks, but you do it. No excuses.

> **Sometimes, not all your equipment is up to snuff. But, you still do your job. You still go out and do your mission. Yeah, it sucks, but you do it. No excuses.**

There have been times when we roll out the gate and only one of the radios in my truck is working, I don't have a map, and the door of my truck was broken leaving me to hold it closed by hand for the entire patrol. But, as easy as it would have been for us to say, "Ya know what, we better not go out. It just isn't a good idea.", we went. Just like in life, you take the good with the bad.

Secondly, their lackluster justification of not having adequate armor on their trucks is not convincing either. I drove around for the longest time with not even a door on my truck. I went through ambushes, RPG attacks, and mortars with nothing between the guardrail and me but air. Don't give me that "not enough armor" line.

Thirdly, and the bottom line is this, they disobeyed a direct order in a combat zone. In wars past, the rules change in a combat zone. Not too many years ago, their actions could have earned them a front row seat at a firing squad. Their actions undermine the foundation of the army. When you are given an order, you follow it. Now, if it is an unlawful order that violates the Geneva Convention or is morally wrong, then that is a different story. If I order someone to shoot a prisoner, and they refuse, it is okay. If I order someone to do their job and they don't do it, then that, folks, is an entirely different story.

These soldiers should be punished. I am talking jail time at the minimum, followed by a dishonorable discharge. Their actions embarrass myself, as well as every other man and women in the military. In addition, it sets a bad precedent for the rest of us here when the leaders above them let them go with a slap on the wrist. In this case, an Article 15.

An Article 15 is a punitive form of punishment that can be administered without a court martial. Some of the things that may be imposed upon those given an Article 15 are reduction in rank, extra duty for up to 45 days, and forfeiture of half a month's pay for two months. Like I said, for what they did, this is a slap on the wrist. An Article 15 is nothing. I can get an Article 15 for not shaving or for being late to a formation. That is what Article 15s are used for. When I was in basic training, the drill sergeants used to hand those things out like they were candy.

What sickens me most about the whole deal is the outpouring of support these pukes got from tree huggers back home. The paper said people back home sent letters of support to those soldiers in question. They praised them for standing up for what is right. How do you figure? All they did was make life harder for leaders at all levels. Both their actions and the actions on the part of the army sent a loud and clear message to troops everywhere they can disobey orders at will and nothing will happen to them.

Hey, wait a minute! That gives me an idea! Maybe I will just complain I am riding around in a Humvee with inadequate protection! After all, we don't have any M1114s in our unit! We are still riding around in old M1025s! Yeah, and I'll whine because our patrol route is dangerous! Good idea! That way, I can just sit in my trailer tomorrow and surf the Internet. That would be great.

No wait, I forgot. I have honor and a sense of duty. I put the needs of others above my own. I have integrity. Guess I had better get my stuff rounded up to go out on patrol. Don't worry fellas, we'll do *your* job for you.

I guess it is a sign of the times that we live in. On page 13 of today's *The Stars and Stripes*, is my favorite cartoon, *Mallard Fillmore*. Today's cartoon is in reference to our society's efforts as of late to remove personal accountability for one's actions. The cartoon shows an old couple sitting in front of a TV and says, "If today's media had been around 63 years ago. The Japanese have just bombed Pearl Harbor...Now, let's examine how we brought this on ourselves."

I couldn't put it better if I tried.

Jason Adams
Camp Cooke, Iraq

Doing What's Right

Today is December 9th

Last night started out like any other night. Patrol for awhile, sit at the police station, tell jokes, play cards, play chess, and most importantly, drink coffee. Late in the evening, as we patrolled the northern half of the small town, we came upon a woman in the road waving her arms. Naturally, we stopped to see what we could do for her. It seems some drunken men with AK-47s came into her home, made sexual advances toward her daughters, and threatened the men of the house. One of the men of the house came back to the police station to make a statement regarding the incident. This man said that he knew the men who had threatened him and where they lived. All this information was taken down and the police prepared a report.

Unfortunately, the wheels of justice turn slow in this country, just as they do in ours. The process for obtaining a search warrant takes about 12 hours at a minimum, *after* the paperwork is filed! The police said in order to obtain such a warrant, they would have to go into Baghdad to see a judge. Sadly, sometimes things cannot be waited upon. Common sense would tell those responsible for this criminal act the victims would most likely go to the police, and they had better lie low for a while.

After SFC Hess and our interpreter finished talking to the man, they took him home. Once back in our police station, we sat upstairs and formulated a plan. The police may have to wait to raid a house, but we do not. SFC Hess, SSG Glisan, SSG Wolford, and I sat in

The police may have to wait to raid a house, but we do not.

the TOC and hammered out a simple plan of attack; an attack that would be carried out at first light. We consulted our map in order to ascertain the best possible locations for our trucks, identified those individuals that would be taking part in the raid, and set a time line for it all to follow. After this, we decided we had better get an idea of how the area looked, versus how it looked on the map.

We left the police station and traveled up to the house the young man had told us contained the suspects. Well, we didn't drive right by it; we parked a couple blocks away and went in on foot. After a brief time, we decided our plan was sound. We returned to the police station to get some sleep prior to the raid.

Five-thirty came early as it always does, and today, it found SSG Wolford kicking me in the rear saying, "Get up man, we gotta go." Thankfully, the coffee was already brewing as I pulled on my boots. SSG Patterson took it upon himself to fix up some java for us. It was good, but he makes it a little strong for my taste. I didn't say anything though; beggars cannot afford to be choosers. And so our day began, a rough awakening and some really strong coffee.

Once downstairs, we began to load the weapons and gear on the trucks, while others made the radio checks. One last little leadership pow-wow and off we went. The target house looked like any other house in that town. The only way to identify it was because it was the only one that had both a satellite dish and a TV antenna. We got our trucks positioned on the cardinal directions in regard to the house. This way, each gunner on the trucks can see two sides of the square, thus enabling our gunners to provide overlapping fire, should the need arise. Unfortunately, we have become surprisingly adept at this whole house raid bit. I say 'unfortunately' because, like the cars, I still do not feel comfortable rummaging through someone's possessions.

By this time, as we were ready to assault the house, the door to the house next door opened, and a man and his little boy came out. They looked at us all standing there in full battle rattle ready to bust open their neighbor's door. The little boy had a startled look on his face, which is not surprising. The man looked at me, and I gestured with my hand for him to return to his home. He nodded his head and retreated through the door. Even though no words were spoken, he understood my intent. Sadly, he is most likely used to it.

We stacked up alongside the outer wall of the home and checked our weapons one last time. That is important. It is a good idea to check your rifle one last time before you go into a building. The reason for this is twofold. One, it is critical you know your weapon is loaded and that a round is chambered. Secondly, even more important is the need to make sure the selector switch is on "safe." Regardless of how sure you are of your weapon status, it is always good to make sure one last time. A lot of things can happen as you go into a building. The one thing you want to avoid at all costs is your weapon firing by accident. As we went in the door through the wall, we found ourselves in a carport and patio-like area. SFC Hess and I stayed outside in the carport to provide security, while the rest of the guys went in the house.

Most mornings when I wake up, the first thing I see is my night stand and my glasses, not the business end of a Mossberg 12-gauge shotgun; but that is exactly what happened to the poor folks who happened to live in this house. I don't remember who it was that went in first, but I remember hearing someone shout "Women and children!" Slowly, as the initial shock of our entrance wore off, the women and little kids started to filter out of the house followed by an older man whom I presumed to be the head of the house. The man was dressed in house clothes with a suit jacket hastily thrown about his shoulders for warmth.

Most mornings when I wake up the first thing I see is my night stand and my glasses, not the business end of a Mossberg 12-gauge shotgun.

SFC Hess motioned to the women to sit down, which they did. The old man nervously drew on his cigarette as our guys finished clearing the house. The men we were looking for were not there. GQ came up on order and started to talk to the old man. We noticed there was another room to the house we could not access from the inside. The door to the room was locked, so GQ asked the man for the key, which he quickly produced. Upon entrance to this other room, it was obvious at least three people had been sleeping there. When questioned about this, the old man said four men lived in that room, which he rented to them.

The old man lit another cigarette and proceeded to tell us the men who lived there were pretty rowdy, and he had kicked them out a couple nights before. We asked GQ if he thought the man was being honest. GQ said he believed the old man, and that is good enough for us.

Unlike our culture, over here, body language is a big part of communication. Gestures, head movements, posture... all are used to convey one's thoughts, intentions, and, in a lot of cases, honesty. GQ, being an Iraqi, can pick up on it pretty quick. I can't. Some movements are so subtle I can't imagine anybody noticing, but I guess when you are raised to speak in this manner, it soon becomes second nature. For instance, when speaking to someone, if I pat my heart while speaking, I am conveying to that person my genuine sincerity regarding whatever it is I happen to be saying. If I touch my right eyebrow while speaking, it is a symbol of great sincerity. If I say to someone how much I enjoyed dinner and patted my heart, it is the same as saying, "I really, really enjoyed dinner." Get the idea?

The whole time GQ was talking to the old man, an old woman whom I presumed to be his wife was talking to me. I have no idea of what she was saying, but if I had to offer a guess, it would be that she was pleading with me. Her tone of voice and, more importantly, her eyes told me she harbored no hatred toward me, or any of us for that matter. She was gesturing with her hands towards my rifle, and then she would put her hands to her face and repeat what she had just said. I felt such pity for her. I felt half ashamed we had to scare them like we did. The problem is we just don't know what is on the other side of that door when we go in. Today it was women and children and an old man. Tomorrow, it could be four men with assault rifles.

As the old woman kept talking to me, I talked to her in as reassuring tone as I could muster. I took my hand off my rifle to show we meant no harm. GQ was finished questioning the old man but before we left, I told him to tell those folks we were sorry for scaring them. GQ also told them we are trying to make their town safe for them to go about their daily lives. We are here to help, not to harm.

After GQ finished speaking, the old woman shook his hand vigorously and kissed him on the cheek. As I passed, I said, "*Masalamah*", which means "goodbye" to the woman. She, in turn, said the same and kissed me, too. To the old man I said *Ahh-sif* followed by *shuk-ran*. That means "I am sorry" and "Thank you." The man smiled and said something I didn't understand. GQ told me later the man had basically said he understands what we are trying to do for his town, and he isn't mad at us.

I walked away from the morning's operation feeling good. We, once again, were able to do our jobs and left a good impression upon the people we dealt with. It is easy to just kick in the door and deal angrily with people. It takes a little more compassion and professionalism to do our jobs and be nice about it. Unfortunately, there are units here who do just that, kick in the door and do not consider the ramifications of their actions. How easy it is to be unkind to people! It takes a special person to do what we do, for as long as we have done it, without falling into the great abyss of cruelty and intolerance.

It is easy to just kick in the door and deal angrily with people. It takes a little more compassion and professionalism to do our jobs and be nice about it.

Jason Adams
Camp Cooke, Iraq

Notice
10/12/03

Training

Deployment
3/1/04

Home leave
9/26-10/14/04

Back Home
3/19/05

Snow Day

Today is December 11th

This morning, as I slept in my little spot on the floor, I was awakened by the sound of people in the hallway. I like to sleep on the floor in nothing but my sleeping bag. All the other guys have cots, but I gave mine up for GQ. I don't mind as the hard floor is better on my back than a cot anyway. I looked at my watch and decided I might as well get up as we had a patrol coming up.

I walked into the TOC room to find a bunch of guys I didn't know standing around. Apparently, our main TOC back at Camp Cooke had lost communications with us, and they sent two Bradleys up to check on us. As it turns out, the problem wasn't with us, but the main TOC. But, until we got the radio problem figured out, we couldn't go on patrol. In plain English, this meant I could go back to bed. There is not a kid alive anywhere on the first snow day of the school year who is happier than a soldier who gets to sleep for another half hour. We finally were able to reestablish communications with our main TOC, and we left the city about an hour later and headed back to our trailers for a hot shower, a real toilet, and some Burger King.

Jason Adams
Camp Cooke, Iraq

Notice 10/12/03   Training   Deployment 3/1/04   Home leave 9/26-10/14/04   Back Home 3/19/05

Circle of Life

Today is December 13th

The last 24 hours have seen a myriad of events. Yesterday, we once again made the trek up to our new home and settled in for another day of boredom peppered with our regular patrol schedule.

The city we are working in has what I would call unreliable electrical service. The police station we call home has a generator, but we have to provide the JP 8 fuel for it. JP 8 is a fancy name for diesel fuel. Another piece of evidence that our unit is constantly screwed by the system is the fact we only have eight or so five-gallon cans with which to transport fuel.

When the city power is up and running, that number of cans is more than adequate. Unfortunately, sometimes the city power is off more than it is on. This then presents a unique problem. We soon find ourselves running low on gas. When this happens, we have to make a flying trip back to the fuel point at Camp Cooke in order to fill up the cans. We have made the trip several times now, and we have the time down to less than 18 minutes one-way. Not too bad, if I do say!

When we pulled into town, we checked the generator and found it to be on empty. We filled the generator, but only left us with five gallons of fuel for the entire day. We decided to make another trip to Camp Cooke for some fuel. The problem is, Third Platoon takes the empty cans with them and we bring up full ones. But, when you are only dealing with eight cans, sometimes that isn't enough. So that is how our day started, making a fuel run.

Around 1600 hours, as we were preparing for our next patrol, the police truck pulled into the compound. SPC Wallenfeldt came in from his machine gun post on the balcony and told me the police were motioning for us to come down to the truck. SPC Wallenfeldt said, "Dude, they got a body in the back of the truck!"

I didn't want to make this into a spectator thing, so I quietly told Ben and SFC Hess. As we put on our body armor to head downstairs, word of the unexpected event ran rampant through the second floor of the cop shop. Soon, there were 10 guys standing around the back of the little Toyota pickup staring at the gruesome remains of a man who had been shot twice in the head. In order to dispense with the obvious, suffice it to say that, yes.... it was messy.

It has been said dead men don't talk. True, but they can yield clues as to events surrounding their death. As most of the guys were stuck dumb at the grisly sight in the back of that truck, I found myself looking at the bigger picture. Ben, always the detective, was doing the same thing. The man, a mid- to late 40s male, had been shot twice in the head. Two entrance wounds could be seen, one in his forehead, the other right above his right eye. I could not see any powder burns on his skin surrounding the entrance wound, which led me to believe the bullets may not have been fired point-blank. Two exit wounds could be seen in the back of the man's head, both of them level with the entrance wounds. The man's wallet, as well as his shoes, was gone. His feet were covered in mud. The rest of his clothes were still on him, and I noticed both his belt, and his pants were pretty nice. Most folks in this town don't dress that nice, leading me to wonder if he wasn't from around here.

As we rolled the man back over, his shirt raised up, revealing his torso. I noticed post-mortem lividity had not yet set in; in addition, neither had rigor mortis. The guy hadn't been dead very long. While we were taking pictures for the forthcoming reports, we tried to question the policemen who had found the man. They said they had found him a few miles outside of town, along a canal. We did not have an interpreter with us, so talking to the men wasn't easy. We told the cops who had found the man to take us back to where they found him. Reluctantly, they agreed.

We drove a few miles northwest of town to a canal road. We turned onto the canal road and went another mile or two and stopped. On the bank of the road by a little patch of scrub brush, we could see a large blood stain. In the branches of the bush, we could see brain matter and pieces of bone. Up on the shoulder of the road, we found where a car or truck had stopped, backed up, and then spun gravel as it left. We looked around the area for shell casings, but found none. We took pictures of the area and used our GPS for precise grid coordinates, and jotted down some notes. There was no one in the immediate area, so witnesses seemed unlikely, and after that was done, went back to the police station to send up a report to our main TOC.

The best we can figure is whoever did this drove the guy out here, stopped, shot him, and left in a hurry. It is sad but what we did probably constitutes the bulk of the criminal investigation. Back home, forensic teams would have had much to do. Many clues are there, waiting to be found. Plaster casts of the tire tracks, latent prints, an autopsy, maybe even a hair or two might have been found either at the scene or on the man which might have yielded clues as to who is responsible for this murder. Unfortunately, a few classes on criminology in college and a number of episodes of *CSI* make up the bulk of my forensic repertoire. The police force here lacks the training, the time, and most importantly, the funding to undertake any real investigation into the events leading up to this man's final minutes on this earth. His death, while sad, is commonplace here.

The police force here lacks the training, the time and, most importantly, the funding to undertake any real investigation into the events leading up to this mans final minutes on this earth.

But, again I find myself wondering why he had to die. What was it that led to this? A family feud? A vendetta? Cooperating with the coalition? Call me crazy, but I think suicide can safely be ruled out. What led this man to be taken out to the middle of nowhere on this lonely road and gunned down like an animal and left in a ditch? Why must the earth spin this way? Can there be no end to this violence?

What's more is the fact he may not be identified. His death may just end up as a John Doe. Somewhere, a woman could be waiting for her husband to come home from work. I can see it, supper is ready, the kids are home, and everyone is just waiting for Dad to come home. But, he doesn't come home, and he never will for he is no more. He has fallen victim to hate; his life snuffed out like a miner's candle at the end of his shift.

I think what will stay with me for the longest time regarding all this is not the blood or the brain matter in the branches of the bush, nor will it be the thought of another senseless murder. What I will remember from this are his eyes. His eyes were open when he was brought in. His eyes were fixed straight ahead. Not to the left or to the right, but straight and level. The spark of life was gone; all that is left now are the biological parts, retinas, corneas, scleras, and optic nerves. Two cold, hollow and haunting eyes that stare at nothing. Eyes that witnessed so much of what this world has to offer, a child's birth perhaps, maybe his wedding or graduation from college. War and peace, happiness and sorrow; these were all witnessed by this pair of brown eyes. The last thing they saw though was the man who pulled the trigger. The last thing this man saw as he lay in that ditch was the blue sky above, the clouds lazily floating past, and the barrel of a gun thrust in his face. This man holds the answer to his murder. He knows who it was that killed him. But, then again, dead men don't talk.

After the dead man incident was handled, the policemen took the body to Baghdad. We went back into our routine of patrolling. Around midnight, SPC Welgat woke me up from my peaceful slumber in my little spot in the hallway and said, "Hey, wanna deliver a baby?" He couldn't have shocked me more if he ran in the building naked and told me aliens had just landed at the local Piggly Wiggly, and they were asking for me by name. In my groggy stupor, I remember asking him what the hell he was talking about. It turns out the police chief's wife was in labor, and they couldn't find the town doctor. The police chief knew two medics (Nick and I) were staying at the police station. He had sent for us to deliver his child.

I have never delivered a baby. I will be honest. I know how, but the thought of such a thing scares the hell out of me. I don't know why, the doc really doesn't do that much. The doctor is just there to catch, cut, and spank. Over here, in rural areas such as this, obstetrics is a pipe dream. Yes, in Baghdad at the hospitals, they have OB/GYNs, but out here in the sticks you are lucky to find a regular doc, let alone, a specialist. Nick had a look in his eye that said, "C'mon buddy, we can *do* this!" I sat up in my sleeping bag, rubbed my eyes, and made sure I had heard him right. Yeah, I heard right.

As it turns out, the town doctor showed up at the last minute and delivered a healthy set of twins. I am relieved that I am not the one who had to do the job of the doc. I am confident I could have managed a normal delivery. But, I have nightmares about breech presentations, prolapsed cords, and any other problem that might arise. I am an EMT, not a doctor. Still though, I am humbled by the fact the chief thought enough of Nick and me to call for us in his moment of need.

As I went back to sleep I couldn't help but see the irony of the day. One man left this world; two more came to take his place. The cycle of life perpetuates and yet, I find myself wondering to what kind of world did these babies enter? What kind of world awaits them? What kind of people will they be?

One man left this world; two more came to take his place. What kind of world awaits them? What kind of people will they be?

Child psychologists debate about several theories regarding development of the human being. Some believe in the theory of Innate Goodness. This holds kids are basically good, but learn to be bad. Another theory is the *Tabula Rasa*. That means blank slate in Latin. This theory holds kids can be either good or bad, depending on outside circumstances. A third theory is called Original Sin. This holds kids are basically bad. I think scholars kind of missed the point on that last one there, but it is only a theory.

I like to believe in people. I believe folks are basically good, but some of us cannot stand up to the world. They cannot weather the storm, so to speak. Greed, lust, hate, and envy consume some people and cause them to turn evil. If you think about it, how many wars in the history of the world have been started because of one or more of the emotions I have listed? Their power is strong, and as I think about the police chief's new babies, I wonder… will they be able to weather the storm? Will they stand like lighthouses against the gale? Or will they crumble like the little pig's house made of straw. Will they live long prosperous lives? Will they be the ones who finally find a way to bridge the divisions in this world and bring a lasting peace to we who so desperately need it, but have thus far failed to achieve? Or… will they wind up gunned down in a ditch?

In the morning, as we put away our sleeping bags and stowed our gear on the trucks for the trip back to Camp Cooke, the radio crackled to life, letting us know our replacements were en route. The other platoon arrived there a short while later, and we hurriedly loaded onto our trucks for the trip back to our trailers. Going in and out of the gate is always a pain in the neck because of the tight fit as well as having to stop the traffic on the street so we can exit in convoy order.

This particular morning, we took an extra minute or so to get out of the police compound. One of our trucks broke down and was being towed by another truck. That isn't a big deal, it just takes longer to get out the gate, and we can't drive as fast as normal when there is a vehicle in tow. As we left the city limits and picked up speed, I heard from behind me what sounded like a jet airplane crashing into a nitroglycerin factory. The explosion sounded like it was far away, but in fact, was only 100 meters or so behind my truck. As the shock wave passed over our truck, we could tell whatever it was, it was big. We stopped the truck and looked to our rear.

The billowing cloud of smoke rolling out of what had only seconds before been a Humvee made my heart skip. Nick and I jumped back in the truck, and I yelled at the driver to floor it. We raced back to the other truck, and as I jumped out I grabbed my medic bags as Nick and I sprinted back to the wounded. The car bomb had exploded only three feet away from its target, the truck towing the broken one. As in nature, the wounded animal is usually the slowest and thus, is an easy lunch.

The billowing cloud of smoke rolling out of what had only seconds before been a Humvee, made my heart skip.

The two Humvees were now off the road, jackknifed in an L-shaped pattern, with the fuel cell of the front truck already on fire. One of the guys was lying in the grass not too far away with his face blackened from the fire and smoke. He wasn't moving very much as we ran to his side, and at first, I feared he was dying. You can imagine my genuine surprise when he started cussing and trying to get up. He was in pain, and as I looked him over I could see his moustache, as well as his eyebrows, was singed off. We began a hasty assessment as I yelled to the others to bring the rest of the wounded over to us so we could treat them. About this time, the Humvee in front really started burning.

We decided we had better move the injured to a safer place for fear the Humvee may explode.

Though most of the events surrounding this latest car bomb are a blur, I distinctly remember two helicopters coming out of thin air. Two Kiowa Warriors came screaming into our aid. Man, those things can really scoot when the pilot stands on the gas! They patiently circled about 50 feet over our heads to provide much needed security for us during our efforts to get the situation under control. I don't know why, but I remember looking up at the pilot of one of the choppers. He was looking down at us with a look of grim determination on his face. He wore an expression that said, "Don't worry boys, we got your back!" I think I will remember that look for quite some time. Every time we get in a pinch such as that one, those guys in the Kiowas show up and cover us while we try to take care of the wounded and recover the trucks. They are literally, a lifesaver.

We moved the men to a place behind another truck and had them sit down. To my amazement, everyone was alive. I couldn't believe it. I still can't. SSG Wolford was the worst of them, and even he only had a partial thickness burn on his forearm and a couple cuts on his wrist. The fact his face was black and his eyebrows and his moustache were singed off caused me some concern. I was worried he may have sustained some amount of damage to his airway. He said his throat felt like he'd been smoking a cheap cigar, but nothing too bad. Luckily, we had another medic riding with us that day. Nick, the other medic, and I worked through each person who had been in the two trucks and found some cuts and bruises on most guys, but no life threats.

The truck that took the brunt of the blast was totally engulfed in flames by this time and from inside the trucks we heard what sounded like popcorn. Only, Pop Secret this was not. It was rounds from the machine gun exploding. We managed to get all the important equipment out of the truck before it was unsafe to approach. The other truck, the one being towed, will be salvaged and live to see another mission. The entire time the truck was burning, Ben was attacking the fire with the little fire extinguishers we carry in all our trucks. He expended at least two before he realized his efforts were in vain. A gallant effort on his part, however.

Once we had all the cuts and burns taken care of, we loaded SSG Wolford onto an ambulance M113, and they took him to the medical station on Camp Cooke. The rest of the men just piled into the remaining trucks that weren't blown up. Third Platoon was on scene to help us get back underway and after a last sweep of the area, I climbed back into my truck and we left for home.

And so the Reaper was cheated out of his prize yet again. He went away empty-handed… this time. But, in the end, death will claim us all. It is only a matter of time. It may be tomorrow; it may be years from now. But, it is only the obtuse person who will say we were lucky today. No, no, I say. We were not lucky. We were being watched over and protected. As in the case of the rocket landing in our midst and knocking my friends down, but causing no harm, we were again protected.

Tell me, a car loaded with howitzer shells, gasoline, and C-4 explosive detonates right by our trucks and we all walk away virtually unscathed. How is that possible? How is it possible no one was killed? For the life of me, I can't get over it! Someone should have died! I can come but to one conclusion, a hand reached down from heaven and shielded us from evil. Luck is winning a hand at cards. Luck is finding a dollar on the sidewalk. In a game where the stakes are this high and the loser has seen his last sunrise, there can be no luck.

Tell me, a car loaded with howitzer shells, gasoline, and C-4 explosive detonates right by our trucks, and we all walk away virtually unscathed. How is that possible?

All we have are the prayers from faithful people the world over to help us. Indeed, when thousands whisper our names on bended knee and ask we be delivered from this evil that surrounds us, God listens. The evidence, to me, is everywhere. It is clear, it is irrefutable and, at the same time, it is perfect. Perfect because I get letters from all over that say the same thing; "You are always in our prayers." Because of this war, people are praying. I know several people who have started going to church again. God works in mysterious ways, we are told. Humans are pretty thickheaded, and sometimes I think it takes a war to get people back into the habit of talking to the big man upstairs. If that is the case, then so be it. The end, in my mind, justifies the means

Tonight finds me in the relative safety of my trailer, lying in bed reading from Homer and listening to Schubert. I think about the day's events. I said a prayer thanking God for sparing my friends yet again. Regardless of the events of the past day, I am confident we can go forth and do our jobs. But, I cannot help but wonder, What will tomorrow bring?

Jason Adams
Camp Cooke, Iraq

Notice
10/12/03
Training
Deployment
3/1/04
Home leave
9/26-10/14/04
Back Home
3/19/05

Christmas Walk

Today is December 19th

As we rolled out the gate yesterday morning, I was already scolding myself for not having packed warmer clothes. It was one of those mornings where you could just tell it wasn't going to get much warmer out. The sky loomed dark with ominous clouds and a hint of rain was in the air. The locals here do not have furnaces in their homes and many build fires outside in order to warm themselves up. The smoke from these fires hung lazily in the air and did not dissipate like usual. I wouldn't have been all that surprised if it would have begun snowing. It was that cold.

Funny, I never pictured myself freezing my tail off in Iraq. I was prepared for the hot temps in the summer, but this cold weather has really surprised me. To put it in perspective, let me say this, true, we have heaters in our Humvees, but the top of the truck is open to accommodate the gunner. So, imagine driving down I-80 in near freezing weather in a convertible. That is pretty much how we ride. When it rains, we all get wet. When it is cold, we all freeze.

I closed my last letter with the musing regarding what tomorrow would bring. That question was answered about 20 minutes after we left the gate. As we turned onto the road that would lead us to our little police station, we passed the burned-out buildings that once served as Iraqi army barracks. From this point onward, we never know what to expect. We were escorting two dump trucks loaded with sand, as well as a heavy equipment transport. They were integrated into our convoy so there was a Humvee in between each truck.

I will get back to the trucks in a bit. Let me just clarify something: convoy intervals. When we drive, we try to keep a certain distance in between each truck. This is a defensive maneuver and it works when done right. Unfortunately, the dump truck dudes didn't feel like taking part in our little defensive efforts. In essence, they were tailgating us. I do not know about all of you, but I don't like having a dump truck riding my bumper as I go down the road.

We couldn't call them on the radio and tell them to back off since they didn't have radios in their trucks. All we could do was grin and bear it, as they say. As we passed the burned-out barracks, we could see two M1 Abrams tanks coming at us. That folks, is a pretty sight– I do not care who you are. Usually, we run right down the center of the road. Oncoming traffic just has to pull to the side and let us pass. It is not that we are some type of arrogant road hogs, this method of driving, like the intervals between vehicles, is a defensive measure.

As the tanks approached us, all the vehicles in my convoy veered to the right side to give the tanks plenty of room. The first tank had just cleared the trailer we were towing when it happened– a bright flash of light, a thunderous explosion followed by the sound of razor sharp pieces of steel hitting the side of our truck. The blast made our truck lurch to the right pretty hard and, **For a moment, time stopped. It was as if I was seeing the world through slow motion.** for a moment, time stopped. It was as if I was seeing the world through slow motion. Then the initial shock wore off, and my mind jumped into hyperdrive.

We had been hit with an IED, and buddy, it was a big one. Immediately after the explosion, during that moment of shock, the cab filled with black smoke and bits of insulation from the roof were flying everywhere. In my mouth, in my eyes, in my ears…everywhere! It was terrible! I remember yelling at the driver to stand on the gas. Nick was yelling at Bill, our gunner, making sure he was okay. Thank God, he was sitting down when it went off; he was unscathed, as were we all.

Our truck, however, was not. Seth, my driver said, "Hey, I think we got some flat tires." "Yeah," I replied, "That figures." I radioed up a status report telling my platoon sergeant we had hit an IED, the truck was damaged, but we were all okay. To say the truck was damaged does not fully give the reader an idea as to the extent of the damage these roadside bombs can inflict. Read the papers! These things account for a large number of casualties, not to mention equipment loss.

We had indeed sustained no less than three flat tires, a punctured gas tank, multiple hits on the driver's side of the truck, and many smaller fragments had gone through our trailer. There are three holes in the back of my truck I can almost fit my fist through. One piece of shrapnel hit right under the driver's window. The door, a solid sheet of armored steel, no less than one-half of an inch thick, is now sporting a nice dent. Both side windows are peppered with shrapnel marks, and our hood has a few holes in it as well. To be quite frank…we were darned lucky. If those tanks hadn't been coming, we would have been right smack in the middle of the road, i.e., closer to the bomb.

Back to the dump trucks. As soon as the sound of the explosion reached the front truck, the driver tried to execute a "J" turn in the middle of the road in order to come to our aid. It is not an easy maneuver in a regular car, let alone a four-wheel drive truck that weighs over five tons. He almost pulled it off though, that is until the dump truck that had been following too close T-boned him. Yep, that's right! The dump truck was riding his bumper, and in the heat of the moment, the driver of the Humvee forgot that important point, slammed on the brakes, and yanked the steering wheel to the left. The driver of the dump truck locked up his brakes in order to avoid hitting him, but he was too late. The bumper of the dump truck hit the rear fender of the Humvee right behind the left rear passenger door and caved in the side of the hummer. No one was hurt and the truck was not totaled, but it could have been much worse.

Once they saw we were still driving, they turned back around and headed for the police station. En route, we started smelling smoke, like rubber burning. We stopped to assess the situation, and we noticed the two tires on the driver's side of the truck were flat as was the left tire on the trailer we were towing. I wasn't about to stop the convoy just to change a trailer tire, so we decided to just limp the trailer the last couple miles into town.

Soon thereafter, I noticed the engine seemed to be struggling. I asked Seth if the engine was loosing power. "Yes," he replied. "I got 'er to the floor and 15 miles per hour is all she's got." "Pull the shifter into Low 2," I told him. "It is," he said. I began to wonder if the shrapnel had hurt the engine somehow. But, we could see the west side of town by this time, so I said, "What the hell, we can always get another truck, keep going!"

When we pulled into the police station, what we discovered was quite funny. The engine was fine. What was causing the engine to struggle was the fact we had been dragging the trailer for at least the last couple miles. The tire had completely been shredded by the blast, and we had been running on the rim. The rim finally stopped turning, slowly grinding the rim down to a nub.

The rim was beyond trashed. So much so that the bearing hub on the axle had a flat spot ground into it.

We spent the rest of the morning fixing our truck back up the best we could to get it back to Camp Cooke this morning. We had to take apart the axle hub and strip the brakes out of there in order for the spindle to turn again. The best part was the fact a piece of shrapnel had hit one of the lug nuts just so that it rendered it mushroomed and the lug wrench would not fit on it. Thus, we couldn't change the tire. Talk about a one in a million shot!

Luckily, the wheel studs were the screw-in type rather than the press fit types. The threads on these are left-handed, so we were able to just pull the whole stud and lug nut at the same time. It took some beating and a pair of big vise grips, but we managed. I thought we might be able to stop the leak in the gas tank as well. I found a self-taping sheet metal screw with a rubber grommet under the head. I thought this might do the trick, but just to be sure, I put some RTV sealant on the screw before screwing it into the hole in the poly-tank.

It didn't work, in fact it leaked more. We wound up placing a bucket under the drip and we just had to go out and empty the fuel back into the tank every few hours. But, in the end, we all lived, I still have all my fingers and toes, and we were able to drive the truck back to Camp Cooke with no further problems. Once again, luck was on our side. Death was cheated, and its angel went away empty-handed once more.

Once again, luck was on our side. Death was cheated, and its angel went away empty-handed once more.

Once our tires were changed, we went into the police station to prepare for the day's patrols. Ben was making up the guard roster, and SFC Hess was telling SSG Glisan what he wanted in regard to the patrol schedule. I noticed on one of the doors were a bunch of white things with people's names written on them. Upon closer inspection, I realized what they were: Panty liners! What a hoot!

You all have seen it in gas stations back home. Around Halloween, they have those pumpkins you can purchase for a buck, write your name on them, and the attendant will tape it up on the wall of the store in a conspicuous location for all to see. It seems someone had sent a care package over here and thought to include feminine hygiene products. Since our unit is made up of all men, we really didn't have any use for them (I hope). So, in the spirit of the holidays, we decided to decorate our police station. We have a single strand of garland, some paper snowflakes that some school kids somewhere made for us and...a door covered with panty liners with all of our names written on them.

The rest of our time in the police station passed uneventfully, and we returned back here to Camp Cooke this morning.

Since it is only a few days until Christmas, some of the guys in my platoon decided it might be fun to do a Secret Santa gift exchange. We drew names the other day and set a $20 limit for the gifts. Christmas day, wherever it finds us, we will exchange the gifts. SPC Rathjen and I decided to hit the PX today and try to find something for our presents. It is hard to find a decent Christmas gift at a forward area army PX, but I think I managed okay. The guy I have to buy for has a great sense of humor so I hope he gets the joke when he opens up his present and finds a turquoise thong.

Well, that isn't all I got for him, I mean we aren't total white trash over here! I just thought a little humor might help offset the feeling of loneliness we all will succumb to on Christmas. I won't tell you what else I bought for him. That is my little secret.

While shopping, Ralphie and I came across a marble chess set. The pieces are handcarved alabaster and onyx, but the board itself is a beautiful brown and white marble. The entire set is enclosed in a red velvet carrying case. It is quite beautiful. I mentioned to Ralphie that GQ, our interpreter, might like something like this. Ralphie agreed, and although it was rather pricey, we figured if we all pitched in a few bucks, we could get it for him. GQ loves to play chess, and I figure someday he can teach his children to play chess on this board. When he does, he can think of us farm boys and the friends we forever shall remain. I hope those memories, for him, are happy.

I haven't really written that much about GQ. GQ has been working with us for awhile now and has quickly become just one of the guys. He is 25 years old, is married, and his wife is pregnant with their first child. Both he and his wife are mechanical engineers. He gets the name GQ from the magazine of the same title. He always dresses preppy and his hairstyle looks like something Brad Pitt would have. He is a really down-to-earth guy. His English is impeccable. In addition, his accent is rather small, and he understands a lot of our slang words.

The other day, he showed up for work dressed up as usual, but today he was sporting blond highlights in his hair. His hair wasn't gaudy or anything like that, just a break from the norm. I told him he looked like a leopard. Then we all started calling him "*dudeckie*." That means homo in Arabic. He just shook his head and said, "Shut up already!"

Some moron in the upper levels of command around here thought letting civilian cars on post was too risky. Never mind they get thoroughly searched prior to being admitted! So, with a stroke of the pen, the interpreter's cars are not allowed here anymore. I still see some civilian trucks here occasionally, but they are mostly workers who work on post. This presents a special hardship for our staff of interpreters. They can't drive here. They have to take taxis from their homes and pay for them out of their own pockets.

Today as I drove GQ to the gate so he could hail a cab, I asked him how much it cost him to get home. "Five bucks," he told me. That means to get to and from work, he has to spend $10. Interpreters get paid around $600 a month. Do the math. I wonder how many folks at home would still work at a place where half of their pay went toward getting to and from their jobs. Today, I tried to give him some money out of my own pocket to help alleviate the financial burden of using taxicabs, but GQ wouldn't hear of it. I feel bad for him, but what can I do? I cannot change policy set by someone high up in the chain of command. Perhaps there is a good reason for their decision to limit the number of cars on post, but in the process they are making life harder for the interpreters. If we lose them, we will be up that well known tributary without a paddle.

After I dropped GQ off at the gate, I came back to the barracks and grabbed the rest of the guys from my team and headed to the motor pool to fix my truck. Well, back up. The mechanics were doing that. I had to get another truck switched over to use in the event they did not get my truck done in time. Luckily though, we got our spare truck mission ready, and the mechanics finished mine. So, at the end of the day, we were once again ahead of the game as far as mission-ready trucks go. I had to help SSG Gade finish installing a new gas tank, as well as lend a second set of hands as we put the drive shaft back on. We finished working around 1700 hours. Just in time for chow!

As I worked in the motor pool trying to get my truck fixed back up, I realized something. Today is my ETS date. That means, had I not been sent over here, I would be eligible to get out of the army. What a kick in the pants.

Christmas is fast approaching. With that, there are tons upon tons of letters and packages streaming into our post office here on Camp Cooke. One night last week I received no less than five boxes! Five! All of them filled with goodies and music. The music is great. Word has gotten out regarding my musical tastes, and the folks back home have really come through for me. The food on the other hand is more than I could possibly eat, so I take it up to the police station with us and we munch on it there. That way, everybody can have some.

As far as mail goes, well, I can't keep up. I am supposed to get 24 hours off in between shifts, but it always seems to wind up being more like 20 or less. Bottom line is this: I don't have time to write to everyone who has sent me a card or a letter. So let me do it this way: Thank you to all of you who have so kindly thought

Thank you to all of you who have so kindly thought of us soldiers over here. Being alone for the holidays is easier when you know you are at least remembered.

of us soldiers over here. The fact you have taken time out of your hectic lives to sit down and send a card to a person whom you may or may not know really means something to us. You don't have to do it, we know. But, because you do take the time to let us know we are thought of and prayed for is truly one of the joys of the season. Being alone for the holidays is easier when you know you are at least remembered.

Walking through the PX anymore is almost depressing. There is holiday stuff everywhere you look. Wrapping paper, bows, and Christmas music, they even have little Charlie Brown Christmas trees! The part that is hardest for me is the music. Back home, around the middle of November, I start to practice the Christmas music so that come December, I am ready. My family is probably so sick of "O Holy Night" they could puke. Anyway, the reason I practice so much is that on Christmas day I like to go out to the Health Center and play for the folks out there. It always saddens me to think there are people right in my own back yard who have no one to be with on Christmas.

I have many buddies out at the health center, and they seem to enjoy listening to me try to crank out "God Rest Ye Merry Gentleman" on their old baby grand. Seeing them smile is payment enough for me. When I am done playing, they all clap and cheer at my efforts. Seeing them so happy is almost an emotional overload for me. I find myself torn between crying at the sheer beauty of it or running up and hugging everyone of them. Usually, I just nonchalantly wipe my eyes and jump into a fiery rendition of "Rudolph the Red Nosed Reindeer."

This year though, there won't be any piano for me. There will be no time spent with my buddies out at the health center. There will be no Christmas tree, no fossilized fruitcake or eggnog. When my kids start thrashing the wrapping paper on Christmas morning, Steph will be the only one to see it. I hope she videotapes it for me. This will be the first Christmas in my life I have not been able to get home.

Here, when I hear "Jingle Bells" or "Silent Night," a wave of sadness washes over me. I have many things I should be rejoicing over, but I tend to focus on the negative aspects of the surroundings in which I currently find myself. For the most part, I am happy. I am content in knowing my efforts here are but a small payment for the freedom I enjoy back home. I know many before me have spent Christmas in much worse surroundings than those in which I find myself now. But, I don't think the surroundings have much to do with my being sad. I could be in a foxhole and be just as sad. Not being home at Christmas time is the same, no matter where you are. One thing is for sure though– I won't be hearing "Silent Night" come over any loud speakers here on Christmas Eve, that's for sure!

The reason I made that last statement is because right by the police station where we stay is a mosque. Five times a day the Imam's voice comes over the speakers singing prayers. There are three mosques up where we are and the Imam at the one closest to us is by far the best vocalist. Not exactly Domingo, but a tenor nonetheless. He can actually sing pretty well.

I've often said I would love to get a hold of the microphone one of these days. Can you imagine the look of utter shock on the people's faces when, instead of the call to prayer, all they hear is me singing Charlie Daniel's "Devil went down to Georgia?" Alternately, can you imagine if all the churches back home had loudspeakers mounted in their belfry? Can you imagine the ACLU freaking out if the pastors started broadcasting the Sunday sermons over them for all to hear? Whoa buddy, that wouldn't be pretty.

Nonetheless, there is one Christmas tradition I can still indulge in. On Christmas Eve for the last few years, I have taken a walk by myself. Sometimes, I just walk around the block, other times I have walked much farther. It depends mainly on how cold it is. It is just a time when I can be by myself and reflect back upon the past year, my accomplishments, my failures, my abilities, as well as my inabilities are all brought to mind as I walk. I sometimes hum Christmas carols to myself and look up at the stars or, if it happens to be snowing, just soak up the peacefulness with which the snowflakes fall.

I contemplate my existence on this earth and then I pray. I thank God for all I have and all I am. I thank Him for sending Jesus to us. I pray for peace, not only for my family, but for all of us. I think about all the people throughout the world who are homeless or hungry on this night. I think about all the little children who dream, not of Christmas trees laden with presents, but of a hot meal and a warm bed. These thoughts weigh upon my mind as I walk, and I realize no matter how bad things get for me, there is always someone who looks at me and wishes they were me.

I realize no matter how bad things get for me, there is always someone who looks at me and wishes they were me.

As I walk, I take in all the peace and solitude I feel from walking by myself late on a winter's night. It is really quite beautiful. Sooner or later, I start to get cold and I turn for home. When I get there and I see the lights of the Christmas tree softly lighting the front window and the smoke lazily drifting up from our chimney, I say one last prayer. Everything is perfect. My family is safe and sound, the bills are paid for the month, the fridge is chock-full of holiday casseroles and other goodies, and in the morning we will go to church together. What more could any human want?

This year will find me walking around Camp Cooke with an M16 slung on my back. It will find me praying for peace more than ever. There will be no snow, but I am betting at least it will be cold. There won't be any Christmas tree lighting my window upon my return, but nevertheless, it will be okay. All of us here will wrestle with our emotions as the holidays pass. Each of us, in our own way, will try to find ways to take our minds off which saddens us all. We are alone on Christmas.

For some, this task will not be easy. For others, it will not be that bad. For me though, I already feel it. I will get by. I will get by because I know it is just another day that must pass for me to finally come home. Each morning I wake is one less I must spend here. If I focus on this simple truth, the separation from all I love is, at least, bearable.

Jason Adams
Camp Cooke, Iraq

Christmas

Today is Christmas, 2004

Today finds the men of Foxtrot Battery hard at it again: No rest for the weary! My platoon has most of the day off, but Third Platoon is still working, as are the mechanics. We managed to get back to our trailers this morning around 0300 hours or so. I had to stop by the PX, which thankfully, is open 24 hours, to do my typical last-minute holiday shopping. I don't know why this always happens to me! Every year, it seems I find myself wandering around Wally World looking for that last-minute gift. I make a list every year, but I always forget somebody, even in Iraq, some things don't change.

My mission to the PX had a dual purpose though. I had to get some Nyquil. Yep, imagine that! I am sick on Christmas. There are about three or four of us that are sicker than dogs. It is always the same, coughing, stuffy head, aches, fever…the whole shebang. As if things couldn't suck any more! I have to go and get the flu! I just can't win.

At least I could sleep though. Nyquil always does the trick for me. It tastes really bad, like a shot of mint-flavored Karo syrup with a hit of rotgut whiskey added for extra misery, but I slept like a baby. Another trick I have learned to rely on when sick is Vicks VapoRub. My mom always swore by "the Vicks," as she would call it. I looked all over the shelves of self-remedy cold cures, but to my dismay, AAFES PX does not put as much stock in the stuff as my mom used to.

So not finding any, I did what any resourceful type soldier would do. I improvised and used Ultra Strength BENGAY. Okay, yeah I admit, not exactly the use that was intended. Using BENGAY in lieu of Vicks VapoRub is akin to using Preparation H instead of Carmex, but I was miserable. People have been known to do some rather strange things to themselves in order to alleviate ailments. My chest felt like it was on fire, and the smell emanating from me was slightly reminiscent of a high school locker room, but at least I could breathe.

As the first rays of light peeked through my window this morning, I could already see it was going to be a nasty day. As I walked over to the bathroom trailer for a shower, it started to rain. The temp hovered around 40 and the sun hasn't shone itself thus far either. As I stepped onto the front steps of my trailer, I thought to myself, "Merry Christmas, Sarge." After my shower, I debated going to Christmas dinner. Since I couldn't taste anything anyway, I opted to go back to bed. I really needed the rest, plus I didn't feel like listening to all the Ho-Ho hoopla anyway.

Our platoon's gift exchange took place at 1500 hours in an empty room in one of our trailers. We all drew names, went to the PX with a set $20 limit and did our best to find the perfect gift for the person whose name we drew. Even in my miserable condition, I confess, I had fun. The manner in which many of the presents were wrapped was hilarious in itself. One package was wrapped in a pair of G.I. underwear. Best part was they were not new either! Another present was securely wrapped in duct tape and took a few minutes to open.

A few guys were wearing Santa hats, but the top prize for that had to go to Ben. Someone made him a camouflage Santa hat, complete with rank! Presents ranged from DVDs and CDs, to panties and a set of DCUs for children that went to SPC Paul Calhoun. He is probably the smallest guy in our unit and is constantly the butt of short guy jokes. The funniest part of his present was the fact they actually fit him! GQ, our interpreter, sent a bagful of presents for us as well. We were all pretty humbled as we opened his gifts and realized he most likely spent half his paycheck on all us. SFC Hess got a box of handmade cigars, which alone was probably 50 bucks! I was given a hand-painted vase with a picture of GQ and his wife on their wedding day stuffed inside.

As we laughed and carried on regarding the humorous nature of many of the gifts, I thought about home. Right now, my girls are probably urging Steph to get up and go open presents. Buddy, my dog, is probably sniffing at his yearly rawhide bone, wondering how to unwrap it. Steph is sitting on the couch with the camcorder capturing these special moments for me to see upon my return. I am sure at this moment, albeit separated by borders and time zones, we share the same emotion– loneliness mixed with a longing to be reunited. Don't worry, babe! The days dwindle with each sunset.

As we sat and laughed with each other, I found myself wondering how much of this laughter was just a weak façade to hide the loneliness all of us feel. I feel it. I would be a liar if I told you otherwise, and I certainly don't consider anyone weak because they feel it too. Emotions manifest themselves in a variety of ways, and sometimes, I think we hide sadness with forced joviality. We finished up with the gifts, wished each other a Merry Christmas, and retired to our trailers.

At this moment, I am just waiting for 2000 hours to roll around. At that time, it will be 1100 hours back home and my family will be gathered over at Mom and Dad's for Christmas dinner. We are going to try to link up on Yahoo! messenger so we can talk. I get such a kick out of my grandma on the web cam. The first time she saw it, she couldn't believe it was really me! She kept saying to my mom, "Is that really Jason?" Mom assured her it was, to which she replied, "That's amazing! How do they do that?" Mom is as dumbfounded with technology these days as I am and the best answer we can collectively come up with is Ancient Chinese Secret.

As far as missions go, time is flying. We have altered our shifts to allow more time here at Camp Cooke. We still put in the same number of man-hours, but we have worked it out so everyone is happy. The police station we now reside in part of the time is progressing nicely. We have hired some locals to fill up sandbags, and we now have reenforced overhead cover for our gun positions. I admit, however, the overhead cover is mainly to keep the rain off the guys manning the guns.

The other day, Ben and I spent the morning arranging our supply room to be more "user-friendly." We organized all the snacks according to what they were, plus, we hauled in another set of shelves to help hold all the junk people have so graciously sent to us. We now have a personal hygiene shelf, a cold remedy shelf, a ramen noodle shelf and, among other things, a microwave popcorn shelf. Being the moronic neat freak I am, I periodically went in to check on the status of the shelves. Every time I went in there, I found things moved around. It drove me nuts putting things back in their appointed spot until I realized as soon as I left the room, some ornery person went in and purposely messed things up, just to irk me! Yeah, it worked. Finally, feeling increasingly sick, I gave up and decided to just go find my bunk and catch some sleep.

Around 0200 hours, our relief showed up, and we began to pack our trucks for the return trip to our trailers. As we carried the machine guns down to the waiting trucks, it felt odd wishing the other men Merry Christmas. I mean, there I was, with a 50-caliber machine gun in my hands and I was wishing someone Merry Christmas. It just doesn't seem to fit. Nevertheless, we are not experiencing anything countless men before us didn't go through.

I am reminded of the books I have at home depicting Christmas in World War I, World War II and other wars. We have it made. I have a warm bed awaiting me as well as some hot coffee. I know I will not have to watch Christmas pass from the bottom of a trench or a foxhole. There is always something to be thankful for. Sometimes, it is just hard to see it.

The holiday did not pass without its share of problems. Christmas Eve is usually a time of preparations, caroling, wrapping presents, and for me, going to midnight Mass. Not here. No, Christmas Eve, 2004, found me watching two more of my buddies being carried to a waiting Medivac helicopter.

Christmas Eve, 2004, found me watching two more of my buddies being carried to a waiting Medivac helicopter.

The road we travel is probably more dangerous than the road we used to patrol in Baghdad. Over the last couple weeks, we have been hit with multiple IEDs as well as a car bomb. Yesterday, to help us celebrate Christmas, the insurgents planted another bomb along our patrol route. This one was hands down, the biggest one I have seen. We have been hit with some rather large IEDs, but I have never seen one punch through the sides of our armored doors.

The truck it hit was the one in which my commander was riding. Two guys were hurt. They will both be okay, but the bottom line is the fact our armor did not stop the shrapnel. See the problem is this, the road that leads to the police station where we stay is not patrolled. The only trucks that roll up and down it are ours, for the most part anyway. And, that only happens every so often as we go to and from our shifts at the police station. So, what that means is the insurgents have nothing but time to plant all the IEDs they want. They even have time to bury them in the ground, thus making them next to impossible to spot. Why no one patrols this particular road is beyond me, but we had better figure something out soon. One of these days our luck is going to run out.

According to the papers, attacks have been increasing here over the last few days. Wow, newsflash! Hey, CNN…it is Christmas! The elections are only a few weeks away! It doesn't take a rocket scientist to have seen this coming. The same thing happened during Easter. Even though this rise in attacks does not surprise me, it still makes me mad. So mad that sometimes, I find myself thinking the best thing for this country is a nuclear warhead. But, just as that thought enters my head, a soft voice comes out of nowhere saying, "Jason, you know that isn't the way." This soft rebuke kicks me back into a logical thought process, and I concede annihilation is not the best idea.

As mad as I get regarding events here, I know there are good people here. GQ, Jaguar, Snake, and all of the other interpreters who gallantly put their lives, as well as the lives of their families, into jeopardy everytime they go out with us to patrol. We owe them nothing less than our best efforts to turn this country into a model society for the rest of the Middle East to follow.

Jason Adams
Camp Cooke, Iraq

DD4

Today is December 26th

The other day, *The Star and Stripes* ran a political cartoon that caught my attention. The cartoon depicted and American soldier standing in front of Donald Rumsfeld dressed as Santa Claus. The American soldier was saying, "All I want is a little armor and to know how long until my tour ends." To which Rumsfeld replied, "Gimme, gimme, gimme! You kids are so spoiled these days!"

Enough!! I can see both sides of the point the cartoonist is trying to make. Yes, there are shortages of equipment here. But, the problem is not that there is not enough armor. The problem lies in the fact it is in the wrong hands. The fact there are not enough troops here is also misleading. I admit, I don't have the numbers in front of me, but I am willing to bet my last buck that for every man that patrols outside the wire, there are two who don't. Moreover, we all want to know when we will finally get to go home. There is no point in whining about it.

I wonder what the rest of the world thinks about all the sniveling coming from our ranks these days. We are soldiers. Lest we forget those who came before us served longer in combat zones than we ever will. We will go home when the army (that we volunteered for, I might remind you) says we can go home. To all those who incessantly complain about being here, I say this, Quit crying! Wipe your little noses, dry your eyes, and cowboy up. Act like adults for crying out loud! Every one of us signed the DD4 in our enlistment contracts. For those of us that have no idea what that form is, I am sorry for you. In a nutshell, the form basically says in a time of war, you can be mobilized for the duration of hostilities, plus six months. Wow, I'll bet your recruiter never mentioned that little tidbit of information, did he?

Jason Adams
Camp Cooke, Iraq

Notice
10/12/03

Training

Deployment
3/1/04

Home leave
9/26–10/14/04

Back Home
3/19/05

Happy New Year

Today is December 31st

Well, there certainly won't be any champagne toast tonight here at beautiful Camp Cooke. Hell, it is probably a safe bet I won't even be awake as 2005 comes.

Usually, on New Year's Eve, I break out my custom made "Kiss the Cook" apron and dust off the ol' Betty Crocker cookbooks and prepare New Year's dinner. I am not really sure how it started, but I know for the past few years, on December 31st, all Steph and my friends get together and I cook a fancy dinner. Steph always lovingly reminds me by saying, "Well, it ought to be fancy, it is the only meal of the year that you cook. The rest of the year, I do it." That is not entirely accurate. I make one heck of a frozen pizza!

The meal preparation starts the day before with a trip to the grocery store and usually, I am still cooking when the first guests show up. I don't mind though, I will admit. The accolades and thumbs-up signs that come my way as our guests dig into the meal make the effort worth every dirty measuring cup. In the first few years of marriage, my wife and I liked to go out on New Year's Eve. We hit the usual comedy clubs and casinos like everyone else, but as we had children, this started to seem like a bad example to set for our kids. So we decided to just stay home. Soon, our other friends started to do the same, and I guess somewhere in there I came up with the idea of cooking a nice dinner for everyone.

Like millions of other Americans, I love to cook. Unlike many men, my idea of cooking dinner goes beyond a phone book and a drive to the nearest pizza place. Man, I like to COOK! I mean fancy Martha Stewart type stuff, too! Trouble is, I only cook like this once a year. As far as the rest of the year goes.... well, if I make a dish of green bean casserole, it is a noteworthy event.

At New Year's though, I get into the whole dinning experience. I make the centerpiece for our table and consult my wine guide to know just what kind of wine to serve with the meal I plan. The first year when I came home from

Wally World with a bagful of cloth and some other stuff, Steph said, "What's all that for?" I said, "Well, I got stuff to make the tablecloth and some candles and some berries and leaves to make a nice centerpiece." The rest of the day I was the butt of Martha Stewart jokes. Even the kids were making fun of me, but I persevered and dinner was a big hit. Our friends even complimented me on the table arrangement. High school home economics really paid off!

For the past couple of years, I have made the same main dish for our dinner. Red wine beef burgundy has been such a big hit with the gang that it is ridiculous to suggest I cook anything else. The recipe I use is rather labor intensive, but the dish is nothing short of fantastic. The meat is the most important part, and I spare no expense when buying it. Then, I enlist the assistance of our neighbor "Buckie" in cutting the meat.

Buckie is a retired butcher. He knows more about quality meat than anybody I know. So naturally I call him when I have a beef- or pork-related issue. For the last few years, I have called Buckie around noon on New Year's Eve and begged him to come help me saw up a roast, make the London Broils or make the fillets. I think anymore, on December 31st, he waits by the phone with his cap and coat already on. I can almost see him sitting in his chair watching TV; the phone rings, he looks at his wife and says, "I bet that's Jason!" Sure enough, it's the neighborhood culinary simpleton trying to bail himself out of another bind. Thanks Buckie, I owe you big time.

My wife tells me there will be no dinner this year. I told her to go ahead and have the party, just without the dinner. She said she has talked to everyone and they are okay with the idea of postponing the dinner until I can be there. Steph and I are very fortunate to have the caliber of friends we do. They have been nothing short of inspiring throughout this entire deployment. She says her mom and dad are coming over tonight, and they and the girls are going to play games and order pizza and just stay in. My parents will probably go ballroom dancing somewhere, but will be home before "all those crazy drunks" get out on the road.

As for me, well...this is my New Year's Eve party. Sitting here typing, drinking coffee, and listening to some music. I've got 20 bucks that says I'll be in bed by 10.

listening to some music. Oh yes, I am the quintessential party animal, am I not? To be real honest, there isn't much alternative. Drinking is not allowed here, there are no clubs, our Internet is down right now, and the only guy who can fix it is on leave for two more days. So this is it: Me and J.S. Bach, Freddy Chopin and Juan Valdez and his pet donkey are going to spend the night together. I've got 20 bucks that says I'll be in bed by 10.

Over the last few days, I, along with the rest of the world, have been watching in disbelief as the coverage of the tsunamis in and around Indonesia via the good folks of CNN. We have a TV and satellite dish up at the police station so we have seen pretty much the whole thing. At first, only the news of the quake itself was broadcast. I am not a seismologist or anything like that but, from the news reports, I guess it was a pretty big earthquake; something like 8.9 on the Richter scale, if memory serves me correct. As we sat and watched the scenes come to us on the screen, it soon became apparent the level of catastrophic destruction that the ensuing tsunamis had caused. Then, the news anchors started to talk about the death toll. At first, it wasn't very many; a thousand or so, but that didn't last for long.

The next morning when we turned on the TV again, the toll had climbed to 56,000. But, most of us started to notice the death toll was all they were talking about. All day long, they showed home video footage of the giant waves and finished the clips with the latest numbers of dead. The anchors kept saying how horrible and tragic this quake was, but they said little about the actual quake. After watching for over an hour, I still had no idea of where the epicenter had been, when the quake occurred, all of the affected regions; but I sure knew how many had died. How callous of the media.

The whole media circus reminded me of a Jerry Lewis telethon. I remember watching them as a kid. Every so often, they had a little party to celebrate another monetary milestone. It seemed like the same thing; like they were hoping the numbers of dead would rise to give them more to talk about. Then after they talked about that until they were blue in the face, they found some experts and started asking them if enough was being done insofar as humanitarian efforts.

One of the anchors sounded more like a lawyer cross-examining some serial killer in the trial of the century than she did a reporter. The poor guy couldn't finish a sentence before she cut him off with some irrelevant question like, "So, do you think this will affect the tourism industry of the area?" Geez! Are you that shallow lady? Multiple tsunamis came ashore, thousands are known to be dead, the place is destroyed, and you ask a question like that?

I could feel my brain cells dying from just watching it. Then it hit me. They hadn't mentioned anything remotely regarding Iraq all day. They hadn't so much as mentioned the current number of deaths or anything! It was kind of nice. For the first time in months, car bombs and dead soldiers weren't at the forefront of their broadcasts.

For the first time in months, car bombs and dead soldiers weren't at the forefront of their broadcasts.

One of the commercials caught my attention though. It showed some reporter going on about why they fight to get to the bottom of every story. Their justification? "So you know the truth." Come on! Do you really believe that? Do you really think Americans believe you report the news for our benefit? Are you so imperceptive you think you are providing a valuable service? Does my knowledge of the fact that 56,000 less people are on this earth today, as opposed to yesterday, really do anything in the grand scope of humanity's existence?

News organizations love telling you how many people died. That folks, is what sells papers. They love reporting one-sided, self-serving, and biased reports. Of course that is nothing new. As far back as the 1730s, when J. P. Zenger was producing the *New York Weekly Journal*, bias, axe grinding, and mud slinging have been the status quo in the media. On the flipside of that coin is this thought, if people didn't crave the knowledge of that type of thing, nobody would be reporting it. So who really is the criminal here; the media that reports stuff like that, or, the audience that wants to know. All in all, I guess my biggest gripe is this: If there is a story to be told, then tell it. But for the benefit of all, tell the whole truth in an unbiased way. Is that really so much to ask?

I guess many of you might be asking yourselves, "If this guy hates the news so much, why does he watch it?" Good question. The answer quickly presents itself if you think for a second. This is the Middle East, right? Even though we have satellite television, it is pretty hard to find a channel that is in English. Most of them are French, Italian or Arabic. CNN is in English, but the anchors are all British and sometimes, even they say something I don't quite understand. It is the best we can do.

About a week or so after we started living in the police station, we decided it was necessary to hire someone to clean. Not so much like one would clean their homes, but just someone to sweep up, take out the trash, police up the grounds of the police station, and other small tasks. The problem started with the general condition of the rooms in the police station we were given in which to reside; they were a mess. I mean, bad. They looked like they hadn't been touched in months. While trying to set up shop, run missions, and do everything else an army has to do, cleaning was the least of our worries. So we hired Lenny.

Lenny's real name is Shehab. Somebody nicknamed him Lenny. I am not really sure where that name came from, but it just seems to fit. Lenny is 26 years old and lives near the police station with his sister and her husband. He has no job, no wife, and no car. He has been out of work since he left the army after we invaded in 2003. I'll get back to that part in a bit.

Lenny shows up every day at 0900 hours and immediately takes out all the trash, sweeps out all the rooms, and then goes outside to burn the trash. He even cleaned one of the bathrooms and that, folks, is no small feat. There are four bathrooms on the second floor of the building we are in, and they were all just nasty as could be upon our arrival. The toilets in this country are not like the toilets in our country. Matter of fact, they are not really toilets at all; more like urinals that are mounted flush with the floor. The people just squat down over the hole when nature calls. I really don't understand it! They don't flush like ours either. They all have a faucet mounted on the wall close by and you just dump some water down the hole when you are done doing your business. The stories you have all heard about nobody over here using toilet paper are true as well (that would be the second reason for the close proximity of the faucet to the toilet, I presume). I really don't understand that one, but I won't go into details.

Anyway, the general himself could have ordered me to clean that latrine, and I would have laughed in his face. There is no way, save for a gun in my face, I would have ventured into that little room

The general himself could have ordered me to clean that latrine and I would have laughed in his face.

with the intent of touching anything. One day, not long after Lenny started working for us, I noticed one of the guys coming out of the bathroom. I asked them what in the world they had been doing in there. "What d'ya think? I had to pee," was the reply. I cautiously stuck my head through the door with my T-shirt pulled up over my nose and was amazed to find the place all spic and span! I asked who had the balls to clean it up, and they told me Lenny had taken it upon himself to clean it. The little toilet was as clean as it was the day it was installed! I couldn't believe it! It even smelled clean! Still though, none of us can figure out how to use it for anything other than urinating. For the other task, we have an ammo crate out back with a toilet seat nailed to it.

Lenny works every day from 0900 hours until 1400 hours or so, and we pay him seven dollars a day for his efforts. Seven bucks a day...doesn't seem like much does it? But to him, it is a good paying job, the most money he has ever made. Lenny doesn't speak English and sometimes it is hard to communicate with him, but he understands a surprising number of things considering his level of education. He went to grade school and that is it. He never had the opportunity to go to high school. Still, what he lacks in schooling, he makes up for in work ethic.

One day, he asked GQ if he could go and get a mop. We told him we had a mop around there somewhere; we just had to find it. We did and he set about mopping the entire place. Then he went and bought a floor squeegee and proceeded to squeegee the floor as well. I guess the mop didn't clean the floors to his standards.

Anymore, he is just one of the guys. The shoes he used to wear were about shot, so one of the guys took in their old running shoes and gave to him. We also gave him a Wal-Mart hat someone had sent in a care package, which he now proudly wears everyday. I get a kick out of watching him go about his tasks. It is nothing to hear him humming some song while sweeping the hall-way. He is happy to clean up after a bunch of GIs, and he takes pride in his work. He takes his job pretty seriously though.

One day, we had been cutting some plywood for a set of doors we were making and I grabbed the broom to sweep up the sawdust. Lenny came over and started talking to me and gesturing toward himself and then the broom as if to say, "Hey, that is my job!" I told GQ to tell him to take a break, and I would sweep up this mess. Lenny insisted it was his responsibility to clean, not mine. Confused, I relinquished my hold on the broom, and Lenny went to work. I guess he likes to feel he is needed. Then again, don't we all?

Before Lenny started wearing the Nikes we gave to him, he wore a pair of beat-up sandals. One day, we noticed some pretty decent scars on the metatar-sal areas of his feet. We asked him (through GQ) to tell us what had happened to his feet. And so began a story I will, for the rest of my life, never forget.

In 1995, when he was 17, Lenny was forced to join the Iraqi army. He, unlike all of us, did not volunteer: He didn't have a choice. For nine years, he served as a porter in an artillery battalion. He was in Al-Basrah when the first units of the marines came into Iraq in 2003. He began his story by explaining he did not want to fight with us. He made it clear he had no choice. He said he liked us and he liked America. I got the feeling he was trying to justify to us why he fought against us, as if we were going to hold it against him.

He told us how some of his friends had decided not to fight. It seems a bunch of his buddies told their superiors they intended to surrender as soon as the Americans got there. The Baath party representative that was a part of his battalion got wind of their seditious intentions and, in a manner analogous to the SS of World War II, rounded them up, tied them together, and proceeded to blow their brains out with his pistol; all in full view of the rest of the men. I guess he wanted to send a message to anyone else that was thinking about desertion.

As Lenny told us about this, his facial expression took on a look of melan-choly reflection and he said, "Those were my friends." And so, it became a matter of choosing the lesser of two evils, disobey your orders and die for sure, or take your chances against the Americans. I found myself wondering what choice I would have made under the circumstances. Lenny went on to tell us about the circumstances surrounding the scars on his feet. In the American army, if you screw up bad enough, you might get put in jail. Hell, you can even disobey a direct order in the middle of a combat zone, and the worst they will do to you anymore is give you an Article 15! Whoa buddy, not in the Iraqi army. Discipline in those ranks is swift and equally brutal.

It seems the favorite tool for instilling discipline in Lenny's old unit was a piece of steel cable about one inch in diameter, two feet long with one end frayed. From Lenny's description, I pictured a cat o' nine tails, only made out of steel cable. The people in need of disciplining were made to take off their boots and socks and stand at attention. Then whoever was in charge of administering punishment proceeded to beat them about the ankles and tops of their feet with this piece of cable.

From the looks of Lenny's feet, it was rather effective. If the person resisted, they were held down and the beatings continued. Once the flesh of your feet was thoroughly ripped open, you were let go. Bleeding and unable to walk, you crawled back to your barracks. The next day, you were expected to be at your post. Not a single day for recovery, and I imagine proper medical care of the wounds was not a major concern either. For the life of me, I can't imagine living like that.

Lenny finally escaped from the clutches of the army and made his way back home, where he lives today. He has nothing; nothing to show for his life thus far, save for some scars. He is 26 years old and in the prime years of his life, and yet his eyes have seen more than most of us would ever see in three lifetimes. He has been witness to things most of us pretend don't happen anymore. I wonder how he has managed to retain his sanity throughout his experiences.

Most 26-year-old people I know are busy trying to work their way up the career ladder and pay off some school loans in the process. They busy themselves trying to figure out how to afford that car they want or how they can get a loan for their first house. They go to the mall and spend money like it is nothing. They aren't worried about the money. They have jobs. They will get paid again soon enough. But hearing Lenny tell his story makes me so sad. My heart feels so heavy when I look at him. I wish there was something I could say or do for him that would take away all the pain he has had to deal with. But, I am powerless to do so.

Sometimes at night I think about him. At times, my eyes cloud with tears as I think about Lenny, with his Wal-Mart hat on, singing a song while sweeping out the hallway. And I say a prayer for him. Why was I given the life I have and others have suffered so? I am certainly no better of a person. Why must some suffer while others do not?

Sometimes, in between missions, I just sit and watch him go about cleaning. I see a young guy who is content to clean up after others. I see a young man who has found the best job he has ever had. I see a guy who, at the end of the day, can reach out his hand in the presence of other men and accept his pay

For some in this world, happiness is simply a Wal-Mart hat, an old pair of Nikes, and seven bucks a day.

with pride, without feeling ashamed. I cannot put into words how happy it makes me to think we have been able to bring happiness to yet another human being over here. Indeed, for some in this world, happiness is simply a Wal-Mart hat, an old pair of Nikes, and seven bucks a day.

Happy New Year!

Jason Adams
Camp Cooke, Iraq

Another Life Lost

Today is January 7th

Around mid-afternoon, while most of us were either playing cards or other games to pass the time, a lone police vehicle pulled into the station. Normally, that happens all the time. Today, however, as the truck pulled into the gate, the balcony gunner could see a pair of feet sticking out of the bed of the little truck. It turned out to be another dead body.

Like the last corpse that showed up here, this was a male person who had been murdered. Other than that, the two murders could not have been more different. This man was much younger than the last one, probably mid- to late-20s, and not as well dressed. This man had not been robbed of his shoes and wallet. The first man had been found outside town. This guy was shot only blocks away from the police station. The first man had been shot twice in the head, execution style. This man, today, was straight up gunned down with, if I had to guess, an AK-47 or some other automatic rifle.

To me, it looked as though he had been hit with a burst of automatic fire from whatever weapon it was that killed him. The sight which lay before me was grizzly: The man had been shot at least six times with wounds forming a general straight line from his feet to his head. I could see bullet wounds on his right tibia, his right quadriceps muscle, and his lower right quadrant of his abdominal region. His chest had two holes in it, but the *coup de grace* had to have been the bullet hole in his forehead.

When a gun fires, regardless of the type, there is recoil. When automatic weapons fire, there are multiple recoils. When the bullet exits the barrel, the gas that propels the bullet down the barrel escapes behind the bullet as it leaves the muzzle, thus doing two things: First it makes a "bang." Second, it makes the barrel rise upward. When firing automatic weapons, the recoil drives the muzzle upward until the gun stops firing. This is one of the reasons the army switched from the fully automatic M16A1 to the M16A2.

The M16A2 only fires a three-round burst, allowing the person firing to reacquire their target more quickly. Another reason for this switch of weapon models was the M16A2, instead of the fully automatic M16A1, would go through less ammunition in a firefight. The shot placement on this man's body leads me to believe it was an automatic weapon that had killed him. Secondly, given the prevalence of AK-47 assault rifles over here, it is safe to assume this was the type of weapon responsible.

Having worked on an ambulance crew for awhile and since I have been in a war zone for almost a year now, I have seen my share of dead people. Sadly, it really doesn't bother me all that much. What does still bother me is dealing with the living. The dead are easy to deal with, but the friends and the relatives of the deceased always look at me as if to say, "DO SOME-THING!" Unfortunately, there are times when, try as I might, there isn't a damned thing anyone short of Jesus himself could do.

> **The dead are easy to deal with, but the friends and the relatives of the deceased always look at me as if to say, "DO SOMETHING!"**

One of my worst memories while acting as an EMT came early on in my career. The ink on my EMT license was still damp, I was full of zeal for my job, I was ready to save the world. In essence, I was a naïve rookie.

One night, while lying asleep in bed, my pager went off. It seems there was an emergency out at the health center. The driver of the ambulance, along with another EMT, pulled into the parking lot at same time as I did, and the three of us rushed out to the nursing home on the edge of town.

Once out at the health center, we unloaded the stretcher, our "first-in" bag, and threw the AED on top of the stretcher, just in case. As we went in through the ambulance entrance, a nurse's assistant directed us to the patient's room. We hurriedly pushed the gurney down the hall to the patient's room and upon entering, I could see two other nurse's assistants performing CPR on an older lady lying in her bed. To make a long story short, this was what the textbooks called a "load and go" situation. In other words, put the patient in the rig and go straight to the hospital. Having spent so much time in the acronym laden parallel universe that is the U.S. army, calling this a load and go just doesn't do it for me. So, I came up with an acronym to describe these particular situations. I call them LSDDs, which stands for lights, sirens, and drive dammit!

Unfortunately, there wasn't much more we could do for our patient than what we were already doing. Once in the trauma room, the doctors and nurses scurried about trying, as we had, to revive this woman. Just like us, they were unsuccessful.

As I walked out of Trauma One, tired and sweaty from 15 miles worth of CPR, I came face to face with the relatives of this woman, whom we had tried in vain to save. News travels at near light speed in a small town, and most of these people most likely pulled into the parking lot of the hospital at about the same time we did. As I looked at them, my heart sank. Some of the women were crying, others looked like they were on the verge of doing so. Even the men had tears in their eyes as they tried to console the women. Obviously, this had been a very special person whom was loved very much.

As the doctors told them what they already had deduced, some of them glanced at my partner and me. There was no mistaking who we were. EMT coats on, stethoscopes around our necks and an idling ambulance parked out under the carport for the emergency room entrance. It doesn't take a rocket scientist to realize that it had been we who had brought the lady to the hospital. I felt the need to offer some words of condolences to the grieving people, but what could I say to them? What, the truth? "Yeah, uh...Hi! I am the guy who was powerless to save the life of your loved one, and it is my fault you are crying right now." I couldn't say that, true as it might have been, so I just told them I tried to save a life tonight, but failed. I told them I was sorry for their loss, and then I made a point to shake everyone's hand.

I shared their sorrow, and as I left the emergency room, I was angry with myself for failing, not so much because the elderly woman had died, but because of the pain her death had caused her family. See, that is the hardest part for me, family grief. I know when we are dead, we feel no pain anymore. The living though, they still hurt and anguish over the loss. Seeing that, bothers me.

And so it was today when, after the dead man arrived, his family showed up. At first, it was only two people, the brother of the murdered man and a witness to the murder. The dead man's brother could hardly walk; he was so shaken with grief. A man of perhaps 20 years of age, he sat down on the curb of the police station and just bawled. Burying his head in his hands, and rocking back and forth, he sobbed.

As the police officers ushered the witness into the police station to make a statement, a large crowd began to form out in front of the gate of the compound. So many people were there that traffic was becoming backed up in the street. Having never seen so many people out in front of the police station, I began to wonder about the deceased man. Who was he? Was he a man of importance, a sheik's son? Why were so many people crowding in front of the police station? More people were still showing up, and by now their numbers had to exceed 100 people. Slowly, like a whisper, a word was repeating in my mind. I tried to ignore it, dismissing it as unlikely, but reason soon got the best of me and the voice in my head became so loud I could not dismiss it any longer. The word? Riot.

Any soldier or police officer that has ever had to deal with crowds will tell you a large crowd can be dangerous, and the potential for catastrophe increases with every person who is added to the crowd. Crowds, especially angry crowds, are dynamic. Fluid like water at times, they constantly change. Seeing the police were preoccupied with the body and the witness, Ben and I decided we had better get some additional men downstairs with us to secure the gate. Soon, there were five guys standing there with our rifles at the low ready. Our fears were unfounded and, as soon as the crowd decided the show was over, they began to disperse on their own.

I turned around and I couldn't help but notice the brother of the dead man still sitting alone on the curb crying. My heart was moved with pity for him, and concluded the right thing to do was to try to comfort him.

I knelt down beside him, put my hand on his shoulder, and said "Asif" or, "I am sorry."

With four men still on the gate and a man on the balcony overlooking the gate, I decided security was adequate. So I walked over to the poor guy sitting on the curb. I knelt down beside him, put my hand on his shoulder, and said "Asif" or, "I am sorry." He raised his head out of his hands, looked at me, and said thank you.

I yelled at the man on the balcony to throw down a bottle of water for the poor guy. One of my buddies brought down a bottle and gave it to the young man, who began to slowly sip the water. Wiping his eyes on his shirtsleeve, he again said thank you. I figured that was about all we could do for him. Besides, he probably just wanted to be alone at the time anyway. I told him I was sorry again and patted him on the shoulder once more and left him with his thoughts. I am rather certain he had plenty to think about.

About this time, more family members arrived. We had tried to find something with which to cover the body, but we live pretty light up here and had nothing. The men who had just come through the gate looked in the back of the truck, saw the horrid remains of their loved one, and instantly began wailing. One older man was clutching his cane with all his might simply to keep his balance as he cried.

At that point in time, I wanted nothing more than to ease their pain. I wanted to find something I could either do or say that would help them. But, what could I do? I couldn't speak to them, and GQ was busy with the police. What if I could have spoken to them? What could I have said? I think the answer here is nothing. Time is the only thing that can help them. The shock of the loss coupled with the gruesome sight in the back of that truck, as well as the violence surrounding the poor man's death, can only be assuaged through time.

Time is a bandage of sorts that can heal both physical as well as mental wounds. Unfortunately, some wounds cut one so deep– that full recovery is not to be found. The sight of those men's family member in the back of that little pickup truck will stay with them forever. Ten eternities could not erase something of that magnitude. In that moment though, these men, whom I had never before met, and I were connected. We were connected because I, too, shared their sorrow. Yes, although I felt only a fraction of the pain they did, we were nevertheless all stricken by what had happened. Even now, as I sit here and type, I am still saddened by what I saw today.

Soon the police came out of the police station, got in the truck, and took off with the body still in the back. I couldn't believe my eyes, however, when the police left. They made absolutely no efforts to either cover the body, nor did they even so much as close the tailgate of the truck! They simply hopped in the truck and tore out the gate with the body just bouncing around as if it were a bale of hay. How utterly disrespectful! No, I think disgusting would be better terminology.

And so ends another day up here in Al-Tarmiyah. I sit in the hallway by my bunk and write these words by the light of a chem stick. Usually, I just make a few notes in my notebook and then sit down at my laptop when I get time. Tonight however, I am compelled to write down my thoughts longhand on a steno pad. Too many thoughts and emotions are running through my head right now. To forsake writing at this moment would be unfair to the people whose lives were damaged today. For in my procrastination, some of what needs to be said would be lost forever.

Twice now, in the short time we have been here, this small town has seen murder. Grotesque as it is, evil has shown its face once again and claimed another victim. But, why must it be? Why must humanity be subjected to such violence, when in every one of us lives the seed of goodness? Sometimes, I find myself thinking what both Iraq, as well as the rest of the world, really needs is that which always seems just out of reach. But, like I have said a thousand times, peace will only come through mutual understanding and love. How easy it is to pick up a gun and kill that which troubles you! I have no idea of the circumstances surrounding the murder of that man today. I really don't care. The bottom line is this, is picking up a machine gun and blowing someone away ever really the right answer?

One time, as a young boy, I remember coming out of church with Mom, Dad and my sister (we always went together). I distinctly remember asking my mom, "What do you think God is doing right now?" My mom was always extremely adept at explaining complicated things to my sister and me, things our young minds couldn't yet comprehend. She used age-old analogies like, "The angels are bowling again!" when trying to calm us during a thunderstorm. This time, however, on the steps of St. Johns church, her beautiful face took on a look of sadness and she said, "I think God is crying." I've never forgotten her words. Even now, I sometimes find myself contemplating the meaning of her answer that day.

These days, as my youthful eyes, which were once trusting and naïve, give way to eyes that are mature, eyes that see the world for what it has become, more and more as I look around and I think my mom, all those years ago, was right.

More and more as I look around me, I think my mom, all those years ago, was right.

Where is it written this is how things must be? Upon what tablet is this law chiseled? Fact is, nowhere is it written we must hate. Nowhere is it written we must not love one another. Humanity has taken care of that on its own. But it doesn't have to be this way! Inside all of us is the seed of goodness. It matters not what religion one subscribes to either. Muslim, Christian, Buddhist, monotheistic, polytheistic, atheist– it doesn't matter! The seed is there. In the history of time, there has only been but one devoid of this seed.

We should not hold this in any longer. We cannot afford to. Let it out! Let the goodness that lives in every one of us shine forth with a light that is brighter than a thousand suns! Let our own goodness and love explode with the force of a volcano and shower all those around us. Is it so hard to do this? It surely is not a sign of weakness. Rather, it is a sign of strength. Like a tiny ship tossed in a whirlpool upon the sea of hatred, I believe our world is in dangerous water. As humans, we have the power to alter our course. After all, humanity's greatest assets are the very hearts that beat in our chests! Let them out! Embrace one another! Help one another! Love one another with all your heart and all your soul, and you will find utopia can exist. Is it so hard to envision this? What better way for us to leave this earth for our children? If we can truly love each other, there would be no more war. Through helping our brothers and sisters, there would be no more people who hunger or thirst. Stop for a second, close your eyes, and imagine what such a place would look like.

But, like the person who makes the brave choice to put down the bottle, the decision to live in such a way is personal. No one can force it upon you. No governing body could ever legislate such a law. You must decide it for yourself. But, I think once one makes the decision to love and serve others, living any other way seems ludicrous.

The irony of what I write is that not three feet from the chair upon which I sit is my rifle. It has a magazine locked in it and, yes, there is a round in the chamber. There are some who may call me a dreamer. I concede they may be right, but I am enough of a realist to know the world I have described seems farther away than ever.

It seems ironic, but it is with that rifle I have been able to help people. That rifle is a deterrent for those who would do violence. In our being here in this small town, we are keeping these people safe from the evil that roams the countryside. Unlike those we fight, I would not use that weapon for violence, unless it was to protect myself or to protect someone who could not do it for themselves. It is sad, but I am willing to fight so others can have peace. Whether or not that makes me a bad person or a good one is debatable.

It is sad, but I am willing to fight so others can have peace.

Sitting here tonight, I write these words on a broken old desk, on the second floor of the police station in downtown Al-Tarmiyah, Iraq. I sit in a dark hallway in the southeast corner of the building. There are no lights above me. Where light bulbs once were, the sockets for them now stand empty. Tonight, the only light by which I am to write comes from two chem sticks suspended from a piece of wood, held in place by a sandbag. The chair upon which I sit has seen better days, too. The cushion is ripped up and one of the arms is broken. It seems fitting these are the surroundings in which I find myself. Outside, the power is off again, the town is dark. And like the desk and chair, this place seems old and broken.

Humor never is far behind in my thoughts though. I am thankful for that as it serves to help keep me sane. As I write here in my hallway, I can't get a vision out of my head. Crazy as it is, I can visualize Thoreau sitting in his buddies' cabin on Walden Pond, writing by candlelight. Ha! Where did that come from? These thoughts bring a smile to my lips, and from the events of today, I could use a good laugh.

Tonight, like B.S. from a barbershop, the words flow with ease. That is not the norm sometimes. There are nights when I try to write, but every sentence I write seems to flounder in space. The meaning of my words is lost amid the adjectives and prepositions. Tonight, the thoughts in my head are easily laid down on paper. But, to think of Thoreau and make any comparisons between us, well, it's just plain wrong. He was a serious writer. Me? I am just a poor sap with pen, paper, and too much time on my hands.

Jason Adams
Al-Tarmiyah, Iraq

Waiting

Today is January 8th

Down in the center of town is Al-Tarmiyah's sole gas station. When we first were tasked with the security of both this police station and the town, the gas station wasn't open. Yes, there were people there everyday, but no gas. Unlike gas stations back home, the only thing these folks sell is gas. No pop, no pizza, no ice– just gas. Personally, coming from a capitalist society, I think somebody is missing out on a huge business opportunity here, but hey, that's another story.

For the last couple weeks, the gas trucks have been showing up on a regular basis. As far as the world goes, this is no big deal. But, here in Iraq, it is a major step in the right direction. The irony here is blinding! For a country that sits over some of the biggest oil reserves known to man, the sight of a gas station should be commonplace. In reality though, the exact opposite has been the reality for the longest time. As well, the gas stations one does see should be overflowing with petrol, but they are not. The reason for this eludes me.

I still cannot get used to the idea that, after almost a year of being here, I can only think of four gas stations offhand. Four! When I was a kid in my home town, I can remember at least five. But, here again, those were private enterprises. Here, I am told, all the gas stations are owned by the government. Over the past few days the line to get fuel has fluctuated, but has never been less than a quarter of a mile in length. At one point, the line was over a

They look more like groupies waiting outside TicketMaster than people waiting in line for something as simple as a tank of gas.

half mile long! At night, people sleep in their cars to not lose their spot in line. They look more like groupies waiting outside TicketMaster than people waiting in line for something as simple as a tank of gas.

Some of them venture out of their cars and congregate in groups of four or five around little fires they have built out of anything that will burn. Cardboard boxes, scraps of wood, garbage– you name it. One night, while driving past the line, we saw a few guys lighting a car tire on fire, right there on the sidewalk! By our last patrol of the night though, most of them are huddled in their cars trying to keep warm and maybe catch 40 winks. In my life, I have yet to witness anything remotely resembling the nightly conglomeration of cars and people, all with the sole intent of buying a tank of gas. Yeah, the gas is still cheap– about eight cents a liter– but the price of this gas must also be measured in time spent getting it.

Yesterday, we saw a fistfight break out between some of the folks in line, most likely over a spot in line. But hey, who knows what they were fighting over. Today, the scene was turning ugly. Cars were jammed into the line at odd angles, some were double-parked, others were stopped on the opposite side of the street, waiting to cut in front of an unattended vehicle as the line moves forward. We could see family members bringing food to the men who had been waiting in line all night.

The sight of this mess just down the street from our police station causes me to think of home. Not that I have ever waited all night for a tank of gas, but rather I have never waited even close to that long. I can remember getting miffed at having three cars in front of me, let alone this many! The gaggle of cars outside certainly brings new meaning to the term, waiting line.

Jason Adams
Camp Cooke, Iraq

Notice   Training   Deployment   Home leave   Back Home
10/12/03   3/1/04   9/26-10/14/04   3/19/05

The Battle of Holy Week

Today is January 12th

Today is January 12th

The following is a brief summary of the events surrounding what history will remember as The Battle of Holy Week. While this is not all-inclusive, it is, however, as I remember it to be.

Sometime during the night of 10 April 2004, the insurgents (hereafter referred to as either insurgents, the enemy, morons, or jerks) planted an IED in a road culvert approximately four miles south of the northern border of our patrol zone. The IED detonated sometime during the night leaving a hole approximately three feet deep and eight to nine feet in diameter in the northbound lane of the MSR. Sometime thereafter, a local motorist happened to hit one of the chunks of asphalt that had been left lying in the road.

On the morning of 11 April 2004, second platoon was tasked with reconnoitering the crater and surrounding area. We arrived on scene, pushed out our security teams, and took pictures of both the hole in the road as well as the car left at the scene. The motorists were not present at this time, so we searched the car for a secondary device with negative results.

Our platoon sergeant led us to a frontage road approximately 300 meters to the east to speak with the locals and ascertain any knowledge of either the blast or those who set the charge. The detonation cord we had observed leaving the crater led to a curve in the frontage road and ended near a house. Upon searching the house and subsequently finding nothing out of the ordinary, we prepared to move onto the next house.

As we prepared to load back into our trucks, we heard a volley of small arms fire. Unsure if it was directed at us, we continued to load up in our trucks when we heard what sounded like bullets zipping through the air, followed by the reports. These were the first shots fired at my platoon since our arrival in country. In other words, we had just lost our virginity, per se.

Every man who has ever marched into battle has asked himself two questions. I don't care who it was, what language they spoke or the amount of training they received prior to their first real combat. All of them asked themselves these two things, Will I survive? followed by How will I react?

> **Every man who has ever marched into battle has asked himself two questions, Will I survive? followed by How will I react?**

For the men of second platoon, that question was being answered that morning. Once it dawned on most of us we were being fired at, we hit the deck and took cover. First thing we had to do was figure out where the morons shooting at us were firing. We could see a dirt berm across the road and logic told me this would be where I would be firing from, so I started to scan the top of the berm. Sure enough, I could see the jerks scurrying around like rats behind the berm. Other guys saw it, too, and soon everyone was yelling, "They are behind the berm!"

SFC Hess had a handle on things from the start. He yelled at our platoon's M203 gunner to come up and lay down some fire. For those of you who do not know what the M203 does, it's pretty simple. It is a grenade launcher. It's perfect for hitting targets behind a wall, a car, or in this case, a berm. I am not going to deprive our M203 gunner of his anonymity here out of respect for him. I will just refer to him as "Barney" His actions that morning were comical. If I hadn't been getting shot at, I probably would have been laughing pretty good.

Canals run everywhere out in the old zone. Imagine the water mains under most city streets being above ground and that would give you an idea of how the canals work. This place is no different. Barney was on the other side of the canal that ran by the frontage road when the shooting started. SFC Hess yelled, "Barney, get over here!" All of a sudden, from behind me, above the gunfire I heard a loud splash, like someone falling in a swimming pool. I spun around and there was Barney flailing in the water! With a look of shock on his face and soaking wet, Barney came running up the other side of the canal bank at full speed.

SFC Hess pointed to where the enemy was and told him to engage them. M203 gunners, unless they have a grenadier's vest, are pretty limited as to the number of grenades they can carry. Barring putting them in their pants pockets, about five or six is all they can carry on their vests by the time they put all the other crap on the army insists we need. Five grenades don't last very long in a firefight, so Barney headed back to his truck for more.

We could hear bullets bouncing off our trucks and we could see ricochets in the dirt all around our trucks. Then all of a sudden- BOOM!! About 50 meters in front of our trucks, a large cloud of dust kicked up! Then another boom and another cloud of dust! Someone started yelling, "Mortars!" It made sense, the enemy could walk a few mortar rounds in on us if they wanted to. That didn't make me feel all that good either. SFC Hess decided to break contact and get us the hell out of there. Then, something weird happened. I could hear SSG Wolford yelling at somebody in the back of one of the trucks. Nobody thought too much about it until later when we got back to base to re-supply our ammo.

It seems SSG Wolford ran by the bed of his truck as we were preparing to leave and found Barney lying in the bed, with his M203 in the air like a mortar tube, launching grenades without even aiming! Those weren't mortars landing in front of us; they were grenades from Barney's M203!

Barney is a nervous type of guy anyway, plus he drinks Pepsi like it is water. Needless to say, he is always wired on caffeine and sugar. SSG Wolford told me later, "I ain't never seen nothing like it! I walk past the truck and there is Barney looking like he just saw an alien, lying on his back, launching grenades out of the back of the truck like they were mortars!"

In other units, actions like this might have drawn ridicule and scorn from some, but we all get along pretty good. Given the fact this was our "baptism by fire," nobody said a word to Barney. Barney is a great guy and a great soldier. But you have to admit, seeing him splash his way through a canal and then shoot grenades so close everyone around him thought they were mortars…well, in a weird way, that's kinda funny.

After we left the ambush site, we drove back to the west gate of our base for more ammo and a chance to unstress. Little did we know our respite would be short-lived. As we pulled into the gate, we were met by a convoy of fuel tankers preparing to leave. We asked them which way they were headed, to which they replied, "South."

Upon hearing their intent, some of the guys in our patrol said, "Hey, umm, that might not be such a good idea. We just came from up north and it's getting pretty stupid out there!" "We'll be fine," was their reply, so we just waved and muttered, "Good luck, suckers!"

We had barely distributed all the ammo when someone noticed several dark clouds of smoke rising in the direction of the morning's ambush. It is not too hard to differentiate a fuel fire from any other type. The smoke was as black as coal and it was *thick*. Pretty soon the radio came to life and the inevitable message came. The fuel trucks were getting ambushed and we had to go save their necks, well, what was left of them.

Upon leaving the gate, we traveled west along a blacktop road that led to the highway. Once out on the highway, we turned north and had gone approximately 2 to 3 km when our patrol could see several damaged and/or destroyed vehicles in the northbound lane of the highway. Black smoke was funneling skyward so much that it looked like pile after pile of car tires alight. Shortly thereafter, our patrol was engaged by enemy small arms from an undetermined distance from our nine, twelve and three o'clock position.

Our patrol began returning suppressive fire with small arms and mounted crew served weapons. At this time our patrol turned onto

Our plan was simple: Divide and conquer.

a dirt frontage road that left the highway to our right (east). Our plan was simple: Divide and conquer. It doesn't make much sense to attack the enemy on both sides of the road. It would be better to sweep one side and then worry about the other.

While traveling on the frontage road to the east, we again took small arms fire from what seemed like our left flank. The road turned to the north and the small arms fire seemed to intensify. It sounded like some enemy crew served was mixed in with the other fire. SGT Sleaford and I were in the back of the last truck of the patrol. We both could observe muzzle flashes coming from a group of reeds to our left flank or, north side of the dirt frontage road before the curve to the north.

While returning fire, with SGT Sleaford on the M249 (mounted) and me with my M249 laid across the tailgate, we both observed what appeared to be an RPG round land approximately 20 meters directly behind our truck. As we turned to the north, the fire seemed to come from all sides. When the RPG landed right behind us, the funniest thing happened, although to be real honest, nobody was laughing at the time!

Ben and I were gunning down everything that was moving with our M249s when the RPG hit. For a second, we stopped firing, looked at each other square in the face, and screamed like little girls! In hindsight, it was hilarious! If the moron who shot the thing had aimed just a tad higher, the thing would have landed in our laps! By the time our truck made the turn in the road, we had each emptied our 200-round drums on our machine guns and were trying to reload. I remember looking at the patch of reeds that had been hiding some of the enemy and, as we drove off, thankfully nobody was shooting at us anymore.

We then proceeded to travel approximately 600 meters farther north on the dirt frontage road before returning to the highway. Upon reaching it, we could see several 915s with fuel tankers staggered on the road and our patrol stopped in among the tankers for cover. At that point, I was witness to the dumbest thing that to this day I have ever seen.

The truckers were lying on top of their tanker trailers with their M16s shooting at the jerks that had ambushed them. They looked like a bunch of cowboys having a good old shootout! I was so shocked at their antics I found myself waiting for one of them to let out a "Yeehaw!" I thought to myself, "Hey retards, do you realize you are sitting on top of a tank full of fuel?"

Upon exiting our trucks, we immediately began taking fire from our nine and three o'clock positions from a distance of approximately 300 meters to the west and 200 meters more or less to the east. The most intensive fire seemed to be coming from a dirt berm that ran parallel to the highway to our west and two buildings located to our west at the same distance. To the west, the fire seemed to originate from the ten to eight o'clock position. We had now found ourselves in the kill zone of nothing short of a fairly well planned ambush.

About this time I observed SGT Vandegenachte engage the enemy located in one of the buildings to the west with the MK19. For those of you who do not know what a MK19 is, it is a fully automatic grenade launcher capable of ruining your whole weekend. When those things are working right, they will do some serious damage, let me tell ya! SFC Hess called for Barney to bring up his M203. SGT Sleaford ordered PFC Douglas to retrieve our vehicle's AT-4 (antitank rocket). PFC Douglas handed off the AT-4 to SGT Ortiz who proceeded to engage the buildings to our west. SPC Wolf also engaged the same buildings with another AT-4.

AT-4s are weapons many soldiers never get to play with- real ones anyway, thus, not too many people realize just how loud they are. On television, when Rambo or some other action star used to launch rockets, it always made a whoosh noise. Not these things! They make a very loud bang when fired.

When SGT Ortiz fired the first rocket, all I could hear was SFC Hess yelling, "Sonofabitch that puppy was loud!" SGT Ortiz has to hold the record for the best AT-4 shot any of us will ever see. As he fired the rocket, we could see it go toward the house he was aiming at. Right before the rocket hit the building, it hit the ground. He had aimed just a bit too low. Instead of blowing up in the dirt, the rocket skipped and continued on right into the side of the house! The hole it left in the house looked to be about three feet wide. Talk about a one in a million shot!

None of us had any time for a victory dance, as we were still being shot at. When we first got to the trucks and the cowboys on top of their trailers, they had already had two people shot. SPC Welgat and I were treating the wounded soldiers

None of us had any time for a victory dance, as we were still being shot at.

from the Transportation Company as somebody else was calling in the Medivac chopper. One of the guys was hit pretty good and had to be carried to the helicopter on a stretcher. The other guy was able to walk to it.

1SGT Sergeant Peterson, SSG Wolford, and myself carried the wounded soldier to the awaiting helo. As we ran the guy on the stretcher out to the bird, we could hear bullets zipping past us and a few even ricocheted off the pavement at our feet. I didn't like that part all too much.

After loading the wounded soldier and another wounded soldier from the Transportation Company onto the Medivac helo, I returned to my truck for more ammo and continued to lay down fire on the buildings and dirt berm to our west. At this time, SFC Hess directed me to assist a soldier who had blood all over his face. I determined the injuries were the result of glass fragments and were not hindering the individual's ability to fight. Upon examination, the individual declined medical care, and I returned to my vehicle and along with SGT Sleaford, continued to suppress the enemy.

At this time, a report was passed along there was an individual to our three o'clock who was waving a white flag. I cannot confirm this act, but, SGT Sleaford and I ceased firing according to the law of war. 1SGT Peterson approached and requested four men to accompany him out to apprehend the enemy soldier. Along with 1SGT Peterson, SGT Sleaford, and SGT Ortiz, I and another soldier from the Transportation Company proceeded to the east approximately 100-120 meters across a field to the building the enemy had been hiding in.

I didn't really have a warm and fuzzy feeling about running across an open field under fire, but what were we to do? SGT Ortiz kept his rifle on the enemy while Top, Ben and I cleared the little building. I was amazed there was anybody alive in the area after all the rounds we had thrown at it, but this jerk who was now lying face down in the dirt managed to survive. I ordered the soldier from the Transportation Company to cover our exposed flank with his M249. There were two Bradleys to our north sweeping and providing security along a tree line, so 1SGT Peterson and SGT Ortiz went out to link up with the BFVs and alert them to our presence. SGT Sleaford and I took charge of the EPOW as Top and SGT Oritz left.

The prisoner was a skinny man of about 20 years of age. He was dressed in a pajama-looking outfit and was covered in mud from lying in the dirt. I knelt down about 10 feet in front of him and aimed the muzzle of my rifle at his forehead. SGT Sleaford approached the man from the side in order to search him for weapons. I could see in his face he was scared out of his mind. Hell, I would be too if a guy had an assault rifle aimed at my face! I figured he didn't speak any English, but I told him if he moved so much as an inch, it would be all over. I think he got the message because he was like a statue. SGT Sleaford patted him down and upon finding no weapons, placed a set of flexi-cuffs on his wrists.

Ben and I decided to wait until Top and Ortiz were back before moving back to the trucks with the EPOW. The enemy soldier was no longer a threat to us, being in handcuffs, so we decided to give him some water. He drank from the canteen we held to his mouth in large gulps. Finally, after his thirst was quenched, he nodded his head and Ben pulled the canteen away from his mouth. We helped him to his feet and moved up toward the building for some cover.

Ben and I decided the guy might want a smoke. So we put one in his mouth and lit it for him. Then the guy started to really freak out. I mean bad! He started rocking back and forth while sobbing and pleading, "No, No, No!" Ben and I looked at each other, not quite sure what was happening. Then it dawned on me. He thought we were going to execute him! I guess he had seen the movies too. You know the ones. They tie your hands behind your back and stick a cigarette in your mouth right before they line you up against a wall and shoot you. Well, I think this guy thought we were going to do just that. He was so worked up by this point I noticed a puddle forming around his feet! The guy up and peed himself!

For the next couple of minutes, Ben and I tried to convince the guy we weren't going to shoot him. Finally, he started to calm down and stopped crying. While we were huddled against the wall of that building, the rest of my platoon was still out on the highway fighting it out with the insurgents. I could see most of what was going on, and it was the most awesome yet, terrible sight I could imagine.

Smoke was rolling out of several fuel trucks, men were tucked here and there shooting their weapons at the enemy who was still behind that berm to our west. I could see the 50-caliber machine guns spitting out empty casings like slot machines spit out quarters. The Bradleys were unloading their 25mm main guns, loaded with high explosive bullets as well. It was the coolest thing I had ever seen. Then, the Apache gunships showed up. Two of them!

They came in low and fast from the south zipping along the berm, just blasting away with their cannon. Even from where we were behind the building, we could see dirt churn along the berm to our west. I don't remember if I said anything while watching the Apaches go to work, but if I had, it was probably something like, "Yeah! Eat that you scumbags!" All of us were running on pure adrenaline.

While the Apaches were making another pass, I remember seeing a cloud of smoke envelope the northern most gunship, followed by a loud explosion.

Right there in front of my eyes, I watched in horror **"Oh my God, Ben,** as the rotor blades folded in half and the chopper **they just shot down** fell straight to the ground. I didn't see the bird **an Apache...this** crash due to some trees that were blocking my **ain't good."** view, but the instantaneous cloud of black smoke told me it wasn't good. I looked at Ben and said, "Oh my God, Ben, they just shot down an Apache...this ain't good."

SGT Sleaford and I waited with the prisoner until 1SGT and Ortiz returned from the tree line and continued back to our trucks. The prisoner was taken to the interpreter for questioning, and SGT Sleaford and I returned to our truck. By this time I could see several M1114s traveling to our west on the other side of the dirt berm to secure the crash site of the AH-64 Apache and sweep the area for any remaining enemy forces.

At this time we were ordered to mount our trucks and return to the gate in order to consolidate and reorganize. The battle had moved on up the road by this time due to the efforts of the Apaches and the Bradleys, so we had a moment of relative safety in which to collect our thoughts. I remember climbing into the back of my truck, rummaging through my backpack and pulling out a cigar. Ben climbed in with a Marlboro he had bummed off somebody. I said, "I didn't know you smoked!" To which he replied, "I do today!" So we sat there for a minute and enjoyed our smokes, along with a bottle of cold water. Yeah, yeah, I know smoking is bad for me, but so are bullets.

Upon entrance to our base, we again took small arms fire to our nine o'clock position from a distance of approximately 200 meters. I cannot estimate enemy strength as I was treating one of our guys who had sustained two wounds from what appeared to be either shrapnel or bullet fragments during the engagement back out on the highway. One wound was to the quadriceps region of the middle thigh, and the other to the distal end of his gastrocnemius. Second platoon and others at the gate laid down heavy suppressive fire from our small arms and crew served weapons.

The Bradleys and M-1 Abrams that happened to be at the gate also engaged the enemy. Boy, did those morons pick the wrong time to attack! The tanks were loaded onto flatbed trucks and were just waiting in line to get in the gate. The enemy obviously didn't figure there would be anyone in the tanks. SUR-

PRISE!!! All of a sudden, the tanks roared to life and the turrets spun sideways! I wish I could have seen the looks on the jerks' faces as they realized the tanks were manned! Man, that would have been priceless!

If everyone thought the AT-4 was loud out on the highway, they were really shocked when the M-1s opened up with their main guns. The enemy had taken up positions in a couple houses out in front of us a ways. The tanks opened up and the houses disappeared. Man, what a show!

About this time, I don't remember how it happened, but I noticed the pistol grip handle was almost ripped off the bottom of my M249! I can't believe it was still working, but it was. Soon though, it started acting up. Ben was having trouble with the feed tray on his weapon as well. After a quick powwow behind one of our trucks, we decided if we field stripped both weapons, we could swap parts and make one good gun out of two broken ones.

So there we were, sitting in the dirt, getting shot at while tearing apart our machine guns! We frantically tore the things apart, switched his good pistol grip for my bad one, put the machine guns back together, loaded the now working one with ammo, and continued to shoot. I threw the broken M249 in the back of my truck and grabbed my M16. The fire from the enemy subsided after approximately 25 minutes, and we were resupplied with ammo.

After consolidation and reorganization, we were again ordered out to secure a road junction approximately 1000 meters north of the gate. We set up security and a traffic blockade at the road junction while other coalition forces swept and searched the area we had taken fire from while at the gate. We stayed out on the traffic blockade for the rest of the day.

After the adrenaline stopped flowing and I realized I was still alive, I noticed my stomach felt like a hollow cavern that hadn't seen food in weeks. We all started to feel it, so we broke out some MREs and ate dinner out there on the hoods of our trucks. We spent the rest of the day talking over the events of the day. Somebody remembered it happened to be Easter Sunday. How ironic! While the rest of America was hunting for hidden eggs, we had spent the day looking for a place to hide!

Around midnight, the radio again crackled to life with the best news of the day. Time to go in! Tired, shaken up and dirty, the men of second platoon once again loaded up in our trucks and headed for home where a well-earned shower and some sleep waited.

And so ended our first day of actual combat. We had been in Iraq less than a month and already had been through one of the worst days of our lives. We all made it through alive. At least one of the questions was answered that day. None of us choked. We all did our jobs and performed bravely under fire. The intelligence analysis that came out later said the force that had ambushed us was in excess of 100 men. I am not too sure if I buy that part, but nonetheless, a lot of bullets, as well as a few RPGs, came at us that day.

We went out to the ambush site a couple of days later and found foxholes dug into the western side of that dirt berm. There must have been 20 or so foxholes, each of which could have held two men. We found the scorch marks on the ground from the crash site of the Apache. All the wreckage had been hauled away, but there was no doubt in any of our minds two pilots died that day on this very spot. They died trying to save our butts. I never knew who those men were until a few days ago.

In our chow hall here at Camp Cooke, there are two private dining rooms. One is the Fortenberry Room and the other is the Colton Room. By the door of each room hangs a picture adorned with the Distinguished Flying Cross. WOs Fortenberry and Colton are shown by their helicopters in their flight suits. The story of their gallant deeds is there for all to see. A fitting tribute to two men who, without being asked, gave the last full measure of devotion to a bunch of Army National Guardsmen out on a highway in the middle of Iraq.

Jason Adams
Camp Cooke, Iraq

Notice   Training   Deployment   Home leave   Back Home
10/12/03   3/1/04   9/26-10/14/04   3/19/05

Captive

Today is January 16th

Today finds us back up in our little clubhouse for another five days straight. Five days, that is a long time to go without a shower or a decent meal. When we first took on this mission, we were told it would be for no more than 10 days yet, here we sit almost two months later. A lesser person would fail to see the humor in that.

Although this mission has lasted considerably longer than we had first planned, it isn't that bad. As of late, we have gotten the chow hall to make us up some lunch meat and cheese platters along with some bread so we can at least have a fresh sandwich. We also have cereal and milk for breakfast, too. Not exactly the five-star cuisine that is featured at the chow hall, but it gets us by. Wow! I never thought I would use the words five-star cuisine and chow hall in the same sentence, but, there you have it sports fans!

One of the guys in our platoon had a rather large parcel of mail the other night. After he and our mail clerk unloaded all 65 boxes, yeah, that's right, 65 boxes, they pretty much closed the door on the mail room and decided they had done enough work for one night. That is a lot of mail, folks. All the boxes were full of food and personal hygiene items we desperately needed up here at our police station. So, aside from going five days without a bath, life isn't too bad up here.

It was last night, however, a tad bit cramped. Third platoon and second platoon rotate our time up here. Usually, when we get here, third platoon heads back to rest and we run things up here. For some reason, our shifts overlapped for almost 24 hours. That meant instead of around 30 guys here, we had 60. Sixty guys and only 30 cots. Do the math on that one, and one can deduce that many men found themselves curled up on the floor for the night.

I was one of the first men upstairs as we arrived, and I found an extra cot in one of the unused rooms. It was missing a couple pieces and had a bent leg, but it was far better than sleeping on the floor. Not too many guys got much sleep anyway. With all those people here, there were groups of men standing around here and there talking most of the night. We are all pretty good buddies and since we rotate shifts up here, we never seem to get more than a parting word before either they leave or we do. It was nice to be able to sit and talk with them for awhile and just kind of catch up on old times.

Today found me on guard duty rather than patrolling. The change of pace was kind of nice, and I find myself enjoying being able to just sit and watch the city out in front of me.

I sit manning a 50-caliber machine gun on the balcony of this police station. Between my legs is a kerosene heater that helps to cut the chill of the January morning air. Grasped tightly in my hands is my Eddie Bauer coffee cup, full of good old Folgers coffee that also helps to both keep me warm as well as awake. Yeah, I bought another one, but this cup works.

My shift starts at 0600 hours and usually I have only been out of my sleeping bag for a matter of minutes when my shift starts. Across Iraq, a curfew has been imposed and the streets are a ghost town from around 2200 hours until first light. Slowly the city comes to life as people venture out of their homes en route to work.

Across the street is a rug merchant who shows up everyday promptly at 0800 hours. First, he unlocks the heavy steel double doors that protect his establishment during the night. Next, he gets out a broom and dutifully sweeps the sidewalk in front of his shop. Next, he proceeds to hang his wares out on the racks that line the front walk. One does not need to watch him very long to learn he is a man who values both punctuality and neatness. The rugs he sells are both beautiful and well made. Some of our guys have purchased several of them, and the very weight of the material is evidence of its quality.

To our north is the shish kebab stand. Around 0830 hours, give or take, the owner shows up and gets his stand ready for the day. Unlike the rug dude, this guy, a former colonel in the Iraqi army, isn't as punctual. As well, I don't think he lives close by as he drives to work everyday. He arrives in his car, a white, late '80s Chevy Celebrity pulling a little trailer upon which rides a little electrical generator. Power is still spotty here and when the lights go out, he just plugs in his generator and it's business as usual.

I don't know the guy's name, I just call him "Bob-kabob." Bob employs two younger kids, and they set about cleaning the tables out front while he gets the day's meat from the lamb butcher down the street. By 1000 hours, he is usually ready to serve the food. He has a stainless steel rotisserie that sits out front and is able to hold several chickens at a time. It runs off propane and is usually fired up and cooking fowl by this time too. Five bucks will get you a whole chicken dinner for two, plus all the fixings. Not exactly KFC, but at least it's sold by a real colonel.

There is an open-air market that sits diagonally across the street from my machine gun position. It, too, is open and full of people by 0900 hours or so. It sells all kinds of vegetables and fruits as well as fish. Out west of town there is a fish farm. Several ponds are dug into the earth and are about 75 meters by 30 meters in area. The man that runs the fish farms nets some fish and brings them to town to sell everyday.

His stand consists of a cooler filled with water mounted upon a little three-wheeled cart. Inside the cooler are the fish, but not for long. He takes several out of the cooler and lays them on the front of the cart for customers to inspect prior to purchase. I am not too sure of the species of fish he sells. Some of them look like some genetic mutation between a carp and an eel. They are some spooky looking fish to say the least! I think there may indeed be weapons of mass destruction hidden here. I think they are buried under the fish farm. Just look what it's doing to the fish!

About 400 meters to the north and a little to the east is a soccer field. Everyday kids playing soccer cover it. They usually don't start showing up until mid- to late-afternoon, but they are there everyday. Playing soccer in Iraq isn't so much encouraged as it is enforced. Soccer fields dot the landscape here. Some of them are nothing more than fields devoid of rocks with goal posts made from tree branches. Up where we are, the soccer field is modest at best, but used as if it were of Olympic quality.

As I sit manning my gun, a pair of Apache gunships fly overhead. First, they fly up the Tigris River that flows on the east edge of town. They bank and turn to the west and cruise over the palm tree grove that is just north of the soccer field. As they bank sharply to the west, I can hear their rotors strain under the force, and it makes a chop-chop-chop sound. They are several hundred meters away, but the noise is loud enough to catch my attention. They then circle the palms a few times and head over the city. Banking again, they head back east.

As I watched the helicopters perform their aerobatics, I noticed none of the people on the street seemed to pay much attention. The people in the market were nonchalantly shopping for vegetables, and Bob across the street was talking to one of his employees. Even the police out at the gate to the compound seemed oblivious to the flying battleships overhead. I guess they are more used to seeing those choppers over their city than I am.

I remember the Cold War. I remember actually fearing a war with Russia; not so much because I would be involved, rather I feared what I didn't understand. I remember watching the movie *Red Dawn* and wondering, "What if this really happened? What if I looked out my window and saw a squadron of MiG-29 Fulcrums fly over." How terrifying would that be to a young kid!

Yet today here I sit, manning my machine gun watching the Apaches fly around, and the folks in town just casually going about their day-to-day lives. It sometimes amazes me when I think about how much this war has impacted my life. Then I stop and realize how much it has impacted that mother and her little girls who are right across the street admiring the rugs. I've little to complain about.

This morning is one of the test days for new applicants for the police force. This city is pretty small as far as most cities go, yet in the lobby downstairs are no less than 40 applicants all wanting, not so much to be police officers, they just want jobs. The age of the applicants ranges from barely needing to shave to ready to retire. They all wait patiently while GQ talks with each one of them.

There is a physical fitness test to be administered and a medical screening to be done as well. We are helping out by taking care of the physical fitness and medical portions of the hiring process. Each applicant must do five pullups, at least 10 pushups, 20 situps, and then complete a short run. Then, they go and see the medic and he takes a set of vital signs. Then they wait in another line for the interview.

The whole process takes a little while and the hopeful applicants pass the time talking and drinking tea. As I surveyed the men, I couldn't help but notice the look of hope in their eyes. I am guessing many of them have been out of work for awhile now and are just hoping to land a job as a cop. I feel a little bit sad because I know there are not 40 job openings, at least here anyway. I have

Either these men do not fear suicide bomber attacks, or their need of work outweighs the risk of being killed as a result of their search for a paycheck.

watched the news and have seen hiring days such as these are a favorite target for suicide bombers hoping to dissuade anyone from applying. Either these men do not fear such attacks or their need of work outweighs the risk of being killed as a result of their search for a paycheck.

Speaking of police, I wrote much in my last letter regarding the police here and their seemingly endless inability to do their jobs. I don't know what happened, but when we arrived here the other night, it was like looking at an entirely different group of men. Perhaps, our leadership got wind of the problems we had with the gas station and made a few phone calls to the head of the police down in Baghdad. It is the same anywhere. The last thing anybody wants is for the head office to stick their nose in and start probing orifices.

Yesterday morning for example, some of the men from third platoon told me the police had taken care of the gas station fiasco. I was incredulous to say the least. When we had left here the last time, the place was a royal mess. My buddies said the cops went down to the gas station and, along with third platoon's help, started cracking heads. They even arrested a few guys and impounded their truck! Kudos to them! It was a job well done that was long overdue. For these police to ever really have an impact in this town, they, first and foremost, must restore order. It would appear this is what they are starting to do. The gas station in the center of town is as good a place as any in which to start.

This morning as I sat there on my gun and sipped my coffee, several men approached the front gate. I sat down my coffee cup and stood at the ready, in front of my machine gun. The men who came to the gate were all speaking at once while simultaneously pointing toward the gas station. As it turns out, a car had been stolen. The men told the cops it had been insurgents who were responsible.

A couple of the police loaded up into their little truck and headed down to the gas station. Soon thereafter, I could hear a siren approaching from the east. The two cops pulled into the gate, jumped out, and started yelling toward the building. All of a sudden, it was if a dam had burst! At least 10 cops came running out of the building with AK-47s in hand, wearing their bulletproof vests! Something was going on!

Four or five of them jumped in the truck and tore off out of town. Even though the siren was wailing, the motorists refused to get out of the way. The police in the back of the truck popped off a few rounds toward the cars and they got out of the way real quick like. I figured it must have been something big, because I had, up till now, never seen them act in such a brazen manner.

Soon, the little truck came back and then more yelling. By now, there were more cops out in the yard handing more ammo to the police in the truck. Then a second truck pulled into the yard with a man in handcuffs, wearing a blindfold. The man was riding in the back of the truck with the other cops and upon stopping, the prisoner was literally dragged out of the back of the truck.

As the cops led the man under the balcony upon which I was standing, I could see he had a pretty good laceration on his head. I, at this time, could only watch and wonder as to what had taken place. I couldn't leave my post to investigate, and since I still haven't mastered Arabic, I had no idea of what the cops were yelling. Soon, SFC Hess and the patrol element were loaded up in the Humvees and followed the cops back out the gate.

As the details of the morning's events slowly came to light, it seemed the man the cops had brought in was, in part, responsible for the stolen car. Apparently there were others, but SFC Hess and the patrol came back empty-handed. At least the cops caught one of the guys.

Later on in the day, a man wearing a desert tan set of body armor and a pistol in a shoulder holster came up to the gate to speak with the police. It seems he is a colonel in the Iraqi National Guard and was recently wounded by an IED, leaving him with only seven fingers. Even more unsettling was the fact the insurgents had killed some of his family recently as well. The reason for his visit was in regards to a rumor he had heard telling of a man in custody that matched the description of the one who was responsible for the deaths of his family members. The colonel wanted to see the prisoner and decide if this was in fact the man.

MAJ Kessel and the colonel opened the cell door, and the colonel recognized the man with the now bandaged head as the one who had killed his family members. So, for the last day or so, this man has been in the prison cell downstairs under guard. Today, the captain of the police asked if they could question the man in order to complete their reports. LT Doubler, our platoon leader, was out patrolling at the time, leaving me in charge of things back here. I didn't see any reason why the cops couldn't interrogate their own prisoner. I mean, he won't be our prisoner until we take him back to Camp Cooke. I came upstairs and got my rifle and returned back downstairs. The cops put the shackles back on the man and led him to the captain's office for a few questions.

One of the things I learned as a recruiter for the Army National Guard was when interviewing an applicant, it is not a good idea to use your desk as a barrier. What I mean is when talking to someone, the desk at which you sit can convey certain things. It is subtle, but the desk is seen as a symbol of power.

The man behind the desk is usually the boss of sorts. When applicants would come into my office, I always had two chairs lined up against the wall, adjacent to my desk. Rather than sit behind the desk and talk to the young people, I would sit beside them on the same type of chair upon which they would be sitting so as to convey the sense of equality. It puts the prospective applicant at ease a bit.

The cops here must have realized this because they did the exact opposite and made the prisoner sit cross-legged in front of the captain's desk on the floor. Surrounding the prisoner were four other policemen. Directly behind him was where I was sitting and, of course, I had my rifle in my lap. Not exactly comfortable surroundings for the man on the floor!

The police talked to the man for about 20 minutes, but they never raised their voices. The whole interrogation seemed very professional, almost cordial, but hey, I don't speak Arabic and had no idea of what it was they were talking about. At times the captain paused and thought silently to himself as if contemplating what the man had just said. After the uneasy silence, he would ask a few more questions while the lieutenant dutifully wrote down the bulk of the interrogation on two sheets of plain white paper with a sheet of carbon paper sandwiched in between them so there would be copies.

As I watched the prisoner talk, I found myself drawn to his body language. He sat slouched with his head hung toward his chest, but when spoken to, he looked the speaker directly in the face. His tone of voice was surprisingly hushed. At times, the captain asked him to repeat himself just so he could hear what it was he had said. The prisoner looked as though he knew his butt was toast and was ready for whatever punishment the cops were ready to deliver.

Through GQ, I asked the prisoner how he felt. The detainee said his head was bothering him quite a bit. That's understandable, I thought. I don't know what it was that hit him on the head, just speculation here, but I'd say whatever it was had a barrel and a trigger on it. I told the man I would come downstairs later on and change his bandage and give him something to help the pain. He thanked me as the cops led him back to the cell.

Later on, after my next shift on the balcony, I went down to the cell with GQ to check on the guy and take care of his head. We unlocked the cell door and the cops went in and put the handcuffs back on. Then we led him to a small office in the back of the police station and sat him down. Three cops were in the room for security as I opened my medical kit. I took off the bandage that was in place and, as I did, I noticed his hair was still matted from his own blood.

The wound was shaped like a T and had seven crude stitches in it. Crude as the sutures were and shoddy as the bandage job had been, I could see no signs of infection starting. I cleaned up the wound a little bit and applied a Telfa pad and some gauze wrap. Satisfied my dressing would hold, I dug in my bag for some Tylenol. I had GQ ask him if he was allergic to any medications, just to be sure. He answered, "No," and I gave him the pills. After taking a few sips of water from the glass I held to his lips, he muttered his thanks.

The man now back in his cell is not what I had pictured when I thought of insurgents. This man is accused of killing others, but he looked too scared in our presence for me to think him capable of such an act. Prisoner or not, guilty or innocent, this man's fate will be decided by a judge. As far as I am concerned, I will treat him with civility and compassion. I will help his wounds heal and I will do what I can to ease his suffering.

That is one of the main things that separates the American army from armies of other countries. We take care of the wounded. We feed them, clothe them, and give them shelter as well as prudent and punctual medical aid. If we fail to do these basic things for others, we are never any better than those we fight.

In some ways, as I took care of the man's wound, I felt sorry for him. If he is convicted, life as he has thus far known it will cease to exist. I don't understand the hate that compels men to act in such a way. I am blessed to not know this. What I do know is he is accused of taking part in anti-coalition activities. The things he is accused of would be just as serious if they had been directed at us.

As I replaced his bandages, I made up my mind I had forgiven him for hating me. His hate stems from ignorance and misguided teachings from others. I cannot hold him totally responsible for that. I think if he really knew the men on the second floor of this police station, he would not hate us. In fact, I believe we could be friends. Perhaps, there are those who would call me an eternal optimist. Is that really so bad?

Jason Adams
Camp Cooke, Iraq

Ambush!

Today is January 22nd

Well, here I sit at my computer again. Typing, correcting, typing some more, and then proofreading. It has been said humans are creatures of habit. One needs look no further than the dolt sitting right here. If we are not on a mission, not busy doing any other thing, and if someone wishes to find me they need only tap on the door of my trailer and they will find me sitting here typing. Maybe it's an email, maybe a letter to a buddy that doesn't see the need for the Internet or perhaps I am typing letters like this one. Bottom line is, if you want me, you know where to find me.

Come on in, grab some coffee if you like, but please, abide by the rules. Rule No. 1: If you empty the pot, it's on you to make more. Rule No. 2: If you don't like Beethoven, then you had better find some earplugs. Rule No. 3: I like my side of the room neat and tidy. If you so much as move my shower shoes, prepare yourself for the forthcoming thunderous oratorical reprimand. Those are the rules. Love it, or leave it.

It's not that I am socially inept. I just prefer to be here writing, rather than engaging in the limited cache of other entertainment options that are available. For the most part, I am not a card player, I don't gamble, and I am not into sports, although I do like to go for a run now and then. I have seen about all of Camp Cooke I want too see, and I am not into nudie books or porno movies. So, the options that lie before me are pretty limited. Plus, and I have said this before, writing is one of the ways in which I deal with the stresses of this deployment. That, and I kinda like to be alone sometimes. It isn't that I am some kind of outcast here. I do have friends. I just enjoy solitude at times.

But, I guess I would have to say I have always been like that. Back home, my favorite time of year is deer season. Every year I go out with my bow and arrows to stalk the wilderness south of Toulon chasing the elusive white tail. Okay, that's a load of manure. I am a lousy deer hunter. Everytime I come home, Steph and the girls run out to the truck and look in the back only to confirm it is indeed empty. Then they laugh at me and remind me if we had lived back in the days of the pioneers, we would be starving. First and foremost, I just like walking through the woods. Secondly, if a deer happens to walk in front of me….well, you know.

I like to get away, out of town, and into a natural setting. I am totally content sitting by a giant elm tree, just watching the rhythm of the forest. The way the wind blows through the trees, the way gravity affects the water in the creek making it flow in a certain direction, the way the squirrels busy themselves by storing food for the winter, the way the hawks float on the air currents and go for great lengths of time without ever flapping their wings– things a lot of folks never get to see.

And somewhere in the midst of all this is a lone deer hunter taking a snooze on a bed of leaves under a tree. When I wake up, I feel refreshed, like I have been asleep for days. I feel as though I am somehow closer to the earth out in those woods. Civilization seems so far away and I like it. Being by myself helps me think more clearly. I have solved many a problem out there in that wood. Sometimes, I pray a little out there. I figure that out among those trees, I am somehow closer to God. My great-great grandfather summed it up best, Why should I go to a church to pray? If I want to be close to God, all's I have to do is go out in the timber. I think he may have had a valid point.

Here, there is no timber and there are no deer. I can't go anywhere here and be totally by myself. There is always a plethora of activity here no matter where one might find themselves. The minute you think you have found the one place nobody else could possibly think to look for you, wham-o! — a chopper cruises overhead. So, having given up hope for finding solitude here, I just resign myself to this laptop and these stereo headphones. But, the result of this self-induced seclusion is a permanent record of most of the high, as well as low, points of this deployment.

Sometimes, I sit and reread some of the letters I had written when we first got here, and I am amazed at the details I had forgotten. Many of the men have not kept journals. Some of the guys have, but I am not sure how dedicated they are to them. Years from now, they may not be able to remember the days we are living here. Perhaps they will not want to.

The other night while getting ready for our last patrol of the night, it was routine stuff. Wake everybody up, load the trucks, load the weapons, line up the trucks, and do the radio checks. We pulled out of the front of the police station and took a left. Cruising down the main drag of Tarmiyah at night is like cruising through a town in which no one lives. The streets are empty, save for the line of cars at the gas station, but that's on the east side of town.

When the power is on, it isn't too bad, but a lot of the times, the power is off and the streets are dark. Saying the streets are just dark doesn't give one an accurate idea of what it is like. Imagine pulling into a town and all the lights were out and no one was to be seen- anywhere. It is that lonesome, uneasy feeling that creeps into your guts like a storm front moving in. First you see it, but it takes awhile before the wind and rain hits. I don't like it, I will admit. The absence of any signs of life puts me on edge, like when you're home alone and get the feeling you are being watched. It's that sixth sense we all have that makes the hair on the back of our neck stand on end. On nights like that, and there have been many, my senses are more perceptive and my heart rate goes up a bit. It's the whole fight or flight thing, I guess. Soon though, my mind starts playing tricks on me, and I start seeing foo fighters around every corner. Drives me nuts.

Tonight, the lights are on, at least for the time being, and the town, for the most part, looks inhabited. We drive down the center of the road, past the girls school. Here, unlike America, the schools are segregated not by race but by sex. The school is old and dilapidated, with windows missing and graffiti spray painted all over the front wall. A newcomer to town might snort at the thought of it being still in use, but I would assure them tomorrow morning it will be full of kids.

Past the school is the new building that is going up. I am not really sure as to what this building will become. Rumor is it will be a bank. The laborers are there everyday toiling with tools their grandfathers most likely used. They get to work either by boots or by bicycle. That, or someone drops them off. One certainly doesn't see brand new Ford trucks with shiny Delta toolboxes in the back parked around these job sites! It amazes me, though, that even with anti-quated tools and homemade ladders, these folks can turn out some amazing work. The building is shaping up quite nicely, and everyday the progress made the day prior is easily seen.

Past the bank the street curves slightly to the southwest and heads out of town. The north side of the street is lined with shops and businesses, too. At this time of night, the steel doors that protect the shops are all aglow under the light provided by a single bare light bulb. On the corner is the veterinarian's place. I know this only because it has a picture of a cow and a chicken on the sign. The rest is in Arabic. I never see too many people come in and out of that shop.

A few doors down is the bakery. Everyday the man who runs the place fills the racks inside his shop with fresh baked breads and glazed sweets, the likes of which I have never seen. Some of his treats look like doughnut holes, but they are crunchy on the outside, soft and sweet on the inside. They are really good, but you can only eat one or two because they are too darn sweet.

Tonight though, we don't go to the edge of town. Instead, we turn and take a mud trail to the south and hit another hard road a couple blocks away by the pile of corncobs.

Navigating this town is easy. It is laid out like any other town and even at night the landmarks stand out. A mosque, a car that hasn't moved since we got here, and a pile of corncobs aid us in navigating the streets. Sometimes though, what looks like a road is nothing more than a pair of tire tracks that lead to a person's abode.

A mosque, a car that hasn't moved since we got here, a pile of corncobs; all aid us in navigating the streets.

Yeah, we feel pretty dumb backing up and turning around. Even in the middle of the night, I am pretty sure somebody, somewhere in the myriad of windows out there, saw us mess up and is laughing at those goofy Americans in their little Humvees. Tonight we don't get lost. We head left at the corncob pile and continue on east until we hit the curve.

The curve is important. It is both a landmark and a warning. It warns us this is the spot where the road is missing. That's right, the road is missing. Just a little ways past the curve, on the west side of the road, a hole is dug. This hole is about three feet deep by two feet wide and about five or six feet long. The east side of the road is intact, but Humvees are pretty wide and you had better hug the east side of the road as you pass. I am not sure if we could get a truck out of that puppy if we had to.

The truck I am in has the rear guard position on this particular patrol. Rather than drive, I opted for the turret and sat manning an M240B machine gun. (The M240B is sorta like the old M60; like the one Sylvester Stallone made famous in his Rambo movies.) It isn't a bad way to ride, but when you're in the rear truck, it is kind of boring. It's akin to riding in the rear-facing seat in an old *Brady Bunch* station wagon. Oh yeah, did I mention it's the coldest spot to ride in a Humvee?

Anyway, we safely navigated the Humvee trap in the road and continued to patrol north. Once up to the main drag, we turned right and headed toward the river. At the end of the main drag, there is a T intersection. The road we were on intersects another, and that one parallels the river on the west side for quite a distance. As we approached the T intersection, I heard a pretty good-sized machine gun open up. At first, I remember thinking to myself, "What the hell is that dufus shooting at?" I stood up from my sling seat and turned around to see what was going on, thinking the gunner in the lead truck had fired a warning burst in the air for some reason.

Once upon a time, the area that lies between the road and the river was a picturesque little garden area with stone benches strategically placed within its walls. As you cross the road, there is a stone railing with ornate little columns supporting it. About two and a half-feet high, the railing is certainly for ornamental purposes only and is broken by an opening for a set of stone stairs. The columns are cement, as is the railing, but to me, resemble some miniature attempt to recreate some Greco-Roman architecture. The whole thing used to be bleach white, but today is showing signs of neglect. Pieces of the rail as well as the columns are chipped, revealing the gray concrete underneath.

The park is sectioned off into squares by sidewalks and there are a few trees growing in the little park as well. About a 100 meters south of the park is a school and to the west of that is a mosque. GQ told us the school "Is bad place" so we are always a little more alert as we pass by. The whole place could be a scene from a postcard if they would fix it up a little. Tonight, however, postcard scenery would prove to be the furthest thought in my mind.

As I stood up in the turret and turned, about 10 tracer rounds went flying by my head. It happened so quickly it almost didn't register: Ambush! And buddy, it was a humdinger.

I remember spinning the turret back around to cover our rear. I didn't want anybody getting any bright ideas about flanking us and boxing us in a kill zone. We were in a tight spot. The enemy had picked the perfect spot to nail us. On each side of our trucks were storefronts, so the only way to go was either into the fire or throw the trucks in reverse and go back the way we had come. That was a bad idea because, from where the enemy was shooting, they could have shot at us all the way back to the police station. We decided to go forward.

I peeked over the side shields of my gun to see if there was any way I could help return fire, even with only my M16. But as I turned, the only things in front of me were the other two vehicles. As the tracer rounds flew past our truck, I could hear SFC yelling on the radio. The volume of fire intensified and I remember thinking, "This ain't good."

Suddenly, two sequential explosions shook the sides of our truck and echoed off the walls of the buildings to our sides. I didn't see what had exploded and I didn't have to– RPGs. What a treat! Luckily, these losers still haven't learned how to work the things, and they both missed our trucks. About this time, I peeked up over the top of my side shields and saw our two front trucks abreast in the road. Good idea, I thought. Double your firepower to the front. What I didn't realize was one of the trucks had taken a bullet through the transmission cooler and radiator, and the transmission was starting to slip.

> **I didn't see what had exploded and I didn't have to: RPGs. What a treat! Luckily, these losers still haven't learned how to work the things...**

As soon as the second truck pulled alongside the first, two bullets hit a couple of the "magic spots"— those are the spots on our truck that aren't armored. Granted, while the likelihood of a bullet ever hitting the front end and going into the cab are slim, it happened twice on the same truck, on the same night, in the same ambush. How's that for dumb luck? One bullet came through the firewall right above the accelerator pedal and struck the driver in the right leg. The other bullet came through the hood, through the radiator reservoir, through the firewall, through the heater vent, and struck the passenger in the left arm. The driver managed to keep the truck moving and continued through the ambush.

The insurgents here know they don't stand a chance against us for very long, so they like to hit and run. They jump out, jack an RPG at your truck, and then run. By the time you get your senses back, they are already gone. The same held true tonight. The attackers didn't hang out long. The machine gun fire had ceased by the time our first truck had gotten to the T intersection. We turned north and headed out of the area. We still had no idea to what extent our trucks were hit, nor did we have any idea of how bad the wounded were.

Once we assessed the situation, it was decided we needed to get the wounded back to the police station for treatment. The fastest way back to the police station was the way we had just come, but that meant going back through the ambush site we had just vacated. The only other option was a dirt road that runs about a mile north of the police station, but due to the situation, we chose to take our chances and go back the way we had just come. One of the guys was bleeding pretty badly, so we decided to just bust through the T intersection and fly back down the road to the cop shop.

As we were turning around, the front truck wouldn't move. Despite the other damage to the truck, the transmission cooler leak had proved to be the *coup de grace*. SFC Hess, thinking fast, told them to put the truck into neutral so we could just push them back to the police station. Thankfully, the insurgents didn't hang around to see if we came back by, and the short trip back to the police station was fast and, thankfully, uneventful. But, once back at the station, we had other problems. We still had two guys bleeding.

The news of our eventful patrol reached the police station right about the time the first tracer rounds went zinging by the balcony machine gun nest. That is almost a mile away from where the ambush took place! The balcony gunner said one tracer even came through the balcony, right above him! Anyway, as we pulled into the gate, our entire platoon was outside waiting for us.

They knew we had wounded, and they were all pulling security for us. The police were out, too, but they all looked like deer in the headlights, which considering they all had automatic weapons in their hands, did little to set me at ease.

As the guys helped the two wounded dudes out of the truck and got them into the cop shop, my driver was already running my medical kits to me. Nick and I each went to work on one of the wounded. One of the men wasn't from our unit and one was. It is ironic but one of the guys who was shot was our medic! Nick and I are both just as qualified as the army medic, but the battalion we are attached to doesn't see it like that. So they insist on sending their own medic with us. Problem is, the army medic, until coming here, had no practical experience. Nick and I each have almost two years of calls under our belts. I guess experience doesn't matter when dealing with some units.

Okay, the whole medic thing is kind of a sore spot with me, if you can't tell, so I won't beat a dead horse.

Once inside the police station, I could see the pants leg of my buddy's trousers was stained crimson. I ripped open my medic bag, grabbed my trauma shears, and went to work. I have gained a rather unsought reputation as a madman when I get out the trauma shears. I can't really help it. If you are hurt bad enough for me to get out the shears, are you really that worried about your shoelaces or pants? I think not. Expose the wound, I say! Let's see that bad boy!

As I cut the pants leg from around the wound, clumps, the size of baseballs, of semi-congealed blood fell out. His boot, sock, and trousers from his knee down were literally soaked in blood. After cutting them all away, I could see a small entrance wound on the anterior side of his calf. Looking on the posterior side of his calf, I could see meat hanging out. Ah, this would be the exit wound, I thought. The wound was clean though and looked as though it hadn't hit the tibia or fibula. But, there was a lot of blood. More than I would have expected. Oh well, back to the basics, pressure and elevation.

I fished around in my medic bag and got out a field dressing. Somebody opened it for me, and as I applied the thing I was thankful I had switched out my old style field dressings for the new Israeli Bandages. These things are about as neat as they could be. The old field dressings were but a small step above a maxi pad with tails long enough to tie around an appendage. These new bandages are top-notch. They are rolled like an Ace bandage so you can darn near apply them with one hand. Two, the wrapping portion of the bandage is elastic, making it a pressure dressing too. Third, and I don't know this for sure, but I am told, the bandage is impregnated with a rapid coagulant powder to aid in the formation of a blood clot. Pretty neat stuff.

I finished bandaging my buddy's leg and then I asked him if he could wiggle his toes. He could, so then I asked him if he could move his foot back and forth and side to side. After doing that, I elevated his feet above his heart and did a hasty head-to-toe exam to make sure I hadn't missed anything. Sometimes, once the adrenaline gets a'flowing, you can be hurt and not know it. So, it is always a good idea to physically check rather than just ask the patient, "Hey, uh…you hurt anywhere else?" That, in the world of EMS, is a dangerous road to go down. I asked him how he felt, and he said he was really cold for some reason. I noticed his face was paler than normal, too. I felt his abdomen and it was cool too. I told him I was going to start an IV. I rummaged around in my bag and got out my IV stuff.

Some of the medics I have seen are not that organized. Some of them are just plain messy. Time is money sometimes, and to have your medic bag neat, organized, and easily accessible could be the difference between life and death. I am pretty picky about my bag and how it is organized. I guess I get that from my boss back home on the ambulance department. He is the master of organization.

The ambulance I usually run in, 1SAM13, is a diesel-powered, mobile monument to the gods of space management and organization. I love it. Even the pens in the cab have Velcro on them and are conspicuously stuck to the dashboard so they won't roll away if you need to write down something en route somewhere. The back of the rig is just plain genius! Every compartment in the entire patient area is marked with a little label showing you exactly what is where. I love it! And just like a well-organized rig, it is also advantageous to keep items that are used in conjunction with each other to perform a certain procedure or task in close proximity to one another as well. For instance, it would not make sense to keep the stethoscope in the back of the rig and the sphygmomanometer in the glove box. No, you use them together, so keep them together!

The same idea came to mind when I got my new medical bag here. I have seen some guys just throw all the necessary items to start an IV in their medic bags, in no specific order, only to fumble around when the proverbial excrement hits the air circulator. So, I got some Ziploc baggies and put all the little junk in the bag, i.e., the needles (two in case I miss the vein on the first try), the alcohol swab, the 2x2 dressing to cover the infusion site, the IV line, a piece of Penrose tubing (for a tourniquet), and a small roll of tape. Then, I tape the Ziploc bag to the bag of IV fluid. That way, all I have to do is grab a bag of fluid and everything I need to start an IV is in the palm of my hand. I am not saying that is the right way per se; I am just saying it works for me, so I use it.

The only thing that miffs me is the new needles they gave us. The ones we used in training were the old style that were just a needle and a catheter. These new chunks of garbage are "safety needles," and after you start the IV, the needle slides into an attached plastic holder to keep it from accidentally sticking someone. The problem is, I am not used to using them. Every time I get a flash in the flash chamber and start to feed the catheter into the vein, the needle moves into the plastic container rather than the catheter into the vein. But, I can't find anyone with the old style needles anywhere.

Needless to say, I was shook up anyway. A few minutes ago, bullets were whizzing past our heads, and we all narrowly escaped getting our behinds shot off. Now, here I am lying on a floor trying to patch up my buddy who is sporting a nice bullet wound. I am kneeling in a puddle of his blood, and my hands are slimy and crimson. Now, I am trying to get a needle into a vein I cannot see, but only feel. No pressure here, folks.

I admit, I missed the first try, flat out, no excuse. The second try, I got a flash, which meant I was in the vein. I dropped the angle of the needle, pushed it in a tad bit farther and started to feed the catheter. Then the darn needle started to slide into the plastic holder. You can't feed the catheter without the needle in the vein as it acts as a guide. So I was pretty much out of luck on the second try, too. Somebody yelled the Medivac chopper was only minutes away and Nick and I needed to hurry. Gee, do you really think we weren't trying?

Moving around to the left arm and applying the tourniquet, a vein popped out at me. I grabbed a third needle and said, "What the hell, why not." I pinched the needle with a death grip so it would not slide out of the vein and as I saw the flash and started to feed in the catheter, it slid right in! Touchdown!

One of my buddies helped me hook up the tubing and cover the infusion site just as the helicopter started to circle overhead.

While I was messing around with the leg wound, Nick had been busy with the medic and his arm. At first it didn't look that bad, he later told me. But, soon it became obvious the medic could not flex his arm. Just so ya know, it ain't supposed to do that. The bullet had grazed his forearm on the anterior side and lodged itself in his bicep. Nick had it wrapped in no time. I think he even put a splint on it, but now I can't remember.

Nevertheless, what I do remember was the calmness with which everyone acted. Nobody was freaking out, well…except for the policemen. They were pretty shook up. At one point, while Nick and I were working, we heard several bursts of gunfire from out in front of the police station. We kind of glanced at each other as if to say, "What's this?" As it turns out, the policemen were shooting at some dogs that wouldn't stop barking. C'mon fellas, now's not the time to be randomly shooting.

Nick and I did not go out to the chopper. The other guys carried both the medic and my buddy out to the bird that whisked them away to the main hospital in Baghdad. Nick and I looked at the floor of the police station that was now a certified mess and slowly began to pick up the garbage from the field dressings, the IV kits, and repack our bags. I went in the bathroom to wash the blood off my trauma shears as well as my hands. Both of the guys will be just fine. In fact, my buddy was back in his trailer the next morning, albeit with crutches, but fine nonetheless.

It is noteworthy to say of my buddy that, while wounded and bleeding, he managed to get the truck and his team back to the police station by himself.

He said he had a hard time pushing down on the gas pedal, but he made it. What a stud.

Once we had a minute to collect ourselves, we went out to look at the trucks. Wow! They were shot up pretty good. One of the trucks had three hits to the windshield– one to the side window, (a couple rounds had narrowly missed the gunner and hit the turret shield), one

While wounded and bleeding, my buddy managed to get the truck and his team back to the police station by himself. What a stud.

through the grill and through the oil cooler, and one through a headlight. The other truck had similar hits to the windshield, a headlight shot out, and two holes in the hood. One came out through the heater vent and the other came out right above the accelerator pedal.

If this had happened eight months ago when we first got here, we would be going to a memorial ceremony for one of us. Back then, we didn't have bullet-proof windshields. As well, if we had M1114s now, we wouldn't have had any wounded. The M1114 has a totally enclosed cabin that is bulletproof. There aren't any "magic spots" on those puppies. But, we still haven't gotten any of them and with only a few weeks left in country, I doubt we will.

The next morning we went down to the little park area to look for any clues the insurgents might have left. What we found was a textbook perfect hasty ambush site. Behind the little railing that adorns the western side of the park, the ground drops off about four and a half feet and is held back by a retaining wall. A guy could stand there, put a machine gun in between the little pillars of the railing, and shoot straight down the road that intersects right there, and the only thing anyone coming down the road would see would be their head. Perfect! Then, after they shot, they were already on their feet and could run along that retaining wall unnoticed until they could hide somewhere else. We got played, big time.

As well, we found three piles of bullet casings in different locations meaning there had to have been at least five guys that ambushed us. Three on the machine guns and two on the RPGs. The casings and links we found were from a Soviet Bloc medium machine gun that is not unlike our M240B. That is quite a step up from the stereotypical AK-47 "shoot'n scoot" ambushes we have seen in the past.

Since we left the airport a couple months ago, we had not seen our old interpreter Jaguar. A few of the guys kept in contact via email but that was it. Unbeknown to me, Jag had lost his job when we left. I am not 100 percent sure of why he lost it, but I think it had something to do with family issues. Anyway, he emailed one of the guys and inquired of his chances of getting his old job back. They told him to come to the police station in Tarmiyah so they could talk.

So one day Jag jumped in his car and showed up at the front gate of the police station. My platoon wasn't there, but Jag filled me in on what had transpired. See, the police didn't know who he was. He showed up and told the cop at the front gate he wanted to see Foxtrot Battery. The cop told him he had no business with them and, "Who are you to come in here demanding...yadda, yadda, yadda."

Jag said he tried to explain to the cop who he was, but the cop wouldn't hear any of it. Finally, Jag looked up onto the balcony where the machine gun sits and, recognizing the guy behind the gun, yelled at him. The guy on the gun yelled back, "Hey Jaguar!" The cop was beside himself.

A long story made short, Jaguar is working with us again. I am glad to see him. Moreover, I am glad to see he was able to reacquire his job with us. He has a family now, and his is the sole paycheck. Times for him are not easy. In the time he has not been employed as an interpreter, he has had to sell many of his things just to provide the bare necessities for himself and his family.

Today, I was on guard duty again. Most of my time was spent in the machine gun nest on the roof, and luckily, I had Jaguar to keep me company. Jaguar is an interesting man. At times, he is hard to understand. Not that his accent is too thick, but rather his word arrangement gets tangled sometimes. Rather than saying "calling card" he will say "card calling." Once you get used to it, it isn't that big of a deal. What he lacks in sentence structuring, he makes up for in common sense.

Jag is a very precocious person, more so than one would think from just talking to him for a short while. He makes it a point to stay current on the issues facing this country, while at the same time dreaming of coming to America to live. The only thing that gets me about him is the uni-brow. His eyebrows form a straight line from the left to the right side of his forehead. We josh him pretty good over it. I mentioned he looked like Michael Dukakis on steroids. He just kind of gave me a blank stare on that one. Jaguar assures us the uni-brow is a family trait and he has no intention of trimming it. Somebody made the joke buckteeth are a family trait, too, and we all had a good laugh. Jaguar is once again just another part of the family.

Having to spend five days straight at our little police station renders one in desperate need of a bath. Matter of fact, one of the high points of my week is getting to come back here and take a scalding hot shower. After parking the trucks and unloading all our junk, I grabbed my toilet bag and headed off to wash up. On the door of the shower trailer was a sign saying there had been a water main break and water rationing was in effect. Oh perfect.

I managed to get one shower while we were back. The next few days we all went without. Then, they managed to get the water back on a week or so later and the power was out for a couple days. The definition of frustration is having no water, but power, and then having water but no power to run the pumps! And to whoever thinks God doesn't have a sense of humor, having spent a week complaining about not having any water, the sky let loose with a veritable torrent of rain that lasted all day long. It rained so hard and the wind blew so hard our trailers were leaking! Now, the whole place is a mud pit. While others cussed our misery, I couldn't help but laugh to myself. We complained about not having any water, then we got more than we wanted, just not to shower with! The Lord works in mysterious (and sometimes humorous) ways!

Jason Adams
Camp Cooke, Iraq

Election Day

Today is February 3ʳᵈ

Well, the elections are over. The moment when the world held its breath has passed. Many people both in Iraq and the rest of the world watched with anticipation as the morning of January 30th came to be. What would happen? Zarqawi and his cronies would probably have a little something planned, but to what extent? None of us knew, but apprehension and conjecture reined supreme as we headed out the gate. We had been tasked with manning a traffic checkpoint both the day preceding the election and through to the day after the election. The checkpoint was setup with barriers, orange traffic cones, concertina wire, and even two sets of those portable light trailers, but it was set up right out in the open. Not exactly a tactical setup if you catch my drift.

Second and third platoons took turns manning the checkpoint for the entire time. Twelve hours on and 12 hours off is a pretty rough schedule, but we managed. The checkpoint was set up on a road is known for its danger around here. Heck, right in the middle of our checkpoint was a hole big enough to lose a riding lawn mower in that was caused by a rather large IED! To make matters worse for us, the checkpoint was right out in the open as well: Perfect for anybody with an RPG to take a potshot at us, but hey, we just follow orders here.

What I don't like about static checkpoints is simple. They are static, they don't move. We set these things up in order to search cars and find weapons, bombs, terror suspects, among other things. The other day while out on our checkpoint, I decided to hand out some stuff my insurance agent, Mike Bigger, had sent to me. He sent me two boxes filled with soccer balls, pencils, crayons and coloring books for the kids. I have had them in the back of my truck for some time now just waiting for the opportune moment to give them out. This seemed like the best time. Sometimes when we search cars, the cars are filled with women and children. The kids are usually pretty nervous about seeing the soldiers, so when we are done searching the cars, I would give them some crayons or pencils to set them at ease. Plus, this is a good public relations thing with the parents.

The other day while my guys were out front searching cars, I was in the rear of my truck, airing up soccer balls. One of my buddies in third platoon loaned me his ball pump, and I set to work. I aired up two balls and handed them out to northbound cars. Two balls, that is it. Every person who came through our checkpoint for the next half hour asked if we had any soccer balls left! I couldn't believe it! If

If they know about some GI handing out free soccer balls down the road, is it not safe to assume that the insurgents know that there is a checkpoint here too?

they know about some GI handing out free balls down the road, is it not safe to assume the insurgents know there is a checkpoint here, too? Bottom line, we are wasting time.

It is necessary, however, to do vehicle searches. I am not arguing that. But, the manner in which we do them is what I am having a problem with. I am a big fan of random, spontaneous checkpoints. In other words, drive around for awhile, stop, set up a checkpoint, search 10 or 12 cars, and then drive some more. It keeps people guessing. Plus, it doesn't expose us to mortar fire. But hey, what do I know? What makes sense and what the army does is proving to be two different things entirely.

The first night out on the checkpoint was rather cold. I don't have a thermometer, but there was frost everywhere as the sun peeked over the horizon. We sat on the north side of the checkpoint all night, huddled in our trucks, trying to stay warm. The heater in my truck leaves a lot to be desired. It only works on one setting, and the fan blower sounds like it's about ready to fly apart. I have taken it to the motor pool many times and complained it isn't working right. The mechanics swear there is nothing wrong with it. Yeah guys, it's supposed to sound like a runaway freight train right before it derails. Anyway, we froze. You would think I would be used to the fact it gets cold here, but I find myself consistently amazed by the weather. Today for example, it is probably in the mid-60s. Really nice weather. Tonight, it could get down to 30, who knows? I was wearing my long johns and my stocking hat under my Kevlar and Gortex boots, but by morning, I couldn't feel my feet.

The government imposed a curfew from 1800 hours to 0600 hours on the day before the election, so needless to say, we didn't search a lot of cars. One man did come through, but his baby was sick and he was taking the baby to the hospital in Baghdad. On Election Day, no traffic was allowed at all. I am not really sure how people were supposed to get to the polling places, but apparently, they managed. I will get back to the election in a bit.

As January 30th dawned, I was a little nervous. We were out on our check-point, but so far had not seen so much as a guy on a bicycle. A few people came through our checkpoint on foot, but we didn't see any cars. Throughout the first hour of daylight, we could hear explosions in the distance, most likely from IEDs or car bombs. Then, as I was standing by my truck talking to SFC Hess, we heard a loud whoosh noise.

We thought at first it was a jet hitting its afterburners, but a few seconds later we heard another. As we discussed the nature of the noises, we heard a third one. Then it dawned on us: rockets. We couldn't be for certain where they had been launched from, but they were pretty close to where we were standing. A minute or so later, we heard three explosions off in the distance. As far as trouble out there that day, this was all we saw, thankfully. The rest of our shift passed without incident.

Of course, the insurgents had to make a show at the polling places though. According to *The Stars and Stripes*, there were a bunch of attacks at the polls, but only 40 or so people were killed. Yes, that is bad, but certainly far less than I had expected. To be honest, I didn't know what to expect. The terrorists were all spouting, "Jihad this and jihad," so who knew what they had planned.

What did surprise me was voter turnout. Seventy-three percent is the num-ber we are getting here. That is pretty amazing considering the fact that nobody could drive to the polls! Seventy-three percent of the registered voters decided to disregard the threats from the insurgents and exercise their right to choose their leaders. I am pretty amazed at this. Here is a people who don't know democracy, have lived the last 30 or so years under a tyrant, were told if they went to the polls, they would be killed, but they went. We can't even get 70 percent of the voters in the United States to go to the polls! That has to say something about the dedication of the general populace here insofar as being serious about democracy.

Yesterday, our old battalion commander came up here to hand out some awards. While he was here, he told us about a polling place in Baghdad he had visited on Election Day. There was no mistaking those who voted. Just look for the purple finger. LTC Morrow told us as the people were leaving the polling place, many of them were holding their now purple fingers in the air as if to say, "Look at me! I am not scared. I voted!" Even hearing this story secondhand as well as after the fact, I was still filled with pride and admiration for those folks.

The second story he told was about a line of people waiting to vote. It seems a mortar round came in close by the polling place and exploded. The people in the line scattered. When the folks realized the attack was over, they came out of hiding and got back in line

> **Many of the Iraqis were holding their now purple fingers in the air as if to say, "Look at me! I am not scared: I voted!"**

to vote. That, in and of itself, is a victory not only for us, but for them as well. Both the soldiers here, as well as the people of Iraq, won a great victory that day. What we all have been striving for these many months culminated with a historic moment: A free people choosing their future. I feel so proud. Yeah sure, I am tired of being here. I want to get on a plane and go home. But a part of me is very glad to be here. I am glad I was able to be a part of this.

As I sat in the chow hall last night eating, I grabbed a copy of *The Stars and Stripes* to read up on the elections. One of the stories I read broke my heart. As I have said before, the enemy here is disgusting and evil. They will stop at nothing to inflict death upon whomever they deem as a threat. I have been witness to the depths to which they will sink to accomplish that mission, but I was not prepared for what I was about to read.

It seems the "no driving on election day" tidbit threw a wrench in the insurgent's gears. I am guessing they had a whole parade of cars laden with explosives to unleash on the voters. So, not being able to use the cars, they improvised. They used good old human bombs. I don't care if some jerk wants to martyr himself for his god. The way I see it, that's just one less butt wad that I have to worry about. Unfortunately, these guys don't just go out into the desert and die quietly. No, they have to wait until the TV cameras are rolling so CNN gets it all on tape. On Election Day, these losers stooped to a new level, one that will surely earn them a spot in a lower cavern of hell someday. They took a kid with Downs Syndrome, in a wheelchair no less, strapped explosives to him and used the kid as the vessel to get the bombs closer to their target.

How can anyone be so blind as to not realize what we are fighting over here and why? How can anyone be that obtuse? The terrorists we are fighting are the essence of evil; they must be destroyed. How can anyone back home say this is not worth it? Some people, with their pacifist rhetoric, try to negate the threat facing the world. I am somewhat of a pacifist as well. I don't like the idea of war. But, I am also a realist. I wonder sometimes how those who speak out against our president and our armed forces for what we are doing here would feel if their loved one had been that kid in the wheelchair, or perhaps a passenger on one of the planes that hit the World Trade Center.

Think about that for a moment. It is easy to damn this war. It is easy to sit, naïve and blinded by a liberal media, in your recliners back home and play armchair quarterback. You are not here. Your eyes have not seen what ours have. It is not your fault. I am not placing blame here, but what I am saying is simple. It is easy to rationalize the threat facing us isn't that bad. It is easy to call us warmongers. It is easy to say, "Let's bring our boys and girls home!" That is, until the terrorists take something from you personally. What have they taken from me, you ask? That is an easy question. The answer is, time (16 months so far), buddies (more on this in a bit), and innocence (until being here, I had never known violence like this). Many of my buddies who are now sporting a Purple Heart, have had their "pound of flesh" taken from them as well.

I must say, though, I am curious. I wonder how many folks at home heard about that little boy in the wheelchair being used as a bomb. It is my belief Americans are not getting the whole story. If they were, I feel folks at home would be more educated as to the reasons behind this war. If folks were more educated regarding things here, I do not think our efforts would be so unpopular.

Last week, as we were leaving our police station, one of the policemen there told Jaguar Lenny's parents had been there wanting to know where Lenny was. The policeman told them Lenny had left and presumably went home. His parents assured the officer Lenny did not come home. In addition, they informed the cops they had found Lenny's sandals in the road en route to the police station. As we left the police station, it was becoming obvious something ugly was afoot. We all feared Lenny had been kidnapped.

They found Lenny's sandals in the road enroute to the police station.

A couple days later as third platoon was manning the traffic checkpoint, some of the police officers that work up north at the cop shop came through the checkpoint. They told the guys they had found Lenny's body. While I cannot verify this personally, it is plausible to think it is true. I mean, why would anyone make up a story like that? When I heard this, it saddened me deeply. Here is a guy who was just trying to make a living, killed for working with the Americans. This again illustrates the depths at which these people will go to accomplish their goals. Of course, we have known for a long time that they were capable of it. This latest murder hits a little close to home for me. Lenny was my buddy. He worked hard for the money we paid him and never once complained. In fact, he was happy and content as he toiled with his broom and mop. I hope the people responsible are caught, but the likelihood is slim.

At times, I like to indulge in revenge fantasies. It is wrong, I know, but I am human, and humans are imperfect. I try to be a good Catholic, but sometimes I fail. I think about Lenny being abducted by his assailants and tied up. I think of the fear he must have felt. I then think about hope, hope his buddies, the men of Foxtrot Battery, will come and rescue him. Hope we will kill the men who took him and reunite him with his worried family. But, like the flame of a candle going out, that hope turned to smoke as they took him out and shot him.

As a Christian, I am taught to forgive, offer the other cheek to those who would strike me. But, it is not easy to do. I think about what I would do to the people responsible for this, and it is evil. I am not going to go into details regarding it. These are my demons, and I, alone, must sort them out.

I know to exact my own revenge on someone is wrong. It is contrary to what I stand for. I would be a hypocrite if I said anything different. People need to pay for their crimes, but I am no judge or jury. Right now though, I don't know how I would react if I came across those people who hurt Lenny. Right now, all I can do is pray for Lenny's soul. I believe God has a little surprise in store for those who took my friend's life. Who knows, if I am unable to forgive those who took my friend, he may have a little surprise for me, too. Do me a favor though. Stop and say a little prayer for Lenny. Pray, too, his family's grief is somehow assuaged and the men responsible will be brought to justice.

The night of the elections, we were again out on the checkpoint. As we set ourselves for another cold and boring night, a car could be seen approaching from the south. The order for no cars to travel was still in effect, so we all became a little nervous as the car approached. The car stopped almost 100 meters from the first set of concrete barriers. Because its headlights were still lit, we had no idea of how many people were in the car. We waved the car forward so we could search it, but it wouldn't move. This piqued my curiosity a little, so SSG Patterson, I, and a couple other guys went out to see what was going on. An old man got out of the car with a white flag tied on the end of a stick, and was furiously waving it back and forth. He was scared out of his mind.

It turns out he had come through this checkpoint earlier in the day when third platoon was manning it. His daughter had been in labor and they were trying to get her to Baghdad and into the hospital. The other men in the car were all family, and they were returning from the hospital. He said he knew he wasn't supposed to be out driving, but "Babies can't wait." He had a point, you know. He was a really nice old man, yeah, we searched his car just to make sure, but I wasn't surprised when it turned up nothing. He said his daughter and her baby were both doing fine. We congratulated him and the other men and wished them well before sending them on their way.

Seeing that poor guy with the white flag made me think about the fear these folks live in. Not only do they have to fear the insurgents, but at times, they are scared of us, too, especially at night. They don't have to fear us. As long as they aren't doing anything stupid, we aren't going to bother them. Matter of fact, we even had a few laughs out on the checkpoint.

At one point, the day before the elections when cars were allowed, some of the guys were goofing around with the motorists. One of the vehicles that came through the checkpoint was a little Toyota pickup. While one of the soldiers was talking to the driver, another soldier set his machine gun in the bed of the truck. Then he yelled at the driver, "Hey, what the hell is this?" The driver turned around, and upon looking at the machine gun in the back of his truck, his eyes became like basketballs. He started pleading, "Ease no my gun, ease no my gun!!" Imagine his surprise when the soldier started laughing and picked up the machine gun and slung it around his shoulder again. They poor guy didn't know what to say! He finally uttered a nervous chuckle and realized we were just messing with him. We laughed with him for a bit and then wished him well and sent him on his way.

We pulled the same trick on others with a hand grenade. One of the guys would reach under the front seat, with the grenade already in his hand, pull it out, and ask the driver, "How do you explain this?" We got the same reaction from the others too. It was pretty fun, and it lightened the mood a little. I think, too, things like this lets the locals know we aren't evil people as many of them have been led to believe. We like to joke around and interacting with the locals like this helps to break down barriers between us.

Anymore, I can't sit still. My thoughts are constantly drawn to the fact we are in our final month of being here. Less than one month from now, we will be out of here and on our way to Kuwait. It seems like an eternity since we crossed the border, but in other ways, it seems like yesterday. Many things have happened, many things could still happen. But, with the day for leaving here fast approaching, I cannot think straight. My thoughts are consumed by what I will do when I get home. A vacation perhaps? I like to think I have earned it. I am thinking about school, going back to work, seeing my family, and getting some stuff done around the house. It is not like I am the only one doing this. We all are and it is not a bad thing either.

I realize, however, we must not lose focus on the tasks at hand either. We still have some things left to do, but like in every war before this one, when the end is in sight, the thought on everybody's mind is one and the same: No more injuries. We are almost done with our tours here and to lose someone this close to going home would be devastating. I would rather get blown up on my first day in country, than to be here an entire year, only to get blown up walking to the plane that is here to **Less than one month from now, we will be out of here and on our way to Kuwait. My thoughts are consumed by what I will do when I get home.**

take me back home. Then again, life is funny that way. So, being so close to packing up, I am unsure of how much longer we will have Internet capabilities. Could be a month, could be two weeks. I don't know the answer to that one. We will just have to wait and see.

Jason Adams
Camp Cooke, Iraq

Remembrance

Today is February 4th

I am freaking out. Yes, it's official. I am losing my mind. In my last letter I spoke of my mind's preoccupation with our return home. Indeed, it grows stronger with each day. I am starting to think more and more about getting home and getting back into the routines that used to encompass my existence. School, for example. I find myself giving serious thought to summer classes in an effort to try and make up for lost time. Some of my friends from school are in their last semester now. Yeah, I guess that burns me a little, but there is not a thing I can do about it. Truth is, this deployment has kind of been like a really long spring break for me anyway. (That is sarcasm, in case you didn't pick up on it.)

In all seriousness though, I am ready to get back to school. Wow! That is a phrase I never thought would cross my lips. Ask any of my teachers as I was growing up, and they will confirm that claim. But, with age comes wisdom, I am told. These days, I look forward to school. I find myself thinking about the classes I still need to take, the exorbitant amount of money it takes to buy a textbook, and the fun I used to have sitting in class. All these things are now coming back into focus, and I like the idea of being back in the classroom in the very near future. As well, I like the idea of tormenting my teachers a little. Hey, I am ornery! Deal with it.

I am thinking about working with the ambulance department again. For some, when the pager goes off in the middle of the night, it elicits groans and grumbles from the person being paged. Not me. Zeal for my work still consumes me, and I have been known to keep a pair of pants, T-shirt, and socks on top of my dresser just so I can get dressed faster. When my pager is not on my belt, it is nestled snugly in its charger base so the battery is always fully charged. Sometimes, I back my truck into my driveway, rather than pull in headfirst because this cuts my response time by a second or two. My blue light that sits on the dashboard of my truck is wired through a toggle switch rather than the cigarette lighter adapter it came with. The reason for this is rather than try to drive and fumble for the cigarette lighter adapter, I just flip a toggle switch and that familiar hue of whirling blue comes to life. Does all this make me a compulsive nerd? Probably, but I stopped caring what others think of me long ago.

The thoughts of getting to spend time with my wife and kids are foremost in my mind. Both the girls are now budding young basketball stars, or so they tell me. Teryl is going to be 11 this summer. Joanna just turned nine. When I left home, Teryl had just turned nine; Joanna was only seven. I have missed so much of their lives.

Whether through Email, web cams, Yahoo! Messenger, or telephones, we have talked (my wife and I) at least several times a week.

Readjusting to them should be relatively easy considering the ease with which we have been able to communicate thanks to the Internet. My wife and I have been in almost daily contact since I was deployed. Whether through email, web cams, Yahoo! Messenger, or telephones, we have talked at least several times a week. This helps lessen the time gone and also lessens the miles that separate us.

My wife and I, along with our closest friends, Dr. Carrie Taylor and her fiancé Kurt Loncka, are planning a getaway as we speak. The four of us get along so well. We all like to do the same things, and our weekend trips we periodically take are always a blast. This time, we are thinking of going to Galena, Illinois. So much history is up there! I have not been through there in years, so it should be a stellar trip. The only bad thing is museums.

When we go away together, we always seem to find ourselves at some museum, even if it is some small, otherwise unknown little place. Steph, Carrie, and Kurt will browse the stuff and look at things here and there. I, on the other hand, will read every little card about every piece that is in the museum. It drives them nuts. Usually, when I come out, they are sitting somewhere close by, casually waiting on me, acting as if I had been lost for days. Then they start with the comments regarding my time spent in the galleries. I can't help it. Steph and Carrie don't realize I do not spend anymore time in a museum than they would shopping, if given the chance. Galena should be fun.

Heaven knows I could use a getaway! Someplace with trees and all the locals speaking English would be nice!

I am also looking forward to getting back with the fire department. I get my local paper from back home via the Internet, and every week I look for fires I had missed. I hate missing a call. Not that I like to see someone's property destroyed. Rather, I like the ability to be able to come to someone's aid in their time of need. Next to the Army National Guard, the volunteer fire department is one of the greatest organizations I have ever had the privilege of being a part.

The thought of a bunch of people putting their personal time and, at times, their personal safety, on the line for the folks in the community is a wonderful thing. We do it not for money, not for recognition or fame. Rather, we just want to help folks. Plus, those big red trucks are pretty nifty as well. For me, the fire department is a manifestation of a childhood dream.

Throughout my waking hours, these thoughts flood my mind. Even in sleep they are starting to creep in! For example, the other night I had set my alarm for 0900 hours. I had the day off, and I had planned on being lazy and sleeping in. Around 0700 hours I could have sworn I heard my pager going off! In a stupor, I jumped out of bed, started to throw on my clothes, and head for the door. The only thing that brought reality crashing down was the fact that, out of habit, I grabbed my rifle.

Then it dawned on me: Where did this M16 come from? Oh wait, it was just a dream. I put my rifle away, took off my uniform, and went back to sleep. Yesterday morning, I dreamed I was in the back of the ambulance on the way to the ER at Kewanee Hospital. I don't remember why I was going to the hospital, or what time of day it was, I just remember hooking up oxygen tubing and taking vital signs. I am almost afraid to fall asleep tonight! Like I said, I am freaking out.

Speaking of freaking out, we had another battery of briefings to sit through the other day. Like all military briefings, these were characterized by a bunch of men trying to stay awake while information was thrown our way at super-sonic speed. When it was all said and done, the person giving the briefing always asks if there are any questions. Hell, I don't even remember what you were talking about, how could I possibly have any questions! It is impossible to take notes like that! I don't know shorthand, and due to funding cutbacks, I had to lay off my personal stenographer, so I guess I am pretty much out of luck.

I do remember the gist of the last briefing. I remember because it had to do with the psychological effects of a long deployment in a combat zone. The effects of long deployments are as different as they are complex. Some of these are, sleep loss, flashbacks, anxiety, grief, anger, loss of appetite, to name a few. The person giving the briefing said, "One in four persons will go home with some type of Post-Traumatic Stress Disorder." One of my buddies made the observation this is due to the fact only one in four people here go outside the wire. We all had a good laugh over that one!

The problem I have with all these briefings about the effects of combat on one's psyche is simple. The way they (the army) try to cram it down our throats makes it almost seem as though they want us to be affected, like the many counselors and headshrinkers employed by the army are, in some way, trying to justify their very existence! I don't get it. I have taken enough psychology classes in school to know almost everybody exhibits at least one or two symptoms of a variety of psychological disorders. Half the guys in my unit exhibit symptoms of narcissism to some degree! Yes, some of us will have problems going home. But, don't make us afraid of it. Educate us, tell us where to go if we decide we need help, but don't make us fear it. That, to me, is just as bad as if they were to forego telling us what to expect.

It is good the army feels the need to help the soldiers in the post-deployment time period. It is better to slowly integrate us back into society rather than to just open up the doors of the bus and say, "Thanks again, fellas!" My buddies and I have seen some pretty messed up things over here.

People constantly ask me, "So what's the most screwed up thing you have seen over there?" Wow, talk about an open-ended question!" Do you mean screwed up, as in funny or screwed up as in… permanently tattooed on my brain? I mean, come on! Clarify your question for me a little!

People constantly ask me, "So, what's the most screwed up thing you have seen over there?"

The funniest thing I have seen over here has got to be the day we tried to help the two men push their car up the overpass only to see it roll down the other side, while the guy was trying to get in the door he had forgotten to open. That, folks, was hilarious.

The weirdest thing I have seen over here is the man marching his women through the desert carrying his family's flag. I still don't get that one. Early on in our deployment, Moqtada Al Sadr, the rebel cleric in what used to be Saddam City (a slum of Baghdad), openly declared war on the coalition. His army consisted of a bunch of nitwits dressed in black pajamas with green bandanas on their heads. After our leaders had had about enough of their shenanigans, we declared war on them.

The order was, if you see anyone wearing black pajamas and a green bandana holding a weapon, shoot them. Period; end of story. Being so far out in the country, quite a few miles from Baghdad, we figured we wouldn't see too many of those guys running around the countryside. Nevertheless, we were on the lookout. One day, while driving up the interstate, we happened to come across a group of people just walking through the desert dressed from head to toe in black. The person in front of the congregation was carrying a large green flag on a pole about six-feet long. They weren't wearing green bandanas, but we decided to stop and see what they were doing.

It turns out the person with the flag was the only man in the group; the rest were his women. When questioned as to why he was marching a bunch of women through the desert, he acted as if it were no big deal, like it happens all of the time! The women were all pretty scared of us soldiers, so we let them be. After we decided that while, *extremely* odd, they weren't breaking any rules we drove away. I remember looking at Ben and commenting, "Well, that's a new one on me!"

The dumbest thing I have seen happened not too long ago. One of the guys in another platoon and I were talking one morning, while shaving, about events of the last few days. He said, "You're not going to believe this one!" To which I replied, "Lay it on me!" He told me about a car they had pulled over while out on patrol. It was a 700 series BMW, with one male occupant. In the subsequent search of the automobile, they found a couple of AK-47s, several hundred dollars of American currency, and 50 blasting caps. The man said he had just bought the car and the money was left over from the sale. He also claimed the blasting caps and the guns must have been in the car from the last owner. Yeah, right buddy, who buys a car without looking in the trunk?

My buddies decided to arrest the man and take him back to camp to be interrogated. They decided to put the detainee in a Humvee and let their interpreter drive the BMW back to camp. When they called this information up to the headquarters, they were told to just let the man drive himself to the base. They were told to sandwich the car in between two Bradleys so the man could not run away. As stupid as this sounds, my buddies had no choice but to follow orders, even though they were pretty ridiculous.

As the interpreter told the detainee what to do, I imagined him thinking to himself, "I can't believe they are stupid!" Anyway, what the "brain trust" up at HQ didn't consider is there are many side roads that intersect the highway they were on, and a BMW can outrun anything the army has on the road. But hey, orders are orders.

Just when you thought this wasn't stupid enough, the HQ told them if the man tried to run, "just shoot him." Hey, Einstein! All we have to do is handcuff him, throw him in the back of a Humvee, and no shots would have to be fired at all! Morons! Can anybody see where this is going?

As they left the scene of the car search, the Bradleys started out for base with the BMW in the middle. Up ahead was a side road that is nice and blacktopped, not to mention flat as a pancake, perfect for an all-out dash. Sure enough, the car pulled a hard left and hit the gas. Couldn't see that one coming! One of the Bradleys swung its turret and shot the car. Without going in to gory details, they got him. So, instead of interrogating a potential source of intelligence, they now got a corpse. Unfortunately, it is not our unit that is calling the shots here. Our commander would never have had us attempt anything so foolish.

The most frightening thing I have seen here has to be the violence with which car bombs explode. Picture a car, maybe a Chevy or a Buick, loaded with artillery shells and some plastic explosive. The man driving it is on a suicide mission. He knows he will not live and he is prepared to die. Now imagine driving along the highway, and this car pulls right alongside of you and detonates. These cars are not marked. There is no way to differentiate a car bomb from a regular car. In essence, as we drive, every car is a potential car bomb.

Imagine driving to get groceries. Now picture every car as a possible car bomb just waiting to kill you. Kinda' makes you feel uneasy, does it not? When these things go off, they don't care who is around. Innocent people who are in the wrong place at the wrong time also get killed. It is terrible.

I was amazed at these people's willingness to martyr themselves for their god. But, after thinking about it for a bit, I realized actions such as these are not wrought by faith in god, but through brainwashing, fanaticism, and hatred. A true believer in God would never do something like this. But, then again, how many times in history have we seen people, both Christian and Islamic alike, kill in the name of God? I just don't get it.

The most sickening thing I have seen is one day when we were still patrolling in Baghdad, a car bomb went off on a convoy of army vehicles. We responded and shut down the road. Unfortunately, one soldier was killed if, I remember right, as well as a taxi driver who just happened to be in the wrong place at the wrong time. The car bomber's car was literally ripped to shreds. Pieces of it were strewn for many yards. That wasn't the most grisly part either. Pieces of the driver of the car bomb were strewn about, too. When we asked what we were to do with the remains of the car bomber, we were told, "To hell with him. Let what's left of his ass rot in the sun." I didn't have too much of a problem with that considering he had, after all, taken the life of a fellow soldier. What I saw the next day, however, was almost too sickening to put into words.

The next day we were back out on patrol on the same stretch of road where the car bomb had detonated the day prior. As we passed the scene of the attack, we could see a couple dogs in the median. They appeared to be eating. As we drove by, we could see the remains of a human leg in the ditch. The dogs had found a repast in what was left of the suicide bomber. If anything I have seen here will cause me to awake at night in a cold sweat that will be it.

But, for now I am only dreaming of pagers going off and trips to the ER. Hopefully, the more horrific things I have seen here will not bother me in later life. If they were going to, I would suspect I would be feeling it by now.

Jason Adams
Camp Cooke, Iraq

Notice   Training   Deployment   Home leave   Back Home
10/12/03   3/1/04   9/26-10/14/04   3/19/05

A Friend Lost

Today is February 11th

Well it is official, Lenny is gone. After the elections, third platoon went up to the cop shop again for a few days. While there, they inquired as to the validity of the reports surrounding Lenny's kidnapping and murder. The police confirmed what we had already feared. It seems they had found Lenny's body out along a canal road. His hands had been tied behind his back and two bullets had been fired through the back of his head. His body was left to rot alongside the scrub brush that parallels the canal. His death came at the hands of men who killed him simply because he worked for us. Lenny was just a simple guy. He just wanted to work and earn a living. Of all the things I have seen here, this has affected me the most. But, I would like to think some of the happiest days of his life were spent working for Foxtrot Battery. From the start, we treated him like an equal rather than a servant. I think he knew this and actually looked forward to coming to work. I have prayed for him at least once every day since I first learned of his death.

As far as the police station goes, a couple days after the elections, the telephone on the desk of the police chief rang. Upon answering, the voice on the other end of the line told him he, along with the other policemen there, had five minutes to vacate the building and surrender their weapons. It seemed the insurgents had figured out big brother was no longer there. The police chief told the caller, if you are man enough to come get them, bring it on. And so they did.

As soon as the caller had hung up, the chief yelled to his men to get their guns and get ready. About five minutes went by, and a rocket struck the balcony where I used to sit and enjoy my morning coffee. One of the policemen who had been standing there

About five minutes went by, and a rocket struck the balcony where I used to sit and enjoy my morning coffee.

was, for the most part, vaporized. Striking right below one of the rooftop positions, another rocket scored a hit. The front of the building was riddled with bullets, and all told, there was one policeman killed and two wounded. But, they stood their ground. They fought back like soldiers and did not allow the insurgents to grab hold of any more weapons. Their steadfast determination in the face of a foe of unknown numbers reflects greatly upon the policemen. I am proud of them. I am saddened by the loss though. I didn't really know the man who was killed very well, but I knew who he was. The insurgents here seem to be a lot like a river; they like the path of least resistance. They won't stand and fight it out with us. They hit us like cowards and scurry away into the night like the vermin they are. Hopefully, they now know the police station will not be for them a free lunch. Knowing this, they may think twice before messing with them again.

Since we are not going up to the police station anymore, our new mission is just plain dumb. We are back patrolling the same few miles of road we had patrolled upon first being reassigned to Camp Cooke. This stretch of road is, for the most part, straight as an arrow. It is split into two zones, north and south, and is now patrolled by no less than 12 trucks, for 12 hours a day. It used to be patrolled by just three trucks for varying hours a day. I am not sure if I am supposed to say the name of the road, you know how the army loves all of that "top-secret" cloak and dagger stuff. Let's just say its name is synonymous with graft and corruption. Sometime when I get home, if you want to know what I mean, just ask me. I will explain it to you.

See, it is like this. We don't need that many trucks out there, we really don't. But, the battalion commander found out with the manpower we have, we were able to get the guys on a schedule of working one 12-hour shift and getting the next day off. That is a great schedule. We have been running ourselves ragged these past months, and now that we are in our final days of being here, a light workload would be most welcome. But the colonel said, "No." So, we drive around like idiots on a road that is covered with other military traffic for 12 hours a day. Driving in circles is basically what we do. Plus, they are small circles at that! The north zone is only about five miles or so, roundtrip. Talk about boring! The other day, I counted our trucks, plus three other trucks that take care of the Iraqi National Guard soldiers who are manning a checkpoint, two M-1 Abrams tanks, two Bradleys and every once in awhile two Apache gunships would fly overhead. Can anyone say "overkill?" But, like always, we just do as we are told and drive on.

So, while we patrol now with the insane schedule we have been given, we have also had to find time to move. We didn't have to move far, only a few trailers away. Matter of fact, I didn't even use a Humvee to move my stuff. I just carried it. The thing that irks me most is they made us hurry up and move, but nobody has even moved into our old trailers! They are just sitting there empty. I don't care about it though. We knew we would have to move like this about a week after we got here, so we can't say we weren't forewarned. Plus, most of our stuff is packed up and moving didn't take me more than a couple hours. We managed to keep our Internet as we moved, which is a plus, and my trailer is right by the showers! In the old trailer, my roommate and I were the only ones there, and we had plenty of room. Now, there are three of us in the same size room, but since we have less junk, we are no less pressed for space. I had to give up my desk and the office chair I found in the dumpster back when we first got here. We had to give up our 29-inch television, DVD player, and PS2 as well. But, because all this was necessary for us to come home, we gladly parted with the luxury items. Now, we aren't quite sure how many days we will have to stay in these trailers, but we are guessing about two or three weeks at the most. So, we get to live out of duffel bags for a little bit– who cares!

For the last few weeks, truck upon truck, trailer upon trailer has been rolling in the front gate here. To say it is like seeing a watering hole in the middle of a desert would be an understatement. You see, these guys are our replacements. They have come in droves for days now! Tanks, trucks, forklifts, bulldozers; you name it! It is such a beautiful sight! Finally, the day we thought would never come is finally on the horizon. But, with the new arrivals come other problems as well. Lines, for example. The chow hall is packed these days. The PX is like Wal-Mart on November 26th! Upon entering the barbershop the other

You see, these guys are our replacements. They have come in droves for days now. It is such a beautiful sight!

day, I took a number and went to sit down and wait. To my surprise, there was nowhere to sit! The number ticket in my hand read "8," I looked at the "Now Serving" sign and it read "45." Needless to say, I didn't get a haircut that day. I went to the other barbershop, and the situation was almost identical. Running out of options, I decided to peek into the beauty salon. Hey, they cut hair, too, right? Besides, I was thinking about a trendy new look anyway.

I stuck my head in the door and it, too, was packed. So, back to my trailer I went, long hair and all, to wait for the next day. As I walked, I decided I would get there well before they opened and be guaranteed a spot in line.

The next morning, I awoke around 0700 hours, went and had breakfast, walked over to the barbershop, and was standing outside the door a full hour before the first lock of hair would hit the floor. I had been standing in line for only about five minutes when a couple other guys walked up and asked if I was in line for a haircut. By 0830 hours, there were no less than 30 guys in line! The barbers showed up, looked at the line, and let out an audible sigh before unlocking the door. I had to laugh. Later in the day, I had to go to the post office to mail a box of junk home. The line at the barbershop should have served as an indicator as to what the line at the post office would look like. I pulled into the parking lot and saw a couple M35A2 "deuce' n halves" filled with boxes sitting in the crowded blacktopped area. Men were unloading boxes and footlockers, all in hopes of mailing them home. Each box has to be inspected, and the paperwork to mail one of those boxes takes a few minutes so each package takes several minutes to prepare for shipping. Then the sender has to wait in another line just to pay for the postage. As I looked at the men unloading the boxes, I did some quick math in my head and realized unless I wanted to wait in line for several hours, I had better beat these guys to the door. Luck was on my side, and it only took me half an hour to mail my package. When I came out from paying the postage, the men I had seen out in the parking lot had now entered the search area and had all their belongings scattered about in disarray. I made it just in time! I can't help but wonder about how much money that little post office takes in a day. Hundreds upon hundreds of boxes go out of there everyday, especially since an entire brigade is leaving here! I myself have spent about $200 just getting some of my stuff home. I can't imagine how much the guys in the M35A2 are about to drop. But, it is money well spent if you ask me.

Speaking of money, since the arrival of our replacements, it has been like one big garage sale around here. My roommate and I had talked about what we were going to do with all our junk because we knew we certainly couldn't take it all with us! We decided to sell what we could, send

> **Since the arrival of our replacements, it has been like one big garage sale around here.**

some home, and throw the rest in the dumpster. Let's just say very little went in the dumpster! For the past few weeks, there have been flyers up at the post office, the phone center, the PX, the chow hall, everywhere! All for the purpose of announcing going home sales. People were selling everything from couches to beanbag chairs to full-sized refrigerators! Carlos and I decided, "If they can do it, so can we!" In a matter of days we had sold most of our junk. The only thing I didn't sell was my desk. I was asking 20 bucks, which isn't bad considering I paid 60 dollars for it. But it would appear no one needs a desk in their room. So, I gave it away. I have never been one for haggling prices. Car salesmen love me.

I was sitting in the chow hall the other night eating what is undoubtedly one of the last meals I will eat here. I grabbed a copy of the *The Stars and Stripes* newspaper to peruse through while I ate dinner. I always like to read *The Stars and Stripes* and then check the news online. The reason I do this is so I can see the difference in what a quasi-military production reports on versus a civilian media service. The difference is always thought-provoking. One thing you all back home might not have heard about is the insurgent's newest tactic: Killing barbers in Baghdad that give western style haircuts. Yes, that's right, folks, western style haircuts! I hadn't realized doing so was punishable by death! If I remember right, it seems the people doing the killing were doing so because men here are supposed to all be sporting long beards. But, many of the guys opt for tightly trimmed beards or just a simple moustache. That, according to some, is a crime against Islam and must be countered by death. To me, I see it as an act of desperation. The insurgents are trying everything they can think of to force their will upon others. They are trying to force their version of the truth onto those who do not see things like they do. But, to what end will this work? The way I see it, why kill the barbers? After all, it is the customer that dictates how their hair and beard should look, not the person doing the cutting! The barbers here are finding themselves between Iraq and a hard place! (Forgive the pun.) They have to make a living and in a country whose economy is still reeling from years of war and tyranny, any job one can find is worth holding onto at all costs, even the threat of death. But, with this latest campaign of terror, how can anyone not see who the real enemy is here? How can one say it is us? How can anyone say it is us, the Americans, who are bringing it on? It is absurd. A blind man could see where the problem lies. It is just that in our current state of mind– appeasement– we are unable to name the enemy. We all know what it is; we just can't bring ourselves to say it. In time though, the world will grow weary of the acts of these terrorists and finally do something. The current policy of some countries is to simply pretend these terrorists do not really pose a threat; some even go so far as to try to kiss their butts. This will not work in the long run and deep down, we all know it. Remember the "Peace in our time" bit? Yeah, we all know how long that lasted. History has shown how appeasement encourages aggressors. Give them an inch and the next thing ya know, they want a foot. How long must my fellow soldiers and I bear the brunt of this fight? We have been called world police. Yeah? Well, somebody has to do it! And if I have said it once, I have said it a million times, I am very glad *OUR* president had the foresight to do it.

As we wrap up our mission here and prepare for our trip back across the ocean, I find myself reflecting back upon this journey that has taken me from my home for these many months. It is almost like a dream when I think in a few weeks I will again be home, back in my rusty old beater of a truck, driving up town to get a cup of coffee, and pester the manager of Casey's about her over-priced doughnuts and greasy pizza. Around the

There is an air of expectation, of excitement, that is electrifying. Conversations consist of what we are going to do when we get home.

trailers here, there is an air of expectation, of excitement, that is electrifying. Conversations consist of what we are going to do when we get home. Most of the younger guys are talking of buying cars, going on vacations, and of course, partying. I plan to kick back and get a little crazy, but I am usually the first one to get tired and go to bed. However, I pity the town we decide to hold our first "coming home" party in, I really do!

Jason Adams
Camp Cooke, Iraq

Notice
10/12/03

Training

Deployment
3/1/04

Home leave
9/26-10/14/04

Back Home
3/19/05

The Light at the End of the Tunnel

Today is February 15th

We are coming to the point in this deployment in which rumors fly at the speed of light. One minute we are leaving here on this day, the next thing you know you are hearing the old "I know for a fact…." bit all over again only this time with an entirely new date and time. As a section sergeant, my guys come up to me and ask constantly about such things as when we are done running missions and when we are moving to the staging barracks. I have to tell them I honestly don't know. Nobody knows. It ain't over 'til the fat lady sings, and she isn't even in the building yet. Trouble is, I want to know, too. We all do. We have been here for a long time and the light at the end of the tunnel is blinding us right now. Unfortunately, we just can't seem to get close to it. Don't get me wrong, time is dwindling here. Our days here are coming to an end. Soon, we will be making that trip back across the pond to our home soil. It is just this endless wondering and waiting that is driving us all batty.

We are done with the moronic patrolling out on the highway. Now, we again head back to the police station, but not to stay. We are just patrolling the area for a set period of time, and then we return back here to Camp Cooke. It is, to me, a rather pointless mission. But, we just do as we are told. Like all wars, when a unit comes close to leaving the theater, all thoughts turn to getting everyone home safe. Well, that isn't happening. Just the other night an IED injured some of our guys. They are all okay, but nevertheless, one of them was evacuated to Germany. Now as we head down the same stretch of road that is pockmarked with craters from IEDs, we wonder who will be next. Everyday I wake up here is one less time I have to.

Third platoon went up to the police station yesterday. They just got back a little bit ago. GQ came into my room shortly thereafter. He and I talked for a little bit. He told me he could see a change in the people up there. They didn't want us around at all.

GQ told me that he could see a change in the people up there. They didn't want us around at all.

They never were the friendliest of people up there, but we managed to get along for the most part. GQ said he stopped over to see Bob-kabob and he wouldn't even sell him any food. He offered no reasons, just "No." The folks up there are scared of the insurgents, yet offer no help to us in their apprehension. They just pretend they don't see them planting IEDs in front of their homes, burying weapons caches in among their fields or abusing the locals.

We never had problems like this back down at the airport. Of course, we are up in what is known as the Sunni Triangle now. People are different up here. They are the minority in this country and with the elections and all, felt they were going to lose considerable control over Iraq (Saddam Hussein is Sunni). They were told by their leaders to boycott the elections, and many did, I suspect. How can your candidate win, when no one votes? At some point in time though, they are going to have to choose. They will have to choose between the insurgents and the Americans. The main difference here is this, the insurgents are just here to fight and kill. We are here to help. One would think these folks see that, but they don't. At what point will these people get the point and realize who the real threat to them and their way of life is? I tell you this, that threat does not drive a Humvee, nor does it speak English as its native tongue.

Since this time here is drawing to a close, some personnel changes are taking place. Since we have been here in country, we have borrowed two platoon leaders from our battalion. Although they were with first and third platoons, I got to know them a little in these last few months. Both of them are great guys and great officers. The other night, our unit had a pizza party and awards ceremony as a sort of send-off for LT Gunn. LT Joey C. as he was known, had to leave early due to a family emergency. We really didn't get to say goodbye to him, but I have a feeling we will be seeing them both again later on this spring at the Battalion Ball. We all crowded into a little room adjacent from our TOC. Soon, most of the battery was crowded into this little room at the position of attention as the commander pinned a Bronze Star Medal onto LT Gunn's DCU jacket. As one of the other men read the citation for the award, LT Gunn shook both the commander's hand as well as Top's. I think he was a little humbled after receiving such an award. He offered a few remarks afterward, saying it was because of the efforts of his platoon he was given that award. I thought his remarks both fitting as well as heartfelt. LT Gunn, as I know him, is a very competent leader and just a really nice guy. He deserves the award, and I am glad we were all there to watch him get it.

SGT Ryan Peterson was also awarded the Army Commendation Medal for actions during the Battle of Holy Week. If I remember right, the truck in which he was acting as gunner was hit by an RPG. Both the driver and team chief were wounded, and the other man in the back of the Humvee had been shot in the mouth. It was an act of God, but the truck was still running as the driver got them out of the kill zone. SGT Peterson managed to help the young soldier that was shot in the mouth while simultaneously laying down return fire with the truck's crew served weapon. The wounded soldier, although now fully recovered, was evacuated to Germany and has not been back here since. The battle that took place that night was the first of many fights we had that week of Easter 2004.

The night the soldier was shot in the mouth was one of the first of many times someone from this unit should have died, but didn't. My team alone has escaped death on a few occasions. The day the rocket impacted a few yards from half my platoon should have killed them all, but not one had so much as a scratch. My truck still bears the scars from the IED that should have killed every man in it. EOD, or "the bomb squad", said it was an aerial bomb that had been buried next to the road! An aerial bomb! Those puppies are dropped from airplanes! How did we survive? I can only look to the sky and give credit where credit is due, for it has been through no efforts of mine, that my team and I are still here.

I can only look to the sky and give credit where credit is due, for it has been through no efforts of mine, that my team and I are still here.

After the awards, we had pizza! There is a Pizza Hut carryout place here on post now, and some of the guys went up there and came back with a ton of pizza. The money for the pies was provided by the Galva American Legion Post. I can't say enough good things about those guys. They have been nothing short of amazing since we deployed. It seems like every time we turn around, they are sending us phone cards, money for pizza or whatever. It is nice to know there are people so dedicated to us back home. It sure makes this deployment a lot easier to stomach.

Jason Adams
Camp Cooke, Iraq

Stetson

Today is February 17th

We went back up to the police station yesterday for 12 hours and ran patrols in Tarmiyah. In some ways, it felt good to be back up there. Most of the guys were complaining it sucked, but it is far better for me to be sitting at the police station than running 12-hour hot laps around a five-mile track out on the highway. Plus, it was good to see some of the cops still alive. Likewise, having seen the damage from the attacks on the police station through pictures, it was neat to be able to survey the damage firsthand. Well, "neat" is probably not the most apt terminology. Perhaps "satisfies my morbid curiosity" would be more accurate. Indeed, the pictures do not lie. The front of the police station is riddled with bullets; the northwest corner is damaged from an RPG impact. The balcony is now sporting a rather nice hole in the front of it from yet a second RPG impact. Above the balcony, splattered on the ceiling, is the remains of the policeman who was manning that position at the time of the impact. Sadly, the police are not unfamiliar with this kind of event. They have seen it all before. This is not the first time this particular police station has been attacked. The main thing is they are still there. They are still there doing their jobs, and to me, this is commendable.

We spent all day up at the police station running patrols in the city. After awhile, we were becoming pretty bored. All the amenities we once had in the police station have since been moved out. All the chairs, weights, television set, and satellite are gone. For the most part, there is nothing to do. Matter of fact, we didn't even spend any time in the building. We sat out in and around our Humvees all day, talking, napping, and aimlessly trying anything to keep our minds occupied. There are some sheets of plywood there we brought up to make our gun positions on the roof back when we first took over the compound. The sheets of wood lying down alongside the building are those that were not needed in the construction of the fighting positions and were left there for the police to use. Bored out of my mind, I walked by and pulled out my knife and threw it at one of the sheets that was leaning up against the building. By luck, it stuck perfectly in the wood! A couple guys saw it and voiced their approval at my deftness with throwing knives. I had to concede it was luck, and my second throw confirmed this fact. Soon, most everyone that had a knife was lined up by a line that had been made in the dirt. A target was drawn on the plywood, and we spent the next hour or so throwing our knives at this innocent sheet of glue and wood chips. Ka-bars, Spydercos, Bucks, and Shrades– even a Gerber or two– were heaved at this wood, all for the sake of amusement. Yes, as a matter of fact, we are pathetic! But, being so close to coming home, yet still running missions, not too many of us can sit still for a second, and every hour we have to feels like an entire day has passed.

Because we have been deployed with the First Cavalry Division, we now are authorized to wear the Cav Stetson hat. It is really pretty cool and certainly unique to the First Cav. The Stetson comes in many different styles, and each comes with a colored band that denotes officer or enlisted. Rather expensive to buy and certainly not something one wears in everyday life, I ordered one online the other day nonetheless. My roommates and I have all ordered ours from the same company, and we are planning on wearing them to our Battalion Ball later on this spring. Many of the men in this unit have purchased them. It should be pretty cool to see a roomful of guys all wearing the Cav Stetson. I am sure it will be a source of animosity with the guys of our battalion who are not authorized to wear them, but hey, they aren't here. They haven't been through all the fun and excitement we have for the past 16 months. I, along with the rest of this unit, really couldn't care less of what others think. To us though, it will serve as a symbol of pride. A bond, if you will, between soldiers from three different units who came together and fought as one. I ordered a hat rack to store it on when I am not wearing it. I am very proud to have served as a member of this division, and it only seems fitting to be the owner of such a recognizable symbol of my affiliation with these soldiers. Forever will the First Cavalry Division's familiar patch adorn the right shoulder of my uniform, and all who see it will know I went to war with the Cav.

Because we have been deployed with the First Cavalry Division, we now are authorized to wear the Cav Stetson hat.

With all of the things going on here between packing, patrolling, thinking about leaving, IEDs, car bombs, and the myriad of other things that occupy my mind, it would seem I am worrying about all one possibly could. Ahh, not so! It seems my little girl is about to have her second surgery since I have been gone. It all started a few years ago with her. Joanna had been having repeated attacks of bladder infections. It seemed as though she would get rid of one, only to get another. Bed-wetting was also a problem and no matter what Steph and I tried, nothing seemed to work. Acting on the doctor's advice, we tried getting her up every few hours at night and taking her to the bathroom. We tried medications designed to relax the muscular wall of her bladder, thus allowing it to fill more before she had to go. We tried not letting her have liquids after six p.m. at night. We tried everything. We had sonograms done, countless doctor visits, drug regimens, but nothing worked. Every morning, Steph and I would find her snuggled in between us in our bed as hers was a soppy mess. Steph and I talked about it as time went on and worried her bedtime problem, if unchecked, might have lingering psychological problems because she wanted to spend the night at friends' homes, but worried she would wet the bed.

Our oldest daughter had the same problem until she was four years old. While four, Teryl had to undergo a tonsillectomy. Amazingly, after the operation, she never again wet the bed. Joanna was different. Last year while I was at Fort Hood preparing to deploy, Joanna developed enlarged tonsils and endured several bouts of tonsillitis. Surgery was scheduled and the operation went off without a hitch. But, unlike her sister, Joanna continued to suffer from bed-wetting. Finally, in desperation, Steph took Joanna to a different urologist in Peoria. After a battery of tests, it was determined one of Joanna's kidneys is enlarged and only functioning at 23 percent. The doctor said urine is flowing backward into the kidneys and causing the majority of her problems. She said surgery is an option and after some more testing, it would be confirmed whether or not it would be advisable. Sure enough, the doctor said surgery was needed. So, once again I am not able to be there for it. Steph has had to do it all. It really sucks I have to be here and all I can do is worry. But, Joanna is proving to be a little trooper and is taking it all very well. I am constantly amazed at the composure kids can possess when told they have to have an operation. The doctor told Steph the problem can be fixed but the damage that is already done cannot. Joanna will not be able to have soda pop or greasy fast-food ever again, according to the doctor. She is taking all of this in stride and Steph has already cleansed the house of soda pop. Steph and I agree if one of us must alter our diet, then we all will. We are a family, and we try to do things together, up to and including dietary restrictions.

For the life of me, I cannot understand why the previous doctor never found Joanna's problem. I would like to ask him, but he died last year. The only good thing to come out of me being gone for this long is the insurance the army has given us. It is great and has covered almost everything Steph and the kids have needed medical-wise. It is comforting to know that is one less thing I have to worry about. If they do get sick, pertinent and prompt care is always very close by. Tricare doesn't pay for everything though! Steph told me she received a bill for anesthetic from the hospital for Joanna's tonsillectomy. After contacting Tricare, it seems anesthetic is not covered. It seems one doesn't need it! Yeah, right, I wonder how the person who made up that rule would like it if a doctor went to carving on them without the aid of a little something for the pain.

Jason Adams
Camp Cooke, Iraq

Notice
10/12/03

Training

Deployment
3/1/04

Home leave
9/26-10/14/04

Back Home
3/19/05

Idle Hands

Today is February 19ᵗʰ

Today, some of our vehicles are to be turned in. Crew served weapons, Surefire Flashlights, two-way talkabout radios, and GPS systems are to be handed into supply. Our time here is rapidly coming to a close. Soon, we will be on helicopters and en route to Kuwait, going out the same way we came in, except this time it will be via C-130s rather than via Humvees. In a few days, we will move into the holding billets, surge housing as it is called, but don't ask me what that means. To us, it is just a ramshackle building we will sleep in until it is time to go. Yes, that is about what we are down to here, the most hated and natural part of army life– waiting around. We have, for the most part, nothing to do.

Camp Cooke has seen a massive influx of people over the last few days, and everything is packed. Phone centers, Internet cafés, barbershops, and the PX are characterized by long lines. The need for going to any one of them must be weighed by how much time one can stand to wait in a line. For most of us, we grow weary of waiting in line for we have been doing so for almost a year and a half now. When contemplating whether or not I need more razor blades, I must balance using a dull one versus waiting in line for an hour. I think I can suffer for another week or two.

> **The need for going anywhere must now be weighed by how much time one can stand to wait in a line.**

Our Internet is off now for good. That wouldn't otherwise bother me, but it is the manner in which it was shut off that irks me. We all knew sooner or later the satellites would be sold, thus our days of emailing and instant messenger would go the way of the dodo. We were prepared for this, and to be real honest, not too many people were that torn up about it. Soon enough, we will all be surfing the net from the comfort of our own homes. We figured they would give us a heads-up as to when the system would be shut down. Yeah, not so! We came back from Tarmiyah the other day, and the little icon down at the bottom right of my computer screen had a little X through it and the infamous words "network cable unplugged" glared at me. While we were gone on a mission, the people in charge of the Internet decided to just rip it out and sell it. No warning, no chance for people to email home one last time and forewarn loved ones. They just came through and cut lines and tore down the satellites. Pretty rude, if you ask me! The excuse they offered upon being called out was weak, "You knew we were gonna sell it!" True, but is 24-hours warning too much to ask? I would bet my last dollar their families all received notice of the forthcoming shutdown. Ahh, that is but water under the bridge now. That was four days ago if I remember right, heck, I am not really sure anymore.

One of the biggest problems we face, but I don't think it bothers all of us the same, is the overbearing feeling that, since having moved up here to Camp Cooke, we haven't accomplished much. This is by no fault of ours, rather, we can only do what we are allowed to do. Allow me to elaborate on this a little.

When we were first tasked with our old zone, we had leeway. This latitude extended throughout our zone, the whole 55-square miles of it. We had assets we could use, i.e.; engineers, civilian labor, money for projects, you name it. This allowed us to accomplish many things that would have otherwise gone undone. At one point, we had a crew of civilian laborers cutting down reeds along a canal that ran parallel to the interstate, that were allowing the enemy to fire at us from concealed positions. The shoulders of the roads were leveled so planting an IED became harder. We took fresh water to folks who otherwise had none. We provided security for medical missions for people who would otherwise not get to see a doctor, much less a well supplied doctor. We built schools, we got to know the locals, and we took wheelchairs to kids who had none. We did these things because we were allowed to! If we felt the need to search a house, we didn't need to get anyone's approval beforehand. If we wanted to detain a suspect or if somebody was acting spooky, we hauled them in, no questions. The battalion we were with, the 4/5 ADA, was great. They trusted us and came to rely on our unit as one that could accomplish whatever task that was needed. But, all good things must come to an end. In this case, the end was a brick wall.

After the time spent at the airport, having made some really good things happen, most of us looked forward to building upon these things as we made the trip up to Camp Cooke. Sadly, our hands have been tied behind our backs since our arrival up here. It isn't our fault. It isn't we do not want to continue doing these good things, we simply aren't allowed. The only thing we have done here is drive around and needlessly endanger our guys. We have done no water missions and we have not helped rebuild infrastructure. Hell, we haven't even gotten to know the locals like we did in our old zone. Our missions have consisted of aimlessly driving up and down the highway, sitting at the police station, and manning assorted static traffic control points. What a waste of time and manpower. I think what torques me most about all this is we could have been doing good things here. For example, we found out pretty quickly the shoulders of the roads are overgrown, just like the ones on the interstate used to be. When the shoulders are bare, it is harder to hide IEDs. In our old zone, we were able to arrange it so a civilian contractor made a little money and return. He brought out his road maintainers and shaved the sides of the road for us. Up here, we just can't seem to get it done. We have even contemplated dumping diesel fuel alongside the road and burning the scrub brush off ourselves. But, I imagine some heads would roll if we did that.

Over the past few days, I have tested the water, as they say, regarding these thoughts. Most, if not all, the men agree. We are wasting our time here. How have we helped the people of Iraq? What positive things have we done since moving up here? Yeah, I suppose our presence here has helped quell the threat of insurgents some. One could make the argument the police station did not get hit until we left.

Most of the men agree. We are wasting our time here. How have we helped the people of Iraq? What positive things have we done since moving up here?

The upper leadership is not out in zone with us. I don't really expect them to be; that is not their job, it is ours. But, they rely on us to be their eyes and ears on the ground and when we make recommendations and suggestions, we should not be ignored. When lower ranking individuals point out the obvious, I would like to think the colonel sees it too. How loud must we yell? Upon what rooftop must we perch ourselves and scream for them to hear our cries? We rely on the brass for orders, leadership, and direction. They rely on us for executing orders and to provide intelligence. Our intelligence is going unused. We know the area we are in is dirty, yet we do not search houses or snoop through the countryside. We could be doing so much more, but we can't. Why you ask? It would be far easier to count the hair upon the back of a grizzly bear than for me to put forth an answer for that question. I simply do not know. The problem is feeling as though we are bound and then told to fight is a helpless feeling. As leaders, we are supposed to inspire the men. We are the ones that are supposed to have answers to the men's questions. So, how do I react when my guys come up and ask me, "Why are we doing this?" What am I to tell them, It's your job? Because we have to? Don't ask why, just do it? Answers such as these only work for awhile. True, we do what we are told. None of us has a problem with the dangers involved in what we do. Sometimes though, and I don't think this is asking too much, we would just like to know why. An honest answer is not asking too much, I do not think. So, lacking answers, we plug on. But, the morale of the men goes down another notch everytime we get stuck with another bullshit mission for no apparent reason. This is only my opinion, but I would like to think while everyone of us would rather be home, since is not an option, if we are going to be here, we might as well be doing something with our time. Our unit has handed out a lot of Purple Hearts. I would like to go home knowing those wounds were payment for something done to help those we are here to protect. We, too, must justify those flag-draped coffins.

Jason Adams
Camp Cooke, Iraq

Notice 10/12/03   Training   Deployment 3/1/04   Home leave 9/26-10/14/04   Back Home 3/19/05

Prayer to St. Joseph

Today is February 20ᵗʰ

Yea, though I walk through the valley of the shadow of death, I shall fear no evil, for thou art with me. — Ps. 23:4

Ever since I left home, I have carried in my wallet a prayer which my dad gave to me upon our activation. Known as the Prayer to St. Joseph, it has been around since not long after Jesus was here. In 1505, it was sent from the pope to Emperor Charles as he was going into battle. It is meant to protect all

All of us in our own way are counting our blessings, and reflecting back upon those moments when we should have died or at least have been mangled. Why is it that we march on unscathed?

those who hear it, or carry it about themselves, from a violent death. As our part of this war comes to a close, all of us, in our own way, are counting our blessings and reflecting back upon those moments when, after all other reasoning fails, we should have died or at least have been mangled. Why is it we march on unscathed? Not all of us are without scars. Matter of fact, we have handed out a ton of awards for wounds received. But, as far as the brutality of what we face here goes, they are but scratches. As I sit here and go through my pictures, I find myself thinking many times we should have lost someone. Only a few guys have had to be sent home as a result of their injuries. Only one is still hospitalized as a result. But, Dusty will pull through (his biggest problem is recovering from being burned so badly). Most of our wounded were RTD'd (returned to duty) in a couple days. I am so thankful that for the most part, we have remained safe throughout this year of being here.

I read a book while I was home on leave titled *A Table in the Presence*. Like the opening sentence of this last entry, the title for this book comes from Psalm 23. The book is written by a marine chaplain who was among the first men to cross the border of Iraq in 2003 when we invaded. The story chronicles the military as well as spiritual journey of a bunch of marines as they go into harm's way. Beautiful, poignant, and very inspirational. At times when I was reading it, I had to stop and pray a little because I was so touched by it. The book talks about how a bunch of guys fought together, bled together, and in some cases, died together, but through it all, the men grew in spirituality and faith. Some were even baptized for the first time! Many stories in the book tell how the men were spared as a result of RPGs failing to explode, RPGs suddenly veering off target, walls of bullets hitting nothing but air. The list goes on. It was as if they were protected from all of it. Well, I shouldn't say "as if." I believe they, like us, have been watched over since the day our boots first hit the sands of Kuwait. So many people have our names on their prayer lists, so many of us pray for our own safety and that of our unit, how can God ignore us? Yes, we are in a war. Yes, people are getting hurt here. But, I have seen surveys that are saying people are praying more these days than in years past. Think about it, more people talking to God! Is the loss somehow worth it? Is my presence here causing more of my friends and family back home to raise up their thoughts to heaven? If it is, then my time here is even better spent than I had previously thought! I am sure some of my buddies here would read this and wonder what the heck I have been smoking, but I assure you, not all of us think alike. Not all of us see in black and white. Some people see things in many shades of gray, but that is not a bad thing. Some of the most interesting people I know have spent their entire lives in the "gray area."

We still have a couple of missions left. Bad things can still happen. It is not unheard of for a person to be killed or badly wounded on their last mission. But, if the past eleven months can serve as an indicator, I am confident we will all make it home just fine. Besides, and I have said this many times, I am the kind of guy who makes it through the hardest of times only to trip and break my neck while exiting the airplane once it is home. That is just about how my luck runs.

Jason Adams
Camp Cooke, Iraq

Losing Hearts and Minds

Today is February 22nd

Well, one mission left. One more pointless trip up to the police station and we will be done. The other day we went up there and sat for 12 hours; what a waste. The entire place seems different these days. It is one of those things you can feel, but can't quite put a finger on. The policemen seem different, the townspeople, while never exactly friendly, these days just stare at us when we pass. The building, once filled with cots, snacks, weight sets, a television, and a satellite is now empty. No sign of the previous occupant can be found, save for the sandbags we stacked up in the window sills. The desk I used to sit and write at is gone, as is the chair. The place seems hollow, empty, lifeless. I don't like it at all.

The other day, I asked one of the cops if he would run across the street and pick me up a soda pop. He nodded his head, and I gave him a couple bucks for the pop. He said something to Jaguar and handed Jag the money. Jaguar then opened up his own wallet, put the two American dollars in, and handed the cop the equivalent back in Iraqi

Jaguar said that the people in town don't like the American money anymore, and if the cop shows it, it means that he has been around the Americans.

dinars. This seemed odd to me. We have never had a problem with the money exchange bit. I asked Jag why the cop had traded money with him. Jaguar said the people in town don't like the American money anymore, and if the cop shows it, it means he has been around the Americans. So much for winning "hearts and minds" as the army likes to call it. That battle was lost before we ever moved up to Tarmiyah.

A few days ago, while my team had the day off, my platoon was up at the police station pulling a shift. While there, another dead guy was brought into the compound. Unlike the others, this guy had been mutilated rather than just shot. While I wasn't there, I did, however, see the pictures and it isn't pretty.

The body was male and looked to be in his 20s. His throat had been slit, but whoever did it didn't know what they were doing. SFC Hess told me they hadn't even cut through the muscles of the neck. He had been stabbed several times in the neck area, and whoever killed him had also gouged out one of his eyes. Pretty grisly stuff, folks. To top it all off, some of the witnesses reported to the cops it had been the Americans who were responsible. Okay, stop right there. My unit is the only one in Tarmiyah. None of us is going to butcher a person and leave them to rot. Furthermore, if we were the ones who did it, why didn't we just shoot them rather than take the time to carve them up? Sounds to me like one of two things. One, somebody is trying to extort money from the coalition. (That one is nothing new.) Two, and this to me is more likely, someone is blaming the death on us to incite more hatred toward the Americans. Either way, I don't really care what motives are behind this poor guy's death. Bottom line is one more life is gone. Someone's son, someone's brother, and someone's friend is gone.

We passed our day playing with some puppies that live next door to the police station. The dogs are great. They haven't figured out yet we are Americans and because of that, they still like us. Well that, and we actually pet them and give them food. The puppies are pitiful, they are underweight, scraggly, and flea-infested. The fleas are so bad the dogs pass their day scratching. Some of the pups have bare spots on them from scratching so much. We felt pretty bad for them, but since we are packing up, we threw out all our flea collars. So, we fed them some MREs and bits of sandwiches we had brought instead. We played with them for awhile and just watched them play with each other for a bit too. I wonder how many of those little pups will live to be a year old. People back home are consistently amazed when they learn you cannot buy a bag of dog food here, nor is there a pet store to be found anywhere. People here just don't keep pets. Dogs sleep wherever they can find a spot and just snoop through the nearest pile of garbage when they need a meal. It is sad to see. Then I think of the big pile of lazy fur that graces my couch back home and I have to smile. I wonder how long my mutt would last over here.

Since we have lost our Internet, the list of things to do has gotten considerably shorter. But, some of the guys figured out when they activated the wireless portion of their computers, they could pick up a wireless connection! Yep, that's right! We have wireless Internet here, probably have had it for some time but nobody knew about it. The service is just as fast as what we had, but is kinda pricey, 25 bucks for 10 hours. If you are downloading junk like music, it gets pretty expensive. But, if you just want to check your email now and then, it's a pretty good deal. Most of the guys picked up on the offer right from the start. Yesterday, it looked like some kind of white trash Internet Café outside in front of the trailers. See, most of the guys cannot pick up a good signal from inside, so they must sit outside to use it. It was pretty funny to see 15 or so men all sitting on the steps of their trailers with their computers in their laps. Hence the term "laptop" I guess!

Jason Adams
Camp Cooke, Iraq

The Last Mission

Today is February 24th

Well, today is our last mission of this deployment. It is a day that for the longest time seemed like it was just a figment of our imagination. At times, it felt as though we would never be done. For awhile, we heard rumors here and there about extension, but given the success with the elections and all, we figured we would be leaving on time. It's weird but some months here have flown by at the speed of light, while others were like digging through granite. The month of January went fast, but this month has dragged on forever.

Today we head up to Tarmiyah one last time. One last run up the gauntlet of bomb craters, IEDs, and anything else the insurgents see fit to throw at us. We have been so lucky thus far in our trip up and down that road. Other units have lost people on it, but for us, we have had a couple wounded, but no deaths. We are very fortunate. But, why are we sitting at a police station with our thumbs in our rears, when the enemy can run free across the battlefield at will? The answer is complex, but to put it in one sentence: We are not allowed. Simple as that. I have yet

Today we head up to Tarmiyah one last time. One last run up the gauntlet of bomb craters, IEDs, and anything else the insurgents see fit to throw at us.

to understand the logic (or lack thereof) behind this restriction. We know where to sit and bag these suckers, but we can't. So, we just drive up and down the same road and pray we don't get hit. The only thing we have done to mitigate this risk is two things. One, we try to drive as much at night as possible so our night vision technology acts as a safeguard against target acquisition. Second, when we do have to go down that road, we run at high speeds, usually as fast as the slowest truck will go. It shouldn't have to be like this.

We should not have to run from the enemy here. But, we do. At times, it feels as though we, in the eyes of our battalion commander, are nothing more than an expendable asset. We call it "cannon fodder." It is a helpless feeling. One thing about it though, nobody can ever say we didn't do exactly as we were told. We ran every mission we were ordered to, regardless of the danger. That, in and of itself, speaks volumes as to the character of the men of this unit. As for our parent unit, their method of clearing that same route is to dismount and walk the road-sides looking for IEDs. Here's a thought, why not look for the scumbags that are planting the IEDs?

We ran every mission we were ordered to, regardless of the danger. That, in and of itself, speaks volumes as to the character of the men of this unit.

We made it to the police station around 0500 hours, unscathed yet again. As we pulled into the compound, we could see where the mortar had hit the day before. While third platoon had been pulling their last mission, a mortar shell came in. It landed right by one of the trucks and hit the very spot where, only hours before, one of the guys had been snoozing. Instead, the only thing it damaged was the puppies that have made the police station there home. There used to be six puppies. One died a few days ago, and one was looking pretty sick on our last trip up there. But there were still four healthy ones. And of course, there was Princess. That is the dog we adopted. Princess is still a pup, but she is about three months old. When the mortar shell exploded, it killed Princess and one other puppy. Those poor little pups didn't stand a chance.

Today was our "right seat rides" with the incoming unit. We thought they might show up around noon or so, but the only one who did show up was the boss. The boss is the guy who makes us pull this ridiculous mission, so most of us went and hid while he was there. While there, the boss decided the place had too much litter lying around, and he ordered us to do a police call. Problem was most of the litter was put there by the police, not us. Some of these folks over here don't believe in trash cans, but what were we to do, other than say, "Yes, sir," and clean the place up. As if that wasn't enough, the guy barked at Jaguar for not having his Kevlar helmet on. Jaguar wears DCUs and all the other junk we have to wear only because it helps him blend in with us, making it harder for a sniper to pick him out of the crowd. But, unlike us, Jag isn't bound by the same rules as we are. If he wants to wear his Kevlar, it is his option. Jaguar told the boss he was the interpreter, not a soldier, to which he replied, "I don't give a f**k, put it on anyway." That, ladies and gentlemen, is professionalism at its best.

Soon, we could hear some Bradleys coming our way. Not long thereafter, five Brads showed up and stopped in front of the cop shop. Great, I thought. Let's get this show on the road so we can go home. Unfortunately, the guy who got out of the track wasn't there for the right seat ride. He was the right guy, he just didn't know his unit would be taking over the police station and surrounding area. He said if he would have known all this, he would have brought more men with him. Usually, on a right seat ride, the leadership all goes out, not just the company commander. Basically, it was a wasted trip for both us as well as him. Oh sure, we showed him around, but as we left the cop shop, we left knowing today would not be our last mission after all. All on the count of a miscommunication.

It never ceases to amaze me that here, in the 21 century, there is still miscommunications. Today, there is a plethora of ways in which to convey information. Email, fax, telephone, walkie-talkie, face to face, via a radio, and yet information still gets jumbled. Kinda makes me wonder how the armies of yesteryear ever got anything right.

What made matters worse for us was everybody else had already turned in their ammo and crew served weapons, which meant the only ones going back out tomorrow will be us. I have to admit, I was angry. When you keep thinking "Tomorrow is it….live through tomorrow and you are home free!" only to find out you have to go on another mission has a serious effect on one's attitude. No one is immune from it. Especially when it is something of this magnitude. It isn't like we have to sweep out the bathroom one more time. No, we have to run the gauntlet again….twice. Once up, once back. Big time fun.

Well, its 2100 hours and word just came in we don't have to go back. Tomorrow we turn our stuff in and we are done. Thank God.

Jason Adams
Camp Cooke, Iraq

Going Home

A Not-So-Subtle Reminder

Today is February 25th

This morning I got up, skipped breakfast, and went to work cleaning all my junk for turn in. My night vision goggles, my smoke grenades, my fragmentation grenades, my antitank rocket, as well as most of my ammo all had to be cleaned prior to turn in. My team and I were the second ones down at the supply warehouse and were a full half hour early for turn in. Seth, my driver, said, "Hey, maybe we should hurry up and turn all this in so they can't make us go on anymore missions!" An excellent idea, I thought. As we walked out of the supply warehouse, recently liberated of so much junk, and, as the realization that for us, this war is all but over, I suddenly began to feel as though a great weight had been removed from about my neck. I felt as though I could breathe easy now. Many of the guys were saying the same thing as we carried equipment into the old dilapidated building that has served as our supply area since we got here. After we turned in equipment, we turned in our trucks, too. This meant we were on foot from here on out, but who cares. We hopped into the back of a five-ton truck and SFC Hess drove us back to our trailers.

As we walked out of the supply warehouse, recently liberated of so much junk, I suddenly began to feel as though a great weight had been removed from about my neck. I felt as though I could breathe easy now.

What we didn't learn until later on in the day was as we were cleaning our stuff for turn in, our parent unit and the new guys were headed up the gauntlet, en route to Tarmiyah. The way they do things to me, is just stupid. There is one area of the road that is flatout blown to hell. There are craters on both sides of the road from various IEDs and at least one car bomb. We blow through there in the dark at about 60 miles an hour. They stop, dismount and walk it. I wish I could say more about the logic behind their actions, but I can't. I simply do not understand it.

Our job is to capture or kill the enemy. The enemy's job is the same. So, it makes sense mounted or dismounted, the enemy is going to blow the IED anyway. It would be more advantageous for the enemy if we *were* dismounted because then we don't have the luxury of an armored truck to protect us, thus inflicting more damage on us. Such was the case this morning. As the men were walking, an IED went off, killing three and wounding nine or 10. Sadly, the dismounted soldiers were walking in front of five M1114 trucks, that up until a few minutes before they had been riding in. Had they been in the trucks, they might have only had a couple injured. We have fought for almost an entire year to try and secure some M1114s for our unit and get rid of the crap we are driving around in now. These morons have brand new M1114s, and they get out and walk. One of the dead is from our higher headquarters unit who is scheduled to leave here about the same time as us.

I just don't get it. Why would you get out of a truck that was specifically designed to protect soldiers from these roadside bombs and walk along a route that is known for IED activity? It makes absolutely no sense. Perhaps, there is less paperwork to fill out for a dead soldier than there is for a blownup truck. I don't know, but it pisses me off to no end when I sit and think there is a man in an office not far from here who sits, in the safety of the base here, and repeatedly sends his men out like lambs to the slaughter. Furthermore, this man will not let anyone do anything about the men who are planting these IEDs. There are plenty of spots to set up a sniper team, over watch positions or even, (hey, here's a thought), roving patrols? Why we repeatedly let the insurgents get a free lunch at our expense is beyond me. I am hopeful, though, the incoming commander can look at what his predecessor has done and say, "What the hell was he thinking?" for if he cannot, many more men shall be hurt on that very stretch of road that we travelled these many weeks.

Jason Adams
Camp Cooke, Iraq

Rules Are Rules

Today is March 1ˢᵗ
Five days until we leave Iraq.

For the past few days we have been like motionless slugs. Most of us have become downright lazy bums, lying in bed until well past breakfast. I am not one to cast judgment here, matter of fact, on more than one occasion I was guilty of this laziness. Ya know what, I kind of liked it. Now that all our equipment is turned over to the new unit and most of our stuff is packed up, there really isn't that much to do. We have daily softball games down at the ball diamond. We spend a ton of time

We have busted our rumps here for a year now. I think that we are entitled to be lazy for a few days.

watching movies and then, of course, we are getting fat from eating three meals a day in the chow hall which is conveniently situated a stone's throw from our trailers. I don't feel all too guilty about it though. We have busted our rumps here for a year now. I think we are entitled to be lazy for a few days. Upon reaching home there will be plenty to do.

Since the new division has assumed command of this post, there has been a slew of new and, for the most part, stupid rules we are required to follow. We have had to put up with a lot of dumb rules since we arrived here last year. Many of these rules are so stupid one just has to shake their heads and wonder who comes up with these things. So, the other day I went around to talk with some of the guys about the rules. I wanted to compile a list of them and I figured if I talked to everybody about it, I might get a better list than if I had tried to think of them myself. I spent a hour or so talking to the guys and writing their recollections down on my steno pad.

What follows is a list of the rules and my explanations of them. It is my intention to show that not only have we fought the insurgents this entire year, we have also fought brainless limitations and obligations given to us by people who have no idea of what the "other side of the fence" looks like.

There has always been a difference between how the active component of the armed forces goes about daily tasks and how the reserve component would do the same task. For the longest time I didn't understand this difference. It wasn't until a few years ago that I fully understood it. The guard only has two days a month to train and two weeks in the summer. The active army has all year, minus the leave time the individual soldier accrues throughout the year. Thus, the guard must maximize the time available to train to standards. This means in order to be at the level of readiness the government sets for us, we must be more focused in allowable time. I call it the "bullshit factor." In other words, it means we have to spend more time on the stuff that matters and less time on the stuff that doesn't.

Time and time again, both the unit I am currently with and the unit I transferred from have proven themselves totally on par with their active duty counterparts. To me that says our way of doing things works, and we as a unit are very efficient in our training and preparation. To do this, one must list the tasks that must be accomplished and prioritize them in order of importance. After all, there is only so much you can do in the span of one weekend.

Time and time again, both the unit I am currently with and the unit I transferred from have proven themselves totally on par with their active duty counterparts.

Luckily, we weren't bothered too much throughout our train-up period at Fort Hood and Fort Polk. No, the real games did not start until we hit Kuwait. Once there, we were told at all times we had to walk at the "low ready." In other words, that meant instead of using the rifle sling to carry the weapon on your shoulder, you had to carry it as if you were getting ready to shoot it. You should have seen it. A bunch of Joes walking to chow with their weapons in their hands as if they were stalking an escaped lion from the zoo. We looked like buffoons. Oh yeah, did I mention this only applied if we were in DCUs? Yeah, if we were wearing PT uniforms, we could just use the rifle sling. Needless to say, we spent a lot of time in PTs.

Once we moved up to the airport in Baghdad, the fun really started. Back when I still had time to go to church, we had to wear our camelback hydration systems as part of our uniform. We didn't need to have anything in them, but we had to wear them. One Sunday as I was putting my hymnal back in the little rack before exiting the tent/chapel, a man whom I had never seen told me to wait outside for him. "Yeah sure, sir," I said. The guy was wearing a florescent vest so I could not see his rank, but given his age, it was safe to assume he outranked me. Once outside, he came up to me and said, "Do you not know who I am?" "No sir, I don't." "Don't 'sir' me, I am a f**kin' sergeant major!" Great, I thought, cussing like a sailor on the doorsteps of a church. Anyway, he told me I was supposed to cut the Camelback patch off my camelback. He said we were not here to advertise for companies back home. Then, he pulled out his pocket knife and cut the patch off for me. By this time I was more than a little steamed. I asked him if this meant I was to carve off the words Goodyear from the tires on my Humvee. A logical question given his reasoning for the camelback, I thought. He gruffly told me not to be a smart ass and sent me on my way. Hmm, so no advertising, huh? That's great. I wouldn't want to offend the locals, most of whom cannot read English anyway.

Next came the debate over eyewear. Upon deploying, we were all issued Wiley X eyewear. They are pretty nice sunglasses, I must admit. The army was supposed to get optical inserts for those soldiers who require corrective lenses. Needless to say, I have yet to see any of those things. So, not being able to wear the Wiley Xs, I wore my BCGs. BCG is a spoof of an acronym which stands for "birth control glasses." Anyone who has ever seen the goofy things would understand what is implied by the name we have given them because no woman would ever be seen in public with a guy wearing them. My wife of 11 years won't let me wear mine at home. They are that goofy. So, I constantly had to explain myself to higher ranking folks as to why I was not wearing my Wileys. I was not the only one either.

Shortly after our arrival in Southwest Asia, we were introduced to the U system of uniform levels. U1 through U5 is how it is designed. U1 means you can wear either DCUs or your PT uniform. U2 means you have to wear your body armor and Kevlar wherever you go, but at a certain time you can take it off. U3 means you are in U2 until further notice. U4 is not used very much, and I think it basically says you are in U2, but with your earplugs in. U5 is the same as U4, but you have your rifle locked and loaded. It is just a simple system that lets the guys know what posture their uniform must be. It makes sense to me. If there is a threat of mortars or rockets that day, it is advantageous to be prepared. But, some people here take it to new levels. For example, for awhile at the airport, you had to be at U2 just to drive a Humvee. Regardless of the U level for those walking. But that was only in a Humvee. If you were driving an NTV or Non-Tactical Vehicle such as a Blazer or civilian truck, you could drive at U1. What, are Humvees *that* dangerous?

For a while, we had to be in U3 after a certain time. For example, for a couple weeks we had to be in U1 up until 1830 hours, but after that we had to be in U3. I guess the head honchos have their reasoning, but to us it just seems silly.

If that wasn't dumb enough, somebody saw fit to limit driving around even more. It was put out we had to have an assistant driver wherever we went, unless the driver was a sergeant or higher. Then, they could drive by themselves. And that rule was enforced too. Some MP guys were setting up checkpoints inside the base and stopping to check rank on drivers! If the driver was alone and less than an E-5, they had to park the truck, walk back to their trailers and get an "A" driver. One of my buddies had to walk about two miles back to the trailers to get someone to go and get his truck. Here is a thought, Why are those MPs not outside the wire helping to catch bad guys?

That rule didn't last very long, thank goodness. Soon though, it was decided seatbelts had to be worn *inside* the wire. That was enforced too. Working as an EMT, I have

> **It was decided seat belts had to be worn *inside* the wire. But when the posted speed limit is 5 mph, what's the point?**

firsthand knowledge as to the value of seat belts. They *do* in fact save lives. But, when the posted speed limit is 5 mph, what's the point? That's right, sports fans; 5 mph. I was yelled at by some puke for speeding one day. I looked down at my speedometer and I was in fact speeding. I was doing about 7 mph. I shall suffer eternal damnation for that transgression, I presume. The speeding thing was mitigated on post by placing a speed bump about every 30 feet. It was kinda refreshing to drive all day on a bumpy road though. It made me think of Illinois highways. The funny part about this is outside the wire, out where it is actually dangerous, seat belts were not required and, furthermore, there was no speed limit to speak of. Many times, we found ourselves flying down a dirt canal road chasing some insurgent. Some of the time, many of us were riding standing up in the back of the trucks with but a machine gun to hang onto. I thought about some poor sap in U3, with their seat belt on, getting whiplash on the speed bumps back on post and I had to chuckle. The irony is endless.

Once our mission was over and we could go back to our trailers for a shower and some chow, we once again had to play the little games. Right by the chow hall was the refueling point. Basically, it is just a truck parked there with fuel hoses. But, unlike filling up your car back home, we had to put on these silly goggles and rubber gloves in order to dispense fuel. Furthermore, the soldiers that ran the fuel point would sit in their little air-conditioned shack and not come out to turn on the pumps. But, as if they were watching some closed circuit televisions cameras, as soon as we would forego the gloves and goggles, BAM! they came out of their little abode and started yelling. It will be so nice to be able to fill up my beater truck back home and not have to put on a clown suit just to do it. Up here at Camp Cooke, we can't even touch the fuel pumps. There are a bunch of guys that do it for us and, in a true reversal of policy, up here we get yelled at if we *do* dispense fuel.

While back at the airport, we had to pull duty in guard towers for awhile. This particular mission was a nice reprieve from the endless driving up and down the interstate. Instead of sitting in a hummer all day, we now sat in a guard tower for 12 hours. But, instead of running autonomous missions within our own unit, the tower guard was in conjunction with another unit. The men of the other unit were great guys. Tower guard was where I met my good friend SPC Jasmin. The duty in the towers was easy. Just stay awake and keep an eye out, pretty simple stuff. But, leave it to some moron to make it difficult.

Back in our air defense days, we ran in teams of two. The towers were manned by teams of two, so this was nothing new to us. The best one could hope for was drawing a tower shift with someone you got along with pretty well. We had hoped we would be allowed to just drive ourselves to the towers by teams and just park the Humvee until our shift was over. No such luck. The other unit had control over this mission so we had to show up at their trailers an hour and a half prior to mission time for guard mount.

Guard mount is retarded. You line up and somebody makes sure you have your weapon and it is clean. They make sure you have your ammo and are in proper uniform. Then, they read to you the mission for the day and the events of the past 24 hours. How do we do it in our unit? Simple, the LT hands me a copy of the mission and the events of the last 24. I let my guys read it for themselves, and we pull out about 20 minutes before we have to be on duty. We leave it to the team chiefs and section sergeants to make sure the guys are ready.

Instead, every morning we had to line up and be treated like children. Talk about a kick in the pants! The 'ol bullshit factor was riding near red-line during that time period. The hardest part for me and the other staff sergeants of my unit was the guy doing the inspecting was an E-6, too. It was pretty demeaning stuff.

Once in the towers it was our gig, but we couldn't get it through to them our guys didn't have to be micromanaged in such a way. Our pleas fell on deaf ears. If that wasn't bad enough, we were told we should take our bottled water and pour it into our canteens to drink from, as drinking out of the bottle just didn't look professional. At first, we had some chairs in our towers in which to sit. Standing for 12 hours with 50 pounds of gear on really sucks. Soon, the chairs were taken away too. So now, we were supposed to stand in full view, not too mention sniper range, of the enemy. The best part of the whole thing was right behind one of the towers was a firing range for the special forces or something like that. Every once in awhile a bullet would go zinging by. That part was great. Matter of fact, while we were in the towers, the only time we got shot at was from *behind* us.

The tower duty is necessary. Perimeter security is a vital thing. I am not belittling its need. I am saying, however, if you are going to do it, do it smart.

We tried over and over to get the firing range either shut down or moved, but like guard mount, our reasoning fell on deaf ears.

While on the tower mission, some of the guys had to do what was called "courtesy patrol." When I was on flood duty during The Great Flood of '93, I had to do courtesy patrols. That meant we drove around and made sure the townsfolk were okay and not in need of anything. It was great to get to go around and meet the folks we were sent to help. Here it was different. We were supposed to walk around, and... well, just walk around. That's it. So, teams of people just walked aimlessly around the base making sure the communist hoards were held at bay, or something like that. In a base of thousands, all with rifles, at all hours, is a few more poor saps walking around in the middle of the night really advantageous? Well, somebody thought so.

Many of us have purchased laptop computers since being deployed. Others simply brought the ones they owned with them when we deployed. I bought mine at Fort Hood in November 2003, and since then it has proven to be the best purchase I have made in a long time. Whether it has been email, movies or games, my laptop has proven indispensable. Most everyone else would tell you pretty much the same thing. The only problem we faced was the dust that would accumulate inside the computers. The only way we could keep them clean was by using canned air we bought at the bazaar. It worked pretty good at keeping our laptops clean. About once a week, I would clean out the fans on my Compaq, and I never had too many problems with it. However, one particular soldier from another unit decided it would be cool to huff the canned air and get high. Bright idea, he died. So, no more canned air. Because of the acts of one moron, we all suffered. We were told to get rid of our canned air and if we were caught with it... yadda, yadda... pain, dismemberment, the whole shebang. Pretty soon we were allowed to have it again, and the whole huffing thing blew over.

One of the biggest pain in our necks came when units started rotating in and out. They kept changing the

When units started rotating in and out, they kept changing the names of the camps that sat at the airport!

names of the camps that sat at the airport! One day it was called Camp Snoopy, for example, and the next thing we knew, it was called Camp Woodstock! Talk about confusing! Of course, when there are so many camps situated in and around the airport, it can get pretty confusing when trying to navigate. One particular time I distinctly remember arguing with somebody over the name of the camp on south post where the other PX was located. Pretty soon, all I could think about was Abbot and Costello's famous routine about, "Who's on First?" Heck, while I was at the airport, the name changed at least three times. Sometimes, I wasn't really sure of what to use as a return address on my postage!

Then we moved up to Camp Cooke, and things didn't really change. It was just different silly rules. For starters, when coming in the gate, there are two to three people we have to show our ID cards to. Like they don't trust us! Or at least they don't trust just one person checking ID cards. C'mon folks, I am in a Humvee. I am with three other guys who are all in uniform. I speak perfect English. I have an M16. and here's the kicker, there are usually at least three other trucks with me all filled with guys just like me. Did I mention I don't look Arabic either? Nevertheless, somebody always scrutinizes our ID cards as if they are fake. I guess I really am glad they *are* checking. I really do not fancy the thought of a bus load of insurgents getting on post with a greyhound full of C4. It just seems funny that checking our ID cards once isn't good enough.

Speaking of ID cards, we have to show them to get into the PX, bazaar, and either chow hall. One of the guys at the chow hall that checks our ID cards is a warrant officer! A warrant officer is checking ID cards at the chow hall! Does this guy not have a job? Are there that many people here the army can afford to let a person of his rank, waste their time checking ID cards just so I can get a plate of grub?

It was put out a couple of weeks ago we must wear some type of eye protection at all times. I am not sure why we must do this. Oh sure, I have heard all the rumors regarding it. One said it was for the dust and wind that isn't blowing yet. Others said it is in case a mortar round hits us. That one makes no sense. If a mortar round hits near enough to damage my eyes, my eyes will be the least of my worries. I don't know why we have to do it, but from walking around post here the last few days, it doesn't look like it is being enforced all that much.

Since we have been in country, the single biggest rule that just makes no sense at all is right outside our trailers. On the south side of our trailers is an area about 100 yards long by about 30 yards in width. It is surrounded by Jersey barriers and has a road that runs in the middle so the water trailers can get to our shower tanks to deposit fresh water. One day some dump trucks showed up and dumped several tons of gravel out there. Then a man in a backhoe showed up and spread out the gravel. For about two weeks, we were able to park our trucks right up by the trailers. It was great. It only took us a few minutes to load up our trucks for missions because they were so close. See, our actual motor pool is over three miles away. Walking there just isn't an option. Well, somebody for some reason thought having the trucks so close to the trailers was a safety risk. Lemme guess, spontaneous combustion?

No reason was ever given, but the rumor mill said it was because the general didn't like the way some units were parking their trucks. I guess it was too messy. So, we all were not allowed to use the parking lots anymore. Imagine going to Wal-Mart, but having to park your car over at Taco Bell– that is about what this is like. So, here we have a perfectly good parking lot that sits unused. And don't think there are not eyes watching to make sure no one parks there either. One day we found papers stuck under our windshields stating if these trucks were not moved, they would be towed. Ha, go on, take 'em. I guess if I don't have a truck, I can't go out on missions anymore. We lost that fight and had to move our trucks. A compromise was reached, and we are now able to park our trucks on the other side of the Jersey barriers that line the parking lot. It just seems ludicrous to me to think the army pays for gravel and the labor to spread it for a parking lot that nobody gets to use. Seems silly to me.

I could go on at length about all the other redundant, silly rules that are in place here. Rules like not having our names in Arabic stitched onto our hats, when there are some pretty high ranking officers running around Baghdad with their names stitched in Arabic. What's good for the gander is not necessarily good for the goose it would appear. Or, how about this one? We cannot go to the chow hall to eat in PT uniform, but we can go there and get a to-go plate. If I can go and get a plate of food, why can I not sit and eat it there? This one is a favorite with a lot of the guys, too. You cannot go to the gym in DCU uniform. But, you can't wear PT uniform when in U3 uniform posture. Think about it. When we are in U3, you can't go to the gym, but the gym is still open.

I guess some of you may think I am growing to hate the army. To the contrary, I still love it. I honestly do. I just think if we are going to go to war, then all our efforts should be aimed at defeating the enemy rather than wasting time making and enforcing stupid rules that do nothing but anger the very soldiers who are

It is going to be so nice to get home and be treated like an adult again.

here fighting. The worst part of it is when these guys get home and the time comes to re-enlist, how many of them are going to remember not the positive things we have accomplished, but the stupid rules and the crap we have had to put up with? When the time comes to raise our right hands, how many of us will be able to put aside the bullshit factor and ante up for another three years? Like my roommate so eloquently puts it, it is going to be so nice to get home and be treated like an adult again.

Jason Adams
Camp Cooke, Iraq

Notice   Training   Deployment   Home leave   Back Home
10/12/03   3/1/04   9/26-10/14/04   3/19/05

Spring Cleaning

Today is March 3rd

The waiting continues here at Camp Cooke. For quite a few days we have sat aimlessly watching the days creep by in hopes of leaving this place. True, that day draws nearer with every passing minute, but time seems to slow to a crawl as our time draws to a close. I guess I don't mind it all too much; we need some time to decompress. Soon however, the time will start to wear on the guys as we wait and wait and wait.

Yes, this time has been put to good use, at least for some of us anyway. The other day I disassembled my Kevlar and cleaned it. The next day I got rid of the last of my junk, well, with the exception of my coffee pot that is. I suspect I will throw that puppy in the garbage only as I walk to the plane. It is 220 V and I can't use it at home, so what's the point of keeping it? Today I stripped my rifle and scrubbed it up good. That killed about three hours, only 21 hours left to kill for today.

Yesterday Ben, SSG Wolford, SFC Kuba, and I went to finance to get some cash for the trip home. That took a little bit of time considering the first of the month is payday, and everybody and their sister wants cash. We walked down to finance after breakfast and got in line. We made it there by 0830 hours and the line was already about 50 yards long. Finance doesn't open up until 0900 hours! The wait lasted about an hour and a half, but since there were four of us, we all had someone to talk to and the time spent in line wasn't bad.

It feels so liberating to be able to aimlessly spend that time in line without thoughts of missions or meetings. No longer must we concern ourselves with the day-to-day tasks of fighting a war. It feels so good to know this. We are in no hurry for anything anymore and to tell you the truth, I feel free. I do not mean to sound melodramatic, but this place

No longer must we concern ourselves with the day-to-day tasks of fighting a war. It feels so good to know this.

feels different these days. It is as if there is a different breeze blowing through here. Even the weather is different. The last few days have been up into the

80s already. The weather is starting to change; the cold is going away and with it, we go too.

The sea of new people that have come in to replace us are out running missions instead of us, and they have already found out what IEDs consist of. We are quickly becoming the forgotten ones, the "who are those guys" of Camp Cooke. I ran into a guy today who was wearing the same patch I wore on my uniform before we were deployed. I stopped and asked where he was from. "Oklahoma," he said. I told him I used to be part of his division and asked him how long he had been in country. "Ten days," he replied, "How long have you been here?" I told him we would be leaving in three days, and I thought for a minute he was going to cry. I felt bad for him at first, but then I realized I was once in his shoes and there were those who left before me, and it was I who watched them go. Now the tables are turned, and it is he who must watch others go home. I know how he feels.

The last couple of days have been spent tying up loose ends here. Jaguar and GQ have left and moved to a new spot on Camp Cooke. Jaguar stopped by today and said goodbye. He was dressed snazzy as always wearing a nice yellow shirt, khaki pants, leather shoes, and a classy black leather belt. His hair looked like he had just stepped out of a salon, and with his sunglasses hung from the breast pocket of his shirt, he looked like something out of Hollywood rather than an interpreter who wears a bulletproof vest when working. We talked for a few minutes and said our goodbyes. We shook hands one last time and he walked away.

As he walked off, I wondered if it would be the last time I ever see him again. I certainly hope not, but I must face reality here and be honest with myself in that the chances of an Iraqi man getting into America these days is slim and none. I have tried to find ways to help Jaguar and GQ, but all of them have been a dead end. Folks like these guys deserve a better life, the kind of life America has to offer. Here, they have to worry about getting killed every time they step foot out of their door. It just doesn't seem fair. Of course, life is not fair, we all know this. It wouldn't be so bad then, if life could be at least equally unfair.

Most of our stuff is either packed up or thrown out. The dumpster out front looks like the end of the year at a college campus, filled to the brim with stuff nobody wants. It is not all junk either. The guys that clean our bathrooms make a daily cruise by our dumpster and are always pulling out stuff to take back to their trailers. It is true what they say, "One man's junk is another man's treasure."

Jason Adams
Camp Cooke, Iraq

The dumpster out front looks like the end of the year at a college campus, filled to the brim with stuff nobody wants.

Notice Training Deployment   Home leave   Back Home
10/12/03   3/1/04   9/26-10/14/04   3/19/05

Absence Makes the Heart Grow Fonder

Today is March 4th

It is hard for me to realize that in two days I will be en route to home. Home, that sounds nice, doesn't it? What does it mean? What is it about a familiar sight, a familiar smell or perhaps a sound that makes a certain area just feel right? Sometimes it is hard to put a finger on. The way the road into town runs through the Indian Creek Valley just west of town is a sight I have seen a thousand times from the cab of my truck or from the side of the road as I jog. Thousands of times I have been over the same bridge and up the same hill as I pull into my home town, but a thousand times I have taken it for granted.

No more. No, I will not take it as a given again for I have come to miss it so. The sight of Gordy Whittaker's farm to the south as I jogged was always a welcome sight that would flood my mind with images of growing up. I spent a lot of time out there with Gordy's son Rob. I was there chucking hay bales in the barn the day the phone call came in saying Rob had been injured and was paralyzed. I held his mom's hand in the waiting room after the helicopter had taken him to Peoria. Perhaps it is the memories that make a place feel like home.

Coming home... what a welcome thing! We just don't realize what it means until we can't have it. Millions before me have known how I and the guys feel and millions after us will know, too, what this feels like. It is just a part of life, but like so many other lessons learned as we walk through our existence, this, too, can be used as a valuable tool to help put into perspective what really matters in one's life. It isn't what we left, it is what we miss most. These are the things that matter most to a person. The only thing that can show us these things is distance from them. Only then do our lives come into focus and only then can we sift through the clutter of everyday life and know what things we hold dearest.

As our time here in Iraq draws to a close, so too closes another chapter in the book that is our lives. We never again will all be together doing the same things we are doing now. It is over. When we get home, we will go our separate ways, back to towns spread all over Illinois and Iowa. We go back to jobs as varied as snowflakes and like the sights one sees as they look through a kaleidoscope. So too will our lives constantly change as the days progress.

Oh sure, we will see each other at drill, and maybe I will see some of the guys from the other units at summer camp now and then. But soon some will get out of the military. Just like a graduating class after the gowns and caps have been taken off, like leaves in an autumn breeze, we will scatter in the months ahead. In a way I am saddened by this. True, I can't say I particularly like all the guys in this unit. I am sure they would say the same about me. But I do know if, during the past year, the time had come to put

If the time had come to put their lives in danger to save another one of us, they would not have hesitated. It is this bond then which will forever bind us, no matter where the roads of life take us.

their lives in danger to save another one of us, they would not have hesitated. In essence, I would crawl through a minefield to help any one of them, and I believe they would do the same. It is this bond then which will forever bind us, no matter where the roads of life take us. Forever more we will all look back and remember that chapter in our life when we were as one. We were Foxtrot Battery, 202nd ADA.

Two days. Two long, long days until we begin the trip back to our loved ones and our homes. It just doesn't seem real, like a dream really. Even though I know we are done here, I still harbor an intense fear that at some point we will be extended. I think we all do. I mean, the unit that was here when we got here made it as far as Kuwait before being recalled. I am not sure who a crushing blow like that would hurt more, me or my wife.

Our families back home have suffered along with us, and they, too, want nothing more than to see us back home safe and sound. Even though we are the ones that have to put up with the IEDs, car bombs and ambushes, it is our families at home that have to put up with the days without word of our safety. They are the ones who must carry on with the daily duties that life requires in our absence. Sure, they are safe, but they also have had to assume an increased workload in our absence.

My wife, Steph, is simply amazing in this respect. I can't imagine what she has had to deal with in the time I have been gone. For one thing, our youngest daughter has undergone two surgeries. She takes care of the house, cooks the meals, goes to basketball games, band concerts, runs the girls to practice, manages to work a full-time job, and manages to pay all the bills on time. Somewhere in there she found time to remodel the kitchen and bathroom too. I joke with her and tell her since she obviously has everything under control, I won't have to do anything upon my return. I can't repeat what she said to that one, but the conversation ended with me saying, "Yes dear, I am a stupid, pathetic example of a man…I'm sorry"– or something like that.

When we wed, neither of us had any idea fate would force something like this upon us. How could we? Two people barely old enough to buy liquor starting out in a three-room apartment above a gun shop. Our thoughts were consumed by the things every young newlywed couple think about, a house, bills, and perhaps a family; certainly not this. But, like all obstacles we have faced in the 11 years since we took our vows, we have overcome them and stayed together. Being gone has taught me yet again how lucky I am to have Steph. Indeed, absence *does* make the heart grow fonder.

Jason Adams
Camp Cooke, Iraq

Farewell Camp Cooke

Today is March 6th

Today was unlike the last few days because we had to be up and moving by 0415 hours. Sure, nobody wanted to get up that early, but when doing so is because we are going home, it is worth every set of red, bloodshot eyes in the unit. For some reason, it feels weird, the thought of leaving. For the past year, this has been our reality. Now, we return to all we left. Some parts of me are as giddy as a racehorse. Other parts of me feel as though all of this is no big deal. I

For some reason, it feels weird, the thought of leaving. For the past year, this has been our reality.

don't understand it to be honest. I thought I would be ready to climb the walls by now, but I am composed and patient. Folks, that just ain't me. Maybe it is because I am getting old?

The morning started by loading our baggage onto a five-ton truck. It was transferred over to a conex shipping container and will be trucked to Baghdad where we will meet up with it tonight. We are flying out of here on CH-47 helicopters, and I guess without the bags, they can cram more people on the short flight. After the bags were loaded, we decided to go and get one last breakfast meal at the chow hall. I had the old standby, Mexican scrambled eggs over potatoes and a plain biscuit with strawberry-flavored milk. I thought about an omelet, but the line was too long.

It was kinda nice to be able to sit among friends and reminisce a little bit about the past year. Soon though, the talk turned to what we ought to do once home. Some of the guys talked of getting together and playing baseball. Others talked of going on road trips together. Heck, on more than one occasion my buddy Ralphie and I have talked of taking a trip up to his home state of North Dakota, but like the rest of the, "Ya know what we oughta do when we get home…" scenarios, these too will most likely never take place. It's okay though. We will always have the memories.

After breakfast we went back to the trailers and did the final cleaning and mopping that had to be done. We hauled loads of junk out to the dumpster until it was overflowing, and junk was stacked around the outside. In the bathroom where we have set up an impromptu PX, there was loads of food, books, odds and ends, and even a set of shelves! The folks that come around and clean our bathrooms thought they had died and went to heaven. Even the dumpster out front saw its share of "dumpster diving" going on. At one point, a guy rode up on a bicycle and picked up a broken chair and rode off with his new find. What anybody wants with a broken chair is beyond me. Wait, I take that back. I have seen my old man do the same thing.

When my sister, Bernadette, was attending Illinois State before grad school, she had to move home for the summer like most college students. Mom, Dad, Steph and I loaded up in the old minivan and drove down to Bloomington, Illinois, to help her move home. If you have ever been on campus around moving week, you will find people will throw out just about anything. You name it, computers, furniture, textbooks, lamps. Whatever they can't fit in their cars, they pitch.

As we had the van loaded up and were about to pull away from my sister's apartment, Dad spied a high-back office chair in one of the dumpsters. Dad said, "Hey, would ya look at that, a perfectly good chair! I've been needing one of those!" Bernadette's face took on a look of horror as the realization of our dad's intentions came into focus. "Dad, please; no!" Dad, always the tight wad, threw the ol' Pontiac into park, jumped out, and snatched the thing from the clutches of the dumpster. I just laughed to myself as we drove home. For some reason, I couldn't get the theme song from the Beverly Hillbillies out of my head. This is my family. This is where I come from. You know what, though? They are the greatest people to have ever walked the earth, and I love them till death.

After Top came by and inspected the rooms, we waited for the five-tons to take us out to the "surge housing" as it is called. Basically, from what I gather, this is where the overflow people as well as those coming or going stay. This is where I sit now. The building is not unlike a machine shed back home. It is about 40 feet wide by about 100 feet long. It is made out of galvanized steel and has a concrete floor. There are bunk beds and small lockers situated throughout the building for the guys to put their junk in. Other than that, there is nothing. It has power, but no bathrooms. For that, we have to go out to another bathroom trailer, but that is nothing new for us. It is going to be so nice to get home and not have to go into another building to shower or use the toilet. I don't think I will ever again look at a porta-john the same. The only bad thing about leaving all this is I will no longer have anybody to talk to when I am sittin' on the stool.

Right now, I am sitting on the floor, with my laptop perched upon a locker I laid onto its side. Under me bum is a nasty old pillow I found upon entering the building. Not exactly primo surroundings for writing a letter home, but not only is it the best I have right now, I also know things could be a lot worse. I am not complaining. After 1600 hours, we are on lockdown; in other words, we can't leave. Some of the guys decided to go to the PX one last time, for old time's sake, I guess. Either that or because they are bored out of their minds. Either way, it kills time.

After 1700 hours, they will start manifesting flights out of here. I am on chock No. 12 and should be leaving sometime after dark. They tell us the first flights leave out of Baghdad at 0700 hours tomorrow morning. I doubt I will be on that plane, but one can always hope. After that, we will spend four days or so in Kuwait and then board another plane bound for the United States. The next few days will undoubtedly try our patience. But, there is nothing any of us can do except wait like everybody else. Time is funny like that. While you are waiting for it to pass, it drags on for what seems like eternity. Once it has passed, it seems like the blink of an eye.

Jason Adams
Camp Cooke, Iraq

Spring Break

Today is March 8th

So far, the trip home has been about what I had envisioned. A lot of sitting around intertwined with moments of "Hurry up!" That, folks, is just how the army does business. I don't mind it all too much. Even if I did, what could I do about it? We moved from the machine sheds out at the surge housing around 1800 hours on the 6th of March. Then, they moved us down to another building where we had to wait yet again. This building, unlike the other ones had no bed, no lockers, and no bathroom trailers. Basically, it consisted of an empty warehouse filled with chairs that were strewn about in no apparent order. This was the manifest building and was just used for those waiting to go to the airfield.

We sat there for maybe a half hour until some five-ton trucks came and took us to the airfield. Once at the airstrip, we sat in long lines called chocks and waited for the birds to come in. Out on the tarmac there were quite a few choppers just sitting. Every once in awhile one of them fired up and sat there with the rotors spinning, mocking those huddled masses yearning for a ride out of there. Soon we found out the choppers that were sitting there teasing us were not the ones that would be taking us to Baghdad. No, ours were coming in from another base up north. Well, that makes sense I thought.

Soon, like manna from heaven, we could hear the faint wump, wump, wump sound a CH-47 makes as it flies. To our dismay, only two birds showed up. Some quick mental math told me given the fact there were 14 chocks and only two choppers, with one chopper carrying one chock, we weren't going any-where for some time. The choppers came in from the north with all their lights off and landed about 30 yards from us. It was such an awesome sight to see those olive drab behemoths come in and land right in front of us!

The noise was thunderous, and I could feel the pulse of the engines against my chest as I stood there in awe. Being so close to those machines I long to pilot made the waiting worth every minute, and in some respects I found myself happy we were on chock 12. That meant I would be able to sit and watch this spectacle again and again before it was our turn to board them. Soon, two more birds came in and grabbed another load of guys. So now there were four CH-47s flying rather than two. I checked my watch as the first birds headed out and upon their return, noted it had taken just a little over half an hour to make the round trip.

As the second set of birds came into land, I noticed they approached the tarmac differently. The first set had landed and then taxied over to where we were. These guys hovered out in front of our chocks and then spun around and set down right there. The pilot of the first bird of the second set actually flew backward and set down even closer to us! It was amazing to watch. I stood there like a child who was watching a magic trick for the first time. At that moment, I wanted nothing more than to fly one of those puppies, if only for a minute.

Our chock lifted off at precisely 1100 hours. The helicopters set down and the rear gunner on the CH-47 dropped the ramp and motioned for us to board. We grabbed our gear, hustled to the ramp, and clambered aboard. Once we were all loaded, the rear gunner (the load master I am assuming) raised the rear deck level and sat back down at his machine gun. I was sitting near the front of the cargo area and had a bird's eye view out of the port side gunner's window. As the pilot throttled up the motors, the fuselage began to vibrate, but once airborne, it calmed down.

The flight was short, only a few minutes really, but it was probably the greatest few minutes of my entire year here. One, we were leaving. Two, we were cruising over Baghdad in the middle of the night with no lights on at about 200 hundred feet or so in the air. It was so cool to see the very roads we had patrolled for so long go skimming by for the last time. Down below, the street lights all twinkled in the cool night air and the city looked rather peaceful. It was all a mirage though, for all of us on board knew firsthand about how peaceful the streets of Baghdad are.

Heck, if they were peaceful, why would the chopper need door gunners?

The port side gunner rode in a little canvas basket for a seat and manned a machine gun throughout the trip. With his night vision goggles on, he constantly scanned the terrain below for the slightest hint of trouble. My buddies and I sat crammed into the belly of the bird like kipper snacks, with our packs on our laps and our rifles pointed to the floor. It felt like what up to this point, I had only seen in movies, a bunch of soldiers riding through the night waiting to jump out and do battle. For some reason, I couldn't get CCR's classic *"Fortunate Son"* out of my head.

We landed at the airport and some buses took us over to the transient tents where we would wait until the next day for a flight to Kuwait. I went to sleep around 0200 hours and slept like a dead dog. You couldn't have awoken me with a cowbell, a cattle prod, and a 90 kiloton nuclear missile. I woke up around 0830 hours and managed to get a warm shower. As I opened my toilet bag to get out my shampoo and body wash, I noticed my shampoo had exploded inside the little bag. Great, I thought, what a mess! So, instead of just brushing my teeth and shaving like everybody else, I had to clean out my toilet bag too. Oh well, it needed washed anyway.

As I got back to my tent, I saw a guy from our old battalion back home standing outside our tent talking with a bunch of guys. I knew he was with the same unit as a good friend of mine whom I hadn't seen since I was home on leave, and that was only over breakfast. I walked up and asked him if he knew where SFC Talbert was and he said, "Yeah, he is here looking for you." I walked into my tent and there stood my buddy, Jerry. Man, it was good to see him. I have known Jerry since the day I first called the armory to see about enlisting.

Jerry stood outside my tent, and we caught up on things for a couple of hours until I had to scoot in order to get my sleeping bag packed up and put on the bus. Jerry and LT Dura followed us over to the airport to see us off. He has only been over here for a couple of months and still has time left before he sees home again for good. Nevertheless, I was happy to have had the opportunity to see him.

We boarded the C-130 aircraft at 1450 hours, but not before one last practical joke was played on the most unsuspecting person.

In order to manifest for the flight, we had to hand over our ID cards to SFC Hess, so he could have the flight roster made. Unbeknown to any of us, SFC Hess and SFC Kuba had cooked up a scheme to mess with SPC Haley. We left the tents in a bus and drove over to another set of tents where the bus stopped and SFC Hess, SFC Kuba and the bus driver, a PFC, got out and walked out of sight.

We boarded the C-130 aircraft at 1450 hours, but not before one last practical joke was played on the most unsuspecting person.

Soon, the bus driver came on the bus with an ID card in his hand and yelled, "SPC Haley, get off the bus!" Haley looked up and said, "Who, me?" "Yes, you!" came the reply and Haley reluctantly moved to the front of the bus and exited. About 10 seconds later SFC Hess, SFC Kuba and the bus driver dove into the bus, and the driver slammed the thing into gear and took off. Driving in a large half circle, he parked on the other side of some buses that were sitting on the other side of the parking lot.

Apparently, they had told SPC Haley there was a problem with his ID card and he had to go into a certain tent and get it straightened out. SPC Haley unassumingly did as he was told and, upon entering the designated tent, soon realized it was a joke, and he was the butt of it. From where we sat hidden, we could see him come out and upon realizing the bus was gone, he began to look around and we could see he was growing angry. Of course, we all had our cameras out and were taking pictures of the whole thing. Pictures which will undoubtedly show up at the Battalion Ball in May. Soon, he figured out what was going on and he spied our bus in hiding. He didn't look too amused as he got back on the bus, and I guess our laughter didn't help matters too much either.

After the pit stop for the practical joke, we headed for the airfield. We got there around 1330 hours and were told our flight would leave at 1450 hours. None of us were holding our breaths, as flights like this, in our experience anyway, are rarely on time. We decided to grab some lunch and got in line for Subway. Jerry was inside the terminal talking to one of the guys as we walked through en route to our plane. I said goodbye one last time and shook his hand. I sure hope he remains safe while he is here.

Call me a liar, but as our plane taxied down the runway, I glanced at my watch. What time was it, you ask? 1450 hours on the nose. I was speechless. Somewhere in the bowels of hell, amid the lakes of burning sulfur, the devil is reaching for a sweater.

I am not too sure of what time we landed, but I do know the landing was pretty rough. We got off of the airplane and went to a waiting area for more people to show up. We then made the trip to Camp Doha via bus, getting here around 2100 hours or so. Having not eaten since lunch, many of us made a beeline for the PX where the fast-food court beckoned like a literal oasis in the desert. Having to choose from so many places to eat, it all came down to how long it would take to get it. The line for Hardees was long, as was the line for KFC. So, having eaten at Subway so many times in the weeks prior to our movement home, where did I go? Yeah, Subway again. So much for variety! But, I did get to have a milkshake from Baskin Robbins, which by the way, tasted like liquid gold topped with half-carat diamonds.

The rest of the day was spent aimlessly wandering through the PX, as well as the other vendors here on post. I went to bed around midnight and didn't get up until 1000 hours this morning. Yes, I am a full-fledged bum.

Today has not been much different. Ralphie woke me up at 1000 hours and wanted to go and play pool down at Uncle Frosty's. Uncle Frosty's place sits adjacent to the PX and is kind of like a community center. For a forward area like Kuwait, it is pretty nice. They have six pool tables, two foosball games, two ping pong tables, some dart boards, and even an air hockey game. They also have several PS2 sets and Xboxes and a ton of games to choose from. Out in the main area is a giant projection screen TV upon which is shown a variety of movies and comedy routines. Over in the corner is a snack stand that serves up hot dogs, hamburgers and pop. All of this, the games, the movies, and the food is free. Not a bad deal if you ask me. Unfortunately, like everything else in the army, there are always lines for everything. Today, Ralphie and I waited for about half an hour to get a pool table. I don't mind it too much; after all, what else do I have to do?

We stayed at Frosty's until around 1230 hours and then headed to the food court at the PX to get some chow. Since then, I have had nothing to do. I am so bored! I walked to the phones a little while ago and called Steph. We talked for a little bit, but she was at work and couldn't stay on the phone for too long.

I am on a spring break of sorts as well. I am not working, school is out, it is warm and sunny here and the ocean is not too far away!

After that, I called a friend from school and told her I was coming home too. I hadn't talked to her for some time, and it was good to hear how things are going. She is set to graduate in December and says her classes are going good. She is on spring break right now and has the week off. I told her I am on a spring break of sorts as well. She asked me what I meant, and I went on to explain, "Well, I am not working, school is out, it is warm and sunny here and the ocean is not too far away!" I think she caught my sarcasm. Trouble is she was only one semester ahead of me in school, and she is set to be done in December. She is two years ahead of me now. It's a bum deal, but what am I to do except go home and jump right back in with both feet.

Since I got back from the phones, I have just been talking with some of the guys out in front of our warehouse. The buildings we are staying in are these giant warehouses that are full of cots for us to sleep on. That's it, just cots. Just like the machine sheds we camped in back at Camp Cooke, these are metal sided, with concrete floors. There are two power outlets in the entire building so extensive use is made of power strips. All our laptops and portable DVD players are crowded onto a couple of tables to recharge. This is where I sit tonight typing. I managed to scam a folding chair, so unlike the other guys, I don't have to sit on a case of water. All of us are just waiting for that day when we can leave here. It seems as though we are stuck in a vortex from which we cannot escape.

The army calls this time "decompression." We call it "depression." The person who thought up this idea of letting us stay here has undoubtedly never had to do it. Personally, I think culprit is AAFES. That is the company that runs the PX. Think about it, the only thing to do here is either Uncle Frosty's or the PX. People are going to the PX for something to do. And when they get there, most of them buy something, even if it is just a soda pop. AAFES is making a killing! Okay, maybe I was reaching a little there. I am glad AAFES is here. Without them, this deployment would have been pretty bad. Speaking of the PX, I am getting thirsty. Perhaps, I will mosey over and get an orange soda before I go to bed. Tomorrow should be another day of fun and excitement. But, it is undoubtedly one less day I have to spend here.

Jason Adams
Camp Doha, Kuwait

Notice
10/12/03

Training

Deployment
3/1/04

Home leave
9/26-10/14/04

Back Home
3/19/05

Deactivation

Today is March 13th (I think)

To be really honest, I am not sure what day it is. Between the weird hours, the time changes, the stops and starts on the jet, I don't know what day it is, nor do I know for sure what time zone I am in. What I do know is this: we are on American soil for good.

I don't know what day it is, nor do I know for sure what time zone I am in. What I do know is this: we are on American soil for good.

Our trip started in Kuwait yesterday. Well actually, it was the night before. Around 2300 hours, we started to go through customs. Wow, what a waste of time. Luckily, we managed to get a hold of a small bus to load our bags onto, otherwise we would have had to carry all 100-plus pounds three blocks to the customs building. I guess it would have made more sense for us to just dump out our duffel bags onto our cots and have the customs people come to our warehouse, but that wasn't an option. So, we again took the most inefficient route we could.

The customs people didn't show up until around midnight or so, and only three of them showed up at that! What that meant for us was simple, a long and painful night– almost 300 troops, each with two bags full of junk... and only three guys to do the searching. Then, to make matters worse, my platoon wasn't the first to go through. While we waited for the other groups to clear, we had to wait outside in the street with our bags. After a bit, it started to rain, and we had to move our bags inside or let them get soaked.

I was in the last group to make it through the baggage search. We walked in, dumped out our stuff, and the searcher walked up to me and asked if I had any ammo or shell casings in among my things. "No, of course not," was my reply. I mean, really! What kind of a dufus would jeopardize getting to go home on account of an empty shell casing? Not this cat, that's for sure. As the guy eyed my things, he never even asked me to unroll my sleeping bag! The number of things I could have hidden in there is limitless! But, that is how things go. By the time the searcher gets to the last group, they really aren't that attentive. That has been my experience anyway. After the half-hearted search we repacked our bags, took them into an adjoining room, and stacked them up in a pile.

We then went back to the warehouse for a couple hours of sleep, which turned out to be a pain in the neck. The first few days in Kuwait had been pretty nice, 80s in the day and 60s at night. Then, after all our sleeping bags were packed up, we had to sleep on a cot with nothing, and it happened to get cold that night, so we froze. But, considering the fact we were spending our last night in Kuwait, none of us were complaining. After crashing out for a couple hours, we got up and started to get ready to go. SSG Wolford and I decided an apple fritter and a latte would be really good for breakfast, so we walked over to the PX one last time and got ourselves some chow. Once again, the apple fritter was excellent, and the latte tasted as though it was made by angels; maybe it was just the fact we were going home, I am not sure.

Soon after we partook of the sugar and caffeine-infused morning's repast, it was time to go and get a couple of briefings and go through the other customs point. One would think they could get all that business done in one shot, but no such luck. So, without an alternative, we sat through more briefings and had our carryon luggage searched. They searched us too. Around noon, we boarded the buses that would take us out to the airfield. The trip took about an hour, but I wouldn't know that for sure, as I was asleep. We were told our flight would be taking off around 1420 hours, which meant we would be sitting out at the airfield for a little bit. As we pulled out onto the airfield, I was very surprised to see our plane sitting there ready to go.

The aircraft, a big DC-10 (I think), was sitting on the flight line with baggage already being loaded into the belly! This meant only one thing, we would be leaving early! Folks, rarely in this deployment has anything (that my unit wasn't directly responsible for) happened on time, let alone early. What a nice surprise for us! We loaded the plane, found an empty seat, and got settled in for what would be a very long flight. The flight attendant's voice came across the intercom and told us, "Make sure the barrels of your rifles are pointed away from the aisles, please." I had to laugh at that one; a flight attendant telling the passengers how to stow their guns! I never thought I would hear that one!!

As the jet accelerated down the runway and took to the skies, I glanced at my watch, 1315 hours! Over an hour early! As the plane gained altitude and with the sands of the Middle East fading in the distance, I settled into my seat and breathed a sigh of relief that was long overdue. Hopefully, that will prove to be the last time I ever see that place. Ben was sitting right beside me, and we chatted for a little bit, then we read our books for awhile before the flight attendant came by with some drinks. I had been waiting for her to make her rounds as I needed something to wash down the Tylenol PM I was about to slam down my gullet. I offered some to Ben, but he declined. "Suit yourself," I said.

As the plane gained altitude, and with the sands of the Middle East fading in the distance, I settled into my seat and breathed a sigh of relief that was long overdue.

As I was trying to get comfortable in the coach seat I was crammed into, the flight attendants were coming down the aisle frantically throwing bags of pretzels to hungry troops who had been up for most of the night, many of which probably hadn't eaten much of anything. As I started to drift into a state of semiconsciousness, I remember thinking the whole scene looked faintly reminiscent of a mother bird feeding her hungry chicks. Without the whole regurgitation thing though. The last thing I remember was thinking when I awoke we would be in Germany.

I don't remember what time we landed, but it was almost dusk when we touched down. The plane taxied away from the main terminal toward a hangar on the far side of the airport. As usual, we were stuck as far away from the rest of the world as possible. The hangar wasn't bad, I guess. I mean the USO was there with coffee and cookies along with cell phones for us to call home. Outside, they had a bathroom trailer set up for us to use and there was about one chair for every five troops. None of us really cared though; we were out of Iraq, out of Kuwait, and now stood in Germany with nothing but freedom on the horizon.

As I stood in the terminal and gazed out at the countryside, I was transfixed at its beauty. Not too far away were some foothills that rose up into the low hanging clouds. The hills were dark green and covered in trees. It looked like a painting. The day was dreary with a cold wind and mist in the air, but to me it was breathtaking. Perhaps it is just it had been so long since I have seen anything like it. I wished I would have had time to see more of Germany, but, as they say, I had a plane to catch.

I know I've said it before, but I live in the past. As much as I read about World War II, I am always fascinated at the sight of an old howitzer, an old Jeep or an old soldier that likes to tell war stories of yesteryear. Now, here I stood on the very ground this war was fought! Imagine the speed at which my mind was going! I wondered for a moment what those hills, which looked so serene, had been witness to. How many soldiers had fought over the very ground upon which I stood? What did this town look like in 1945? How much time passed before everything was peaceful again?

Time, though, is a funny thing. I mean, there I was, an American soldier again standing in a land that had once given birth to my enemies. Now, I can stand there in peace, rather than in war. As our plane refueled, I pondered these things. In Iraq, it was the same way. Many of the people we worked with had, at one point, fought against us. Now, we are friends. Jaguar had been a weapons instructor in the Iraqi army for a few years. Today, we email back and forth! It is funny, but sometimes it seems like if one wants peace, they must first make war.

After a couple hours, our plane was once again ready for the transatlantic flight and so were we. As I climbed to the top of the portable truck-mounted stairway, I took one last look at the countryside. It was dark by then, but it didn't matter. I knew what was out there and I could see it in my mind. The elation I was feeling coupled with the historical significance of the land I was leaving, left me almost giddy as I greeted the flight attendant at the door. I knew the next time I felt fresh air on my face, it would be American fresh air.

Once seated and buckled in, the gigantic monstrosity of an aircraft once again lumbered down the runway and took flight. As the landing gear went up and the aircraft began to climb, a cheer went up from the soldiers packed in like sardines. Many emotions were crammed into that cheer, too, elation, relief, accomplishment. We all felt it, and you could hear it in our hoots and hollers. Indeed, I

As the landing gear went up and the aircraft began to climb, a cheer went up from the soldiers packed in like sardines.

felt it, too, and as Europe disappeared in the night sky, I let out a sigh of relief. As I reached for the Tylenol PM, I figured as long as the plane doesn't decide to burst into flames, I should have a nice long, uninterrupted snooze.

I am not quite sure what time we touched down in Baltimore. It had to be about 2300 hours or so local time. As I woke from my chemically induced coma and staggered down the narrow aisle of the plane, I could hardly keep my eyes open. What I needed awaited me inside the terminal: Starbucks! I figured since I had made it through a year of bombs, bullets, and RPGs, what's a little caffeine going to hurt? Much to my dismay, Starbucks was nowhere to be seen, and since most of the other kiosks were closed up as well, my choices of a beverage were limited to whatever I could find in a vending machine. We managed to find a lone pizza place open, and SFC Kuba and I each purchased a Diet Coke. There is nothing better than a good old American fountain pop, I dare say.

We wound up being stranded at the airport for about three hours. Folks, there just ain't much to do at midnight at the Baltimore International Airport. We mainly just walked around aimlessly and drank our Cokes until they were gone. Then, once again having nothing to do, we went and bought a couple more. About 0130 hours, we decided we had better find our way back to our gate and get on the bird. This was one flight none of us could afford to miss! SFC Kuba and I returned to the international terminal and sat down with some of the other guys until the gate opened. At 0200 hours, the TSA folks opened up the gate and prepared to let us board our plane again.

As we lined up to go through the security checkpoint, a TSA employee instructed us to take off our boots and empty our pockets. MAJ Kessel went ballistic saying, "Are you serious? These guys have spent a year fighting the very people you are trying to keep off this airplane! Are you going to subject them to the same searches the general public has to endure?" The TSA guy tried to explain rules are rules, and that while he could see we were soldiers in uniform, he had guidelines to follow and could not deter from them on account of our status as returning soldiers.

Both men had a valid point. Arguing that point at 0200 hours in the morning in Baltimore International Airport on a red-eye flight home was neither the time nor the place for such an argument. True, taking our boots off is a pain in the neck. Especially when there are a 100 or so men trying to get on the same aircraft, trying to empty pockets, and get our carryon bags onto that little conveyor belt. Yeah, it was a pain, and that is the first time I have had to take my boots off to get through a checkpoint. I told the guy the particular boots I was wearing would not set off the metal detectors, but he would not be dissuaded from his duty. That part irked me a little. I wore those boots solely because they would not set off the metal detector, thus making my trip home less of a hassle than it already was. But, I was past the point of engaging in an argument I could not possibly win. In this case, if I wanted to get on the airplane, I would have to play by the TSA rules, regardless of how ridiculous they are.

MAJ Kessel, on the other hand, stood there and argued with the guy for a few minutes, and at one point, had his notebook out writing down names and badge numbers, I presume (I was busy putting my boots back on and vaguely recall the exchange that took place). Both guys stood their ground and neither gave an inch. In the end, the major had to go through a secondary search, and it took him longer to get through the checkpoint.

A letter to the Department of Homeland Security seemed in order, but what would it say? If troops in uniform should not be subjected to these searches, how long would it take for some terrorist to wise up to that little loophole? Personally, and certainly after the fact, I have come to realize I am glad the guy didn't relent and let us through without adhering to protocol. I *want* that guy standing there doing his job. I *want* to know the airways are safe from dirt bags with bombs in their shoes or from fanatical jackasses armed with box cutters.

The flight from Baltimore to Lawton, Oklahoma, is about three hours. I vaguely remember the flight attendants serving beverages as I was asleep most of the trip. We touched down at 0500 hours. It was dark still, but it didn't matter. Our travels were over, well, for a few days anyway. As we disembarked from the aircraft, I could hear a band playing outside on the tarmac. I remember thinking, "Man, I'll bet those guys are ticked off about being here at 0500 hours!" But hey, they were there for us and it really didn't matter to me what time it was. As I walked down the portable stair steps and as my boots hit asphalt, I looked up and saw a row of men standing there in a line to greet us. A couple generals were first, followed by a couple colonels and some other officers and a sergeant major. We shook their hands and headed for the buses.

The buses took us to some building a few miles away where hot coffee and free dough-nuts awaited us. We formed up into our respec-tive units and prepared to turn in our M16s. As we lined up to hand in what had been our per-sonal "ball and chain" for the past year, I thought for a moment of how weird it would

As I stood there in line to give up my M16, I had to smile; one more check mark on the "list of things to do in order to go home."

feel in the coming days to not have that eight-pound lifesaver near me. Rarely in the past year had that M16 been out of my sight. Now, as I stood there in line to give it up, I had to smile; one more check mark on the "list of things to do in order to go home."

The rifle turn-in went pretty fast, and we were chugging down free coffee within minutes. As I savored the thought of being one step closer to home, I realized there was no one checking the rifles to make sure they were clean! What the heck…you mean I cleaned that thing for nothing? What a rip-off. Usually, when we turn in weapons, they have to be spick and span. I guess they will be sent somewhere and be reworked and steam cleaned anyway. Oh well, that certainly wasn't the first time in my life I had exerted effort for no apparent reason, and I am fairly certain it won't be the last. At any rate, one less hurdle cleared.

From the weapons turn-in facility we loaded back up onto the buses and headed for the welcome home ceremony. Most of the guys were jet lagged and tired, wanting only to relax and unwind. None of us wanted to go to some big ceremony, that's for sure. Fortunately, the ceremony was very short and sweet. A couple generals made a few remarks and a band played the "Army Song" and the "National Anthem."

Over in the corner of the big gymnasium we were in was a small group of Veterans of Foreign Wars (VFW). World War II, Korea, and Vietnam were all represented. I felt humbled to think these guys traveled out here in the wee hours of the morning just to welcome us home. They made a point to come up and say thank you to as many men as they could, and I felt very grateful to have them there. Compared to the days of sustained combat that is tattooed into their memories, I have seen nothing. To have them welcome me home and thank me for my service ranks right up there with getting to have lunch with President Bush back at Fort Polk.

We hung around the gym for a few minutes chatting with the old men, and then headed back out to the buses. We drove across post to our new home for the duration of our time at Fort Sill. As we drove, I noticed how pretty Fort Sill is. Well, maybe it was just I hadn't seen America for so long, coupled with the realization I was home for good. Anyway, we wound up in front of an old building that was numbered BLDG 2471: Home.

Our bags were all piled up out in front of the barracks, and people started milling about in vain attempts to find their bag. I decided to wait until most of the guys found their bags so when I went down to get mine, I wouldn't have to rummage through 200 duffel bags. Once I had found my room and gotten my bags hauled up the stairs, I moseyed down to the day room to see what was going on. Rumor was there was some beer already on ice somewhere close by.

Sure enough, for once the rumors were true! Beer! Ice cold, American beer! The best part you ask? Free beer, free, ice cold, American beer! I am not a big drunk, but after a year of fun and adventure in the sands of the Middle East, a little Budweiser action seemed to be in order. Plus, I enjoy the camaraderie that comes from a bunch of guys, who have endured so much for so long, sitting down and having a beer with one another. As the guys sat and talked, I could almost

For once the rumors were true! Free, ice cold, American beer!

hear the stress exit from their words as they spoke. For too long we have been uptight and unsure of what tomorrow would bring. Now, here in Fort Sill, the curtain of uncertainty was lifted, and all of us knew the danger of being hurt was gone. The only thing that stood in our way of going home was a week's worth of psycho babble; more on that in a bit. To be honest, that was the best-tasting Bud Light I have ever had.

Top came in and told us we had the rest of the day off, but we had to be ready to go by 0630 hours for the first day of briefings. I looked at my watch and it wasn't even past 0800 hours! The only question that was in my mind at this time was, "What am I going to do first?" That question was soon answered as SFC Kuba and Ben walked up. SFC Kuba asked if we wanted to go to the mall and grab some new clothes to wear. It seemed like a good idea, so we called a cab and went outside to wait.

As the cab pulled up to get us, I couldn't help but chuckle at the thought of us choosing to go to a shopping mall on our first day back from war. If only my wife could see us now. I would never hear the end of it! As it was, we did need some clothes to wear. We made it to the mall and went into the Dillard's store. I wound up buying some socks and a new shirt to wear. Ben got a shirt, as did Kuba.

After shopping, we decided to grab a bite to eat at Garfield's Restaurant. We started out with another beer and some appetizers. Soon, other guys from the unit showed up and sat down at the other end of the bar. I guess they had to go shopping, too. Pretty soon our food arrived and we all dug in. I had a nice steak and some shrimp scampi. Man, talk about good stuff! We stayed in Garfield's for a couple of hours and then decided we had pestered the poor girls behind the bar enough for one day.

Having called another cab, we went outside to wait. One of the things that was becoming painfully obvious was our entire existence was becoming dependent upon the taxi services of Lawton, Oklahoma. Soon though, our cab showed up and we went to a place called Mike's Sports Grille. Mike's was a pretty nice place, kind of a cross between Applebee's and a neighborhood pub. As we walked in, we heard people yelling "Yo, Kuba; Yo, Adams. Over here!" Wouldn't ya know it, but most of third platoon had already found the place. I laughed when I realized we had been on the ground only for about four hours and most of the guys had managed to find a bar already!

As we ordered our drinks and sat at the table with the rest of the guys, I surveyed my surroundings. There must have been at least 15 televisions, many of them big screens, situated throughout the joint, all showing various basketball, NASCAR, and other sporting events! It was really a pretty neat place to be! In the back of the building was the game room. I admit, even though I am a 31-year-old father of two, I still love playing video games. I guess this stems from the fact that growing up, Mom and Dad kind of put the kibosh on Atari and Nintendo. I still remember Dad saying, "Those damn things will melt your brain." Dad gave in one time and got us a Nintendo machine. Bernadette and I were so happy to think we could play "Duck Hunt" and "Mario" whenever we wanted! Imagine our disappointment when Mom and Dad bought a defective Nintendo! Dad, smiling inwardly I am sure, said, "Well, that's enough of that!" and took the thing back to the store and got his money back. And so, my sister and I were able to enjoy a poorly manufactured video game for about three days and then no more. So ever since then, I have been trying to make up for lost childhood memories, I guess.

Anyway, I meandered back to the game room. As I approached the double doors that led to the pool tables and arcade games, I began to hear a loud "bam…bam…bam" noise coming from within. Curious, I opened the

I could see SSG David Jensen standing at the "Whack-a-Mole" game with a beer in one hand and a big padded whacker stick in the other.

door and decided to investigate. As I rounded the corner by the door to the banquet room, I could see SSG David Jensen standing at the "Whack-a-Mole" game with a beer in one hand and a big padded whacker stick in the other. He had a look of grim determination on his face, and when the poor little mole stuck out its head, Dave let loose with all his might and slugged the sucker as hard as he could.

I stood there and watched him for a second, secretly wondering if he wasn't suffering from some sort of mental breakdown. Soon though, I started laughing at this pathetic display of pseudo-childhood amusement. Dave looked over at me and shrugged his shoulders as if to say, "What are you looking at?

Haven't you ever seen somebody beat the hell out of an inanimate object before?" I said, "Dude, you're pathetic!" Dave just smiled and took a draw on his beer and waited for the mole to get brave and show its face again.

As I sat in the main area of the restaurant and talked with the other guys, I remember commenting to somebody with regards to the likelihood of one or more of our guys winding up in jail before the night was over. We concluded, that while jail was unlikely, one or more people still being legally drunk at first formation was a pretty good bet. I looked at my watch and saw it wasn't even 1300 hours. Secretly, I was betting on somebody in jail. These guys have been cooped up with each other for a year. Now, we were cut loose to roam the town. There was no telling what kind of trouble we were going to get into, especially when you mixed unlimited amounts of alcohol into the equation. Fortunately, and only by the grace of God, everyone was at first formation. I won't lie and say all were standing tall, but we were all there. I managed to be good. I didn't go home drunk, and I didn't wind up in jail.

The next morning, or to put it in better terms, "The morning after the booze," we set in for a day of briefings aimed at easing our return to civilian life. I could write at great length about what took place in our last week on active duty, but I will try to be concise so as to not bore you.

I don't remember all the briefings we went through. What I do know is they lasted all of two days. Then we went through what they call a Reverse SRP. SRP, if you remember is the acronym for Soldier Readiness Processing. Basically, they make sure you are fit to return home. Shots are updated, HIV tests are done, finances are looked over, deactivation orders are cut, and you get your DD214, which is probably one of the most important documents we have ever gotten. Back to the briefings.

First, we broke up into groups at first formation. LT Doubler was our group leader, and I was the NCOIC or non-commissioned officer in charge; in other words: baby sitter. The group thing was just to keep us more organized and was aimed at making the whole process more efficient. Yeah, whatever. We loaded up onto some buses and were shipped over to a nice building called Gunner's Hall. The facilities for the briefings were pretty nice and the interior

of the hall was very tastefully decorated. Free coffee and soda were set out for
the guys as we got there.

We sat around these large round tables and spent the day listening to a battery of speakers who spoke on topics ranging from dental care to GI Bill benefits. Some of the speakers were mediocre, some just plain stunk. One of the
guys talked like Mr. Garrison off the irreverent television series "South Park."
After Mr. Garrison finished telling why we should not kill ourselves and our
families, some lady who sounded like Mary Poppins with a North Dakota
accent got up and told us about the ACAP program, which is designed to help
us find jobs, if we need them. Trouble is, they are in Oklahoma, and we all
live in Illinois. Indeed, most of the presentations were geared for the soldiers
from Arkansas. True, they make up the vast majority of the soldiers in the 39th
Brigade, but for us, a lot of the info wasn't relevant for guys from the Land of
Lincoln. As we were released for the day, we left knowing we had to sit
through it all again the next day.

One of the biggest pains we had to endure was getting chow. See, we
couldn't eat at the regular mess hall with the other troops from Fort Sill. No,
we had to eat in the chow hall with all the basic trainees. Of course, this chow
hall was all the way across post. There was supposed to be a bus that took us
there, but no bus showed up, ever. In the morning, we could take the bus over
to the chow hall, but rather than walk from the chow hall over to the Gunner's
Hall for our briefings (a three-minute walk), we had to get back on the bus and
ride back across post, only to get on another bus and drive back over to the
Gunner's Hall for the briefings. Confused yet? Don't worry, it gets better.

After the meal debacle, it was decided a pack of Twinkies out of a vending
machine beat having to spend an hour on a bus at the butt crack of dawn just
to get a bad plate of S.O.S. and powdered eggs. Many of the guys just went
without breakfast. On a couple of days, I just had the cabbie run through the
drive-through of McDonalds so I could get a burger to eat the next morning.
Yeah, burgers for breakfast– what a great idea. What were we to do? Take a
cab to chow? We would have had to wait for the cab and then pay the cabbie

both ways, just to eat! Forget that! We always went out for dinner anyway, so it really worked out better than waiting for the stupid buses.

I just do not understand where the logistical screw-up happened insofar as getting us to chow. I mean did they not realize people get hungry? And whose bright idea was it to bus us clear across post to eat with the newbies? Not that I have a problem with new recruits, but are we, as Army National Guard soldiers, not good enough to eat with the regular soldiers who are stationed there?

The next day it was the same thing, briefing after briefing after briefing. The thing that made me laugh the most – aside from the fact the active component soldiers who had gone to Iraq with us were already home – was the people who led the briefings handed out pamphlets and then read them to us. Are we unable to read?

Now here we were, in America, a scant 12 hours by car from our loved ones, but we were stuck in that building.

Some of the briefs were necessary though, especially the ones about our GI Bill benefits. Others were just time fillers it seemed. All of us had but one goal – getting home. Now here we were, in America, a scant 12 hours by car from our loved ones, but we were stuck in that building listening to Mary Poppins and Mr. Garrison. Luckily, the next day was the beginning of our out-processing.

The out-processing took a little bit of time to do, which came as no surprise to any of us. If there is one thing I have learned about the army, it is inefficiency. The army thrives on it. One of my buddies works in management at a large manufacturing facility. He told me one day if his people worked like the people at the SRP, he would fire them all. But, in retrospect, I wouldn't go that far. They get burned out too. They are the ones who sit there day in and day out listening to soldiers gripe about having to be there. I think if the tables were turned, we would be the same way. We all know when you are looking forward to something as much as getting to go home, minutes seem like days. In reality, the people there did a pretty good job of shuffling us through. In the end though, the busing to chow thing, coupled with the redundancy in briefings, really made me mad. Some of the briefings overlapped in their topics. We have had no less than four briefings about suicide prevention! Come on, folks, that's a bit of overkill, don't you think? We even told the people leading the briefs we had already had them, to which they replied, "Well, you're getting it again!"

One of the nice things about getting bused all over Fort Sill was it satisfied some of my curiosity. I love old military posts. So much history lives there. Some of the guys aren't into history, and I can appreciate that, but for me, I love it. Fort Sill is probably the neatest fort I have ever been to. Many old stone buildings still stand, and the museum there is rather extensive. Many old cannons and field guns are sitting here and there for people to stop and look at.

One day as we drove over to the Gunner's Hall, we rounded a curve and I noticed a small display of old rockets and missiles. Being a World War II freak, as I am, you can imagine my surprise when I noticed a familiar shape there on the end of a row of missiles. The fuselage of the rocket was about seven or eight feet in length, the middle of the fuselage had some stubby wings protruding out of its sides, and mounted on top of the fuselage was a large motor. It was painted green and had the fin flash of the U.S. Air Force on it, but there was no mistaking what it was. Right there in front of me was a World War II German V-1 rocket! I was struck dumb there for a second as the realization of what I was seeing sank in.

I jumped to the other side of the bus for a better look, while somebody said, "Dude, what are you all excited about?" "That's a V-1, man!" I said. "Yeah, so?" they said. Nevermind I thought. I don't have time to explain it, so I just sat back down and was thankful we were riding the bus after all. Otherwise, I might not have had the chance to see the predecessor to the V-2, which was the forerunner of today's ICBMs. Seeing that piece of history made the day's briefings worth every minute.

Sitting here in my room on the second floor of building 2471, I can look out my tiny window and see the foothills that grace the horizon a few miles away. In between the hills and the barracks is a construction crew digging and moving dirt for some new construction. Yet again, the face of the earth is changed. We call it progress, but sometimes I am just not sure if "progress" is the most apt phraseology. Many years ago, when this post was first built, there was nothing here but open ground. Slowly, buildings were put up, and over time, you get the Fort Sill of today. As I gaze out my window and look to the hills, I wonder. I wonder what mark I will leave. What great things have I done to make this world better for the Americans of tomorrow?

I am sure for years to come, politicians will argue over what we are doing in this War on Terrorism, and historians will certainly postulate all the "what ifs" as well as the "if they would've done that" kind of stuff. Things like that make for good book fodder and should keep writers busy for at least one or two generations. As far as I am concerned, what we did

As far as I am concerned, what we did was right. I am proud of my unit and of my fellow soldiers.

was right. We did what others said was impossible and unnecessary. We went where others did not want to go and did what others were unwilling to do. I am proud of my unit and of my fellow soldiers.

As I walked back to my room, I thought if the ghosts that now walk these hallways were here today, they would be proud of me and my unit too. That is all that really matters to me, being able to stand in the midst of other soldiers from other wars and not feel ashamed. I couldn't care less what the general public thinks of me anymore. They were not there as the bullets whizzed by our heads. Only my brothers in arms can ever really understand what goes on in a war, and only they can really appreciate what it was the men of Foxtrot Battery accomplished.

Jason Adams
Fort Sill, Oklahoma

| Notice | Training | Deployment | | Home leave | Back Home |
| 10/12/03 | | 3/1/04 | | 9/26–10/14/04 | 3/19/05 |

Final Briefings

Today is March 18ᵗʰ

Well, I have made it through the Reverse SRP and the army has deemed me fit to reenter society. Whew! What a relief. I will tell you what, if I had to sit through another suicide briefing, I would have chewed my own toes off. We have to go through some moronic briefing this morning. I think it has something to do with mental health awareness or something like that. Honestly, I couldn't care less. All I know is in less than 24 hours, I will be on a plane home. That is all that matters to any of us.

> **Well, I have made it through the Reverse SRP, and the army has deemed me fit to re-enter society.**

Well, one last painful briefing is out of the way. We just got back from the mental health awareness brief. What a waste of taxpayers' money. The poor lady that tried to lead the class was lucky they broke our guys down by rank. She led the E-6s and E-7s. I feel bad for the folks leading the lower-ranking men! Well, actually, that's not true. What these folks do not realize is we have heard this all before. It is redundant. We couldn't care less about it. All our minds are fixated on returning home, and yet they preach on.

Our briefing was scheduled to last until 1100 hours. Thankfully, the instructor gave up around 1030 hours. We went into this room and sat in a circle and started out by hearing what the class was all about. The whole thing had an AA feel to it. Needless to say, none of us felt like "sharing." Part of the problem stems from the fact we are men as well as soldiers. Not to sound too chauvinistic here, but I just don't feel comfortable standing up in front of other guys and saying, "Hi, my name is Jason, and I have a problem dealing with anxiety and stress." Moreover, the second reason most of us had made up our minds to remain silent throughout the class came from the fact we had about had it with ridiculous briefings such as this one. At one point, we had to stand up and say our name, where we were from, what we wanted to do when we got home, and lastly, and I really don't get this part, what kind of car we drive. I felt like I was back in Boy Scouts and it was the first day of summer camp!

One could make a decent argument saying as long as we were there, why not make the best of it? Okay, I will give you that, but that person was not there. That person had not been away for a year and a half. That person was not forced to sit through countless people, who had never been to Iraq, telling me, "I know what you are going through. Ha!, yeah right, bucko." Unless you were there with us in Iraq, you don't have a clue as to what we are going through. Secondly, where will you be tonight? Oh, I see, home with the wife and kids, huh? Guess where I will be? Yeah, that's right, in the same barracks I have lived in for the past week while listening to you tell me all about how I feel! I tell ya what, run on down to Wally World, aisle four I think it is, and get yerself one of them thar clues!! Man, I wanted to say all that, but I figured they would make me stay longer for further evaluations, so I held my tongue.

Although at one point, when asked how I felt, I told the lady, "I feel fine, nothing is wrong, everything is good." To which she replied, "Would you tell me if anything *was* wrong?" "Nope, because it would cause me to stay here longer," I said. I don't think she liked that reply, and my intention was not to sound snotty, but that response of mine encapsulated what everyone of us in that room felt. Enough is enough. Send us home! I feel as though I am a prisoner here. The only thing missing is the orange jumpsuit or perhaps the electronic ankle bracelet.

"I feel fine, nothing is wrong, everything is good." To which she replied, "Would you tell me if anything *was* wrong?" "Nope, because it would cause me to stay here longer."

At one point, the lady was telling us statistics and research suggest groups as large as ours happened to be are traditionally unproductive, but it would be a logistical nightmare for this kind of meeting to take place at our home armories. I couldn't let that one pass unchecked. I raised my hand and asked, "So what you're telling us is this meeting will be unproductive, but you can't do anything about it?" Have I told you about how cynical these briefings have made me? Many other guys said the same thing, and I wasn't the only heckler in the crowd.

I can appreciate what the army is trying to do for us. It is far better to try to educate us regarding our feelings and emotions as we make the transition to civilian life, rather than just patting us on the head and wishing us luck as we exit the aircraft. This system of re-entry is fairly new, and many of the bugs have not yet been identified and done away with. Plus, in a way, I can kind of see the army's thoughts about giving us some time to de-stress after being in Iraq for so long. But, we spent darn near a week in Kuwait de-stressing, and now we are at Fort Sill for another week de-stressing. For me, and I certainly do not speak for everyone here, but all this sitting around has raised my anxiety levels threefold. There has to be a better, more effective and certainly less counterproductive way in which to get troops from Iraq back into society.

Yes, there are problems guys will face upon going home. For many it's the feeling of being out of the loop insofar as parenting. For others, they will have trouble with intimacy with their spouses or girlfriends. Some guys might just stress out as the pressures of daily life start to creep back in. But, I am not convinced sitting so far away from home attending mandatory briefings is the answer.

Many of the men suggested it would be better to get us home and then hold these classes at our home armory a couple days after we return. In doing things this way, they argued, it would allow the family to be a part of it too. They have been apart from us for just as long as we have been away from them. They, too, will have issues that need to be dealt with, I am sure. Secondly, having been home for a couple days, it might serve to help identify potential problems, thereby helping the army provide more focused help to individuals rather than blanket applications of therapy to all, the likes of which are being applied now.

Hopefully, the multitude of surveys and questionnaires we have filled out in the past five days will be taken seriously, and some positive changes will come as a result. For now though, as I sit here staring out my little window at the darkness, I am just angry, angry at the system keeping me from my home. In time it will pass, and this all will seem like it only lasted but a second. But here and now, I am mad. My wife is mad. My family wants nothing more than to see me, and I wish for nothing more than to see them. I keep telling myself, "Tomorrow, tomorrow– tomorrow you will be home!"

Jason Adams
Fort Sill, Oklahoma

The Day of Days

Today is March 19th

Wake-up came early here at Fort Sill this morning. By 0200 hours we were up and hard at it; cleaning the barracks, trying to cram last-minute items into our duffel bags, shaving, brushing our teeth, and so on. We had to get a lot of things accomplished in a very short amount of time. But, in doing so, one can see the impossible is, in fact, obtainable if the right motivational tools are employed. The motivation in this case was the idea we weren't getting on any plane until the barracks were clean. Fair enough, we thought, and gladly we got out of bed and started scrubbing. Soon, the building was acceptable, and we loaded up on the buses to go over and get weighed in.

Not many people had much sleep last night. Most of them I think didn't even go to sleep. Me? Well, I have to admit I managed to get about four restless hours of shut-eye. At my age, sleep is a mandatory thing, you know. After loading up on the buses one last time, we went over to a building right next to the one where we turned in our rifles on the first day. We had to have our carryon baggage with us so they could get an accurate idea of the total passenger weight.

We formed up into two lines and went across some little scales that were set up. After that, we went into another room where coffee and doughnuts were being served. As it turns out, the folks that work at that little building during the week had pitched in and gotten the pastries for us, a very nice gesture I thought. Most of us made a point to thank the folks for the chow as we hastily filed through the line and got back onto the buses.

We made it out to the airport about 0530 hours and prepared to get on the plane. The aircraft, a 737 I think, looked beautiful to me, and I could feel the excitement building in me as I stepped off the bus. Obviously, I wasn't the only one feeling this. We all were!

As we waited in line to board the plane, I couldn't help but notice the design of the plane was such that the engines were round from the seven o'clock position all the way around to the five o'clock position, but from five to seven o'clock, they looked flat. To me it looked as though the pilot had forgotten to put the landing gear down a time or two and accidentally belly landed. I mentioned this to Ben, to which he replied, "I don't care if we belly land or not, as long as we do it in Moline, Illinois!"

I also noticed we were able to walk right onto the plane without going through some goofy security checkpoint! They drove the buses right up to the door of the plane and we just walked on! Not that I was complaining, but the fiasco in Baltimore was still pretty fresh in my mind. I figured it would be okay, because if anyone was stupid enough to try and hijack this particular flight, I would personally beat them to death with my free bag of pretzels.

If anyone was stupid enough to try and hijack this particular flight, I would personally beat them to death with my free bag of pretzels.

Once on board the plane and in our seats, it came time for the flight attendants to give their safety briefing. Personally, I had heard this briefing so much in the past few days, I could recite it verbatim. As it turned out, I wasn't alone in that respect. SGT Anderson decided to ask the flight attendant if he could do the safety talk. To my amazement, the flight attendant said, "What the hell, why not!" And so, SGT Anderson got up and gave us our safety briefing. What a hoot! He had a little trouble with the seatbelt thing, but other than that, he did a very good, albeit animated, job of telling us what to do should the aircraft suddenly burst into flames while simultaneously losing cabin pressure and pitching into an irrecoverable nose dive. The flight attendants were actually pretty funny. They were cracking jokes over the intercom for most of the flight, and I have to say it was probably the most fun I have ever had on an airplane.

The flight left Lawton, Oklahoma, around 0600 hours and landed in Moline, Illinois, around 0730 hours. As the plane touched down, a cheer went up in the cabin and people began clapping and high-fiveing each other. We were at the tail end of a long and arduous journey that had spanned almost a year and a half of our lives. The best part was we had brought every person home.

As we taxied to the waiting charter buses for the trip to Galva, we went between two big airport fire trucks that, as we passed, fired up their deck cannons and showered the plane with water. Things like that just never get old for me. Sure, they did the same thing for us when I went on leave, but I still was rendered mesmerized as the big trucks doused our plane with water. Maybe it is because I am a fireman, maybe it is because it is a salute to us for our achievements, I do not know. What I do know is the guys in those trucks certainly didn't have to be out there doing that for us, but they were. That is the important thing. In retrospect though, what they did was but a small taste of what had yet to take place. We had no idea of what awaited a scant drive from the airport. It truly would become a day of days.

As the flight attendants cracked a few last-minute jokes, we grabbed our carryon luggage and pushed for the door. Outside on the tarmac were a couple buses and a group of guys in BDUs (BDUs differ from DCUs in that the BDUs are green camouflage and the DCUs are desert camouflage). As I descended the steps of the plane, I recognized the guys standing there. They were my buddies– the ones who had been wounded and sent away for treatment! They made it home to be with us! How cool is that? Well, they all didn't make it home. SGT Dustin Hill is still in the hospital, but we all knew he was there in sprit. We said our, "Hellos," and got on the buses for the trip to Galva.

Outside the airport there were a couple of Henry County squad cars waiting for us. There were some unmarked cars there, too, but I am not sure from what department they came. As we headed out of the airport and onto Interstate 80, the squad cars were out in front with there lights going, and I have to say, I felt pretty darn important right then and there! As we traveled down I-80, we came to one of those turnaround spots that are reserved for official traffic only which was now occupied by a Colona City fire truck. Up on top

Up on top of the truck stood a lone fireman at the position of attention, and as our convoy passed, he rendered a salute to us.

of the truck stood a lone fireman at the position of attention, and as our convoy passed, he rendered a salute to us. I remember thinking how cool it was the city of Colona had thought enough to send out a fire truck to help welcome us home.

As we passed the next turnaround point, we saw another fire truck sitting there with its lights going. At the next overpass, another fire truck waited for us with its lights flashing. There were a few people standing on top of the overpass as well. As we passed underneath, we could see they were all bundled up against the cold and stood there with their homemade banners just waiting for us to come by. What a nice gesture! And so it went all down the interstate! Many fire trucks from the surrounding community were out in force to welcome us home. My buddy Ben is a fireman, so as we passed the town of Geneseo, we saw a nice new truck sitting there with a sign that read "Welcome home, Ben!" Of course, being the kind, considerate men we are, upon seeing that we all started in with the "Aww, isn't that cute!" bit.

Once we made it to the town of Annawan and our exit from the interstate, we were met by no less than five or six more squad cars from Henry County. They were lined up on the off-ramp, pulled out in front of our convoy, and led the way into Kewanee, which was only a few miles down the road. As we went through the small town of Annawan, the streets were lined with more people than I had ever seen in that

It looked as though the president's motorcade was passing by! Everybody was waving and holding little flags in their frozen hands.

town. It looked as though the president's motorcade was passing by! Everybody was waving and holding little flags in their frozen hands. Some folks had banners and signs, while others just gave us the thumbs up and waved their hats at us.

On the outskirts of town is the Hatzer-Nordstrom farm implement dealer. Twice a year they hold a giant equipment auction that draws people from all over the Midwest. If you are looking to buy or sell any type of farm equipment, it is the place to be, that's for sure! As our buses passed by, all the farmers had left the auction rows and were standing out along the road! Folks, that is a pretty big thing. I mean auctions usually don't stop for just anything! It was an awesome sight though to see a wall of flannel shirts and Carhart jackets standing there waving as we passed. It may not seem like much to you, but to me it was a great honor.

Somebody mentioned to me that in the 25 years or so this particular auction has taken place, this was the first time they had stopped the auction for any reason! I cannot vouch as to the authenticity of that claim, but anyone from the Midwest will tell you once an auctioneer gets down to selling, come hell or high water, they are not stopping until everything is sold.

The rest of the way into Kewanee was just like the interstate. People were everywhere! All along the highway, in stopped cars, in their front yards. You name it, they were there! It was truly amazing to see the support we were getting from the folks we left those many months ago. It is funny, but up until we got off the airplane in Moline, I wasn't that excited. For some reason, it just felt like another day to me. But, as we neared Kewanee and as I began to realize just how much this bunch of tired soldiers were loved by our community, I felt myself growing increasingly anxious, like a child on the night before Christmas.

As our motorcade entered Kewanee, I was stunned. People were everywhere! Fire trucks were everywhere! Police cars were blocking streets and barricades had been thrown up, just for us! All the marquees, on all the stores in town said, "Welcome home F-Battery, we love you!" Some of my friends from school were standing down by the video rental store and were waving so hard they looked like a bunch of jack rabbits with epilepsy! I remember thinking to myself "Did they truck these people in from other towns? Where did they all come from?" Literally, there were hundreds of people out– I couldn't believe it!

When we got out to the south end of town, out by the new Sullivan's Grocery Store, Ratliff Brothers Construction had one of their big cranes set up with a giant American flag hoisted up high into the air. That giant symbol of our

I noticed the American flag was fluttering ever so gently in the wind, and I remember thinking to myself I was seeing one of the most beautiful things in the world right then.

country, those simple pieces of colored fabric sewn together to represent the greatest nation on earth was being flown in our honor! What tribute to us could be more fitting? As we passed the giant flag, I noticed it was fluttering ever so gently in the wind, and I remember thinking to myself I was seeing one of the most beautiful things in the world right then. Our flag flying free in the wind, to me is perfect. That rectangular piece of cloth means so many different things to me I would have a hard time listing them all.

South of Kewanee is the local John Deere dealer. Kline Equipment sits along Illinois Routes 34 and 78 and has sold John Deere tractors and combines for years. Today however, they had a brand spanking new combine sitting right out front with its auger extended and an American flag hanging from the auger tube. In addition, someone had tied yellow ribbons all over the gargantuan machine. The one thing that came to my mind as I saw that display was how right it felt. Sure, it was patriotic, but it was also more than that. The juxtaposition of two of the biggest symbols of Americana one could find, combined on our behalf, is something that will stay with me for a long time. An American flag and a John Deere, you just can't get much more American than that! Well, perhaps if there had been some of Mom's apple pie on the driver's seat, but let's not go overboard!

A mile or two after Route 34 splits from Route 78, out by Black Hawk Community College, or as some people call it "The University of Southern Kewanee," sat a couple more fire trucks. But these were special to me because they were from Toulon. Just past the college, at the next crossroads, sat our brand new tanker truck and one of our city trucks. On the side of No. 7, the tanker hung a giant sign that read, "Welcome home Jason." Over the mirror of the truck someone had hung my turnout gear as if it had been sitting there all along, just waiting for me to come and put it on. A bunch of my buddies were standing there wearing their turnout gear as well, and all of them were waving as we passed. Unfortunately, the windows in the bus were tinted, so they couldn't see me waving back, but they knew I was on one of the buses at any rate.

On the side of the No. 7 tanker hung a giant sign that read, "Welcome Home Jason." Over the mirror of the truck someone had hung my turnout gear as if it had been sitting there all along, just waiting for me to come and put it on.

One of the fringe benefits that comes from living in a small town is the "small town values" that seem to be slipping from our country these days. I am very fortunate to live where I do. I am also very fortunate to be a member of a fire department that is staffed by such wonderful people. In the winter of 2003-2004, while I was at Fort Hood, we had a pretty good snowstorm back home. Steph is not one to ask anyone for help and would have been out in the driveway with a snow shovel had it not been for my buddies standing there in their bunker pants and helmets. I happened to have called home one night and was talking with Steph as she was telling me about how much snow they had received. About that time, I could hear my youngest daughter, Joanna, yell out "Mommy, there is a fire truck in front of our house!" "What the…?" Steph said as she opened the side door and peeked out. I asked what was going on, to which Steph replied, "You are not going to believe this, but the equipment truck just pulled up and Jerry, John, Andy, and a few more guys are in our driveway shoveling snow!" I told Steph to put one of them on the phone so I could thank them. Jerry came on the line and I thanked him for helping Steph out. Jerry, always the mischievous one, said, "Don't worry, we told you we'd take *care* of your wife while you were gone, didn't we?" "Yeah," I said. "But I was thinking you meant something else." As I said, I serve with some of the best guys in the world. It is just understood that anyone of us would be there for anyone else in their time of need. That is just something we do. Oh yeah, we put out fires too.

It is hard to remember everything folks had done for us once we reached Galva. What I do remember is the city looked as though they had spent days preparing for our return. Yellow ribbons adorned almost everything I could see. The Kewanee Corporation's parking lot had three large dump trailers hoisted up into the air with their empty beds visible from the road. Inside the beds were the words, "Welcome Home Troops." Farther up town as we drove by the park, people continued to line the streets!

As we drove down a side street toward the armory, it became apparent to me, judging by the lines of parked cars, that there must be several hundred people waiting for us at the armory. Sure enough, as our charter buses pulled up in front of the armory, there were too many folks to count. The American Legion Color Guard was standing out front of the building and all were standing at attention with rifles and flags. I was on the first bus and was probably the fifth or sixth guy off. I figured my dad would be somewhere in the crowd, trying to get a picture of me as I first stepped through the doors of the bus. I didn't see him, but I knew he was there. Heck, I didn't notice anyone hardly, there was too much to take in. It was almost a sensory overload, and I do not think I was the only one who felt it either. I must have had the "deer in the headlights" look on my face because I don't remember walking into the armory doors.

Once past all the well-wishers, I made my way into the gymnasium where we used to hold our formations. As I walked through the doors to the gym, people were screaming, banners were everywhere, and a band was playing. The roar from the crowd was deafening. So loud were the cheers that had Ben been yelling in my ear, I most likely would not have been able to understand him.

All along the walls of the gym hung homemade signs welcoming us home. There was an area of the gym that had been taped off with that yellow caution tape like they use at construction sites. It is good someone had the forethought to do this. Otherwise, there would have been no place for us to stand! I am quite sure the building capacity was exceeded at least twofold that day, but no fire marshal in the world could have enforced that little rule, not that day anyway!

I looked around for Steph and the girls, but I didn't see them. I must have had blinders on because as it turns out, they were screaming at the tops of their lungs while holding a giant yellow banner our buddy Kurt Loncka had made. We had been told once we get off the bus, to go into the gym, set down our carryon bags and form up in a mass formation. In case you are wondering, a mass formation is where the whole unit lines up en masse, rather than in our respective platoons.

As we lined up, I noticed someone had even taken it upon themselves to decorate the backboards of the basketball hoops with red, white, and blue foil! As more soldiers filed into the gym, the place erupted with even more cheers. Some of the family members were crying, some were waving, and others just stood there stunned and relived all at the same time. I guess it goes without saying it was a very emotional time for all of us. So many weeks of worrying and praying paid off as my fellow soldiers and I strode into that armory.

It was a dream come true! Just think *all* of us came home! *All* of us! That is a miracle in and of itself. When we left, we were flat out told, statistically speaking, *at least one* of us would be killed while deployed. "That's nice," I thought. "Way to start our deployment out on a high note!" But, there we were defying that very macabre prediction!

National Guard Armories, at one point in history, were the social magnets of small towns everywhere. Dances were held there on a regular basis. In fact, for those of you who remember, Duke Ellington played at my armory in Dixon, Illinois, in 1952, I think it was. But, with everything else, things change. Armories gave way to drive-in movies, drive-ins gave way to skating rinks, skating rinks gave way to discos, discos gave way to mosh pits. I am not really sure what kids are doing these days, but going down to the armory on a Saturday night for a dance is certainly not on the list of "things to do and places to be."

Like the old army posts I spoke of, whose glory days live only in unit histories and old faded photographs, so too have the armories faded into obscurity insofar as a house of celebration or an occasional courtship. Today, they are home to Army National Guard units, true, but their glory days are long gone. Newer armories are not even built with stages anymore. It is a shame. But, for a few hours last Saturday, the armory in Galva was once again transformed into a place of festivities and music. Once again, the old stage housed a band. Once again, the building which had seen many troops come and go in the years since its construction, was able to watch its boys come home. On many different levels, it was a grand day all around.

Once the cheering stopped and we were all standing at attention, several people made a few short remarks. Chaplain Prain said a nice prayer and read from the Bible. We gave thanks to our Lord for bringing us home to those we love. We gave thanks for the honor and ability to use our talents to make the world a better place. We gave thanks to the families, for they, too, made sacrifices in our absence. But, the most important thing for me was the fact we all stood together in silence and gave thanks to our Lord, who so mercifully delivered us from so much.

So many times in the past year, the powers of our enemies tried in vain to take our lives. But each time, they went home empty-handed. There were many times when a few of us should have died, but there we stood at home, with our loved ones. How amazing is that? What more proof does anyone need that our God is an awesome God?

> **There were many times when a few of us should have died, but there we stood at home, with our loved ones. How amazing is that?**

After Chaplain Prain finished with the prayer, both 1SGT Peterson and MAJ Kessel made a few remarks outlining some of our accomplishments. Top then brought the battery to attention, and we saluted as the band played our national anthem. As I stood there with my hand raised to the brim of my hat, I could see an American flag on the far wall of the gym. As the music played, and the bass from the tuba resonated in my head, I felt a wave of pride wash over me as if I had been doused with water dumped from a bucket.

We were there being honored for our accomplishments, but it was we who had also given honor as well. We honored our nation, our way of life, our Constitution, and certainly our fellow Americans by our service. How great it is to be part of something so much bigger than ourselves! How marvelous it feels to be able to stand proud and say to the world, "I did my duty; I did not falter." Regardless of anything anyone might say about me, no one can deny me these things. History will remember us as it sees fit. But for us, in those few moments, with our heads held high and our hands raised in that age-old sign of respect, we were on top of the world. Indeed, I now know the feeling of being king for a day.

After the music had ended, amid the deafening roar of an adoring hometown, MAJ Kessel took command of the formation and uttered the one command we had yearned for so long to hear: Dismissed!! The millstone had been lifted from my neck and the shackles hit the floor as we broke ranks and began to search out our family members. Dad was the first to find me, and in a flash, I was holding Steph in a tight embrace. Teryl and Joanna were jumping with joy and hugging me around my waist. Mom was trying to capture the whole thing on the camcorder as Steph and I kissed for the first time in months. Both of my grandmas were beaming with a mixture of relief and love as I went over and hugged them. My sister had flown in from Boston and was waiting for her turn to hug me. Steph's mom and dad were there, as were our closest buddies, Kurt Loncka and Carrie Taylor. The moment was complete; it was everything I had dreamed it would be and it was perfect.

Soon, I found myself trying to carry on a conversation with Steph and the girls, but it was rather pointless as so many people in that small gym were attempting to do the same thing. A couple of reporters for the local papers whom I have gotten to know through the fire department

The moment was complete; it was everything I had dreamed it would be and it was perfect.

and from my weekly letters came up and started to ask me questions. As I tried to put into words what I was feeling, they were both dutifully scribbling notes in their little paper tablets. At one point, I glanced at Steph, who just rolled her eyes as if to say, "You are such a media hound!" After a brief battery of questions from the reporters, I excused myself and told Steph it was high time we headed home. As we navigated our way through the swarming crowd, people whom I didn't even know came up and either shook my hand or hugged me. To be honest, it was a bit overwhelming. We made it out to the car and loaded up for the 15-minute trip back to Toulon.

When we pulled into the drive, the first thing I noticed was my truck was parked in its same old spot! Ol' Betty was back on the road! Steph informed me she had taken the liberty of reinstating the insurance on it plus, she updated the license plate sticker! Mom and Dad had vacuumed the interior and washed it as well, not that you could tell. Rust doesn't clean up all that well, you know!

As I opened the kitchen door and went in, my whole family was there! Dad was taking play by play pictures of me to the point it started to freak me out a little. We sat and talked for awhile, but what I wanted most was to put on my old jeans and my wornout running shoes. I excused myself and went down in the basement to change. When I arrived at the top of the basement stairs a few minutes later, I grabbed my old ball cap from the coat rack and put it on. Then I went into the bedroom, grabbed my pager for the fire department, clipped it to my belt and, like a butterfly that has just burst from its cocoon, my metamorphosis was complete. I was once again Joe Q. Civilian and it felt great.

When I had come home for leave, I was pleasantly surprised with the changes Steph had made around the house. Our buddies, Carrie and Kurt were such a godsend in helping Steph remodel. I had no idea they could all be so handy around the house. Now, as I stood in my living room, I noticed the floor was sporting some new carpeting and, where our old couch had once sat, now stood two brand new leather-bound Lane recliners! His and hers! As if she possessed psychic abilities, Steph could tell as I looked at the leather recliners, all I could see were dollar signs. Steph said, "Well, go on! Have a seat in one!" As I sat into the new piece of furniture and tilted it back, I thought to myself, "Wow, this *is* kinda nice!" "Well, what do you think?" Steph asked. "Oh, I *suppose* I could get used to it," I replied. All in all, the house looks great. The best part is I didn't have to do any of it! What a deal!

Mom, Dad, Bernadette and my in-laws stayed for a little while before returning home. Steph asked me what I wanted to do first, to which I replied, "Let's go to the Kaiserhof for dinner!" The Kaiserhof, situated in downtown Bradford, Illinois, is one of our favorite places to eat. So, we called Kurt and Carrie and told them to meet us there around 7:30 p.m. for dinner. Steph and I decided to invite Bernadette, as well as Carrie's parents.

Around seven, Steph and I loaded up into our Impala, grabbed my sister and headed to Bradford for some of the best German food this side of Berlin. Carrie's folks showed up not long after we got there and proceeded to pay for the entire night. Judy, Carrie's mom, came through the door carrying a beautiful tulip plant for me. Barry, her dad, bought me my favorite drink, and we all sat and chatted while waiting for the other two. Soon, we were all seated at a table eating Jaeger schnitzel, roasted duck and all the fixings.

Every Saturday night, the restaurant has a man who comes in and plays the accordion for entertainment. He was dressed in a white shirt and khaki pants, with a Bavarian style cap on his head complete with a little feather in the hatband. He played polkas, he played old drinking songs, he played 1950s type music– you name it. At one point, after the food and the after-dinner liqueur had been consumed, we found ourselves singing along with his music. Then, one of the cooks came out of the kitchen and sang a song in Spanish! I was having such a good time! This is what I had been missing for the past year and a half! It was everything I had wanted and more. The food was fantastic, the music was uplifting, and I was in great company– what a perfect end to a perfect day.

We stayed and sang along with the accordion for quite awhile. Matter of fact, most of the waiters and waitresses had already left by the time we put our coats on to leave. I reached into my pocket for my wallet and walked up to the owner, Gary, and asked for our bill. Gary told me it had already been taken care of. Confused, I glanced at Carrie's mom, who was sitting quietly with the slightest hint of a smirk on her face. I certainly did not expect anyone to pay for our meals and drinks. But, I guess it is their way of saying thanks for serving my country. I am so lucky to be surrounded by such wonderful friends and neighbors.

Carrie and Kurt invited us over to their house for a dip in the hot tub after dinner. It was one of those days that was so much fun, that one didn't wish for it to end. Here I thought only kids experienced feelings like that! I had been up since two that morning, but I didn't care. Sleep would come later. And so we went and sat in the hot tub until well past midnight. When we dropped Bernie off and finally went to bed, I was flat-out exhausted, but what a day it had been! As my head hit the pillow, my mind, albeit exhausted, was still reeling from the events of the day. What a trip it had been. Such an emotional and patriotic hero's welcome followed by a great day with friends and family. Indeed, March 19th, 2005 will not fade in my memory anytime soon.

The next morning I woke up and went out in the kitchen. Steph had made coffee and its aroma lifted my eyelids as soon as I smelled it. "Ah, gourmet coffee! Steph, you thought of everything!" Buddy, my dog, was already up and had come out to see me. Well, he doesn't really care who he sees, he just wants somebody to pet him. As I sipped my coffee and played

One thing I was sure of was the feeling that I had gotten my wish. I made it home and I had my life back. What I do with it from here is another story.

with Buddy, I realized something. I realized that the past year and a half didn't really seem like that long of a time. It felt somehow like I had never left. I can't really explain it. All the pain and suffering we had gone through in Kuwait and Fort Sill seemed like a distant memory to me for some reason. It certainly didn't feel like I hadn't even been home for 24 hours yet! I couldn't put my finger on it. But one thing I was sure of was the feeling I had gotten my wish. I made it home and I had my life back. What I do with it from here is another story. Nobody knows how that one will turn out. It will be what I decide to make it. I am standing on a road with many forks. I can choose any one I wish to travel down. I don't know what one I will choose at this time. What I do know is I am going out to the college and get enrolled in summer classes ASAP.

My goals are still the same. The only way I will ever achieve them is to jump right back in the fire with both feet. As for work, well, I have several options on the table. I do not know which one I will choose, but prudence demands I explore each one.

After I had my coffee, I decided the one thing I hadn't done yet was fire up Ol' Betty. My neighbors are pretty fond of that old Ford, you know. Every once in awhile they will say, "I see you had a fire the other night, huh?" "Uh, well…um, yeah, at three a.m.. How did you know? Did you see my blue light flashing as I went down the street or something?" I would ask. "Oh no, we heard you go by!" they'll say. "What were you doing up at three o'clock in the morning?" I would ask. "Oh, we weren't up." they replied. Yeah, I guess my truck is pretty loud and unmistakable, as I live in a neighborhood of Buicks and other cars that actually have mufflers.

Since I have been home, many people have asked me if I plan on getting rid of the old jalopy. Are you nuts? Why on earth would I want to part with such a pristine example of automotive engineering perfection? Besides, what trucks like mine lack in chrome and leather, it makes up for threefold in character! Plus, I have a great stereo in there, and the heater works, too! I have to laugh at the looks on folks' faces sometimes when I pull up in the old girl. There I am, in faded blue jeans, a camouflage hat, an old pair of Reebok running shoes, sitting in my truck. When I roll down the window, people expect to hear something like an old Garth Brooks song coming out of the cab. Much to their surprise, they hear something more along the lines of Wagner or Puccini. But that's just who I am. I can fit in with just about anyone. I can make a three-piece suit work, just as easily as I can do the Polo shirt and Dockers routine. I can tell you what wine is best with fettuccini alfredo, or I can probably fix your lawn mower. I am who I am, and I am happy as such.

I put on my shoes and headed out the door. I climbed in that old familiar seat, put the key in the ignition, pumped the gas pedal three times, and turned the key. Without hesitation, Betty fired up as if I had only parked her yesterday. I hadn't driven a stick shift for quite awhile so I ground reverse a little, but I don't think my old friend cared much. With a rev of the engine and a cloud of blue smoke, we headed out the driveway and up town. It was cold out Sunday, but I didn't care. I rolled the window down anyway. I can afford to do that now since I don't have to worry about IEDs or car bombs any longer. I hung my arm out the window in hopes I might catch a little bit of a trucker tan again, but given the fact it is March, I may have to wait a couple of months for that one.

I drove past the county highway garage and turned north, up the six-mile stretch. The six-mile is long and straight and just like my future, it is wide open. I pressed in the clutch and slipped the shifter into fourth gear and pushed on the gas. The air coming in the window is cold and moist, but I don't care. It felt like a bath, like it was washing the husk off my soul and helping to change me from a soldier back into what I once was. I am not sure where I am driving to right now. Perhaps, I'll run up to Wally World and see what's on special…

Jason Adams
Toulon, Illinois

Glossary of Terms

9 mm handgun – standard issue sidearm of the U.S. military.

AH-64 Attack helicopter – gunship primarily designed to take out enemy armor.

AK-47 – mass produced relic of the Soviet bloc nations; standard issue rifle for many countries around the world; lightweight, easy to use and maintain, this rifle carries a high capacity magazine and has a good rate of fire.

Article 15 – Nonjudicial Punishment (NJD) that can be administered without a court martial; usually for minor disciplinary offenses.

AT-4 – Rocket Launcher

BDU (Battle Dress Uniform) – standard outfit for U.S. soldiers.

Battalion – an army unit typically consisting of a headquarters and two or more companies, batteries, or similar subunits.

Brigade – a group of several battalions (typically two to four), and directly attached supporting units (normally including at least an artillery battery and additional logistical support).

Browning M-2 (Ma Duece) – 50 caliber heavy machine gun used in WWII, still used today; heavy weapon for most Motorized Infantry Platoons.

Bradley Fighting Vehicle – transports infantry on the battlefield; provides fire cover to dismounted troops and suppresses enemy tanks and fighting vehicles. The M2 carries three crew, commander, gunner and driver, plus six fully equipped infantry men. The M3 performs scout missions and carries three crew plus two scouts.

C-130 Hercules – military transport airplane.

C-17 Globemaster – military transport/cargo airplane.

CAV (cavalry) – highly mobile army unit using vehicular transport, such as light armor and helicopters; originally mounted on horseback.

CH-47 – twin-rotored helicopter used to transport troops and/or equipment.

Combat lifesavers – soldiers with basic emergency medical skills.

Company – a military unit, typically consisting of 100-200 soldiers. Most companies are formed of three or four platoons although the exact number may vary by country, unit type and structure.

CSH – Combat Surgical Hospital

DCU – Dessert Combat Uniform

DD4 – enlistment contract; the form basically says that in a time of war one can be mobilized for the duration of hostilities, plus six months.

Demobilize – release from military service or remove from the active list of military service (fancy word for going home).

EMT – Emergency Medical Technician

EPOW – Enemy Prisoner of War

ETS – Estimated Time of Separation

Green Zone – part of Baghdad where Saddam Hussein had all of his governmental buildings.

GPS (Global Positioning System) – allows soldiers to obtain up to the second positions in the form of grid coordinates.

Guidon bearer – usually a lower ranking soldier given the task of carrying the units flag in front of the unit's formation.

Humvee (HMMWV – High-Mobility Multipurpose Wheeled Vehicle) – a light, highly mobile, diesel-powered, four-wheel-drive vehicle.

ICDC – Iraqi Civil Defense Corps

IED – Improvised Explosive Device

IP – Iraqi Police

Insurgents – bad guys.

JRTC (Joint Readiness Training Center) – designed to get different branches of the services used to working together; focused on improving unit readiness by providing highly realistic, stressful, joint and combined arms training across the full spectrum of conflict.

LSR (Left Seat Rides) – current patrols ride with leaders of a new unit during their first missions; final phase of transition from one unit to another.

M16 – standard issue rifle for the U.S. military.

M145 optical scope – offers magnification and range reticles (grid or pattern placed in the eyepiece of an optical instrument, used to establish scale or position) for quick aiming.

M-1 Abrahms – 76 ton main battle tank; carries crew of four; driver, gunner, loader and TC; while not invincible, the M-1 is arguably the best tank that the world has ever seen.

M240b – medium machine gun which replaced the aging M60.

M249 (SAW) – belt fed light machine gun.

Menard's Armor – homemade attempts at making trucks bullet proof; consists of sheets of plywood, nails, bungee cords, sandbags, banding material and other items.

MK-19 – fully automatic, belt-fed grenade launcher.

MRE (Meal, Ready to Eat) – military ration.

MOS – Military Operating System

MP – Military Police

NCO – Noncommissioned Officer

NVGs (night vision goggles) – amplify available light allowing one to see in the dark.

NTV – Non-Tactical Vehicle

OH-58 Kiowa – small, agile and quiet helicopter used to scout the battlefield.

Platoon – unit composed of two or more squads; typically consisting of 50 soldiers; a sub unit of a company; four platoons make up a company.

PT Uniform – Physical Training Uniform

PX (Post Exchange) – a store on a military base that sells goods to military personnel and their families or to authorized civilians.

QRF – Quick Reaction Force

Reticles – grid or pattern placed in the eyepiece of an optical instrument, used to establish scale or position.

RSR (Right Seat Rides) – leaders of a new unit ride on current patrols; gives incoming units a chance to see what the current units are doing.

SIB – Separate Infantry Brigade

SP – Start Point

Squad – A squad is a military unit consisting of several soldiers, larger than a fire team but smaller than a platoon. In most armies a squad consists of between eight (8) and twelve (12) soldiers, sometimes as many as fourteen (14).

TC – Track Commander

TCP – Temporary Check Point

TMC – Troop Medical Clinic

TOC – Tactical Operations Center

Tracer Bullet – ammunition that glows red when traveling through the air thus, allowing the firer to see where the rounds are going; effect is twofold, it also lets person being fired at, see where the bullets are coming from.

UAV – Unmanned Aerial Vehicle

UH-60 Blackhawks – utility helicopter also used as the medivac choppers.

Unit – an organization within an armed force; usually consists of several platoons of soldiers totaling 100 to 200 soldiers, depending on unit.

VBIED (Vehicle-bourne Improvised Explosive Device) – also known as a car bomb.

Wally World (Wal-Mart) – large department store.

A Few Statistics from Foxtrot Battery

During their tour in Iraq, Foxtrot Battery impacted countless lives in an effort to help the Iraqi's secure their freedom. Below are just a few of our accomplishments:

Estimated Number of Rounds Fired

- 33,000 5.56mm rounds fired from M16's
- 10,000 5.56mm rounds fired from M249's
- 10,000 7.62mm rounds fired from M240B's
- 8,000 .50 caliber rounds fired
- 6,000 MK-19 grenades launched
- 30 40mm HE M203 grenades launched
- 2 AT-4 rockets launched
- 2 Hand Grenades

Car Bombs

- 2 VBIED's (Vehicle-Borne Improvised Explosive Device) hit us directly
- 1 VCIED (Vehicle-Concealed Improvised Explosive Device) hit us directly
- Cleaned up after 6 detonated VBIED's
- Located and contained 3 VCIED's

Improvised Explosive Device's

- Located 150+
- Located and detonated 80+

Commendations and Awards

- Service Awards
  - ★ 11 Bronze Star Medals (BSM)
  - ★ 108 Army Commendation Medals (ARCOMs)
- Action Awards
  - ★ 12 Army Commendation Medals w/V Device (ARCOMs w/V)
  - ★ 18 Army Commendation Medals ARCOMs

★ 26 Purple Hearts

✪ Everyone in Foxtrot Battery received:

★ GWOT (Global War on Terrorism) – Service Medal

★ GWOT (Global War on Terrorism) – Expeditionary Medal

★ Armed Forces Reserve Medal w/"M"

Accomplishments

✪ Delivered over 100,000 gallons of water

✪ Built 1 school

✪ Refurbished 6 schools

✪ Built 6 water treatment plants.

WANT TO SHARE *ACTIVE DUTY: LETTERS TO HOME FROM IRAQ* WITH SOMEONE ELSE?

CHECK YOUR LEADING BOOKSTORE OR ORDER HERE

YES, I want copies of *Active Duty–Letters to Home from Iraq.*

____ hardback copies at $24.95 each, plus $4 shipping per book.
(Indiana residents please add $1.50 sales tax per book).

____ paperback copies at $14.95 each, plus $4 shipping per book.
(Indiana residents please add $.90 sales tax per book).

$ _____ Total enclosed   Allow 10-12 days for delivery

Ship To:

Name_____
Address_____
Address_____
City_____ State_____ Zip_____
Phone_____ E-Mail _____

Payment Information:

☐Visa   ☐Master Card   ☐Discover   ☐Am. Express   ☐Check

Credit Card Number _____ Exp. Date _____

Name on Card _____

Signature _____

Make checks payable to Learnovation

CALL toll-free 1-888-577-1190 or 317-577-1190
M-F, 9 a.m. to 5 p.m. EST.

FAX your order to 317-598-0816

MAIL your order form to:
Learnovation®, LLC - P.O. Box 502150
Indianapolis, IN 46250   **Call for quantity discounts!**

ORDER ON-LINE www.learnovationpress.com

Adding "Menard's Armor" to our truck in Kuwait.

Welcome to Iraq - Our first rockets.

Home sweet home - my half of the trailer in Camp BlackJack.

Handing out candy to the kids along a canal road.

Team Destroyer 86, from left: SGT Ben Sleaford,
Jaguar, me, and SPC Richard Douglas (in truck).

Team Destroyer 86 enjoying burgers in our mortar bunker. From left:
SGT Carlos Ortiz, SPC Richard Douglas, me, and SGT Ben Sleaford.

A chunk of ordinace we found laying out in the country. From left:
1LT Tracy Doubler, SPC Mark Rathjen, SGT Ben Sleaford,
SPC Jon McKirgan, SSG Troy Wolford, and SGT Carlos Ortiz.

A family that lived by one of our rest stops.
They always came over to visit when we stopped by.

SGT Ortiz won a bet by jumping in the canal. SGT Sleaford looks on. You can see the details of the "Menard's Armor" on our truck.

The Batmobile – One of the few armored M1114 Humvees in our unit.

The parade grounds in the Green Zone, Baghdad.

SGT Mike Finney checks out the hole left from
an IED. This one is about average size.

Gathering provisions for a cookout. From left: SSG Derrick
Glisan, SGT Mike Finney, SGT Bruce Hartman.

The Second Platoon, Foxtrot Battery, 4th Battalion/
5th Regiment, 1st Cavalry Divison

This man brought us water and tea after the Iraqi National Guard searched his home. He had an interesting antique Russian submachine gun.

Here I am having fun with some of his kids.

The men deployed from Dixon, Illinois, sporting T-shirts
from Zero's; a tavern back in Dixon.

The school we spearheaded under construction.

I met this Iraqi National Guardsman at the airport while on tower duty.
We shared our MRE's with him and his buddy.

My buddies Omar and Ahmed.

Back side of my "deer stand." Tower guard at OP4.

10/12/2004

Doing our part. Pre-election campaigning in downtown Baghdad.
From left: SGT Ben Sleaford, SGT Carlos Ortiz,
SPC Brian Beckman, and SPC Richard Douglas.

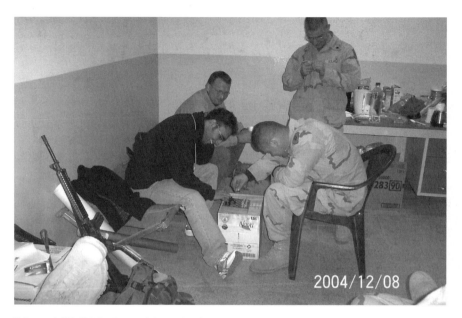

GQ and SPC Mark Rathjen playing chess at the police station in Tarmiyah.

One of our humvees after a car bomb on the outskirts of Tarmiyah.
Luckly, no one was seriously hurt.

Princess getting a bath at the police station. From left: SGT Tyler Andersen, Lenny, SPC Hipkins (standing), and SPC Beckman.

Happier times. SPC Richard Douglas with our friend Lenny.

On the back of Geryon, we ride deeper into hell.
The battle of Holy Week, 2004.

We were investigating this bomb damage when we came
under fire for the first time. The Easter Sunday assault, 2004.

Welcome home at Galva.
from left: Steph, Jason, Teryl in front.

Joanna and Teryl showing off their welcome home signs for Dad

The home support. From left: Me; Stephanie; my Mom, Joanne;
my Dad, Howard. Front: Teryl and Joanna.

SGT Ben Sleaford and myself sporting our Cav Stetsons
at the Battalion Ball in May, 2005